Continuities in the Sociology of Religion

Continuities in the Sociology of Religion:

Creed, congregation, and community

J. Alan Winter

Connecticut College

Harper & Row, Publishers
New York   Hagerstown   San Francisco   London

This book is dedicated to

my parents, Herman and Rose Winter, from whom
my own religion comes;

my wife Gail, with whom I share it;

my daughters Wendy and Miriam, to whom
I hope to pass it on;

and to the memory of Jacob and Libby Kavkewitz,
Mattus and Rifka Winter,
Harry and Bertha Weck,
Dave Mogel,
Yetta Kavkewitz and Jack Miller.

Sponsoring Editor: Dale Tharp
Project Editor: Renée E. Beach
Designer: Andrea C. Goodman
Production Supervisor: Stefania J. Taflinska
Photo Researcher: Myra Schachne
Compositor: Maryland Linotype Composition Co., Inc.
Printer and Binder: The Maple Press Company

Continuities in the Sociology of Religion: Creed, Congregation, and Community

Library of Congress Cataloging in Publication Data
Winter, Jerry Alan.
    Continuities in the sociology of religion.

    Includes index and bibliographies.
    1. Religion and sociology.   I. Title.
BL60.W56   301.5′8   76–27674
ISBN 0-06-047158-1

Contents

contents

the sociology of religious communities   195

Preface

This book examines three of the many phenomena which constitute religion: creed, congregation, and community. *Creed* refers to a body of beliefs and practices concerning the sacred, in general, or of the divine and supernatural, in particular. *Congregation* refers to an association or social organization in which social actors seek to attain a desired relationship to the sacred, in general, or to the divine or supernatural, in particular. *Community* refers to a social organization in which social actors affirm their identification or relationship to the people with whom they share a common religious heritage or history.

This book does not seek to be either a comprehensive or an encyclopedic study of religion. Rather, it is selective as to the aspects of religion discussed. (I have attempted, however, to provide comprehensive bibliographies with each chapter. I trust these will be of use both to students for term papers and to instructors for lectures or however readers may wish to use them as they pursue the sociology of religion beyond the scope of this book.) The choice of content was dictated by the fact that this is a work in the *sociology* of religion. Its focal concerns are the focal concerns of sociology as they bear on the study of religion. Specifically, this work focuses, as does any sociological work, upon the *cultural* and *social organizational* aspects of the phenomena under study. Hence, the book concentrates on the cultural aspects of religion, as manifested in a creed, and on the social organizational aspects, as manifested in congregation and community.

There are nine chapters, divided equally among three parts, and an

introduction, which discusses Emile Durkheim's classic sociological definition of religion and the relationship of that definition to recent attempts
to measure or operationalize the dimensions of individual religiosity.
The introduction also discusses the rationale used for the selection of the
topics in the body of the book.

Part I begins with an examination of the social sources of theism,
one of the creeds of greatest interest to sociologists of religion. Chapter
1 identifies two approaches to the study of the social sources of theism:
functionalism, the view that theism helps meet the needs of both societies
and individuals; and metaphorical parallelism, the view that theism is a
metaphorical or symbolic representation of basic social facts. Chapter 2
focuses on another creed of great interest to sociologists of religion, the
so-called Protestant Ethic. It begins with an examination of Max Weber's
classic statement of the relationship between the ethic of early Protestantism and the spirit of entrepreneurial capitalism. Efforts to test Weber's
theory empirically are discussed. Weber's theory is then updated through
an examination of the relationship between a contemporary ethic and
the spirit of modern capitalism. The third chapter, which discusses the
role of religion in the integration of advanced industrial society, pays
particular attention to the process of secularization and the possible
presence of a civil religion.

Part II turns attention to social organizational aspects of religion as
manifested in congregations or religious associations. Chapter 4 examines the basic issues facing any congregation or religious association,
as these issues are presented within the framework of Ernst Troeltsch's
sect-church typology. An alternative approach to the study of congregations, the choice-point approach, is offered and its use illustrated.
Further applications of the choice-point approach are made in Chapter 5,
where attention is focused on the rise of sectlike congregations and
hypotheses concerning their development into churchlike congregations
formulated by Reinhold Niebuhr and Liston Pope. Chapter 6 seeks to
understand how clergy who lead or represent churchlike congregations
may nevertheless engage in the unchurchlike behavior of joining reform-
oriented sociopolitical movements.

The third part of the book begins, in Chapter 7, with a review of
Will Herberg's analysis of America's three main religious communities,
Protestants, Catholics, and Jews. Empirical evidence bearing on the
validity of Herberg's analysis is presented and discussed. Chapter 8 examines tensions between church and state inherent in the norms of the
three- community system described by Herberg. Chapter 9 discusses the
applicability of the concept of religious community, as developed by
Herberg, to the understanding of religion among black Americans.

Throughout the book an effort is made to provide coherence in the
field of the sociology of religion by stressing two forms of continuity

within it: continuity between theoretical concepts and statements on the one hand, and empirical studies on the other; and continuity in the development of the theoretical concepts and statements themselves. Since the sociology of religion is, as Demerath and Hammond describe it in *Religion in Social Context* (1969:5), "an area known more for its disparate—one may even say 'schizophrenic'—character than for its unity," the efforts to attain coherence by stressing continuity may seem to some more valiant than successful. Still, it is an effort which must be made if the sociology of religion is to advance as a scientific discipline and is to make worthwhile contributions to the understanding of religion as it is manifested in creed, congregation, and community.

The study of creed, congregation, and community undertaken here is largely confined to contributions made by studies of religion as it exists in the United States. Admittedly, there is no good theoretical justification for such a relatively narrow focus. Indeed, the resulting limitation on the scope of the book constitutes the chief shortcoming of which I am aware. Nevertheless, there are practical and pedagogical reasons for the concentration on religion in the United States. From a practical point of view, since the vast majority of available research has been done in the United States, the focus of this book follows the focus of the field. Pedagogically, concentrating on religion in the United States presents the student with material that is familiar and with which he or she can identify. Such familiarity and identification should facilitate learning.

This book is intended as both an introduction and an invitation to the sociological study of religion. As an introduction, it does not seek to catalogue all of the myriad of works in the field but rather to concentrate on pivotal concepts and studies. As an invitation, it focuses not only upon what is known, but on what is still to be discovered. It is my hope that the book may serve those who wish to undertake further study of sociology as well as those who wish a deeper understanding of religion, be they in departments of sociology, departments of religion, or seminaries and congregations.

It is my hope, too, that those who read this book will join with me in acknowledging the assistance and support of all those who helped make it possible for me to write it: Connecticut College, which provided funds through its Faculty Research, Travel, and Study Grants to help defray some of the costs of typing the manuscript; Patsy A. Duran, who typed much of the initial drafts; Margaret Cibes, who so ably typed all of the final drafts and the manuscript itself; Gilda Walker and Robert Cutler who helped me so greatly with proofreading the pages, Helen K. Aitner, Interlibrary Loan Librarian, and James MacDonald, Reference Librarian, of Palmer Library, Connecticut College, each of whom helped me obtain essential bibliographic materials; and my students at The University of Michigan, Rutgers College, Temple University, and especially at Connecticut College, whose interest and questions during more than a decade have led me to deeper and deeper study of the sociology of religion. I wish also to thank the editors of the *American Journal of Sociology*, the *Review of Religious Research*, and *Sociological Analysis*, for granting permission to use portions from the following of my previously published articles: "Elective affinities between religious beliefs and ideologies of management in two eras," *American Journal of Sociology* 79 (March, 1974):1134–1150; "Quantitative studies of the applicability of the Weber Thesis to post-World War II U.S.A.: a call for redirected efforts," *Review of Religious Research* 16 (Fall, 1974): 47–54; and "The metaphorical parallelist approach to the study of theistic beliefs: theme, variations and implications," *Sociological Analysis* 34 (Fall, 1973):212–239. Thanks should also be given to my sponsoring editors at Harper & Row, Alvin Abbott, Ron Taylor, and Dale Tharp, and to my project editor, Renée E. Beach, whose interest and encouragement helped me to keep my nose to the grindstone, my shoulder to the wheel, and my ear to the ground—an awkward posture indeed— long enough to complete this work. But above all I hope everyone will join with me in thanking my wife Gail and my daughters Wendy and Miriam for tolerating a husband and father in that awkward posture which all too often precluded my attending properly to the responsibilities and joys of family life.

J. ALAN WINTER

New London, Connecticut

Continuities
in the Sociology
of Religion

Emile Durkheim

Max Weber

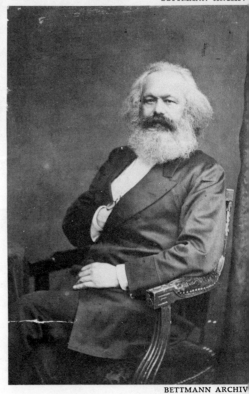

Karl Marx

Introduction

Continuity in the Sociology of Religion

The aim of this book is to further the understanding of the sociology of religion in its present stage of development. This aim can best be accomplished by focussing attention on three forms of continuity in the development of the sociological study of religion: empirical continuity, theoretical continuity, and substantive continuity.

Empirical continuity, is that between theoretical concepts and statements, on the one hand, and empirical findings, on the other. A focus on the continuity between theory and data is, of course, commonplace in the study of any discipline, such as the sociology of religion, which lays claim to the status of a science. Moreover, understanding the relationship between theory and data in a given scientific discipline constitutes an understanding of the main contribution of the discipline to the study of the phenomena in question. For the most part, the relationship between theory and data which will be discussed takes one of two forms: the relationship between theoretical concepts and attempts to measure or operationalize them, and the relationship between theoretical predictions or hypotheses and empirical findings. For example, the discussion of Herberg's three-generation hypothesis (see Chap. 7) will deal (1) with the problems of measuring religious identification,

1

one of the key variables in the hypothesis; and (2) with empirical findings which bear on the prediction of the hypothesis that religious identification is lower among the second-generation Americans, the children of immigrants, than it is among the first generation, the immigrants themselves, but rises among third-generation Americans, the grandchildren of immigrants, to a level equalling or surpassing that of the first generation. Of course, there are areas within the sociology of religion where virtually all the work which has been done is theoretical or speculative. Such areas include the study of the processes of secularization, discussed in Chapter 3. Within such an area, interest in the continuity between theory and data is subverted by the general lack of appropriate empirical studies. Moreover, such a lack indicates that the sociological study of the phenomenon in question, here secularization, is at a very early stage of development—a stage prior to that of infancy, somewhere between conception and contact with reality after birth.

Theoretical continuity is continuity in the development of theoretical concepts and statements. Here attention is paid, first, to the continuity between recent works and classic works, such as those of Karl Marx, Emile Durkheim, and Max Weber, who are primarily responsible for establishing the field of the sociology of religion within the larger discipline of sociology.[1] Attention to this aspect of theoretical continuity will facilitate the understanding of the current state of the sociology of religion. However, the future development of the sociology of religion requires more than an understanding of how present work is related to the classic statements of the founding fathers of the field. As Alfred North Whitehead once quipped, "A science which hesitates to forget its founders is lost." That is, the future development of the sociology of religion also requires a conscious and concerted effort to update and improve upon the work of its founding fathers. Such effort should, of course, draw on their insights but it should also take care to abandon their mistakes and break free of any time-bound limitations in their work. For example, an attempt will be made (see Chap. 2) to revise and update Weber's famous Protestant Ethic thesis, which relates developments in religion and economics, specifically, the development of Protestantism with the ethos of a nascent capitalism. The revision or update offered in Chapter 3 takes into account changes which have occurred both in religion and in the economy since Weber first presented his thesis more than seventy years ago. It seeks to relate recent developments in Protestantism with the use of an established or mature capitalism.

An attempt is also made, in Chapter 4, to update Troeltsch's classic discussion of the *sect* and the *church* as forms of Christian religious organization. This attempt seeks to lower the barriers between the study of religious organizations and that of other forms of organiza-

2

tion. Such barriers may have been appropriate given the state of sociology in the early twentieth century, when Troeltsch was examining the differences between *church* and *sect*. However, the development of the sociology of religion would be furthered if these barriers were now lowered to encourage the advances which normally ensue from the cross-fertilization of ideas flowing freely among the various fields within a given discipline. Barriers should be lowered not only as they pertain to the study of the concepts of *sect* and *church*, but, more generally, between the sociology of religion as a whole and other fields within sociology if the sociology of religion is to develop as much as possible.

Such a lowering of barriers constitutes the third form of continuity stressed in this book, namely, *substantive continuity*, the continuity between the sociology of religion and other branches of sociology. Such continuity would be enhanced if it were generally accepted that the sociology of religion and the *sociology of* any other aspect of human life are all studies of the same two processes: (1) the processes by which culture infuses social relationships with meaning, that is, reduces their absurdity, and (2) the processes of social organization which fuse social actors into ordered or patterned social relationships, that is, reduce their randomness.[2] Thus, to understand the *sociology* of religion in a manner which enhances the possibility of its continuity with other branches of sociology, attention should be focussed on the two basic aspects of the social activity of interest: (1) the components of culture which infuse these activities with meaning; and (2) the social organizations which fuse them into recognizable patterns. Interestingly, these aspects may be regarded as facets of the three religious phenomena, *creed, congregation,* and *community,* on which this book focusses, since *creed* refers to the cultural components of religious activity, and *congregation* and *community* refer to different forms of the social organization of religious activity. Thus, in order to enhance the linking of the sociology of religion with other branches of sociology, Part I of this book will focus on *religious creeds,* that is, on religious beliefs and practices which social actors accept or give credence to and which provide their social relationships with meaning; Part II will focus on *religious congregations,* the social organizations or associations in which social actors seek to attain religious ends or goals, such as salvation; and in Part III will focus on *religious communities,* the social organizations or communal groupings in which social actors affirm their religious identity, their relationship to the people with whom they have a common religious heritage or history.[3]

The remainder of this introductory chapter will serve two purposes. First, it discusses the term *religion* as it is defined in Durkheim's classic work, *The Elementary Forms of the Religious Life* and relates

3

that definition to the study of creed, congregation and community. Second, it illustrates the concern with empirical and theoretical continuity by examining the relationship between Durkheim's classic definition of religion and recent attempts, following the work of Glock (1965:18–38), to identify the dimensions of religious commitment.

Durkheim's Definition of Religion

Durkheim (1965:37–63) discusses the problem of defining the term *religion* and finally offers a definition which stresses activity relating to the *sacred* as the defining characteristic of religion.[4] Activities relating to the supernatural, or to divinity, gods, or spirits, are also accepted as religious, but are viewed as less elemental than those referring to the sacred (Durkheim, 1965:39–50).

Durkheim's definition of religion involves clear reference to cultural and social organizational elements and indirect reference to the three aspects of religion of central concern in this book—creed, congregation and community. The definition reads (1965:62):

> A religion is a unified system of beliefs and practices relative to sacred things, that is to say, things set apart and forbidden—beliefs and practices which unite into one single moral community called a Church, all those who adhere to them.

There are, then, three basic elements of religion: (1) a system of beliefs and practices; (2) a community or church; and (3) sacred things, in its generic or elementary form, the form which Durkheim believed he could identify from his study of the simple preliterate society of the Arunta of Australia. The first elements, the system of beliefs and practices relative to sacred things is, of course, the cultural component of religion. It is what this book refers to as *religious creed*. The second element is the social organizational component. That is, the community and the church are what this book refers to as, *congregation*.[5] Durkheim clearly regards the organizational component as crucial and refers (Durkheim, 1965:62–63) to it as "no less essential than the first, or cultural component." "The idea of religion is inseparable from that of the Church [congregation] . . . religion [is] an eminently collective thing." In our terms, Durkheim is arguing that creed, congregation, and community are inseparable, that the social functioning of one cannot be differentiated from the other. However, such a lack of differentiation or inseparability is largely true only of religion in its elementary or most primitive form, the form which Durkheim described on the basis of his study of the simple, preliterate society of the Arunta in Australia. Durkheim recognized that in more complex and modern forms,

4

religion could well involve a differentiation of its cultural and social organizational components.[6] Others have since suggested that there could also be a separation of the religious community and the congregation.

Durkheim noted that as he wrote (in 1915) there were "contemporary aspirations towards a religion which would consist entirely in internal and subjective states, and which would be constructed freely by each of us." Such internal and subjective states could, of course, include the tenets of one's own religious creed. Should such "aspirations" be realized, there would be what Durkheim regarded as a spread of "religious individualism" (1965:62). He acknowledged, "It is possible that this religious individualism is destined to be realized in facts . . ." (1965:62). Some contemporary sociologists of religion, for example, Peter Berger and Thomas Luckmann (see Chap. 3), believe that religious individualism has indeed become the most characteristic form of religion in modern industrialized societies. They contend that religious creeds may be adhered to apart from any membership in a religious congregation or community, that the systems of beliefs and practices relative to sacred things held by various individuals do not necessarily unite them into a single community or congregation, no matter how similar these systems may be.

Contemporary sociologists of religion, then, recognize that the cultural and social organizational elements of religion may be functionally differentiated. Similarly, there are some who claim that the religious community, the arena in which one affirms his religious *identity*, may function apart from the religious congregation, the arena in which one seeks religious *goals* such as a communion with God. Herberg (1960:39) whose work forms the basis of the discussions in Part III, especially Chapter 7, contends that in a modern society, membership in a religious community "does not necessarily imply actual affiliation with a particular church" or congregation. That is, according to Herberg, the religious community and the religious congregation may function as separate or differentiated organizations. Such differentiation would not, of course, be found among the Arunta of Australia from whose study Durkheim inferred his definition of the elements of religion. Among the Arunta, as in other simple preliterate societies, there is little, if any, differentiation between the "community" and the "congregation." One organization, namely, the total society, provides both religious identity (community) and the arena in which religious ends are sought (congregation). In the complex modern societies which are of interest to sociologists of religion, there are, however, generally separate and distinct social structures performing each of the various social functions (see Chap. 3). In short, there is a tendency for a given organizational form to focus on one central function, a tendency which

5

Durkheim recognized and stressed in his study of the division of labor in modern societies (1964). Thus, in a complex differentiated modern society, it is generally necessary to distinguish between religion in the community, where religious identities are affirmed, and religion in the congregation, where religious ends are sought.

The sacred as defined by Durkheim. If Durkheim's definition of religion is to be used in research, it is necessary to turn attention to what is meant by *sacred*, for it is concern with sacred things which characterizes given communities and congregations, and for that matter given creeds, as religious. It is quite clear that Durkheim regards it as fruitless, even impossible, to identify any intrinsic attributes which characterize or define the *sacred*. To the contrary, he argues (1965:52–57) that the sacred can only be understood or defined in relation to something extrinsic to it, namely, the *profane*. "There is nothing," he claims (Durkheim, 1965:53) "with which to characterize the sacred in its relation to the profane except their heterogeneity." That is, the *sacred* can only be defined in terms of its differences from the *profane*. Since sacred things do not have any necessary or intrinsic properties, "anything can be sacred" (Durkheim, 1965:52). Thus, Durkheim admonishes (1965:52), "by sacred things one must not understand simply those personal beings called gods or spirits," but must recognize that "a tree, a spring, a pebble, a piece of wood, a house," and even such abstractions as the four noble truths of Buddhism may be sacred. It is not its intrinsic properties which make something sacred, but rather its being viewed as different from, or apart from, the profane.

Moreover, Durkheim contends, whatever the distinction between the sacred and the profane, "*it is absolute*. In all the history of human thought there exists no other example of two categories of things so profoundly differentiated, so radically opposed to one another" (1965:53, italics in original). He adds (1965:54) that, "the sacred and the profane have always and everywhere been conceived by the human mind as two distinct classes, as two worlds between which there is nothing in common." Between the sacred and the profane, "there is a break of continuity" (1965:56), a break so great that "the mind irresistibly refuses to allow the two corresponding things to be confounded, or even to be merely put in contact with each other." (1965:55). Thus, "the sacred thing is *par excellence* that which the profane should not touch, and cannot touch with impunity" (Durkheim, 1965:55). More generally, "sacred things are those which . . . interdictions protect and isolate; profane things, those to which these interdictions are applied and which must remain at a distance from the first" (Durkheim, 1965:56).

Reference to the *sacred*, then, is merely a shorthand way of referring to belief in a fundamentally dualistic world. Beliefs and practices that are religious, that is, related to sacred things, divide the world into two absolutely distinct classes. As Durkheim (1965:56) asserts, "the real characteristic of religious phenomena is that they always presuppose a bipartite division of the whole universe, known and knowable, into two classes that embrace all that exists, but which radically exclude each other." These two classes are "generally designated by two distinct terms, which are translated well enough by the words *profane* and *sacred*" (Durkheim, 1965:52). In specific religions the two classes may be designated as supernatural and natural, or divine and human, or spiritual and material. Whatever the specific terms, the essential characteristic of religion is that it divides all things into two absolutely opposite categories.

In sum, given Durkheim's understanding of the sacred and the previous discussion of the possible separation of creed, congregation, and community, the elements of religion in the complex modern societies of interest to sociologists, may be identified as (1) a creed, or body of beliefs and practices which pertain to the division of all things into two absolutely opposite classes, one of which, the sacred, is set apart from and forbidden to the other, the profane; (2) a congregation, or social organization in which social actors seek to attain a desired relationship with the realm of the sacred; and (3) a community, or social organization in which one affirms a relationship to people who have a common history or heritage with respect to some creed or congregation.

Recent Attempts to Identify Empirically the Dimensions of Religion

Recent empirical investigations into the dimensions of religion have largely followed guidelines suggested by Glock (1965:18–38) in his discussion of a conceptual framework for studying the components of religiosity.[7] This section will first briefly characterize the relationship of Glock's framework to the Durkheimian approach to the study of religion and to the study of creed, congregation, and community. Glock's discussion of the dimensions of religion will be summarized.[8] The section will then review empirical studies which follow the guidelines suggested by Glock and which seek to operationalize or measure the dimensions he identifies. This section, then, will illustrate the concern with continuity in the development of the theoretical or conceptual framework of the sociology of religion and in the relationship of empirical investigations to that framework.

Glock on the dimensions of religiosity. The Durkheimian approach to the study of religion stresses two points: (1) religion is an "eminently

7

collective thing," that is, the basic units of analysis should be the social organization and its culture rather than individuals; and (2) substantively, a religious outlook is characterized by a view which regards reality as bipartite or dualistic—one part sacred, the other profane. Glock's approach to the study of the dimensions of religiosity diverges somewhat, although not entirely, from the emphases of the Durkheimian approach both with respect to the units of analysis and the substance of religion.

First, Glock (1965:19) makes it clear that he is interested in "the different ways in which *individuals* can be religious" (italics mine). Unlike Durkheim, Glock treats religion as a phenomenon in which individuals, rather than the social organization and its culture, are the basic units of analysis. Although Glock's emphasis is on the individual and his creed rather than on the congregation or the community, he does not claim that what Durkheim called "religious individualism" is an established or fundamental fact. He neither affirms nor denies that one's religion is freely constructed by the person and consists entirely of internal and subjective states. Indeed, Glock takes no position concerning the source of the different ways in which individuals can be religious. However, as a sociologist, Glock is aware of the influence of various social processes in shaping the religion which a given individual may construct. For example, he alludes consistently to the influence of culturally provided expectations.[9] Nevertheless, the dimensions which he identifies refer primarily, albeit not exclusively, to internal and subjective states. He identifies five dimensions of individual religiosity: ideological, intellectual, ritualistic, experiential, and consequential.[10] Since Glock's approach to the study of the dimensions of religion is somewhat more concerned with the individual, that is, more psychologistic, than the heavily sociologistic approach of Durkheim his work represents something of a departure from, rather than a continuation of the Durkheimian approach, at least with respect to the basic units of analysis.

Glock's departure from Durkheim's conception of the essential substance of religion, however, is minor. For Durkheim, it may be recalled, the essential substance of religion is the division it makes between the sacred and the profane. None of Glock's dimensions deals directly or explicitly with assessing the existence or extent of any perceived division of reality into the categories of the sacred and the profane. Indeed, the term *sacred* appears only once in Glock's discussion, (1965:20) in a passing reference to sacred scriptures. Glock defines religion in terms of "a divine essence," "ultimate reality," "transcendental authority," (1965:20) and "divine purpose" (1965:24). These may, of course, be regarded as manifestations of the sacred or even synonyms for it. They pertain to important components of what

Durkheim took to be the substance of religious beliefs and practices, namely, describing "the nature of sacred things" and " the rules of conduct which prescribe how a man should comport himself in the presence of . . . sacred objects" (Durkheim, 1965:56). In short, while Glock fails to refer to the essence of the religious perspective, as Durkheim understood it, namely, the distinction between the sacred and the profane, he does, by referring to the divine, the ultimate, and the transcendent, allude to important, derivative, components of a religious outlook or creed. His five dimensions—ideological, intellectual, ritualistic, consequential, and experiential (1965:20–35)—may be thought of as presupposing a dualistic conception of the world but focussing explicitly on the nature of the sacred and one's relationship with it. Thus, the substance or content of the dimensions are within the Durkheimian approach to the study of religion, even if the units of analysis are not.

Glock's ideological dimension consists of the set of beliefs which the individual holds concerning the divine, or whatever he takes to be the ultimate reality or transcendent authority. The ideological dimension consists of three subsets of beliefs: warranting beliefs, purposive beliefs, and implementing beliefs. Warranting beliefs are "beliefs whose primary role is to warrant the existence of the divine and to define its character" (Glock, 1965:24). These beliefs include beliefs in miracles which prove (or warrant) belief in the god who performs them. Purposive beliefs are "those which explain divine purposes and define man's role with regard to that purpose" (Glock, 1965:24). For example, one may believe that it is a god's purpose to bring all men to judgment at some appointed time in the future. Implementing beliefs arise (1965:25) out of purposive beliefs and consist of those beliefs "which bear on the means by which the divine purpose is to be implemented." They "establish what is the proper conduct of man toward God and toward his fellow man for the realization of the divine purpose."

The intellectual dimension consists of what one knows about the beliefs of a given religion and the content of its scriptures. While the intellectual dimension is related to the ideological dimension, Glock (1965:21) notes that "belief need not follow from knowledge nor, for that matter, does all religious knowledge bear on belief." Furthermore, he adds (1965:32), "It is certainly not inconceivable, and perhaps, even likely, that the atheist will tend to be highly informed religiously." The atheist may know a good deal of what a given religion asserts about God, but not believe any of it himself. One may know the content of some scriptures, such as the Gospels of Matthew, Mark, Luke, and John, and not believe it warrants belief in the divinity of Christ.[11] While the intellectual and ideological dimensions may be related, they are distinguishable from each other. Yet, each may be regarded as bearing on the cognitive aspects of religious creed, or belief. Indeed, Glock's discussion of the ideological and intellectual dimensions may be regarded as clarifying or amplifying the definition of the belief component of religious creeds. The remaining three dimensions, the ritualistic, the consequential, and the experiential, all bear more on the noncognitive component of religious creeds.

The ritualistic dimension encompasses "such activities as worship, prayer, participation in special sacraments and the like" (Glock, 1965:20). Although Glock provides no more explicit or connotative definition, it would appear from the context of his discussions that the ritual dimension encompasses the practices through which one seeks to communicate with the divine or otherwise come in contact with something divine. However, the dimension does not appear to include obeying rules, believed to be of divine origin for the practice of mundane behavior. For example, the Jewish laws of the Kashrut, which specify the kosher foods one can eat and the unkosher (*treif*) foods one cannot, would not fall within the ritualistic dimension. They would, instead, come within the scope of the consequential dimension.

The consequential dimension includes "what the individual can expect to receive as a result of being religious and . . . what he is expected to give" (Glock, 1965:35). What one may expect to receive might include such rewards as a long and happy life, eternal salvation, or reincarnation in a higher status of life. What one may be expected to give might include obedience to divine injunctions, which typically include both proscriptions and prescriptions. As Glock notes (1965:35), in the Ten Commandments, there are . . . both Thou Shalt and Thou Shalt Not injunctions." The consequential dimension refers to the consequences of being religious, but especially to the "secular effects of religion," (Glock, 1965:21), to the import of religion practical conduct. The primary focus of the consequential dimension is "man's relation to man rather than . . . man's relation to God," (Glock, 1965:21); the latter being primarily included within the ritualistic dimension. Together, the ritualistic and consequential dimensions define what a religious person does; the intellectual dimension defines what he knows; and the ideological dimension defines what he believes.

The experiential dimension refers to what a person feels, specifically, to feelings experienced as involving some communion or contact with the divine. These vary widely, as Glock notes (1965:20), "from terror to passionate union with the universe or the divine,"[12] and may result from the performance of some ritual or other act. The ritualistic, consequential, and experiential dimension refer to different, although related, aspects of the practices denoted by a given religious creed. Thus, Glock's discussion of the dimensions of individual religiosity may be understood as clarifying or amplifying the meaning of religious creed within the Durkheimian approach to the study of religion. He suggests that religious creeds be understood as including not only what one believes and does, but what one knows and feels with respect to the divine (or sacred); and what the consequences of such belief, action, knowledge, and emotions are for mundane, practical, and secular (profane) affairs.

Empirical studies within Glock's framework. Glock suggests that empirical investigation within the framework he developed follow two lines of inquiry (1965:22–23): (1) to discover the subdimensions within each of the five dimensions of individual religiosity which he identified; (2) to determine the extent and pattern of interrelations or correlations among the various dimensions and subdimensions. Glock's (1965:23) preference is to undertake the first line of inquiry and essentially complete it before undertaking the second:

> The premise which will inform our efforts is that insofar as the comprehension of religiosity in its whole is possible, this can only follow from an understanding of its parts. Consequently, principal attention will be given to considering how religiosity may be studied within each of its core dimensions.[13]

Other researchers have tended to concentrate upon the question of the interrelations among the five core dimensions before turning attention to the detailed understanding of the internal components of these dimensions. The summary of relevant research which follows will begin, as has most research, with studies of the interrelations among the core dimensions.

Faulkner and DeJong undertook the first study whose explicit purpose was to "empirically test the interrelationships among the scales for [the] dimensions of religiosity as identified by Glock" (1966: 252). Their study of the questionnaire responses of 364 introductory sociology students at Pennsylvania State University in 1964 found that the correlation of the scores on any one scale or dimension were positively related to the scores on each of the other scales or dimensions to a statistically significant extent. However, the pattern of interrelations or correlations varied from dimension to dimension: The highest correlations were, in every case, associated with the ideological dimension, while the lowest correlations were associated with the consequential dimension.[14] This pattern of results is viewed by Stark and Glock (1968:174–182) as consistent with the results of their own study of two random samples of Christian adults, one consisting of three thousand church members in four Northern California counties and the other of nearly two thousand persons in a nationwide study. Using measures different from those employed by Faulkner and DeJong (1966), Stark and Glock found that theology, an aspect of the ideological dimension, correlates most highly with the other dimensions of religiosity, while concern for person-to-person ethical responsibilities, which can be seen as an aspect of the consequential dimension, is least correlated with other dimensions of religiosity.

Similarly, Gibbs and Crader (1970), although critical of the scales devised by Faulkner and DeJong (1966) and using some scales of their own design, find support for the Faulkner and DeJong results in their own study of questionnaire responses from 250 undergraduates at Emory University. They report (Gibbs and Crader, 1970:111) that "with the use of improved experience and consequential scales, the data . . . tend to support the patterns of relationships reported by Faulkner and DeJong," namely, that the ideological dimension is most strongly and the consequential dimension most weakly correlated with the other dimensions. The factor analytic study by Clayton and Gladden (1974) of responses to the Faulkner-DeJong items by samples of 873 students in 1967 and 656 students in 1970 at Stetson University in Florida also tends to support the Faulkner-DeJong finding. Clayton and Gladden find that an ideological factor is clearly highly related to other aspects of religiosity and accounts for most of the common variance among the items used, while the consequential dimension is poorly related to other items, accounting for virtually none of the common variance.

In sum, the studies of Faulkner and DeJong (1966), Stark and Glock (1968), Gibbs and Crader (1970), and Clayton and Gladden (1974), having examined the interrelations among the five core dimensions of religiosity identified by Glock (1965), all find a similar pattern: The ideological dimension is the most central, and the consequential, the least. There seems to have been some progress along one of the two lines of inquiry suggested by Glock, albeit not the one he thought primary. However, the progress has been slight since all but one of the studies (Stark and Glock, 1968) was restricted to one segment of the total population, namely, college students, and the results may not be representative of any larger population. Consequently, no firm understanding of the interrelations among the core dimensions can be claimed.

As Glock advised, sociologists of religion may improve their inquiries into the interrelationships among the various core dimensions of individual religiosity by a careful consideration of possible components of each dimension. Such a careful consideration precedes the examination of interdimensional relations in Davidson's extension (1975) of his own earlier work (1972). In a study of questionnaire responses from members of two Baptist and two Methodist congregations in Indiana, Davidson (1975: 85–86) identified and defined two subdimensions within each of the five core dimensions discussed by

12

Glock (1965). For example, within the ideological dimension, two sets of beliefs were identified, "vertical beliefs" and "horizontal beliefs." Vertical beliefs are beliefs pertaining to a supernatural order, such as belief in God or an afterlife. Horizontal beliefs are those which pertain to one's social relationships and one's activities in social institutions. They include beliefs such as that in loving one's neighbor. Within the intellectual dimension, "religious knowledge" is distinguished from "intellectual scrutiny." Religious knowledge is measured by the extent of knowledge one has about sacred scriptures and the historical roots of a given religion. Intellectual scrutiny is measured by the degree to which questioning and doubt, as opposed to acceptance of belief by faith, is regarded as permissible. The two components of the ritualistic dimension are "private practices" and "public practices." Private practices, such as praying and reading scriptures, are those which need not require participation in a group setting. Public practices are those which ". . . derive their meaning from a group context" (Davidson, 1975:85). On the consequential dimension, "personal consequences" are distinguished from "social consequences." Personal consequences are those which "benefit the individual by providing a sense of inner-strength and peace" (Davidson, 1975:86). Social consequences are those which increase both "concern about other people and . . . activity in social groups designed to benefit others" (Davidson, 1975:86). Davidson distinguishes between the desirability of having religious experiences and the frequency with which they occur as separate aspects of the experiential dimension.

The data of the Davidson study (1975:88–90) indicate that (1) vertical and horizontal beliefs are negatively related within the ideological dimensions; (2) religious knowledge and intellectual scrutiny are negatively related within the intellectual dimension; (3) there is a positive relationship between private practice and public practice, the components of the ritualistic dimension; (4) there is no relationship between personal and social consequences; and (5) experiential desirability and the frequency of religious experiences are positively related within the experiential dimension. Moreover, having examined the relationships between the two components within each of the five dimensions, Davidson proceeded to study their relationships across the various dimensions. He found two clusters of relationships, one which he contends denotes religious conservatism, the other, religious liberalism:

> Those components which are most often associated with religious con-
> servatism . . . were positively related to one another and negatively
> related to the components most often associated with religious liberalism
> . . . [which] were positively related to one another and negatively re-
> lated to the other dimensions (1975:90).

13

The components of religious conservatism are identified as vertical belief, private and public religious practice, religious knowledge, experiential desirability and a high frequency of religious experiences, and personal consequences. The components of religious liberalism are identified as horizontal beliefs, intellectual scrutiny, and social consequences.

Davidson notes that the reason Faulkner and DeJong (1966) found a pattern of high positive correlations with their measure of the ideological dimension may have been the absence of measures of *horizontal* beliefs. The high positive relationship they found between the ideological and ritualistic dimensions is also found in Davidson's study, if one looks at the relationship between *vertical* beliefs and either private or public practice. However, no such relationship is found between *horizontal* beliefs and religious practice; indeed the latter relationship is negative, not positive. Similarly, the low relationships involving the consequential dimension may have resulted from a stress on social rather than personal consequences. In short, as Glock (1965) suggested, understanding the relationships among the various dimensions of individual religiosity can be greatly advanced by a more complete understanding of the components of each core dimension. Moreover, by first modifying Glock's framework for the study of individual religiosity and then submitting the modifications to empirical test, Davidson's study (1975) evidences a concern with continuity in both the development of theory and the relationship between theory and empirical study. Such a concern will also be evident in the body of this book as it considers the sociology of religion as the sociology of creed, congregation and community.

Summary

The aim of this book is to further the understanding of the sociology of religion and to provide a basis for enhancing its future development. This aim will be accomplished by focussing attention on three forms of continuity in the development of the sociological study of religion: (1) continuity between theoretical concepts and statements, on the one hand, and empirical measures and studies on the other; (2) continuity in the development of the theoretical concepts and statements themselves, that is, between the classical statements of the past and conscious and concerted efforts to update them by freeing them of any time-bound limitations; and (3) continuity between the sociology of religion and other branches of sociology. This last form of continuity is to be enhanced by concentrating on the processes by which *culture* infuses social relationships with meaning

14

and by which *social organization* fuses social actors into ordered or patterned social relationships. Consequently, the book will focus on the study of religious culture as manifested in creeds, and religious social organizations as manifested in congregations and communities.

In this chapter, a definition of religion based on Durkheim's (1965) discussion of the problem of defining religion was offered. The relationship of that definition to the study of creed, congregation, and community was discussed, as was Glock's (1965) theoretical attempt to identify and define the dimensions of individual religiosity. To illustrate the concern for continuity in the development of the sociology of religion, Glock's theoretical framework was related both to Durkheim's definition of religion and to empirical efforts to measure its key concepts.

FOOTNOTES

1. For a discussion of the classic works of Marx, Durkheim, and Weber and subsequent progress in the sociology of religion based on their work, see Glock and Hammond (1973, esp. chaps. 1–4, and the Epilogue). For another view of the classics in the field, see Parsons (1944).
2. This definition of the subject matter of sociology draws upon that offered by Olsen (1968:3, 55).
3. The distinction between *congregation* and *community* as aspects of religious organization is suggested by Lenski (1963:18–24) in his discussion of the associational and communal aspects of religious groups. Lenski's term *association* is not used since it is rooted in Toennis' distinction between *Geminschaft* and *Gesellschaft* and thus implies that religious associations are "without regard for the affective character of the social relationships required by their collective effort" (Lenski, 1963:20). However, as discussed in Part II, one form of religious congregation (or association), the *sect*, is indeed characterized by a concern for the affective character of the relationships within it. In short, the term *congregation* is preferred not only for its alliterative quality as a companion of *creed* and *community*, but as a less restrictive term than *association*. As discussed in Part III, congregation subsumes both the *church* and the *sect* as types of religious organizations.
4. Durkheim's definition of religion, as it is presented here, is a substantive rather than a functional definition. It focusses on the substance or content of religious activity rather than on functions or consequences for the individual or the society. For a discussion of some of the relative advantages of the substantive definition, see Berger (1974) and Weigart (1974) who give a critique of the functional definition of Luckmann (1967). For other examples of functional definitions of religion, see Geertz (1966) and Yinger (1970:5–16). See Yinger (1969) for an attempt to measure religion defined functionally. For a definition of religion which, like Durkheim's, stresses the role of the sacred, see Eliade (1959).
5. The term *congregation* is substituted for Durkheim's term *church* in order to avoid confusion when discussing organizations in which social actors seek to attain religious ends. As is noted in Part II, the discussion of such organizations is dominated by Troeltsch's distinction between the *church* and the *sect*. The word *congregation* is used here as a generic term to refer to both types of religious organization. Using the term *church* both as the generic term and as the

term for a specific form of organization would lead to unwarranted terminological confusion.

6. For an overview of the process of differentiation as it affects religion, see Bellah (1964). For a discussion of differentiation in modern societies, see Chapter 3 of this book.

7. Of course, not all sociologists of religion interested in the dimensions of religion have stayed within the framework provided by Glock (1965). King and Hunt, for example, have conducted a series of studies outside of that framework (King, 1967; King and Hunt, 1969, 1972a, 1972b, 1975). Some of the dimensions found in their most recent study seem related to those discussed by Glock. For example, what King and Hunt call "creedal assent" may be an aspect of what Glock calls the "ideological dimension"; while what they call "devotionalism" and "church attendance" may be aspects of the ritualistic dimension discussed by Glock, especially as reinterpreted by Davidson (1975). However, King and Hunt's discussion of organizational activity and financial support seem to fall outside Glock's framework. Alternative approaches are taken by Allport (1954: 451–453); Campbell and Coles (1973); Fichter (1969); Ludwig and Blank (1969). Verbit (1970:24–38), offering an approach similar to Glock's, discusses ritual, doctrine, emotion, knowledge, ethics, and community as aspects of religion. Various approaches to the study of individual religiosity are reviewed in Demerath and Hammond (1969:127–154) and in Johnstone (1975:29–58). For a critical evaluation of Glock's approach, see Moberg (1967).

8. This discussion is based on Glock's (1965) original version which first appeared in 1962 as a research supplement to the July–August issue of *Religious Education*. A slightly modified and briefer version is found in Stark and Glock (1968:11–21).

9. The impact of social or demographic variables on a person's location on dimensions of religiosity defined by Glock (1965) is studied by Fukuyama (1961). See also a related study by Putney and Middleton (1961). Factors influencing the location of one particular group, college faculty, on dimensions defined by Glock are studied by Lehman and Shriver (1968) and Lehman (1972, 1974). See also DeJong and Faulkner (1972).

10. The order in which the five dimensions are discussed has been changed from that followed by Glock (1965) to highlight their relationship to the definition of religion offered in this chapter. It should be noted that Glock himself discusses the dimensions in one order when he first defines them (1965:20–21) and then in another when he expands upon his initial definitions (1965:24–38). Hence, the order of discussion apparently is not fixed within Glock's framework.

11. Hunt (1972) devised a scale which distinguishes those who, for example, know and accept a literal interpretation of Christian doctrine, of various miracles, from those, on the one hand, who know the literal doctrine and reject it outright, and those, on the other, who reject the literal interpretation, but accept a nonliteral interpretation.

12. In a related paper, Stark (1965:39–66) identifiies and defines four modes of religious experience: (1) awareness of a divine or sacred presence, (2) a sense that the divine is aware of you, (3) intimate and affective contact, and (4) a sense of being a confidant or agent of the divine. Analogous experiences with the demonic are also defined. Burger and Allen (1973) have attempted to operationalize or measure the typology of religious experiences offered by Stark. For an alternative approach to the measurement of religious experience, see Hood (1970, 1972, 1973, 1975).

13. Glock's own research with Stark follows the pattern he suggested, examining, first, the components of each dimension and then the relationships among them (Stark and Glock, 1968:57–62; 174–182). Their study also includes an examination of religion as community which includes measures which fall outside Glock's original (1965) scheme, but which pertain to the conception of religion as creed, congregation, and community developed above.

14. Weigart and Thomas (1969:262) are critical of the methodology of the Faulkner

and DeJong study (1965). They believe that "Faulkner and DeJong's results may be more an artifact of the equivocation involved in the similarity of the semantic categories of the items than of defensible results from valid responses." Faulkner and DeJong (1969) reject the point made by Weigart and Thomas and assert that their work meets accepted methodological standards. Other criticisms of the Faulkner and DeJong items are found in Gibbs and Crader (1970). However, whatever their methodological purity, Clayton (1968) has replicated Faulkner and DeJong's results, insofar as the scalability of the items is concerned, in a study of 873 students at Stetson University in Florida, although a further analysis (Clayton, 1971:39) indicates that "religiosity as measured by these scales may be empirically unidimensional" rather than five-dimensional as Faulkner and DeJong believe.

REFERENCES

Allport, Gordon W.
1954 "Two kinds of religiosity." In *The Nature of Prejudice*. Reading, Mass.: Addison-Wesley.

Bellah, Robert N.
1964 "Religious evolution." *American Sociological Review* 29 (June):358–374.

Berger, Peter L.
1974 "Some second thoughts on substantive versus functional definitions of religion." *Journal for the Scientific Study of Religion* 13 (June):125–134.

Burger, Gary K., and John Allen
1973 "Perceived dimensions of religious experience." *Sociological Analysis* 34 (Winter):255–264.

Campbell, Colin, and Robert W. Coles
1973 "Religiosity, religious affiliation and religious belief: the exploration of a typology." *Review of Religious Research* 14 (Spring):151–158.

Clayton, Richard R.
1968 "Religiosity in 5-D: a southern case." *Social Forces* 47 (September): 80–83.
1971 "5-D or 1?" *Journal for the Scientific Study of Religion* 10 (Spring): 37–40.

Clayton, Richard R., and James W. Gladden
1974 "The five dimensions of religiosity: toward demythologizing a sacred artifact." *Journal for the Scientific Study of Religion* 13 (June):135–144.

Davidson, James D.
1972 "Religious belief as an independent variable." *Journal for the Scientific Study of Religion* 11 (March):65–75.
1975 "Glock's model of religious commitment: assessing some different approaches and results." *Review of Religious Research* 16 (Winter):83–93.

DeJong, Gordon F., and Joseph E. Faulkner
1972 "Religion and intellectuals: findings from a sample of university faculty." *Review of Religious Research* 14 (Fall):15–24.

Demerath, Nicholas J., III, and Phillip E. Hammond
1969 *Religion in Social Context*. New York: Random House.

17

Durkheim, Emile
1964   *The Division of Labor in Society.* Translated by George Simpson. New York: Free Press (paperback).
1965   *The Elementary Forms of the Religious Life.* Translated by Joseph W. Swain. New York: Free Press (paperback).

Eliade, Mircea
1959   *The Sacred and the Profane: The Nature of Religion.* Translated by William R. Trask. New York: Harcourt Brace Jovanovich.

Faulkner, Joseph E., and Gordon F. DeJong
1966   "Religiosity in 5-D: an empirical analysis." *Social Forces* 45 (December):246–254.
1969   "On measuring the religious variable: rejoinder to Weigart and Thomas." *Social Forces* 48 (December):263–267.

Fichter, Joseph
1969   "Sociological measurement of religiosity." *Review of Religious Research* 10 (Spring):168–177.

Fukuyama, Yoshio
1961   "The major dimensions of church membership." *Review of Religious Research* 2 (Spring):154–161.

Geertz, Clifford
1966   "Religion as a cultural system." In *Anthropological Approaches to the Study of Religion,* edited by Michael Banton. New York: Praeger.

Gibbs, James O., and Kelly W. Crader
1970   "A criticism of two recent attempts to scale Glock and Stark's dimensions of religiosity: a research note." *Sociological Analysis* 31 (Summer):108–114.

Glock, Charles Y.
1965   "On the study of religious commitment." In *Religion and Society in Tension,* edited by Charles Y. Glock and Rodney Stark. Skokie, Ill.: Rand McNally.

Glock, Charles Y., and Phillip E. Hammond, eds.
1973   *Beyond the Classics? Essays in the Scientific Study of Religion.* New York: Harper & Row.

Herberg, Will
1960   *Protestant—Catholic—Jew.* Garden City, N.Y.: Doubleday (Anchor Books).

Hood, Ralph W., Jr.
1970   "Religious orientation and the report of religious experience." *Journal for the Scientific Study of Religion* 9 (Winter):285–291.
1972   "Normative and motivational determinants of reported religious experience in two Baptist samples." *Review of Religious Research* 13 (Spring): 192–196.
1973   "Forms of religious commitment and intense religious experience." *Review of Religious Research* 15 (Fall):29–36.
1975   "The construction and preliminary validation of a measure of reported mystical experience." *Journal for the Scientific Study of Religion* 14 (March):29–41.

Hunt, Richard A.
1972   "Mythological-symbolic religious commitment: the LAM scales." *Journal for the Scientific Study of Religion* 11 (March):42–52.

Johnstone, Ronald L.
1975   *Religion and Society in Interaction: The Sociology of Religion.* Englewood Cliffs, N.J.: Prentice-Hall.

King, Morton B.
1967   "Measuring the religious variable: nine proposed dimensions." *Journal for the Scientific Study of Religion* 6 (Fall):173–190.

King, Morton B., and Richard A. Hunt
1969   "Measuring the religious variable: amended findings." *Journal for the Scientific Study of Religion* 8 (Fall):321–323.
1972a "Measuring the religious variable: replication." *Journal for the Scientific Study of Religion* 11 (September): 240–251.
1972b *Measuring Religious Dimensions: Studies of Congregational Involvement.* Studies in Social Science, no. 1. Dallas: Southern Methodist University Press.
1975   "Measuring the religious variable: national replication." *Journal for the Scientific Study of Religion* 14 (March):13–22.

Lehman, Edward C., Jr.
1972   "The scholarly perspective and religious commitment." *Sociological Analysis* 33 (December):199–213.
1974   "Academic discipline and faculty religiosity in secular and church-related colleges." *Journal for the Scientific Study of Religion* 13 (June): 204–220.

Lehman, Edward C., Jr., and Donald Shriver
1968   "Academic discipline as predictive of faculty religiosity." *Social Forces* 47 (December):171–182.

Lenski, Gerhard
1963   *The Religious Factor.* Garden City, N.Y.: Doubleday.

Luckmann, Thomas
1967   *The Invisible Religion.* New York: Macmillan.

Ludwig, David J., and Thomas Blank
1969   "Measurement of religion as a perceptual set." *Journal for the Scientific Study of Religion* 8 (Fall):319–321.

Moberg, David O.
1967   "The encounter of scientific and religious values pertinent to man's spiritual nature." *Sociological Analysis* 28 (Spring):22–33.

Olsen, Marvin E.
1968   *The Process of Social Organization.* New York: Holt, Rinehart and Winston.

Parsons, Talcott
1944   "The theoretical development of the sociology of religion." *Journal of the History of Ideas* 5 (April):176–190.

Putney, Snell, and Russell Middleton
1961   "Dimensions and correlates of religious ideologies." *Social Forces* 39 (May):285–295.

Stark, Rodney
1965   "A taxonomy of religious experience." In *Religion and Society in Tension* edited by Charles Y. Glock and Rodney Stark. Skokie, Ill.: Rand McNally.

Stark, Rodney and Charles Y. Glock
1968   *American Piety: The Nature of Religious Commitment.* University of
        California Press.

Verbit, Mervin F.
1970   "The components and dimensions of religious behavior: toward a re-
        conceptualization of religiosity." In *American Mosaic: Social Patterns
        of Religion in the United States,* edited by Phillip E. Hammond and
        Benton Johnson. New York: Random House.

Weigart, Andrew J.
1974   "Whose invisible religion? Luckmann revisited." *Sociological Analysis*
        35 (Autumn):181–188.

Weigart, Andrew J., and D. L. Thomas
1969   "Religiosity in 5-D: a critical note." *Social Forces* 48 (December):260–
        263.

Yinger, J. Milton
1969   "A structural examination of religion." *Journal for the Scientific Study
        of Religion* 8 (Spring):88–99.
1970   "On the definition of religion." In *The Scientific Study of Religion.*
        New York: Macmillan.

I

the sociology of religious creeds

The Social Sources
of Theism

One of the central problems for the sociology of religion is, to use
Emile Durkheim's phrase, "the old problem of the origins of religion"
(1965:20). Of course, the search for the very first beginnings of
religion has largely been "resolutely discarded," as Durkheim (1965:20)
himself urged. Sociologists have, instead, followed his suggestion
and sought "the ever present causes upon which the most essential
forms of religious thought and practice depend" (1965:20). The search
for such ever present causes has generally moved along the two paths
blazed by Durkheim in his classic study, *The Elementary Forms of the
Religious Life*. The first, and by far the more common path, is taken
by those who ask, "What functions does religion serve?" The second,
less common path is taken by those who ask, "To what do religious
symbols *really* refer?" I shall call those who take the first path
functionalists and those who take the second, for reasons which will be
apparent later, *metaphoric parallelists*. Those who follow the first path
search for the ever present causes of religious beliefs and practices
(religious creeds) in the consequences these have for their adherents.
Those who follow the second path search for the truth-value of religious

symbols as representations of humankind's environment and experiences. This chapter first summarizes the relative positions of the functionalists and the metaphoric parallelists on one key question: What are the ever present social sources or causes of theism, a religious creed about the nature of a god or gods?[1] Theism refers, of course, to but one of the many categories of things and beings regarded as sacred by one or another human grouping. The decision to focus on theistic creeds follows from the tendency of sociologists, including sociologists of religion, to concentrate on the study of industrial societies. Within such societies, theism is the most common creed pertaining to the sacred.

The chapter concludes with an examination of the Marxian view of the social sources of theism. The Marxian view employs, in modified form, a combination of the functionalist and parallelist positions. Thus, an examination of Marxian theory facilitates an understanding of these two positions and of the possible relationships between them. More importantly, the discussion of the Marxian view will highlight continuity in the development of theoretical concepts and statements in the sociology of religion. Unfortunately, the virtual absence of empirical studies testing the functionalist and parallelist positions precludes attention to continuity between theory and empirical data.

Theories of the Ever Present Sources of Theism

The functionalist approach. As indicated above, the functionalist approach seeks to identify the ever present social sources of theism by answering the question, What functions does theism serve? The basic tenet of the functionalist's answer is the assertion that the main function of theism is to help people cope with "the points of maximum strain and tension in human life," when "expectations, in the fulfillment of which people have acquired a deep emotional investment, are doomed to frustration" (Parsons, 1964:164, 167). These frustrations result when one comes face to face with the consequences of the uncertainty, powerlessness, and ethical indifference which characterize the Human Condition (Parsons, 1964:164–166): *uncertainty*, in that "men are 'hit' by events which they . . . cannot foresee"; *powerlessness*, in that even in those human endeavors where energy and skill undoubtedly count for much "unknown and/or uncontrollable factors may and often do intervene to upset any 'reasonable' balance between action and success"; and *ethical indifference*, in that "men must endure deprivation and pain . . . so unequally and so haphazardly . . . 'the good die young while the wicked flourish as the green bay tree'."

24

The conditions of uncertainty, powerlessness and ethical indifference referred to by the functionalists are perhaps best illustrated by the preindustrial or primitive societies studied by the founders of functional theory (see: Radcliffe-Brown, 1948; Malinowski, 1954). In such societies, the vagaries of weather or other natural phenomena beyond the rational control or understanding of its members are capable of frustrating all one's efforts and dreams and, as in all societies, the distribution of rewards and punishments often seems profoundly indifferent to the concepts of justice and morality held by the society, for "the sun rises on the evil and the good and the rain sent on the just and the unjust." However, it would be a mistake to deny that uncertainty, powerlessness, and ethical indifference pervade modern, industrial societies as well as more primitive ones. Even with the advances of science and technology, earthquakes may threaten whole cities, as they do in southern California, and tornadoes may destroy whole towns, as they do in the southwestern United States. Disease and accidental death still strike in unpredictable and uncontrollable ways, and social injustice is far from eliminated. Thus, even in the most advanced modern industrial state, one may suffer the strains and tensions of the frustration of the most dearly held expectations due to the unpredictability, uncontrollability and ethical indifference of the world.

On a more individual level, the conditions the functionalists speak of are very much like those facing the soldier in a foxhole. Important events, indeed the very safety of life and limb, are at the mercy of *unpredictable* shelling by unseen forces: one may do what he can to protect himself, move from foxhole to fortified bunker, yet one remains *utterly helpless* in the face of a direct hit. The mortar and rocket shells *do not care* how moral or immoral their victim's life has been, they simply strike when his "number is up."[2] And just as there are reputedly few atheists in the foxhole, the functionalists contend that theism in some form is widespread, given the uncertainty, powerlessness, and ethical indifference of the Human Condition.

Moreover, according to the functionalist point of view, theism, that is, any set of beliefs in the existence of a god or gods responsible in some way for events in this world, is not only widespread, it helps one cope with the inevitable frustrations of life by providing an explanation of *why* the world is as it is. In the words of Davis (1949:532), "By giving him a world beyond this one, a sort of invisible shell around the factual sphere, the culture enables the individual to interpret any catastrophe." The interpretation, it should be noted, need not make sense intellectually or rationally. It suffices, according to the functionalist, if it makes sense emotionally and is emotionally satisfying. In other words, one can cope with the uncertainty, powerlessness, and ethical indifference of the Human Condition if one can *feel* he knows why the world is as it is, and one can if he believes that some god or gods is responsible for it. One can cope with his frustrations if one believes there is a reason for them, say the functionalists, even if the reason is the action of a god who is itself unpredictable, uncontrollable, and indifferent to human ethics. The *felt* sense of the intelligibility of the Human Condition is the important fact; it is not necessary for the feeling to be defended on rational and intellectual grounds; sufficient faith is all that is needed. Theism provides a framework of meaning within which to cope with the frustrations of an otherwise meaningless existence in which one is hit by events which cannot be foreseen, in which action and success are not in balance and in which deprivation and pain are unequally and haphazardly distributed.

Furthermore, it must be noted that the theism which serves the individual also serves the society of which one is a member. It does so in two important ways. First, by helping individuals cope with their moments of frustration and despair, theism enables them to pursue their normal duties. Without theistic beliefs, then, society would be unable to function, since its members might be continually incapacitated by intolerable and unmanageable frustration. For example, if there were no theistic beliefs to help bereaved parents cope with the death of a very young child, the rest of their lives might be spent in grief rather than in the performance of their normal roles. Thus, theism helps prevent an individual's reaching a breaking point, the point beyond which the burdens of life are too great and normal functioning becomes impossible. Theism, then, can help make conformity to the dictates of society possible.

Theism may also support and legitimate the content of the dictates of society. As Parsons reminds us (1944:188), "if we can speak of a need to understand ultimate frustrations in order for them to 'make sense,' it is equally urgent that the values and goals of everyday life should also 'make sense.'" With the support of theistic beliefs, and thus of the gods, the values and goals of everyday life can make sense in that they can be viewed as consistent with divine will. Everyday values and goals may be seen as ordained by the gods. Such support is important since one set of values or goals may have no intrinsic or universally accepted advantage over another. For example, in some societies, particularly in the Orient, loyalty to one's family is the highest value, while in other societies, particularly in the West, achievement is the highest value. Thus, while an Oriental businessman would prefer to hire a close relative, even if he is not quite the most qualified candidate, in the West the most qualified candidate is preferred over a close relative. For the one, the interests of the family take precedence, even at the expense of the business, while for the other, business interests prevail over family loyalty. Were there no theistically based legitimation for each person's decision, one might find oneself torn between conflicting values, unable to decide whom to hire. However, in the Orient it is generally clear that the gods value family above all else, while in the West, it is generally clear that the gods help those who help themselves. The Oriental and the Westerner can make their decisions with relative ease and remain untroubled by conscience. Indeed, it is just such differences, according to Max Weber, that helped account for the rise of capitalism in the West but not in the East. Thus, a society's theistic beliefs may not only help make conformity possible by helping one cope with the inevitable frustrations of his own powerlessness in an uncertain and indifferent world, they may help shape the direction of his conformity by legitimating the values and goals of the society.

The approach of the metaphoric parallelists. All the approaches to be examined in this section agree that the true (naturalistic) referents of theistic discourses are social facts rather than the supernatural beings the speakers may believe in.[3] All also agree that theistic assertions are *metaphorical* representations of social facts, that is, that there is a *parallel* between the characteristics attributed to the gods and real properties of the social world. Thus, I call this school of the sociology of theism the *metaphoric parallelists*.[4] The three representatives of the school discussed in this section, Durkheim, Swarson, and Simmel, differ as to which assertions about gods are examined and which social facts are seen as their referents.

In *The Elementary Forms of the Religious Life* (1965), Durkheim provides the most general, albeit not the first, of the metaphorical parallelist statements on the social referents of theistic discourse.[5] Swanson's works (1964 and 1967) represent a conscious attempt to refine Durkheim's original formulations. Simmel's work (1957) represents an alternative development of Durkheim's basic thesis.

DURKHEIM'S NONFUNCTIONALIST SOCIOLOGY OF THEISM. Durkheim (1965) describes the social facts which he believes are the true referents of three basic theistic statements: (1) "God is transcendent over the individual"; (2) "God is immanent in the individual"; and (3) "God occupies a world fundamentally different from that which the individual occupies." The key to Durkheim's views on the specific referents of each of these three statements lies in his general proposition (see: 1965:237) that a god stands in the same relationship to his worshippers as does a society to its members. Each of the three relationships between the gods and the individual is said to refer to a similar or parallel relationship between society and the individual. In short, Durkheim implies (1965:257) that before all else, theism is a system of ideas with which the individuals represent to themselves the society of which they are members, and the obscure but intimate relations which they have with it. . . . Though metaphorical and symbolic, this representation is not unfaithful.

Specifically, Durkheim argues that the belief in a god's transcendence is a metaphoric representation or symbolic parallel of the moral authority and superiority of society over its individual members. "In a general way," Durkheim asserts (1965:236–237),

it is unquestionable that a society has all that is necessary to arouse the sensation of the divine in minds merely by the power that it has over them. . . . At every instant we are obliged to submit ourselves to rules of conduct we have neither made nor desired, and which are sometimes contrary to our fundamental inclinations and instincts. . . . The empire which it [society] holds over conscience is due . . . to the moral authority with which it is invested.

In short, experience with the control that society has over their actions, thoughts, and even desires, has convinced people (and correctly so, in Durkheim's view) that there is an entity which is transcendent over them. If they err, it is only in the belief that the entity is a god rather than their society.

However, society is more than a source of authority and controls over its individual members. It is the source of their distinctly human qualities. "A man is a man only because he is civilized," Durkheim says (1965:240–243). Society is the source of his language, his instruments or tools, and his knowledge. Moreover, there are occasions, Durkheim asserts (1965:240), on which the "strengthening and vivifying action of society is especially apparent." Durkheim regards some of these occasions as exceptional, such as those in which one is buoyed by a crowd. However, he also cites less exceptional cases, such as when one experiences a sense of satisfaction and confidence as a result of having performed one's moral duty. Such exceptional and unexceptional occasions coupled with one's learning of and dependence on the methods and traditions provided by society indicate that the

collective force is not entirely outside of us; . . . this force must also penetrate us and organize itself from within us; it thus becomes an integral part of our being and by that fact this is elevated and magnified (Durkheim, 1965:240).

That is, the force which is called *god* or *society* is not only outside and above the individual, it is within him; god is immanent within the individual.

Furthermore, Durkheim notes, the being that is thought to be both transcendent and immanent is also thought to occupy a world fundamentally different from the world of which the individual is a part. He also notes that the individual occupies the world of simple visual objects and that his relationship to such objects is unlike the one he has with society. Simple visible objects are not respected, nor do they "raise us outside ourselves." (Durkheim, 1965:243). Since society is respected and does raise us outside ourselves, Durkheim concludes (1965:243),

> we get the impression that we are in relations with two distinct sorts of reality and that a sharply drawn line of demarcation separates them from each other; on the one hand, is the world of the profane things, on the other that of sacred things.

The individual occupies the former, and the gods, the latter, a fundamentally different world.

SWANSON'S DEVELOPMENT OF THE DURKHEIMIAN THESIS. Swanson (1964) accepts Durkheim's basic tenet that theistic assertions are metaphorical representations or symbols of social facts, and advances the Durkheimian formulations by describing the specific components of society which he holds to be the referents of theistic beliefs.

Swanson uses three properties commonly attributed to gods to aid in identifying the social facts to which theistic assertions refer. He notes that gods are said: (1) to have life spans greater than that of humans, (2) to be orderly and predictable individuals, not diffuse conditions, and (3) to have distinct purposes. Their greater life span suggests to Swanson that gods represent groups rather than individuals, since social facts about the former persist for relatively long periods, while those about individuals do not. The fact that gods are seen as individuals with an identity rather than as diffuse conditions indicates to Swanson that they symbolize particular groups rather than groups in general. Moreover, the distinctive nature of the purposes of each god suggests that each represents a group with distinctive purposes. One class of groups with distinctive purposes is that which has sovereignty over some particular sphere of life. Swanson suggests insofar as a group has sovereignty, it may provide the model for conceptions of the deity (1964:18–21).

Swanson makes it clear, however, that sovereign groups per se are not the model for gods. Gods are, instead, modeled on the social arrangements which constitute sovereignty. He calls these arrangements "constitutional structures," and says they are "what men often conceptualize as personified and supernatural beings" (1964:27). Constitutional structures are the social arrangements which "define those affairs with which [an] organization may legitimately concern itself . . . and 'state' the proper procedures for making and executing decisions" (1964:23). In Swanson's view, gods are metaphoric representations or symbols which parallel not the total society as Durkheim argues, but

29

the "structures by which goals are chosen, and rewards and responsibilities allocated" (1964:190); that is, the structures by which decisions are made in the areas of legitimate concern to the society's sovereign groups. That is, a *god* is a metaphorical representation of some given structure of the political regime. The properties attributed to the gods have their parallels in the structures of the regime.

In Swanson's *The Birth of the Gods* (1964), differences in theistic beliefs from one primitive society to another are shown to be related to differences in the structure of their respective political regimes. Particular theistic doctrines are regarded as metaphorical or symbolic representations of basic facts of the political life of the society. For example, the presence or absence of monotheism is related to the presence or absence of a political or decision-making structure, for which monotheism is a reasonable metaphoric or symbolic representation.

Monotheism, by Swanson's definition (1964:56), is a belief in a single deity or "high god" who is "considered ultimately responsible for all events, whether as history's creator, its director, or both." Swanson goes on to argue (1964:92):

> If we search for the conditions which correspond to the idea of a high god, and if we assume that these conditions will involve the actions of sovereign groups, then we seek situations in which such groups bring unity to the world's diversity.

He contends (1964:63–64) that such a situation, that is, one in which a sovereign group brings unity to the world's diversity, exists when the ultimate sovereign group to which the individual gives allegiance has two or more other groups subordinate to it. The subordinate groups must themselves be sovereign groups with distinctive purposes of their own for then the *super*ordinate group can clearly be seen as modifying them and bringing them together in some fashion. In his later work, *Religion and Regime* (1967:22), Swanson notes that the requisite conditions exist where

> a council of elders from several villages . . . coordinate[s] decisions affecting all of those villages, and in every village, a local council may develop policies affecting several organized clans of which each village is composed. Under these conditions, one overarching source of decision and purpose provides unity among groups diverse in purpose.

Under such conditions, people will come to believe that there is a single spirit or deity who is "considered ultimately responsible for all events." That is, they will develop a monotheism which is a metaphoric representation of the structure of the political regime which governs them. They will come to believe in a god with such attributes as the ability to serve as "the overarching source of decisions and purpose" and to "provide unity among groups diverse in purpose," attributes which have their parallels in the political structure of their real world.

Swanson (1967) seeks to identify the variations in political structure in the countries of Reformation Europe which account for the presence or absence of belief that a high god (monotheistic deity) is immanent in history and in his creations, controlling and directing them. Following the line of reasoning established in his earlier work (1964), he begins by noting that "in explaining a high god's characteristics, one should look at some properties of central government" (1967:23). He continues (1967:28),

> If such [high] gods represent experiences with the unifying activities that central governments exercise over groups subordinate to them, then whether an actively governing high god will be judged immanent should depend on whether the actions of such a government are believed to embody only that government's purposes. . . .

Government, he adds (1967:30), will not be seen as embodying only its own purposes when

> the exercise of government is not, in principle, separated from the influence of special interests [for then] the common purpose, that is, the regime's own distinctive purpose, is difficult to separate from the special.

That is, God is not seen as immanent, controlling, and directing his creations in those countries where the political structure does not protect the regime from the influence of special interests. Such protection is lacking where (1967:42)

> men or groups participate legitimately in a regime not solely as its officers or agents but also in their status as . . . promoters of legitimate special interests that exist independently of the common interest. . . .

Where the purposes of the regime and the purposes of the special interests commingle, there may be one authority that is ultimately responsible to create unity out of diversity, but it will not control and direct that diversity. If such is the case, a belief in a high (monotheistic) god who is not immanent in history or in his creations is a reasonable metaphoric representation of the basic political structure of the regime. Such a belief posits that while there is an authority which is ultimately responsible for creating unity out of diversity, it does not direct or control all the diverse beings in its creation. Other lesser authorities, such as human individuals and groups, may often go their own way, following their own special interests.

SIMMEL'S VARIATION. In contrast to the Swansonian position, Simmel's (1957) formulations do not find parallels for attributes of gods in any specific component of society. Rather such parallels are found with social relationships in general. "[R]eligious ideas could

31

never," claims Simmel (1957:336), "have obtained their influence upon men if they had not been the formulas or embodiments of previously existing relations for which consciousness has not yet found a more appropriate expression. . . ." The relationships Simmel speaks of are clearly *social* relationships: "Religion, whatever else it may be, consists of forms of social relationships which, separated from their empirical content, become independent and have substances of their own attributed to them" (1957:339). Simmel contends that the development of religious thought passes through three stages. First, one experiences some form of social relationship. The attributes of the social relationship are then abstracted and labeled, and become formulae standing for the attributes in question. Having been abstracted, the formulae are "separated from their empirical content," and become concepts in the minds of men. Finally, the abstractions are reified and said to be the *real* attributes of a *real* being. That is, they "have substances of their own attributed to them."

Simmel's approach is illustrated by his explanation of the origin of the assertion that God is a being in whom one can believe (1957: 336–337).

> When I say, "I believe in God," the assertion means something entirely different from the statement, "I believe in the existence of ether waves." . . . It means not only that I accept the existence of God, even though it may not be fully demonstrable, but it implies also a certain subjective relation to him; . . . in all of which there is a peculiar mixture of faith as a kind of method of knowledge with practical impulses and feelings.

He goes on (1957:336) to note that the relationship between a believer and his god just described has its analogy in much of human interaction.

> We do not . . . base our mutual relations by any means upon what we conclusively know about each other. Rather, our feelings and suggestions express themselves in certain representations which can be described only as matters of faith . . . which we illustrate when we "believe in someone"—the child in its parents, the subordinate in his superior, friend in friend, the individual in the nation, and the subject in his sovereign.

To summarize, Simmel begins his explanation of the origins of a belief in God by describing forms of social relationships in which one experiences other people who have a similar believability. He then goes on to argue that the social relationships involved are first abstracted, or conceptualized, then "separated from their empirical content," and finally reified. Thus,

> In faith in a deity the highest development of faith has become incorporate, so to speak, has been relieved of its connection with its social counterpart. Out of the subjective faith-process there develops, contrariwise, an object for that faith (Simmel, 1957:337).

Thus, the three-step process—experience with relationships based on faith, representation of such relations in abstractions, and attribution of substance to those abstractions—is completed, and individuals assert they believe in God. The formula for, or embodiment of, a previously existing social relationship has found an appropriate expression, a metaphoric representation, that symbolizes attributes which have their parallels in the social world.

The Marxian View of the Social Sources of Theism

At the outset, two points should be made clear about the Marxian viewpoint in order to keep it in proper perspective.[6] First, it should be clear that Marx sought only to explain the rise of Protestant Christianity as a concomitant of the industrialization of western Europe. His views, unlike the functionalist and parallelist views, are not intended as a general theory of the social sources of theism ever present across societies, time, and cultures. On the contrary, the Marxian view is intended as a specific theory of the social sources of a given set of theistic beliefs, namely, Protestant theology, in a specific time and place, the period of industrialization within the societies and cultures of western Europe. Secondly, it should be made clear that the Marxian view contains not one, but two distinct, albeit related, theories. The first combines, in modified form, aspects of the functionalist and parallelist approaches. The second centers on one aspect of the functionalist approach, namely, the claim that theistic beliefs may be used to buttress or legitimate everyday values and goals. Both theories will be considered.

Marxian theory: functionalist and parallelist approaches combined. The first of the two Marxian theories of the social sources of theism seeks to explain why bourgeois society, emerging with the industrialization of western Europe, saw God as an alien, inexplicable, and dominating force. The Marxian explanation begins, like the functionalist, with the view that the function of religion, in which theistic beliefs are often a central part, is to help individuals cope with the inevitable frustrations of life. For the Marxian, "Religion is the sigh of the oppressed creature, the heart of the heartless world, just as it is the spirit of a spiritless situation. It is the opium of the people" (Marx and Engels, 1964:42). Religion, and with it theism, is seen as helping to sustain human happiness in the face of the distresses which life brings. The Marxian theory continues with the assertion that theistic beliefs are to be understood as a set of symbolic or metaphorical representations of social conditions, thus fusing the approach of the parallelist to that of the functionalist. The Marxian view, like Swanson's but unlike Durkheim's, argues that theistic discourse is a symbolic or metaphorical representation of specific components of society rather than society as a whole. However, for Swanson the components are political and in the Marxian view they are economic.[7]

The Marxian view introduces an evolutionary scheme not present in either Swanson or Durkheim[8], but not unlike that found in Simmel. This scheme posits a three-stage process in the evolution of theistic beliefs which culminates in monotheism. In the first stage, theistic beliefs reflect the mysterious nonsocial forces of nature. That is, initially theism "is nothing but the fantastic reflection in men's minds of those external forces which control their daily life, a reflection in which the terrestial forces assume the form of supernatural forces" (Marx and Engels, 1964:147). However, in the second stage, theism comes to reflect social as well as nonsocial forces.

> It is not long before, side by side with the forces of nature, social forces begin to be active—forces which confront man as equally alien and at first equally inexplicable, dominating him with the same apparent natural necessity as the forces of nature themselves. The fantastic figures, which at first only reflected the mysterious forces of nature, at this point acquire social attributes, become representatives of the forces of history (Marx and Engels, 1964:147).

Finally, in the third stage, monotheism replaces polytheism as the symbolic representation of the alien forces which dominate man.

> All the natural and social attributes of the numerous gods are transferred to *one* almighty god, who is but a reflection of the abstract man. . . . In this convenient, handy and universally adaptable form, religion can continue to exist as the immediate, that is, sentimental form of men's relation to the alien natural and social forces which dominate them . . . (Marx and Engels, 1964:148; italics in original).

To explain why bourgeois society sees its monotheistic God as an alien, inexplicable, and dominating force, the Marxian now need only to identify the forces which dominate the society. Bourgeois theology can then be shown to attribute to God the properties of these alien forces. It is claimed that the forces which dominate the members of a bourgeois society are "the economic conditions created by themselves, by the means of production which they themselves have produced, as if by an *alien* force" (1964:148; italics added). The parallel between the alien, inexplicable, and dominating monotheistic God of the bourgeois Protestants on the one hand, and the nature of their economic order, on the other hand, is clear:

> It is still true that man proposes and God (that is, the alien domination of the capitalist mode of production) disposes . . . [only when society] by

34

taking possession of all means of production and using them on a planned basis has freed itself and all its members from the bondage in which they are now held by these means of production. . . . When therefore man no longer merely proposes, but also disposes—only then will the last alien force which is still reflected in religion vanish; and with it will also vanish the religious reflection itself, for the simple reason that then there will be nothing left to reflect (1964:148–149).

In sum, the Marxian position is (1) that God, as conceived by the bourgeoisie, is a metaphoric representation of the basic characteristics of the economic order, that is, of the alien inexplicable domination of the capitalistic system over the members of bourgeois society; and (2) that belief in such a God helps one cope with the distresses or frustrations of life in such a society. The approach of the parallelist and of the functionalist are thus combined to help explain the rise of Protestant theology during the industrialization of western Europe.

Marxian theory and legitimation. The second of the two Marxian theories of theism focuses attention on the role of theistic beliefs in buttressing or legitimating everyday values and goals. However, whereas functionalists tend to see theism as supporting the values and goals of the total society, the Marxian stresses its role in supporting the values and goals of one part of society, namely, the ruling class. In the case of the societies of industrializing western Europe, with which Marxians are concerned, the ruling class is the bourgeoisie. Protestant theology is seen as having served two purposes for the bourgeoisie, it helped them get into power and it helped them remain in power. In order to understand how Protestant theology helped the bourgeoisie gain power, it is necessary to recall that the rise of the bourgeoisie meant the end of feudalism and that the Roman Catholic Church was a crucial source of support and legitimation for the feudal system (Marx and Engels: 299).

> The development of the middle class, the *bourgeoisie*, became incompatible with the maintenance of the feudal system; the system, therefore, had to fall. But the great international centre of the feudal system was the Roman Catholic Church. . . . Before profane feudalism could be successfully attacked in each country and in detail, this, its sacred central organization had to be destroyed [italics in original].

According to the Marxian view, the bourgeoisie opposed the Church because it supported and legitimated feudalism and because it failed to support and legitimate the rise of science. The bourgeoisie needed science to ascertain the physical properties of natural objects and the modes of action of the forces of nature in order to develop its industrial production. "Science rebelled against the Church; the bourgeoisie could not do without science, and, therefore, had to join in the rebellion" (Marx and Engels, 1964:300). When the long struggle against the Roman Catholic Church and the feudal system was eventually completed, Protestantism replaced Catholicism in most of industrial Europe, and democracy and capitalism replaced the political and economic institutions of feudalism. Nevertheless, the bourgeoisie did not abandon their theological system. Instead, they soon discovered (1964:303) that the theistic beliefs which legitimated their rise to power offered

> opportunities . . . for working upon the minds of . . . natural inferiors, and making them submissive to the behests of the masters it had pleased God to place over them. In short, the . . . bourgeoisie now had to take a part in keeping down the "lower orders," the great producing mass of the nation, and one of the means employed for that purpose was the influence of religion.

The Protestant theology which helped bring the middle class into power was used to help keep it there by discouraging workers from efforts at social, political, and economic change. Such discouragement resulted from (1) the belief that doing one's job well was a sign of eventual personal salvation, and (2) the importance of the individual and his individual efforts.

For the Protestant, during the industrialization of western Europe, the most meaningful sign that an individual, worker or owner, could attain personal salvation was the ability to perform one's own functions well. Material rewards and material comforts were not of any particular religious or theological significance. Even the poor could reach Heaven, if only they did their jobs well. There was no need to agitate for a better life on this earth. Salvation would come in the next to all good workers, rich and poor, alike. Workers were thus encouraged to focus on the next life, rather than agitate for changes in this one.

Among those who wished for a better earthly life, Protestant theology discouraged the joining of organized efforts which pressed for desired changes by stressing the importance of individual achievement. What one did by virtue of one's own efforts and talents was what mattered. God would judge the individual, not his group. Individual achievements, for which the person could take full credit, would be weighed in the balance, not the accomplishments of the groups to which one belonged. If an achievement was a cooperative effort, the individual would get that much less credit in the final judgment. Thus, workers were encouraged to go it alone, to develop their personal talents, and especially their self-discipline and self-reliance. Since personal salvation could not be advanced by organized group effort, there was no theological reason for joining organized efforts such as those of the socialists or labor unionists which eventually led to the political and economic changes that eased the life and working conditions of the working class in bourgeois capitalist societies.

Summary

This chapter reviewed the positions of two approaches, the functionalist and the metaphorical parallelist, to answering one key question: What are the ever present social sources of the theistic beliefs in a given society? The functionalist answer is based on the tenet that theism helps the individual cope with the inevitable frustrations which result from the powerlessness of the individual in the face of the uncertainty and ethical indifference of the world. To the functionalist, theism helps the individual to feel he understands why the world is as it is, and why deeply held expectations and dreams are repeatedly frustrated. A felt-sense of being in a meaningful universe helps the individual cope with his own frustrations and helps prevent his reaching a breaking point beyond which he could not function as an adequate member of society. Thus, theistic beliefs help make conformity possible and can help shape the direction of that conformity.

The metaphoric parallelists find the key to understanding the ever present sources of theism in the parallel between the characteristics attributed to the gods and real properties of the social world. They contend that theistic assertions are metaphorical representations or symbols of social facts. The relationships which are believed to exist between the individual and the gods are said, by the parallelists, to be symbolic parallels or metaphorical representations of the relationships between specific social organizations and their members. Parallelists may differ on just which theistic assertions to focus upon and on just what social structures these assertions represent, but they all agree that theistic assertions, while metaphorical and symbolic in character, are not an unfaithful representation of the Human Condition.

The chapter also examined two aspects of the Marxian view on the social sources of theism. The first combines modifications of both the functionalist and the parallelist approaches. It holds that theistic beliefs are symbolic representations or metaphoric parallels of the basic economic structures of a society, but yet help one to cope with the distresses and frustrations of living within those structures. The second aspect of Marxian theory focusses attention on the role of theistic beliefs in the support or legitimation of everyday values and goals. It holds that the same theology which is used by a subordinate class to gain power at the expense of its rulers may then be used by them to maintain their own newly found position as the ruling class.

FOOTNOTES

1. Throughout this book, the term *theism* is used in its general sense to refer to beliefs about any god or gods, rather than in the more specific sense which refers to a belief in one God as the creator and ruler of the universe. The term *theology* has not been used since it refers not only to beliefs about the attributes of a god or gods per se, but to the study of other religious issues, such as sin and salvation, as well. (See *The American College Dictionary*, 1966:1255, 1256).

2. Feifel (1974) and Nelson (1974) provide empirical studies of the role of religosity in general, rather than of theism in particular, in helping one face the prospect that his number is up, for example that one has a terminal illness and death is imminent. Lewis and Lopreato (1962) examine the relationship of aspects of individual religiosity and mechanisms of coping with serious but not necessarily fatal illness.

3. Others, such as Freud (1955, 1960, 1964) and Feuerbach (1957), have agreed with the metaphoric parallelists that theistic statements involve representations of humankind's experience and environment, but contend that the true (naturalistic) referents of theistic discourse are to be found in psychological, rather than social, facts. See also Benson and Spilka (1973).

4. The term *metaphorical parallelism* was coined in Winter (1973) and is used in place of the term *social involvement approach* coined by Swanson (1971:178) for two reasons. *Metaphorical parallelism* refers very clearly and unambiguously to the central thesis of the approach in question, while *social involvement* could well be misleading due to the ambiguity of the term *social*. For example, social involvement could be interpreted as referring to involvement in such social groups as voluntary associations, an involvement not directly nor generally of interest to the approach in question. Bellah's use of the term *symbolic reductionism* (1970:248–250) to refer to the Durkheimian and Marxian positions discussed here is avoided since I do not think the positions in question *need be* reductionistic, although they may be. A metaphoric parallelist need not reject the claim that theistic symbols, in particular, and religion, in general, are a reality *sui generis*. All the metaphorical parallelist need claim is that just as *sui generis* sociological phenomena are not completely independent of psychological processes, neither are *sui generis* theistic symbols completely independent of social processes. To argue that two sets of phenomena are interdependent is not to argue that one is necessarily reducible to the other.

   For a discussion of the reductionist and nonreductionist tendencies within Durkheim, see Wallwork (1972:62–64, esp. 185). For a discussion of such tendencies in Marx, Weber, and other leading theorists in the sociology of religion, see Garrett (1974). Further consideration of the relationship between theistic and sociological discourse as seen from the vantage point of metaphorical parallelism is found in Winter (1973:220–222). The relationship between theistic and sociological discourse as seen from the vantage point of the functionalist approach is also discussed by Shepherd (1972). Basically, it can be said, the metaphorical parallelist approach is more amenable to the possibility of a mutually facilitative relationship between sociological and theological discourse than is the functionalist approach. Examples of such possible mutual facilitation are given in Winter (1973).

5. It should be noted that in his later works, Durkheim did not directly address himself to the development of what I have called the metaphorical parallelist approach. He was apparently more interested (see Durkheim, 1965) in the functions of theism as an integrating factor in society than in the development of the metaphoric parallelist's interests in its symbollic nature. Moreover, the typical summary of Durkheim's sociology of religion moves quickly from noting that Durkheim, as a metaphorical parallelist, held that god was a symbollic representation of society and goes on to emphasize the role of such a symbol

in the processes of social integration (see: Parsons, 1944, and Greeley, 1972:32–34). In any case, the focus of this paper is on the metaphorical parallelist approach taken in one of Durkheim's works and not on the corpus of Durkheim's work. That is, the focus is on an approach once taken by Durkheim and not on the whole of Durkheimian thought. For an alternative view of Durkheim (1965) see Parsons (1973:156–180).

6. The phrase "Marxian view" is used since the works cited are those of Engels as well as Marx. For further discussion of Marxian sociology of religion and of critiques of it, see Birnbaum (1973:3–70).

7. Underhill (1975), in a study of a file of 1168 so-called primitive societies, seeks to determine if belief in a high god (monotheism) is more closely related to one aspect of a society's economic structures, as the Marxian view holds, than to one of its political structures, as Swanson would hold. Underhill finds (1975:859) that with respect to one aspect, the complexity of such economic and political structures "each have effects on monotheism that are independent of the effects of the other, even though part of their effects is shared." Of the two, Underhill believes that the complexity of the economic structure is the more important. Swanson (1975), however, believes that use of more appropriate measures of economic and political structure than Underhill's supports his own position on the social sources of monotheism. He contends (1975:869) that "variation in the number of sovereign groups in hierarchy explains a significant amount of the variance in monotheism" whereas economic factors do not.

8. Of course, as Wallwork (1972) notes, Durkheim did develop an evolutionary scheme in the course of his career. However, the development of such a scheme is not part of his version of the parallelist position and, hence, is not pertinent to the concerns of this chapter.

REFERENCES

1966   *The American College Dictionary.* New York: Random House.

Bellah, Robert N.
1970   *Beyond Belief.* New York: Harper & Row.

Benson, Peter, and Bernard Spelka
1973   "God image as a function of self-esteem and locus of control." *Journal for the Scientific Study of Religion* 12 (September): 297–310.

Birnbaum, Norman
1973   "Beyond Marx in the sociology of religion?" In *Beyond the Classics? Essays in the Scientific Study of Religion,* edited by Charles Y. Glock and Phillip E. Hammond. New York: Harper & Row.

Davis, Kingsley
1949   *Human Society.* New York: Macmillan.

Durkheim, Emile
1965   *The Elementary Forms of the Religious Life.* Translated by Joseph W. Swain. New York: Free Press (paperback).

Feifel, Herman
1974   "Religious conviction and fear of death among the healthy and the terminally ill." *Journal for the Scientific Study of Religion* 13 (September):353–360.

Feuerbach, Ludwig
1957   *The Essence of Christianity.* Translated by George Eliot. New York: Harper & Row.

Freud, Sigmund
1955 *Moses and Monotheism.* Translated by Karen Jones. New York: Random House (Vintage Books).
1960 *Totem and Taboo.* Translated by A. A. Brill. New York: Random House (Vintage Books).
1964 *The Future of Illusion.* Translated by W. D. Robson-Scott. Garden City, N.Y. Doubleday (Anchor Books).

Garrett, William R.
1974 "Troublesome transcendence: the supernatural in the study of religion." *Sociological Analysis* 35 (Autumn):167–180.

Greeley, Andrew M.
1972 *The Denominational Society.* Glenview, Ill.: Scott, Foresman.

Lewis, Lionel S., and Joseph Lopreato
1962 "Arationality, ignorance and perceived danger in medical practices." *American Sociological Review* 27 (August):508–514.

Malinowski, Bronislaw
1954 *Magic, Science and Religion.* New York: Free Press.

Marx, Karl, and Frederic Engels
1964 *On Religion.* New York: Schocken Books.

Nelson, L. D.
1974 "Functions and dimensions of religion." *Sociological Analysis* 35 (Winter):263–272.

Parsons, Talcott
1944 "The theoretical development of the sociology of religion." *Journal of the History of Ideas* 5 (April):176–190.
1964 "Motivation of religious belief and behavior." In *Religion, Culture and Society,* edited by Louis Schneider. New York: Wiley.
1973 "Durkheim on religion revisited: another look at The Elementary Forms of the Religious Life." In *Beyond the Classics? Essays in the Scientific Study of Religion,* edited by Charles Y. Glock and Phillip E. Hammond. New York: Harper & Row.

Radcliffe-Brown, A. R.
1948 *The Andaman Islanders.* New York: Free Press.

Shepherd, William C.
1972 "Religion and the social sciences: conflict or conciliation?" *Journal for the Scientific Study of Religion* 11 (September):230–239.

Simmel, Georg
1957 "A contribution to the sociology of religion." In *Religion, Society and the Individual,* edited by J. Milton Yinger. New York: Macmillan.

Swanson, Guy E.
1964 *The Birth of the Gods.* University of Michigan Press (paperback).
1967 *Religion and Regime.* University of Michigan Press.
1971 "Life with God: some variations of religious experience in a modern city." *Journal for the Scientific Study of Religion* 10 (Fall):169–199.
1975 "Monotheism, materialism and collective purpose: an analysis of Underhill's correlations." *American Journal of Sociology* 80 (January):862–869.

Underhill, Ralph
1975 "Economic and political antecedents of monotheism: a cross-cultural study." *American Journal of Sociology* 80 (January):841–861.

Wallwork, Ernest
1972   *Durkheim: Morality and Milieu.* Cambridge: Harvard University Press.
Winter, J. Alan
1973   "The metaphorical parallelist approach to the sociology of religion: theme, variations and implications." *Sociological Analysis* 34 (Fall): 212–229.

DALE THARP

2

The Weber Thesis:
Its Applicability
to Post—World War II
America

Since it first appeared some seven decades ago, Max Weber's treatise, *The Protestant Ethic and the Spirit of Capitalism* (1958a), has served as a seminal work in the sociology of religion. It has done so despite scathing criticism (e.g., Samuelsson, 1961), sympathetic revision (e.g., Little, 1969), modifications relating the Protestant Ethic to developments in science (e.g., Merton, 1957), in psychiatry (Rotenberg, 1975) and in politics (e.g., Hill, 1973:183–204; Walzer, 1965);[1] and despite much continual debate and analysis (e.g., Andreski, 1964; Bendix, 1967; Birnbaum, 1953; Fischoff, 1944; Forcese, 1968; Green, 1959; Luethy, 1964; Schneider, 1970:95–119; and Wagner, 1964). As a seminal work, it has also spawned numerous empirical studies, both quantitative and qualitative, using data from historical and contemporary settings.[2]

This chapter first summarizes Weber's Thesis concerning the relationship between one particular religious creed, the Protestant Ethic, and a given economic development within Western civilization, namely, the rise of capitalism.[3] In the spirit of highlighting empirical continuity in the sociology of religion, the continuity between theoretical statements and empirical study, this chapter then reviews studies which seek to test the applicability of the Weber Thesis to the United

States after World War II. Since the review concludes that such studies have been largely fruitless and misdirected, the chapter discusses revisions in the Weber Thesis which render it more applicable to conditions in the United States since World War II. Such revisions are offered in the hope of furthering theoretical continuity in the sociology of religion, that is, continuity in the development of theoretical concepts and statements.

The Weber Thesis

Put very briefly and simply, the Weber Thesis, holds that belief in predestination and the doctrine of work as a calling, supported by the theology of certain Protestant sects, was conducive to the development of an ethic of worldly asceticism which, in turn, facilitated (1) the individual's commitment to and attainment of worldly or financial success and (2) the rise of capitalism as an institution with a prevailing ideology or spirit that superseded the ideology of traditionalism that dominated the feudal era. The spirit of capitalism to which Weber referred is an example of what Bendix (1956:2) later termed an *ideology of management*, that is, a set of "ideas which are espoused by or for those who exercise authority in economic enterprises, and which seek to explain and justify that authority." Since the capitalism of which Weber spoke took the form of entrepreneurial capitalism, I refer to the spirit of capitalism which he discussed as the *entrepreneurial ideology*. The term *managerial ideology* is used to refer to the ideology of management[4] in the contemporary era of managerial capitalism.

In his later works, Weber modified his original thesis concerning the relationship between the Protestant Ethic and the entrepreneurial ideology (or spirit) of early capitalism to take into account organizational as well as ideological factors (Weber, 1946; see also Berger, 1971; and Johnson, 1971). In a series of comparative studies (Weber, 1951; 1952; 1958b; see also Eisenstadt, 1973; Warner, 1970), Weber focused more on the progressive rationalization of all areas of Western civilization than on merely the rationalization of the economic realm represented by capitalism (Eisenstadt, 1968a; Luethy, 1964; Nelson, 1973; Swidler, 1973; Wrong, 1970). However, since the quantitative studies reviewed here all purport to test aspects of the original Weber Thesis and rarely, if ever, refer to later developments in his work, and since the revision proposed here pertains only to the original version of the Thesis, the summary which follows deals only with the Thesis as put forth in *The Protestant Ethic*.

It should be clear at the outset that no claim is made that Weber was correct in all aspects of his treatment of the relationship between

44

the Protestant Ethic and the ideology or spirit of entrepreneurial capitalism. It is no doubt true, as Demerath and Hammond (1969:109) have asserted, that "Weber is guilty as charged of historical inaccuracies."[5] However, this chapter focusses on Weber's "fundamental theory" which "continues to be both stimulating and sound," as Demerath and Hammond (1969:109) recognize.

Furthermore, it should be noted that the concept of *elective affinity* is central to Weber's fundamental theory. As Bendix (1962:63) notes,

> Weber stated explicitly that he was investigating "whether and at what points certain '*elective affinities*' are discernible between particular types of religious beliefs and the ethics of work-a-day life. By virtue of such *affinities* the religious movements have influenced the development of material culture, and [an analysis of these *affinities*] will clarify as far as possible the manner and the general direction of that influence . . ." (italics added).[6]

As Gerth and Mills (1958:62–63) recognize, the concept of elective affinity is a decisive concept often used by Weber to relate ideas and interests, a concept he used rather than the more Marxian notions of correspondence, reflection, or expression. Furthermore, they continue (1958:62–63),

> for Weber, there is hardly ever a close connection between the interests or social origin of the speaker or of his following with the content of the ideas during its inception. . . . Only during the process of routinization do the followers "*elect*" those features of the idea with which they have an "*affinity*," a "point of coincidence" or "convergence" [italics added].

In other words, as Stark observes (1958:257), use of the concept of elective affinity implies that

> human groupings, of whatever kind, will, for their part, always be on the look-out for appropriate ideas to give expression to their essence and their strivings. . . . Thus there will be a gradual convergence between substructures and superstructures, not coherence *ad initio*. Like will search for like, and when found, link up with like.

Thus, Weber's fundamental theory makes no claim as to the causal relationship between the rise of a given religious creed, for example, the Protestant Ethic, and the rise of given economic principles and practices, as embodied in the ideology or spirit of entrepreneurial capitalism. However, it is claimed that over time, after the initial rise of the religious creed and economic ideology in question, "like will search for like, and when found, link up with like" on the basis of an elective affinity which gives expression to the essence and strivings of those concerned.

One result of the linking of like with like is that religious beliefs become supportive of an ideology of management which explains and justifies the authority of the capitalist. Consequently, by positing a supportive role for a religious creed in the legitimation of social norms, the Weber Thesis can be regarded as a form of the functionalist approach (discussed in Chapter 1). The Weber Thesis, like the functionalist approach, stresses the role of a religious creed in legitimating the prevailing norms in a given society, such as, the norms embodied in the principles and practices of entrepreneurial capitalist society.

The practices and principles of entrepreneurial capitalism as defined by Weber. For Weber, the practices of the entrepreneurial capitalism of the post-feudal period are "identical with the pursuit of profit, and forever *renewed* profit by means of . . . utilization of opportunities for exchange that [are] (formally) peaceful . . . [and] by means of money" (1958a:17–18, italics and parentheses in original). Entrepreneurial capitalistic practices are, thus, defined in terms of both their goal and the means used to attain it. The goal is not merely profit, but "forever renewed," that is, continuous, profit; the means are peaceful exchanges involving money not, for example, acquisitions by force or barter. The quest is for a steady profit not for a one-shot windfall; the arena is the marketplace not the battlefield or the trading post. In addition, "capitalistic enterprise would not have been possible without two other important factors . . . the separation of business from the household . . . [and] rational capitalistic organization of labor" (Weber, 1958a:21–22). However, Weber's study of the relationships between religious beliefs and capitalism is less concerned with the practices which constitute capitalism than it is with the principles or spirit which provide their rationale for being, that is, with the ideology of management, which explained and justified the authority of the entrepreneur.

The entrepreneurial ideology of management, or spirit of capitalism, as Weber conceived it, consists of three principles: (1) economic rationality, (2) worldly asceticism, and (3) occupation as a calling. Economic rationality, that is, the directing of all activity in terms of its effect on the making of money, is "the idea which gave the way of life of the new entrepreneur its ethical foundation and justification" (1958a:75). Weber goes on to add (1958a:76), that "one of the fundamental characteristics of an individualistic capitalistic economy [is] that it is rationalized on the basis of rigorous calculation, directed with foresight and caution toward economic success." That is, the hallmark of the entrepreneurial ideology is that it gauges all actions in terms of their impact on profit. An entrepreneur may take risks, but they are rational or calculated risks. Moreover, through foresight and caution, that is, through gathering facts and a distaste for impulsive action, he seeks to minimize his risks. The entrepreneur is a businessman, not a gambler. Continuous profitmaking is his main concern. As Weber says (1958a:53), the entrepreneur

> is dominated by the making of money, by acquisition as the ultimate purpose of life. Economic acquisition is no longer subordinated to man as the means for the satisfaction of his material needs.

Nevertheless, while not restrained by its relationship to material needs, the acquisitive drive of the capitalist is restrained by the spirit of capitalism. The spirit of capitalism, the entrepreneurial ideology, was not content to define the good or proper life merely in terms of financial success. It also specified how the successful man should comport himself. As Weber (1958a:71) described him,

> the ideal type of capitalistic entrepreneur . . . avoids ostentation and unnecessary expenditure, as well as conscious enjoyment of power, and is embarrassed by the outward signs of the social recognition which he receives. His manner of life is, in other words . . . distinguished by a certain ascetic tendency. . . .

True, the asceticism of the entrepreneur did not involve the other-worldliness of the monk. It was a "worldly asceticism" (Weber, 1958a: 79–184), that is, practiced in the everyday, secular, work-a-day world, not in a monastery; but an asceticism, a doctrine of self-denial, none-theless. Moreover, the principles of asceticism were so powerful within the spirit of capitalism that they could override the domination of money and acquisition. The tenet of worldly asceticism demanded that the entrepreneur get "nothing out of his wealth for himself, except the irrational sense of having done his job well" (Weber, 1958a:71). The successful, that is, wealthy, man was not to indulge in conspicuous consumption, not to enjoy his power or his prestige. For the entrepreneur, the businessman, the *summum bonum* (supreme good) was "the earning of more and more money, combined with the strict avoidance of all spontaneous enjoyment of life" (1958a:53).

The third, and for Weber most distinctive, component of the ideology or spirit of entrepreneurial capitalism is the "conception of labor as an end in itself, as a calling" (1958a:63). To regard one's work as a calling, is to suggest, at least, that it is a task with spiritual as well as material rewards. It is to regard "the fulfillment of duty in worldly affairs as the highest form which the moral activity of the individual could assume" (1958a:80). The spirit of capitalism held, "The only way of living acceptably to God . . . [is] through the ful-fillment of the obligations imposed upon the individual by his position in the world. That was his calling" (1958a:80). Moreover, what Weber calls "this peculiar idea . . . of one's duty in a calling" (1958a:54) is, in his view, what is most characteristic of the social ethic of capitalistic culture, and is in a sense the fundamental basis of it. It is an obligation which the individual is supposed to feel and does feel towards the content of his professional activity (the German term Weber uses is *Beruf*), no matter in what it consists. . . .

In short, to do your job, to follow your profession, to excel in your chosen career is to be supremely moral; it is to lead the good and proper life.

The concept of the calling was so central to Weber's understanding of capitalism that he held (1958*a*:55) one could not understand how "capitalism could be . . . a way of life common to whole groups of men" unless its origins were understood. Thus, he defined his task as that of discovering "whose intellectual child . . . the idea of calling and the devotion to labor in the calling [is] (1958*a*:78). His search led him to examine the Protestant Ethic to which we now turn in hopes both of understanding it, and, more importantly, of understanding why adherents of the entrepreneurial ideology, the spirit of (early) capitalism, might develop an elective affinity for it.

The Protestant Ethic and the spirit of entrepreneurial capitalism. Weber's thesis can be understood to hold that the fundamental existential problem facing the entrepreneur in the early stages of capitalism was to justify or explain why he regarded success in business as a calling worthy of his great devotion and virtually total commitment. For Weber such devotion and such commitment was neither natural nor rational. Quite to the contrary, he regarded it as "an attitude . . . by no means a product of nature (1958*a*:62), and "irrational from a standpoint of purely eudaemonistic self-interest" (1958*a*:78). Since neither natural nor rational, one's devotion to commercial success was not self-evident and had to be explained. Moreover, an explanation was sought not merely by Weber or other observers, but by the entrepreneur himself. Any belief system which could help provide the entrepreneur with a rationale for his own deepest commitments, with means to express his essence and strivings, would be most welcome. Indeed, it would be a belief system for which he could hold a deep and abiding elective affinity. The Protestant Ethic, according to Weber, was just such a belief system, one which could give expression to the essence and strivings of the entrepreneurial capitalist as well as fitting his material interests, one towards which he could have an elective affinity.

The Protestant Ethic, as understood by Weber, is rooted in the concept of *predestination*. Before defining or discussing this concept, it would be well to restate Weber's disclaimer of interest in the official doctrines per se of Protestantism in favor of a focus on the unintended consequences of accepting them. As Weber (1958a:97) expressed it,

> we are naturally not concerned with the question of what was theoretically and officially taught in the ethical compendia of the time. . . . We are interested rather in something entirely different: the influence of those psychological sanctions which, originating in religious beliefs and the practice of religion, gave a direction to practical conduct and held the individual to it.

We turn now to a consideration of predestination, with an eye toward discovering the "direction to practical conduct" which belief in it gives.

The doctrine of predestination holds, in terms quoted by Weber (1958a:99–101) from the Westminster Confession of 1647, that "by decree of God, for the manifestation of His glory, some men and angels are predestined unto everlasting life, and others foreordained to everlasting death." That is, humanity consists of two broad classes, the elect and the damned. The elect will, when it pleases God, be "taken out of that state of sin and death, in which they are by nature" and be given "that which is good." The damned, on the other hand, face the withdrawal of the "gifts which they had" and will be exposed to the evil consequences of "their own lusts, the temptations of the world, and the power of Satan." Moreover, the status of being one of the elect or one of the damned is a result of the decree of God and that decree alone. It is not dependent in any way on any action or good works an individual may perform. It is a status decreed by God "before the foundation of the world was laid," and is "eternal and immutable." The individual can do nothing, absolutely nothing, to change his status. One can only express or demonstrate it. According to the doctrine of predestination (Weber, 1958a:103):

> We know only that a part of humanity is saved, the rest damned. To assume that human merit or guilt play a part in determining this destiny would be to think of God's absolutely free decrees, which have been settled from eternity, as subject to change by human influence, an impossible contradiction.

However, whether or not one could do anything about his status, "the question, Am I one of the elect? must sooner or later have arisen for every believer and have forced all other interests into the background" (1958a:110). Moreover, as one attempts to discover if he is one of the elect or not, he must face "a feeling of unprecedented inner loneliness" (1958a:104). In his search for a determination of the most important issue of his life, the future of his eternal soul, Reformation man, according to Weber (1958a:104),

. . . forced to follow his path alone to meet a destiny which had been decreed for him from eternity. No one could help him. No priest, . . . no sacraments . . . no church. . . . Finally, even no God.

The decision had been made by God, it had been settled from eternity. No earthly act, not even performing a sacrament, could alter it. No earthly person, no priest, no layman could change it. There simply were no means whatever of attaining grace for those to whom God had decided to deny it. Yet, even though there were no means of changing one's status, one might at least seek signs to alleviate the fears of damnation. That is, Weber notes (1958a:110),

. . . wherever the doctrine of predestination was held, the question could not be suppressed whether there were any infallible criteria by which membership in the elect could be known.

In short, while one might be unable to change one's status, one might at least hope to determine what it was. Moreover, adherents of the Protestant Ethic did eventually develop a consensus as to what criteria were acceptable as indicating that one was among the elect. According to Weber (1958a:114) these criteria encouraged one to determine if

. . . his conduct, at least in its fundamental character and constant ideal, . . . rested on a power within himself working for the glory of God; that it is not only willed of God, but rather done by God.

In other words, one could believe one had attained the "highest good towards which this [Protestant] religion strove, i.e., the certainty of salvation" (Weber, 1958a:115), if one could but convince oneself that one's conduct was fundamentally and ideally what God would have it be, that one was living acceptably to God. What was such a life? As noted above, "the only way of living acceptably to God . . . [is] through the fulfillment of the obligations imposed upon the individual by . . . his calling" (1958a:80). Hence, the best available sign of being among the elect was to fulfill the obligations of your calling, to do your job, to follow your profession, to succeed in your chosen career or business. Thus, the great devotion and virtually total commitment to one's calling, the keystone of the entrepreneurial ideology, was given religious sanction. Devotion and commitment to business was not merely good business, it was a sign of being among the elect. Thus, "the emphasis on the ascetic importance of a fixed calling provided . . . [a] providential interpretation of profit-making [and] justified the activities of the businessman" (Weber, 1958a:163).

There is, then, an elective affinity between the religious beliefs which constitute the Protestant Ethic, with its concept of predestination, and the spirit of (early) capitalism, the entrepreneurial ideology. A belief in predestination provided, through its linkage to the concept of the calling, an expression of the essence and strivings of the entrepreneur, a desire for profit (Weber, 1958a:176–177):

> With the consciousness of standing in the fullness of God's grace and being visibly blessed by Him, the bourgeois businessman . . . could follow his pecuniary interests as he would and feel that he was fulfilling a duty in doing so.

In addition, a belief in predestination supported a concept of calling compatible with the entrepreneur's material interests, particularly in relationships with workers and with the impoverished within entrepreneurial society. The commitment to a calling not only buttressed the entrepreneur's devotion to business, it required an equal devotion on the part of workers to their jobs. All people were to be committed to their calling no matter in what it consisted, whether boss or worker. Thus, "the power of religious asceticism provided him [the entrepreneur] in addition with sober, conscientious, and unusually industrious workers, who clung to their work as to a life purpose willed by God" (Weber, 1958a:177).

Finally, a belief in predestination, in humanity's being divided into the elect and the damned, fit the material interests of entrepreneurs, and freed them from any obligation to care for the impoverished members of society and from any claim that some capital be diverted from business to welfare programs. That is, the Protestant Ethic gave the entrepreneur, as Weber notes (1958a:177),

> the comforting assurance that the unequal distribution of goods of this world was a special dispensation of Divine Providence, which in these differences, as in particular grace, pursued secret ends unknown to man.

In sum, the Protestant Ethic, with its concept of predestination, could converge with the entrepreneurial ideology, the spirit of (early) capitalism; it could be accepted or elected as one of the ideas which sought to explain and justify the authority of the entrepreneurial capitalist. The Protestant Ethic helped give expression to the essence and strivings of entrepreneurs and was compatible with their material interests; it was, in short, a religious belief for which the entrepreneur could hold an elective affinity.

Quantitative Tests of the Applicability of the Weber Thesis

The quantitative studies reviewed here, as noted above, all purport to test aspects of the original Weber Thesis and refer rarely, if ever, to later developments in Weber's work. The studies in question focus on the relationship between Protestantism and an individual's commitment to or attainment of worldly or financial success. The studies do not share Weber's interest in organizational or institutional analysis, but remain almost exclusively on the ideological and individual levels of analysis. As such, they may be regarded as attempts to replicate, in the America of their own time, the study by Offenbacher (1901) to which Weber refers early in the body of his treatise.

Among other things, Offenbacher's findings suggested that "business leaders and owners of capital, as well as the higher grades of skilled labor, and even more the higher technically and commercially trained personnel of modern enterprises" are more likely to be Protestant than Catholic (Weber, 1958a:35). In addition, Offenbacher's study suggested that Protestants were more likely than Roman Catholics to select the type of higher education which facilitated entry into the occupations just cited. Weber (1958a:39) attributed the differential educational and occupational choices of Protestants and Catholics to "the religious atmosphere of the home community and the parental home," and then committed himself to an investigation of ". . . religions with a view to finding out what peculiarities . . . might have resulted in the behavior we have [just] described" (1958a:40). However, as indicated above, the studies reviewed here do not so much seek to improve upon or develop the Weber Thesis, as they seek to determine if the findings of the Offenbacher study which occasioned Weber's initial inquiry can be replicated in the America of their own time. The studies seek to determine the validity of two general assertions, (1) that Protestants achieve higher occupational status than do Roman Catholics due to the distinctive beliefs of ascetic Protestantism, and (2) that for similar reasons, Protestants make better use of educational opportunities than do Roman Catholics.

Much of the recent research relevant to the Weber Thesis was stimulated by the appearance of Lenski's study (1963).[7] Lenski was reacting to a study by Mack, Murphy, and Yellin (1956) which indicated that there were no differences in occupational achievement between Protestants and Catholics, and another by Lipset and Bendix (1959) which held that there were no differences between the rates of occupational mobility between Protestants and Catholics. According to Lenski (1963:84–85) close scrutiny indicates that the data of these two studies do not necessarily support their conclusions. Moreover, he cites data from his own study and that of Weller (1960) which suggest that Protestant-Catholic differences in occupational status and mobility had, in fact, persisted to the end of the fifties, the period of his research. Thus the debate over the replicability of the Offenbacher study cited by Weber was renewed and with it came a renewed interest in the applicability of the Weber Thesis to post-World War II America. Unfortunately, research has done little to resolve the debate or to advance the Weber Thesis.

Research relevant to differential occupational status, deals with three specific subissues: differences in achieved status; differences in intergenerational mobility; and differences in intragenerational mobility. Studies of possible Protestant-Catholic differences in occupational status were done by Burchinal and Kenkel (1962), Crespi (1963), Crowley and Ballweg (1971), Glenn and Hyland (1967), Gockel (1969), Goldstein (1969), Lenski (1963), Morgan et al. (1962), Mueller (1971) and Mueller and Lane (1972). A review of these studies (Bouma, 1973:144) indicates that "in terms of both numbers of studies and quality of research . . . Protestant-Catholic differences in social [occupational] status have become negligible in contemporary North America."[8] Research on differences between Protestant and Catholic intergenerational mobility also fails to yield support for the Weber Thesis (Crowley and Ballweg, 1971; Jackson, Fox, and Crockett, 1970; Mayer and Sharp, 1962; Schuman, 1971; Weller, 1960). Furthermore, in the results of studies by Alston (1969), Featherman (1971), Greeley (1969), and Greeley and Rossi (1966) "there appears to be little evidence in the area of intragenerational mobility to support hypotheses derived from the Weber Thesis" (Bouma, 1973:146).

In sum, available evidence does not support the general assertion, suggested by Weber's use of the Offenbacher study, that in post-World War II America, Protestants achieved higher occupational status than Roman Catholics due to the distinctive beliefs of ascetic Protestantism. First, the assertion that there are differences between the occupational status of Protestants and Catholics is not supported by the evidence. Second, as Bouma observes (1973:147), while it is true that researchers generally fail to measure actual religious beliefs, nevertheless,

> what relevant evidence can be gleaned from the research of the sixties suggests that differences in belief are not the most likely cause of the small and inconsistent differences observed in status and mobility.

A similar lack of support for the Weber Thesis is found in research on differences between the educational attainment of Protestants and Catholics, much of it done by Greeley and his associates (Greeley, 1963a, 1963b, 1967, 1969 and Warkov and Greeley, 1966) but also in the work of Elder (1965), Mueller and Lane (1972), Lenski (1963), Morgan et al. (1962), and Steinberg (1974). A related study by Rhodes and Nam (1970) finds Protestants are not consistently more likely than Catholics to plan to attend college. Indeed, a recent study by Fox and Jackson (1973:83) concludes that

> the small magnitude of the religious differences reported in this and
> past studies clearly suggests that, with the possible exception of men of
> high-status origins, the major branch of Christianity [Protestant versus
> Catholic] one prefers does not exercise an important influence upon
> educational attainment in the contemporary United States.

The past studies alluded to by Fox and Jackson include, in addition to
those already cited: Nam, Rhodes, and Herriot (1968); Warren (1970);
Featherman (1971); and the unpublished works of Laumann (1971)
and Organic (1963).

In sum, efforts to support the two general assertions concerning
differences between Protestant and Catholic occupational status and
educational attainment suggested by Weber's use of Offenbacher's
study have largely failed. Thus, there is reason to support Greeley's
decade-old conclusion (1964:20) "that the Protestant Ethic hypothesis
has no relevance to the study of contemporary America."[9] Indeed,
the temptation is strong to agree with Greeley (1964:33) that "it is
high time for a moratorium" on attempts to apply the Weber Thesis
to post-World War II America. However, since tests of the Thesis
have been inadequate, the sociology of religion could be better served
by a redirection rather than cessation of efforts to so apply the Weber
Thesis.

One line for such redirected efforts would call for more adequate
testing of the Weber Thesis itself rather than mere attempts to
replicate two findings which were only the occasion for work which
led to stating the Thesis and were never intended as proofs or tests
of the Thesis (see Bendix, 1967). A second line of redirected efforts
would take more seriously Weber's own admonition (1958a:181–182)
that his Thesis need not apply to the United States where capitalism
was "victorious" and had attained its "highest development." This
second line of effort would, then, be based on attempts to reformulate
and update the Weber Thesis so as to make it applicable to and
testable in post-World War II American society.

Despite their claims to be doing so, it is highly doubtful that any
of the studies cited above actually test the Weber Thesis. The central
defect in virtually all of the studies cited is a failure to properly operationalize the key independent, intervening, and dependent variables
in the Thesis, respectively, the Protestant Ethic, worldly asceticism,
and the spirit of capitalism. The same failure applies to more specific
derivative concepts, such as belief in predestination, viewing one's
job as a calling, or rationality (see Bouma, 1973:151–153).

Commitment to the Protestant Ethic has generally been opera-
tionalized simply in terms of one's religious identification, that is,
Protestant versus Catholic. Few, if any, studies directly measure
acceptance of the tenets of the Protestant Ethic as defined by Weber.

Indeed, with few exceptions (e.g., Morgan et al., 1962; Rhodes and Nam, 1970; Schuman, 1971), studies even fail to differentiate affiliation with one branch of Protestantism from that with another and merely group all Protestants together as one. However, as Weber made clear, not all Protestants accept what he called the Protestant Ethic. He noted that such acceptance was prevalent primarily among Calvinists, Pietists, Methodists, and Anabaptists, but not among Lutherans. Thus, before efforts to test Weber's thesis are abandoned during some moratorium, it would be better first to direct efforts at improvements in the operationalization of the religious variables. Furthermore, if the Thesis is to be tested against alternative explanations, as scientific procedure requires, it is necessary to determine the possible influence of Protestant beliefs not included in Weber's conception of the Protestant Ethic. Such beliefs would include an emphasis on transcendence, on the Bible as the Word, and on the brotherhood of all men (see Means, 1966). In any case, as Jackson et al. (1970:61) urge,

> it would seem especially important in future research to distinguish among Protestant denominations, to measure religious socialization in childhood as well as current religion, to measure degree of religious involvement, and to assess directly the extent to which economically relevant religious values have been internalized.

Attempts to operationalize the nonreligious variables in the Weber Thesis have been somewhat less rudimentary. Ball (1965) used a measure of belief in the efficacy of rational, personal control, but failed to find support for the Thesis. Goldstein and Eichorn (1961) used measures of the importance of work, attitudes toward health, work, and leisure, and measures of the rationality of one's approach to farming in a study of 260 farmers. Their results (1961:564) suggest to them that

> modern remnants of the Protestant Ethic [may] still contain the need to feel mastery and control over one's life but are no longer accompanied by rational economic behavior. . . .

In a different context, namely, a population of Catholic undergraduate males, Kosa and Rachiele (1963) used measures of occupational, educational, and mobility aspirations as well as a preference for self-employment over a salaried position as indicators of the spirit of capitalism. However, they found that religiousness was not correlated with the spirit of capitalism.

Lenski (1963:83–114) devised other relevant measures, and the use of measures of achievement motivation has been suggested by McClelland (1961). Lenski's measures include those of work values, use of family income, concern with thrift, and attitudes toward installment buying which pertain to one or another element of worldly asceticism. However, Schuman's study (1971), which sought to replicate

Lenski's study, generally failed to reproduce the original results involving these measures. McClelland (1961:47) observes, "Certainly, Weber's description of the kind of personality type which the Protestant Reformation produced is startlingly similar to the picture we have drawn of a person with high achievement motivation." Moreover, as McClelland goes on to note, Weber's reference to the belief that one ought to get "nothing out of his wealth, except the irrational sense of having done his job well" (1958a:71) is remindful of the definition of achievement motivation and is, indeed, "exactly how we define the achievement motive in coding" (McClelland, 1961:47). However, studies by Veroff, Feld, and Gurin (1962), Carney and McKeachie (1963), and Featherman (1971) find no consistent relationship between achievement motivation and religious variables relevant to the Weber Thesis. Moreover, as Featherman (1972:139) observes, "No support appears for the hypothesis that achievement orientations are highly relevant to . . . status attainment." If measures of achievement motivation do operationalize variables in the Weber Thesis, then according to that thesis, such motivation should be highly relevant to status attainment. In short, the use of measures of achievement motivation may lead up yet another blind alley in attempts to support the Weber Thesis with data gathered in post-World War II American society.

Indeed, it may well be, as Lenski (1971:50) concedes, that since Vatican Council II "such differences as existed between Catholics and Protestants [in status attainment] a decade ago have been seriously eroded and likely to diminish in the decade ahead." In other words, the Weber Thesis, as originally stated, may simply not apply to post-World War II American society (see Wagner, 1964; Lane, 1965). Consequently, however adequate their measures of relevant variables, any attempt to test the Weber Thesis in America today may well prove fruitless and misdirected. Moreover, I think it clear that Weber himself would not expect his thesis to apply. Weber's *The Protestant Ethic and the Spirit of Capitalism* is a treatise on the genesis of capitalism. Today, capitalism in America is not in its genesis. To the contrary, it is "victorious" and in its "highest development," to use Weber's own terms (1958a:181, 182). If the Weber Thesis is to be applied it must be updated, that is, reinterpreted and reconceptualized in a fashion which will facilitate application to a society incorporating a highly developed form of capitalism.

Updating the Weber Thesis

The first of three steps needed to update the Weber Thesis is simply to recall that Weber's discussion of the spirit of capitalism can be regarded as a treatment of but one instance of what Bendix (1965:2) has called an *ideology of management*, that is, a set of "ideas which are espoused by or for those who exercise authority in economic enterprises, and which seek to explain and justify that authority." The spirit of capitalism, then, can be seen as the ideology of management which sought to explain and justify the authority of capitalists during the period of the genesis of capitalism. Moreover, it can then be recognized that modern, highly developed capitalism might have a different spirit or ideology of management.

The second step in recasting the Weber Thesis is to acknowledge, as was done above, the centrality of the concept of elective affinity in Weber's work. One is then in a position to update the Weber Thesis by looking for a set of modern religious beliefs for which adherents of a modern ideology of management may hold an elective affinity.

The third and final step is to identify the appropriate modern beliefs and ideology. In so doing, one is merely following the steps taken in Weber's original analysis which first identified the prevailing ideology of management (the spirit of capitalism) and the prevailing set of religious beliefs (the Protestant Ethic), and then sought to find the elective affinity between them. To reinterpret and reconceptualize the Weber Thesis, so as to make it applicable to contemporary society yet consistent with the logic, albeit not the content, of the original, one need only retrace Weber's analysis, replacing the original content with content from the current era. That is, to render the Weber Thesis applicable to post-World War II American society, one must first identify the prevailing ideology of management and the appropriate religious beliefs, and then identify the elective affinity between them.

The practices and principles of managerial capitalism.   In the more than seven decades since the initial publication of *The Protestant Ethic and the Spirit of Capitalism*, the capitalist economy has been altered. An economy characterized by a multitude of small firms, each with a small fund of capital and each under the control of a single entrepreneur, has been supplanted by an economy dominated by relatively few enormous corporations, each with massive capital investments and each under the control of a corps of managers. In short, entrepreneurial capitalism has been superseded by managerial capitalism.

The practices of managerial capitalism may be said to be characterized (as Weber said of entrepreneurial capitalism) by a pursuit of profit in a moneyed economy. Both are capitalistic systems; however, profit making on the part of large corporations is no longer significantly problematic. As Galbraith (1967:93) observers, "big corporations do not lose money." In 1970, a very poor year by all accounts, only 5 of the 100 largest industrial corporations failed to return a profit. Only

10 of the largest 200 and only 34 of the top 500 had losses. Again in 1974, another very poor year, only 4 of the 100 largest industrial corporations failed to return a profit, while only 5 of the top 200, and 21 of the top 500, had losses. In other words, in two of the worst years since the Great Depression of the 1930's, 93 percent or more of the 500 largest industrial corporations still made a profit (see Fortune, 1971:190; 1975:231).[10]

The technical, financial, and marketing aspects of corporate enterprise are, more or less, self-sustaining and successful regardless of who occupies the managerial positions. In a study of 167 large corporations over twenty years, Liberson and O'Connor (1972) found that much of the variance in sales, earnings, and profit margins can be explained by factors other than the impact of management. Hence, it is difficult, if not impossible, for managers within large complex corporations to determine to what extent, if any, their own individual efforts influence corporate profit or loss. Thus, while profit making is by no means ignored, it is not the central focus of the day-to-day concerns of managers nor an adequate gauge of their personal success. Their attention is focussed not on profit making, but on the problems of coordination and direction in a large-scale organization. Concurrently, the principles or spirit which explain and justify the manager's authority differ from those which explain and justify the entrepreneur's authority. Celebration of the entrepreneur's economic rationality has been "superseded by the ideal image of the manager as the skillful organizer of cooperative effort" (Bendix, 1956:441). The manager is judged primarily in terms of skills in dealing with the realities of human interrelations not pecuniary standards. In short, a principle of human interrelations[11] has supplanted economic rationality as a basic principle or component of the spirit of capitalism. In addition, with respect to the two other main principles of early capitalism, worldly humility has superseded worldly asceticism and work as satisfaction has superseded occupation as a calling. In sum, the managerial ideology, or the spirit of modern capitalism, consists of three principles:[12] (1) human interrelations, (2) worldly humility, and (3) work as satisfaction.

The first principle of managerial ideology is the stress on human interrelations within the corporation.[13] This principle recognizes the need for the manager to be a skillful coordinator of cooperative effort and reflects the more complex division of labor, and ever increasing specialization, within the corporation. Corporate endeavor is essentially the endeavor of specialists, each with expertise in a narrow and incomplete portion of the total effort. The reliance on such specialists requires that the corporate manager contend with two important realities. First, there is the fact that all effort within the corporation is basically team effort. Specialists, by the very nature of the narrowness and partiality of their expertise, must join together in a team effort to complete a given task. Teamwork and coordination are simply the other side of the coin of specialization. Secondly, managers must contend with the fact that specialists are experts and know more about their area of concern than any nonspecialist. Thus, managers are placed in the delicate position of attempting to supervise work on matters about which they may know relatively little. These two factors, teamwork and the problems of supervising experts, have important consequences for managers.

The attempt to coordinate a team of specialists cannot succeed if it deals only with matters directly and rationally related to the task at hand. Potential interpersonal problems stemming from various social and emotional factors must also be considered. Even trained specialists may fail to confront each other solely in terms of their common task. Personality clashes, emotions, and pressures from family life and other outside factors affect their efforts and must be considered if the team is to be effective (see White, 1961:127). A manager must deal not only with the requisites of the formal task, but with human interrelations. He must be concerned with worker morale.

The concern with worker morale has very significant implications for the maintenance of the manager's authority. As Miller and Swanson (1958:53) observe,

> a concern with worker morale suggests that managerial skills are now directed toward enlisting worker desires and aspirations. But it also assumes that it is in the worker's power to grant or refuse such enlistment. If he refuses, management will have to continue trying to gain his support . . . [his] loyalty. . . .

If their support or loyalty is not gained, workers may disturb the routines or procedures of productive effort, for example, by transferring to another company or, less overtly, by inefficient or half-hearted work. The problem of gaining worker loyalty is heightened by the fact that workers may often be engaged in specialized efforts where adequate evaluation is beyond the competence and expertise of the manager. As Miller and Swanson note (1958:53–54),

> . . . where supervision is extremely difficult [the worker] must be self-supervised. He must want to perform with high proficiency. . . . There is required a devotion to the welfare of the enterprise and a satisfaction with its procedures. . . . No known technique of supervision could compel such behavior. This kind of loyalty and devotion does not come solely from good pay. . . . [It comes from] a situation in which people find each other's presence to be so mutually rewarding and, simultaneously, so lacking threat, that they feel wholly comfortable and spontaneous and seek to preserve their happy and productive state.

In sum, where managers must supervise specialists whose work they cannot personally evaluate, they must, if they are to succeed, create or organize a rewarding and nonthreatening environment in which the loyalty and devotion basic to self-supervision can flourish. Moreover, they must do all this without undercutting their own authority and while creating an environment conducive to cooperative team effort.[14] Thus, the manager must be a skillful organizer of cooperative team effort. Successful managers have learned how best to structure the relations among the human beings with whom they work. They have learned that an organization which depends on the dedication and discretion of its employees can only succeed if, as Swanson says (1968:823), it "respects its participants as persons and . . . nurtures them not merely as employees . . . but as independent men and women; nurtures their personal growth and personal power."[15] The manager has developed an ideology of management and a definition of the successful manager which focus on the value of human interrelations rather than on economic rationality. The new definition of a successful manager is aptly summarized by Likert,[16] whose research leads him to conclude (1961:102–103) that

> . . . the general principle which the high-producing managers seem to be using and which will be referred to as the *principle of supportive relationships* . . . can be briefly stated: The leadership . . . must be such as to ensure a maximum probability that in all interactions and all relationships with the organization each member will, in the light of his background, values and expectations, view the experience as supportive and one which builds and maintains his sense of personal worth and importance [italics in original].

Worldly humility is the second component or principle of the spirit of corporate capitalism. Like the second component of the spirit of entrepreneurial capitalism, worldly asceticism, it pertains to how one comports oneself after one has achieved success. In the era of early entrepreneurial capitalism, success meant commercial success, and there was a doctrine of comportment vis-a-vis accumulated wealth. In the current era of corporate capitalism, success means success in the management of human interrelations, and a doctrine of comportment is developing with respect to the skillful coordination of the efforts of a team of specialists.

Worldly humility, like worldly asceticism, is a doctrine of self-denial. However, whereas worldly asceticism called upon one to forego the joys which could come from spending accumulated wealth, worldly humility calls upon the successful manager to forego any claim of personal or individual credit. The doctrine requires managers to be humble, to avoid claiming personal credit for the group's success. They cannot claim to be heroes or that their success is a direct result of any unique personal characteristics. They cannot claim sole or even primary responsibility for the successful effort over which they presided as manager.[17] To take personal credit would be, first of all, imprudent. It would invite subversion of future efforts, evince ingratitude towards one's co-workers, and be insensitive to their need to be rewarded and thanked for their efforts. It would be bad for worker morale and thus, bad human relations which could turn success into failure.

The humility of a successful manager is, however, more than a mere expedient. It is a reflection of the realities of his situation. Managers are not heroes. They do not succeed due to their own unique personal characteristics. Their authority is based not on charisma, but legal rationality. Humility, with respect to their role in their own success, is an appropriate, empirically sound response. Moreover, it is a worldly humility, not the humility of an individual before God. It is not the Calvinist doctrine of the worthlessness of the individual in the eyes of God. It is not a humility rooted in doctrines of Original Sin and the inherent depravity of the ungraced human soul. Quite the contrary, it is a humility of this world, a humility in the face of a secular and human reality: the enormity and complexity of corporate endeavor. It is a humility based on the realization that one is esteemed primarily because of one's affiliation with the organization, and only as long as it is maintained. It is a humility based on what Galbraith (1967:107–108) calls the infallible test of whether credit belongs to the individual or the organization, namely, to

> . . . observe what happens to the individual when he leaves the organization. The great physician is not greatly diminished by being separated from his hospital. . . . Nor is the great scientist. . . . They sustained, and were not sustained by, the organization to which they belonged.
>
> By contrast the politician . . . the ambassador . . . the university president . . . [are] sustained by the organization; on losing its support they pass permanently into the shadows. . . .
>
> But for none is the transition more dramatic than for the great business executive. . . . The great entrepreneur lived out his last days disposing of his wealth or resisting those who sought to have him do so. The modern executive does not have . . . such [a] . . . recessional. The conclusion requires no undue emphasis. Preeminently, *the organization man is sustained by the organization* (Italics added).

The success of managers is preeminently tied to the success of their teams, and they cannot take personal credit for it. They are just another part of the organization. To claim personal credit for the group's success would approach hubris. The manager must walk humbly within his organization.

The third component of the managerial ideology, like the third component of the entrepreneurial ideology, is a statement of the reasons why people work. It is a doctrine of the proper reasons or motivation for entering a given occupation or accepting a particular position. Whereas the entrepreneurial ideology proffered a doctrine of work as a calling, the managerial ideology proffers the doctrine of work as satisfaction. As Bendix (1956:441) observes, "the fashionable vocabulary of motives by which the economic conduct of Everyman is 'explained' has shifted from . . . work as a virtue to work as a source of satisfaction." People are now expected to choose their occupation not because they are called to it, or from a sense of obligation or duty, but because they believe they will find it enjoyable or satisfying; because they want to, not because they ought to. One's choice of work is more a matter of personal preference than of ethical obligation.

The doctrine of work as satisfaction, at least as it applies to managers, contains some guidelines for determining what occupation or job one ought to find satisfying. The selection of one's work is left to personal preference, but not to mere personal whim. One's choice is to be guided by the possibility of maximizing *identification* and *adaptation* (see Galbraith, 1967:142–143). Identification is a process whereby one accepts as one's own the goals of the organization one seeks to join. Adaptation is a process whereby one seeks to accommodate or adjust the goals of the organization more closely to one's own. Thus, using the concepts of identification and adaptation as guides, the satisfying occupation or position is defined in terms of the degree of compatibility between the goals of the corporation and one's own. A good job is one in which people are able to attain simultaneously their own goals and the company's. Thus, the relationship between the manager's goals and the corporation's is viewed as a dynamic process of mutual adjustment. Individual managers do not merely adopt the corporation's goals, they seek to have the corporation adapt to their goals as well.

Thus, the managerial ideology holds that managers are motivated to seek a position with an organization in which, by serving its goals, they are increasingly serving their own. This ideology implies that the corporation and its managers are cocreators of the goals they serve, the goals of the manager modified by the corporation through identification, and the goals of the corporation, modified by the manager through adaptation. Thus, the manager does not seek the irrational sense of having done a job well, as much as the satisfying sense of having a good job.[18]

A new Protestant theology and the spirit of managerial capitalism. The fundamental existential problem facing managers in the present stage of capitalism is to justify or explain why they are "organization men" —forever concerned with and sensitive to the needs and feelings of others, denying any personal credit for the successful endeavors in which they participate, finding satisfaction in serving the goals of the organization. Why is one not on one's own and for oneself? Any belief system which could help provide managers with a rationale for their deep commitment to the organization and thus provide a means for expressing their essence and strivings would be most welcome. Indeed, it would be a belief system for which they could hold as deep and abiding an elective affinity as their predecessors, the entrepreneurs, held for the older Protestant Ethic. Significantly, there are developments within theology which can provide the manager with such a belief system.[19] The central feature of these developments, and those which may lead to a theology towards which the manager may turn, is the doctrine of the interdependence of the individual and a loving God in the performance of a common task.

The roots of this doctrine may be found in the effort during the World War I era of the Social Gospel theologian Walter Rauschenbusch to "democratize the conception of God" (see Livingston, 1971:265). Rauschenbusch sought to replace the feudal monarchical categories in theology with the notion that God "works *through* humanity to realize his purposes." "Our universe is not," writes Rauschenbusch (quoted in Livingston, 1971:265), "a despotic monarchy, with God above the starry canopy and ourselves down there; it is a spiritual commonwealth, with God in the midst of us." The new doctrine also draws upon the view of Martin Buber, a Jewish theologian. As expressed in Buber's work, *I and Thou*, in 1923, God could not be known in absolute, non-relational terms, but only within the context of an I-Thou relationship, (see Livingston, 1971:350–353). These two strands of theological thought—that God's work is done in a commonwealth, that is, in a cooperative relationship with individuals, and that God can only be known in a loving, I-Thou relationship—have been developed by the so-called secular theologians of today ranging from the relatively mild radicalism of Cox (1966), Vahanian (1966), and Robinson (1963, 1965) to the "Death of God" theologians, Altizer and Hamilton (1966) and Van Buren (1963).[20] The development in question is evident in the words of widely known secular theologian Harvey Cox. Cox writes (1966:224), "We speak of God in a secular fashion when we recognize man as His partner. . . . Speaking of God in a secular fashion . . . entails our discerning where God is working and then joining His work." He continues (1966:230–231),

> a new type of interhuman relationship seems to be emerging, one that is just as human as I-Thou, but qualitatively different. . . . [I call] this . . . phenomenon the I-You relationship. It describes very well the rewarding relationship one has with a fellow team member, with whom one has worked on a research project. . . . It derives from work that is

> done together by two persons for whom the work is the key to their mutuality. . . . It may be that in addition to the I-Thou relationship with God, . . . contemporary man could meet God as a "you."

A similar view, that is, one which also stresses the cooperative relationship between the individual and a loving God is found in the works of the so-called process theologians (Cobb, 1965; Pittenger, 1968; Ogden, 1967; and Williams, 1968). Process theology itself has been most directly influenced by the writings of Alfred North White-head and Charles Hartshone. Among the central tenets of process theology are the beliefs that (1) "God and the world . . . constitute a society of interdependent entities" (Livingston, 1971:486); and (2) "what we are and do really makes a difference to God. Love is the key to our understanding of God" (Cobb, 1971:135). In short, process theology, like secular theology, stresses the interdependence of the individual and a loving God.

The doctrine of the interdependence of the individual and a loving God in the performance of a common task it will be argued below, is one towards which managers may hold an abiding elective affinity. I turn now to a consideration of this doctrine with an eye towards discovering, as Weber did for the old Protestant Ethic, the "direction to practical conduct" which belief in it may give.

The new theology, with its stress on the interdependence of the individual with a loving God, differs from the old Protestant Ethic in two regards, in its conception of the relationship between God and the individual, and in its conception of the true or basic nature of God.

Within the old Protestant Ethic, the individual is clearly subservient to God. However, within the new theology, God and the individual are equals, mutually dependent upon each other in the performance of a common task. In other words (Swanson, 1968:825),

> . . . in Reformation Protestantism, men were identified as God's creatures or dependents, or servants or worshippers. The most dignified role allotted them was as God's images or as children in his household. . . . New trends in [theology] . . . make another role the chief one, namely, the role of man as equally dependent with God in a common task.

Moreover, the task referred to is not the one which the old Protestant Ethic stressed. It is not the sorting of humanity into the elect and the damned. God is no longer seen as "an overseer or recorder of imperfections" (Swanson, 1968:828). The true or basic nature of God is no longer understood to be that of Divine Judge. God is now regarded as a loving God, whose basic nature is to love, and to nurture human beings. Without human beings to nurture, God cannot be God. By His very nature, God must help individuals develop their creativity, their initiative, their skill and their involvement in

64

the continuing creation or development of a just world. As individuals develop themselves as unique beings they are performing the same task to which God's nature draws Him. Thus, God and the individual perform a common task, and, with Swanson (1968:826), we see "that the proper name of the common task is love. . . . Nurturing men as persons is loving, and the nurturance obtained is love itself."[21]

From the vantage point of seeking a basis for an elective affinity between the manager and the new theology, the import of a doctrine of the interdependence of the individual with God in the nurturance of human beings is that it subordinates both to the exigencies of their common undertaking. As a consequence, as Swanson (1968:818) notes,

> . . . and despite God's divinity, there emerges a significant equality with man because . . . when all participants are subordinated to the exigencies of a common principle—a common undertaking—a hierarchical subordination of one collaborator to another is justified only by the technical requirements of their work, this leaving them equal as persons and equally necessary as fellow workers.

In short, God and the individual become co-workers, or more accurately, colleagues. They are related much as managers are to the team of specialists over whom they preside. First of all, the hierarchical subordination of others to God or to a corporate manager is justified because of their expertise in the technical requirements of their respective positions—God as nurturer, the manager as coordinator of cooperative endeavor. Secondly, both must seek to enlist the loyalty and devotion of their co-workers if they are to be fulfilled in their undertaking. Both are concerned with interrelations among human beings; both must seek to nurture the hierarchical subordinates who are their co-workers. Finally, neither can claim sole responsibility for the success of the endeavor over which they preside for it is a cooperative endeavor, not an heroic exploit. Whatever satisfaction or honor one can draw from one's efforts is justified only to the extent to which one has subordinated oneself to the common cooperative undertaking.

In other words, managers believing in the doctrine of the interdependence of the individual with a loving God, can believe that in their own relationship to their organization and coworkers, they are like God. The manager's relationship to co-workers is analogous to their relationship to God. To aspire to be a skillful coordinator of a cooperative endeavor is to aspire to a God-like skill. Under the new secular theology, the best way of living acceptably to God is to nurture one's co-workers in a cooperative endeavor. To be completely on one's own and for oneself, is to be totally self-reliant and independent, callous and insensitive to the needs of others, and afraid of love.[22] Now if asked, "If you are for yourself alone, what are you?" the corporate manager can respond, "I would be less than I should be, for, made in the image of God, I must strive to cooperate with and nurture my fellow human beings."

In conclusion, the new theology, with its doctrine of the interdependence of the individual with a loving God, could converge with the managerial ideology, the spirit of modern capitalism; it could be accepted or elected as one of the ideas which sought to explain and justify the authority of the corporate manager. The new theology could help give expression to the essence and strivings of the corporate manager. It is, in short, a religious creed to which the corporate manager could hold an elective affinity. Whether corporate managers do in fact hold such an elective affinity remains a matter for future empirical study. Such study would be clearly in the tradition of the Weber Thesis. Moreover, such research would require "sociologists to worship Weber the less and to emulate him the more," as Wax has called upon them to do (1972:279). It would be research which regarded the original Weber Thesis as a modifiable, testable, scientific hypothesis and not as a "revealed doctrine" which, as Means (1965) has pointed out, many have taken it to be. Such research would require sociologists of religion to see beyond the works of a giant such as Weber. It would require that they stand on his shoulders rather than kneel at his feet in unreflective reverence for the master, while fruitless and misdirected attempts to replicate minor aspects of his work in an inappropriate historical setting proliferate. Finally, such research would advance the cause of empirical continuity in the sociology of religion, just as the discussion of this section has sought to advance the cause of theoretical continuity by suggesting how the original Weber Thesis might be revised and updated to make it applicable to conditions in the United States in the post-World War II era.

Summary

This chapter summarized Weber's Thesis concerning the relationship between a religious creed called the Protestant Ethic and an economic development within Western civilization, the rise of entrepreneurial capitalism. In a vein similar to that of the functionalists (discussed in Chapter 1), Weber asserted that a religious creed could become supportive of a prevailing ideology of management and help explain and justify the authority of the early capitalists. Specifically, Weber's Thesis holds that there was an elective affinity between the Protestant Ethic, with its doctrines of predestination, and the ideology or spirit of (early) capitalism, with its principles of economic rationality, worldly asceticism, and work as a calling.

Research seeking to test the applicability of the Weber Thesis to post-World War II American society has concentrated on testing the validity of two hypotheses derived from Weber's work: (1) that Protestants achieve higher occupational status than do Roman Catholics due to the distinctive beliefs of the Protestant Ethic, and (2) that Protestants make better use of educational opportunities than do Roman Catholics for similar reasons. The research was found to be largely fruitless and misdirected lending little, if any, support for the Weber Thesis. Two lines of improved research were called for, one based on improved measures of the variables in the original Weber Thesis and another based on a revision and update of the original thesis so as to make it applicable to the corporate, rather than entrepreneurial, capitalism of American Society today. The revised or updated Weber Thesis argues that there is a basis for an elective affinity between a new theology, stressing a doctrine of the interdependence of the individual with a loving God, and the ideology or spirit of managerial capitalism, with its principles of human interrelations, worldly humility, and work as a satisfaction.

FOOTNOTES

1. Hill (1973:183) reviews the Halevy thesis, offered by a French contemporary of Weber's (Halevy, 1924, 1926, 1927), and regards it as, "in many respects the political corollary . . . of the broader thesis put forward by Weber."
2. Extensive bibliographic material on works bearing on the Weber Thesis are found in Eisenstadt (1968b:385–400) and in Little's bibliographic essay (1969: 226–259).
3. Birnbaum (1953) discusses the relationship between the Marxian views on the rise of capitalism (see Chapter 1) and Weber's views.
4. The term *ideology of management* is used rather than *spirit of capitalism* because I wish to focus on changes in rationales of control or authority rather than on changes in justification of ownership. Reference to capitalism is, at best, equivocal in this regard, that is, it confounds ownership and control.
5. The many criticisms of Weber are reviewed in Fischoff (1944), Green (1959), and Little (1969:226–259). More recently, scholars have accepted the general outlines of Weber's Thesis, but they see the relationship between the rise of Protestantism and the early developmnt of capitalism as more indirect. For example, Demerath and Hammond (1969:103–109) and Jacobs (1971) contend that the rise of Protestantism had no direct impact on the development of capitalism but facilitated the growth of secularism, which in turn aided the growth of capitalism. In any case, regardless of how direct or indirect the link between the Protestant Ethic and the spirit of capitalism *ab initio*, an elective affinity between them may have developed later. It is the possibility of just such an affinity which this chapter explores (see note 6 below).
6. Curiously, as Bendix (1956:64) notes, "the same passages are translated some-

what differently" by Parsons (Weber, 1958a:91–92). The Parsonian version substitutes "correlation" for "elective affinity" and reads, "we can only proceed by investigating whether and at what points certain *correlations* between forms of religious belief and practical ethics can be worked out" (italics added). The original German (Weber, 1947:83) reads, "dass zunaechst untersucht wird, ob und in welchen Punkten bestimmte *Wahlverwandtschaften* zwischen gewissen Formen des religioesen Glaubens und der Berufsethik erkennbar sind" (italics added).

7. There are, of course, studies which predate Lenski's work: such as those by Cantrill (1943), Pope (1948), Bogue (1959), Lazerwitz (1961), and Wagner et al. (1959). However, recent research, as Bouma recognizes (1973:141), stems mainly from Lenski's, rather than from the earlier work. In any case, the results of the earlier studies do not qualify the conclusions or discussions offered here.

8. Bouma reviewed one study in Canada (Porter, 1965) not directly relevant to our present interest in the United States.

9. Indeed, there is debate over the applicability of the Thesis to the colonial era discussed by Weber (1958a). See Hertz (1962) and Little (1969:232–234) for the pro, and Homans (1962) and Kolko (1965) for the con side of the debate. Weber's views on the applicability of his thesis to America at the turn of this century are presented in his essay on the Protestant sects and the spirit of capitalism (1946) and discussed by Johnson (1971).

10. Galbraith (1967:93) provides somewhat less recent figures to support his observation. He notes: "In 1957, a year of mild recession in the United States, not one of the one hundred largest industrial corporations failed to return a profit. Only one of the largest two hundred finished the year in the red. Seven years later in 1964, a prosperous year by general agreement, all of the first hundred made money; only two among the first two hundred had losses and only seven among the first five hundred."

11. Human interrelations is a generic term including both the human relations and human resources approaches identified by Miles (1965) as alternative approaches to management. The human relations approach values the participation of co-workers as a means of gaining their cooperation and their acceptance of the manager's decisions. The human resources approach values the participation of co-workers as a necessary component of quality decision making. The human relations approach tends to view the participation of co-workers as a necessary evil, or means to an end, while the human resources approach tends to view such participation as an intrinsically valuable end in itself. Both approaches, recognize that the successful manager must deal with the realities of human interrelations.

12. I do not claim that the new managerial ideology has been universally accepted, only that it has become the prevailing or predominant ideology. For a discussion of sources of resistance to the new ideology, see Lee (1971) and Miles (1966).

13. In this discussion, managerial ideology is defined so as to highlight parallels and contrasts with Weber's definition of the entrepreneurial ideology (1958a). The present definition has its roots in discussions of managerial ideology (Bendix, 1956); the managerial grid (Blake and Mouton, 1964); motivation-hygiene theory (Herzberg, 1966); man incorporate (Kaufmann, 1969); the system-four approach to participative management (Likert, 1961 and 1967); theory Y (MacGregor, 1960); and the welfare bureaucrat (Miller and Swanson, 1958). See also the commentary of Swanson (1968) and Whyte's analysis of the social ethic (1957).

14. I do not claim all corporate managers are at all times cooperative, collectivity-oriented saints. Competitive and selfish endeavors may remain. However, such endeavors come to be viewed as idiosyncratic, even by managers who engage in them. They become activities to be undertaken *sub rosa* and discussed only

with one's most intimate associates, rather than as customary or normative *modus operandi* that one engages in openly and discusses with anyone.

15. See also MacGregor (1967:13), who contends that "man must seek to create conditions (an organization environment) such that members of the organization at all levels can best achieve their own goals by directing their efforts toward the goals of the organization."

16. A similar view, and one which refers to Buber's concept of the I-Thou relationship to be referred to in this chapter, is noted by Mullen (1966:41). "The successful leader in the modern business organization . . . generally puts the welfare of his subordinates before his own personal advantage; . . . attempts to utilize employee knowledge and initiative . . . as much . . . as he possibly can . . . and tries at all times to maintain with subordinates the 'I-Thou' relationship, the person-to-person approach, and eschews the 'I-It' relationship, the person-to-thing approach. . . ."

17. That is, as Slater and Bennis (1964:55) put it, "more and more, large corporations . . . predicate their growth not on 'heroes,' but on ideal management teams." Similarly, but in more picturesque language, Kaufman (1969:142) observes, "there are still tyrants and tin gods flying corporate colors, . . . but as a working philosophy, autocratic management is on its way out. Little Caesar is an anachronism." For historical case studies of the passing from one-man rule to the reign of more humble management teams, see Dale (1960).

18. For a more traditional account of managerial motivation, but one which nevertheless recognizes the importance of the relationship between corporate and personal goals, see Patton (1971), who speaks of the "excitement factor": "the excitement generated by the purposeful pursuit of a demanding goal" (1971: 194). See also Porter (1962, 1963).

19. Attention here focusses on developments in Protestant theology in America. For a discussion of analogous developments in German Catholic theology and the potential of an elective affinity between this new Catholic theology and the managerial ideology in Germany, see Merck (1975).

20. For a more extensive review of the roots of secular theology, see Gilkey (1967) and Livingston (1971:479–484). See also Johnson (1971:481–484).

21. Interestingly, the development of a new theology is not a process confined to theologians. Stark and Glock (1968) find analogous changes among the laity (see esp. chap. 11). That is, they find a decline in the belief in a judging God in favor of views more akin to those of secular theologians. They also find the rise of a new ethic concerned with the nurturance or love of one's fellows. Finally, they suggest (1968:206) that the pattern of denominational switching indicates an erosion of the old Protestant faith. Specifically, they find a movement from denominations, such as the Baptists, which remain committed to the traditional faith, into denominations, such as the Episcopalians, the Congregationalists, and the Methodists, which have more liberal theologies. Unfortunately, Stark and Glock do not make any occupational breaks. Hence, it is not possible to determine if corporate managers are more or less involved than others in switching denominations or in forsaking traditional beliefs in favor of a new theology.

22. A similar view is developed by Oppen, a sociologist on the theological faculty of Marburg University. He writes (1969:117): "If we . . . remark that the manager, in contrast to the earlier entrepreneur, is today generally not a lonely figure at the summit, but a member of a directing body with which he must collaborate in reaching decisions, the new nature of personal existence embodied here becomes evident: . . . there is now added the crucial question of one's relationship to one's counterpart, a person who stands on his own feet and who, like his superior, also bears responsibility. The individual who stands vis-à-vis another, however, is *more a person* than was the solitary individual who was able to demand unconditional obedience" [italics added].

REFERENCES

Alston, Jon P.
1969 "Occupational placement and mobility of Protestants and Catholics, 1953–1964." *Review of Religious Research* 10 (Spring):135–140.

Altizer, Thomas J. J., and William Hamilton
1966 *Radical Theology and the Death of God.* Indianapolis: Bobbs-Merrill.

Andreski, Stanislav
1964 "Method and substantive theory in Max Weber." *British Journal of Sociology* 15 (March):1–18.

Ball, Donald W.
1965 "Catholics, Calvinists and rational control: further explorations in the Weberian Thesis." *Sociological Analysis* 26 (Winter):181–188.

Bendix, Reinhard
1956 *Work and Authority in Industry.* New York: Wiley.
1962 *Max Weber: An Intellectual Portrait.* Garden City, N.Y.: Doubleday (Anchor Books).
1967 "The Protestant Ethic—revisited." *Comparative Studies in Society and History* 9 (April):266–273.

Berger, Stephen D.
1971 "The sects and the breakthrough into the modern world: or the centrality of the sect—Weber's Protestant Ethic thesis." *Sociological Quarterly* 12 (Fall):486–499.

Birnbaum, Norman
1953 "Conflicting interpretation of the rise of capitalism: Marx and Weber." *British Journal of Sociology* 4 (June):125–141.

Blake, Robert, and Jane S. Mouton
1964 *The Managerial Grid.* Houston: Gulf Publishing Co.

Bogue, Donald J.
1959 "Religious affiliation." In *The Population of the United States.* New York: Free Press.

Bouma, Gary D.
1973 "Beyond Lenski. a critical review of recent 'Protestant Ethic' research." *Journal for the Scientific Study of Religion* 12 (June):141–155.

Burchinal, Lee G., and William F. Kenkel
1962 "Religious identification and occupational status of Iowa grooms, 1953–1957." *American Sociological Review* 27 (August):526–532.

Cantril, Hadley
1943 "Education and economic composition of religious groups: an analysis of poll data." *American Journal of Sociology* 48 (March): 574–579.

Carney, Richard E., and Wilbert J. MacKeachie
1963 "Religion, sex, social class, probability of success and student personality." *Journal for the Scientific Study of Religion* 3 (October): 32–43.

Cobb, John B., Jr.
1965 *A Christian Natural Theology.* Philadelphia: Westminster Press.
1971 "Alfred North Whitehead." In *Twelve Makers of Modern Protestant Thought,* edited by George L. Hunt. New York: Association Press.

Cox, Harvey
1966   *The Secular City*, rev. ed. New York: Macmillan.

Crespi, Irving
1963   "Occupational status and religion." *American Sociological Review* 28 (February):131.

Crowley, James W., and John W. Ballweg
1971   "Religious preference and worldly success: an empirical test in a midwestern city." *Sociological Analysis* 32 (Summer):71–80.

Dale, Ernest
1960   *The Great Organizers*. New York: McGraw-Hill.

Demerath, Nicholas J., III, and Phillip E. Hammond
1969   *Religion in Social Context*. New York: Random House.

Eisenstadt, S. N.
1968a "The Protestant Ethic thesis in an analytical and comparative framework." In *The Protestant Ethic and Modernization*. New York: Basic Books.
1968b ed., *The Protestant Ethic and Modernization*. New York: Basic Books.
1973   "The implications of Weber's sociology of religion for understanding processes of change in contemporary non-European societies and civilizations." In *Beyond the Classics? Essays in the Scientific Study of Religion*, edited by Charles Y. Glock and Phillip E. Hammond. New York: Harper & Row.

Elder, Glen H., Jr.
1965   "Family structure and educational attainment." *American Sociological Review* 30 (February):181–196.

Featherman, David L.
1971   "The socioeconomic achievement of white religio-ethnic subgroups: social and psychological explanation." *American Sociological Review* 36 (April):207–222.
1972   "Achievement orientation and socioeconomic career attainment." *American Sociological Review* 37 (April):131–143.

Fischoff, Ephraim
1944   "The Protestant Ethic and the spirit of capitalism: the history of a controversy." *Social Research* 11 (February):53–77.

Forcese, Dennis P.
1968   "Calvinism, capitalism and confusion: the Weberian Thesis revisited." *Sociological Analysis* 29 (Winter): 193–201.

Fortune
1971   "The five hundred largest U.S. industrial corporations: the money losers." *Fortune* 83 (May):190.
1975   "The five hundred largest U.S. industrial corporations: the money losers." *Fortune* 91 (May):231.

Fox, William S., and Elton F. Jackson
1973   "Protestant-Catholic differences in educational achievement and persistence in school." *Journal for the Scientific Study of Religion* 12 (March):65–84.

Galbraith, John Kenneth
1967   *The New Industrial State*. New York: New American Library (Signet).

71

Gerth, H. H., and C. Wright Mills
1958   "The sociology of ideas and interest." In *From Max Weber: Essays in Sociology*, edited and translated by H. H. Gerth and C. Wright Mills. New York: Oxford University Press.

Gilkey, Langdon
1967   "Social and intellectual sources of contemporary theology in America." *Daedalus* 96 (Winter):69–98.

Glenn, Norval D., and Ruth Hyland
1967   "Religious preference and worldly success: some evidence from national surveys." *American Sociological Review* 32 (February):73–85.

Gockel, Galen L.
1969   "Income and religious affiliation: a regression analysis." *American Journal of Sociology* 74 (May):632–647.

Goldstein, Bernice, and Robert L. Eichorn
1961   "The changing Protestant Ethic: rural patterns in health, work and leisure." *American Sociological Review* 26 (August):557–564.

Goldstein, Sidney
1969   "Socioeconomic differentials among religious groups in the United States." *American Journal of Sociology* 74 (May):612–631.

Greeley, Andrew M.
1963a "Influence of the 'religious factor' on the career plans and occupational values of college students." *American Journal of Sociology* 68 (May): 658–671.
1963b *Religion and Career.* New York: Sheed and Ward.
1964   "The Protestant Ethic: time for a moratorium." *Sociological Analysis* 25 (Spring):20–33.
1967   "Religion and academic career plans: a note on progress." *American Journal of Sociology* 72 (May):668–677.
1969   "Continuities in research on the 'religious factor.'" *American Journal of Sociology* 75 (November):335–359.

Greeley, Andrew M., and Peter H. Rossi
1966   *The Education of Catholic Americans.* Garden City, N.Y.: Doubleday.

Green, Robert W., ed.
1959   *Protestantism and Capitalism: The Weber Thesis and Its Critics.* Lexington, Mass.: Heath.

Halevy, Elie
1924   *A History of the English People in 1815.* Translated by E. I. Watkin and D. A. Barter. New York: Harcourt Brace Jovanovich.
1926   *A History of the English People: 1816–1840.* Translated by E. I. Watkin. New York: Harcourt Brace Jovanovich.
1927   *A History of the English People: 1830–1841.* Translated by E. I. Watkin. New York: Harcourt Brace Jovanovich.

Hertz, Karl H.
1962   "Max Weber and American Puritanism." *Journal for the Scientific Study of Religion* 1 (April):189–197.

Herzberg, Frederich
1966   *Work and the Nature of Man.* New York: Harcourt Brace Jovanovich.

Hill, Michael
1973   "The Halevy thesis." In *A Sociology of Religion.* New York: Basic Books.

Homans, George C.
1962   "The Puritans and the clothing industry in England." In *Sentiments and Activities.* New York: Free Press.

Jackson, Elton F., William S. Fox, and Harry J. Crockett, Jr.
1970   "Religion and occupational achievement." *American Sociological Review* 35 (February):48–63.

Jacobs, Jerry
1971   "From sacred to secular: The rationalization of Christian theology." *Journal for the Scientific Study of Religion* 10 (Spring):1–10.

Johnson, Benton
1971   "Max Weber and American Protestantism." *Sociological Quarterly* 12 (Fall):473–485.

Kaufman, Carl B.
1969   *Man Incorporate.* Garden City, N.Y.: Doubleday (Anchor Books).

Kolko, Gabriel
1965   "Max Weber on America: theory and evidence." In *Studies in the Philosophy of History,* edited by George H. Nadel. New York: Harper & Row.

Kosa, John, and Leo D. Rachiele
1963   "The spirit of capitalism, traditionalism, and religiousness: a re-examination of Weber's concepts." *Sociological Quarterly* 4 (Summer): 243–260.

Lane, Ralph, Jr.
1965   "Research note on Catholics as a status group." *Sociological Analysis* 26 (Summer):110–112.

Laumann, Edward O.
1971   "The persistence of ethnoreligious differences in the worldly success of third and later generation Americans." Paper, American Sociological Association Meetings, Denver, as reported in Fox and Jackson (1973).

Lazerwitz, Bernard
1961   "A comparison of major United States religious groups." *Journal of the American Statistical Association* 56 (September):568–579.

Lee, James A.
1971   "Behavioral theory and reality." *Harvard Business Review* 49 (March–April):20–28; 157–159.

Lenski, Gerhard
1963   *The Religious Factor.* Garden City, N.Y.: Doubleday (Anchor Books).
1971   "The religious factor in Detroit: revisited." *American Sociological Review* 36 (February):48–50.

Lieberson, Stanley, and John F. O'Connor
1972   "Leadership and organizational performance: a study of large corporations." *American Sociological Review* 37 (April):117–130.

Likert, Rensis
1961   *New Patterns of Management.* New York: McGraw-Hill.
1967   *The Human Organization.* New York: McGraw-Hill.

Lipset, Seymour M., and Reinhard Bendix
1959   *Social Mobility in Industrial Society.* University of California Press.

Little, David
1969   *Religion, Order and Law.* New York: Harper & Row.

Livingston, James C.
1971   *Modern Christian Thought.* New York: Macmillan.

Luethy, Herbert
1964   "Once again—Calvinism and capitalism." *Encounter* 22 (January):26–39.

MacGregor, Douglas
1960   *The Human Enterprise.* New York: McGraw-Hill.
1967   *The Professional Manager.* New York: McGraw-Hill.

Mack, Raymond W., Raymond J. Murphy, and Seymour Yellin
1956   "The Protestant Ethic, level of aspiration and social mobility." *American Sociological Review* 21 (June):295–300.

Mayer, Albert J., and Harry Sharp
1962   "Religious preference and worldly success." *American Sociological Review* 27 (April):218–227.

McClelland, David C.
1961   *The Achieving Society.* New York: Van Nostrand.

Means, Richard L.
1965   "Weber's Thesis of the Protestant Ethic: the ambiguities of received doctrine." *Journal of Religion* 45 (January):1–11.
1966   "Protestantism and economic institutions: auxiliary theories to Weber's Protestant Ethic." *Social Forces* 44 (March):372–381.

Merck, Gerhard
1975   "Managementideologie und theolgische Lehrmeingungen: aktuelle Wahlverwandtschaften." *Die Neue Ordnung* 29 (3):221–229.

Merton, Robert K.
1957   "Puritanism, Pietism and science." In *Social Theory and Social Structure,* rev. ed. New York: Free Press.

Miles, Raymond
1965   "Human resources and human relations." *Harvard Business Review* 43 (July–August):148–163.
1966   "The affluent organization." *Harvard Business Review* 44 (May–June):106–115.

Miller, Daniel R., and Guy E. Swanson
1958   *The Changing American Parent.* New York: Wiley.

Morgan, James N., Martin H. David, Wilbur J. Cohen, and Harvey E. Brazer
1962   *Income and Welfare in the United States.* New York: McGraw-Hill.

Mueller, Samuel A.
1971   "The new triple melting pot: Herberg revisited." *Review of Religious Research* 13 (Fall):18–23.

Mueller, Samuel A., and Angela V. Lane
1972   "Tabulations from the 1957 current population survey on religion: a contribution to the demography of American religion." *Journal for the Scientific Study of Religion* 11 (March):76–98.

Mullen, James H.
1966   *Personality and Productivity in Management.* New York: Temple University Press.

Nam, Charles B., A. Lewis Rhodes, and Robert E. Herriot
1968   "School retention by race, religion and socioeconomic status." *Journal of Human Resources* 3 (Spring):171–190.

Nelson, Benjamin
1973 "Weber's Protestant Ethic: its origins, wanderings and foreseeable futures." In *Beyond the Classics? Essays in the Scientific Study of Religion*, edited by Charles Y. Glock and Phillip E. Hammond. New York: Harper & Row.

Offenbacher, Martin
1901 "Konfession und Soziale Schichtung: Eine Studie Ueber die Wirtschaftlische Lage der Katholiken und Protestanten in Baden." *Tuebingen and Leipzig*, vol. IV, pt. V, of the *Volkwirtschaftliche Abhandlungen der badischen Hochschulen*, as reported in Weber (1958a).

Ogden, Schubert
1967 *The Reality of God*. New York: Harper & Row.

Oppen, Dietrich von
1969 *The Age of the Person*. Philadelphia: Fortress Press.

Organic, Harold
1963 "Religious affiliation and social mobility in contemporary American society." Ph.D. dissertation, University of Michigan, as reported in Fox and Jackson (1973).

Patton, Arch
1971 "Motivating tomorrow's executive." In *The Arts of Top Management*, edited by Roland Mann. New York: McGraw-Hill.

Pittenger, Lyman W.
1968 *Process Thought and Christian Faith*. New York: Macmillan.

Pope, Liston
1948 "Religion and class structure." *The Annals of the American Academy of Political and Social Sciences* 256 (March):84–91.

Porter, John
1965 *The Vertical Mosaic: An Analysis of Social Class and Power in Canada*. University of Toronto Press.

Porter, Lyman W.
1962 "Job attitudes in management. I. perceived differences in need fulfillment as a function of job level." *Journal of Applied Psychology* 46 (December):375–384.
1963 "Job attitudes in management. II. perceived importance of needs as a function of job level." *Journal of Applied Psychology* 47 (April):141–148.

Rhodes, A. Lewis, and Charles B. Nam
1970 "The religious context of educational expectation." *American Sociological Review* 35 (April):253–267.

Robinson, Bishop J. A. T.
1963 *Honest to God*. Philadelphia: Westminster Press.
1965 *The New Reformation*. Philadelphia: Westminster Press.

Rotenberg, Mordecai
1975 "The Protestant Ethic against the spirit of psychiatry: the other side of Weber's Thesis." *British Journal of Sociology* 26 (March):52–65.

Samuelsson, Kurt
1961 *Religion and Economic Action: A Critique of Max Weber*. New York: Harper & Row.

Schneider, Louis
1970   "Religion and the extrareligious spheres: the case of the Protestant Ethic." In *Sociological Approach to Religion*. New York: Wiley.

Schuman, Howard
1971   "The religious factor in Detroit: review, replication and re-analysis." *American Sociological Review* 36 (February):30–38.

Slater, Philip, and Warren G. Bennis
1964   "Democracy is inevitable." *Harvard Business Review* 42 (March–April):51–59.

Stark, Rodney, and Charles Y. Glock
1968   *American Piety: The Nature of Religious Commitment*. University of California Press.

Stark, Werner
1958   "The theory of elective affinity." In *The Sociology of Knowledge*. New York: Free Press.

Steinberg, Stephen
1974   *The Academic Melting Pot: Catholics and Jews in Higher Education*. New York: McGraw-Hill.

Swanson, Guy E.
1968   "Modern secularity: its meaning, source, and interpretation." In *The Religious Situations: 1968*, edited by Donald R. Cutler. Boston: Beacon Press.

Swidler, Ann
1973   "The concept of rationality in the work of Max Weber." *Sociological Inquiry* 43 (1):35–42.

Vahanian, Gabriel
1966   *No Other God*. New York: Braziller.

Van Buren, Paul
1963   *The Secular Meaning of the Gospel*. New York: Macmillan.

Veroff, Joseph, Sheila Feld, and Gerald Gurin
1962   "Achievement motivation and religious background." *American Sociological Review* 27 (April):205–217.

Wagner, Helmut R.
1964   "The Protestant Ethic: a mid-twentieth century view." *Sociological Analysis* 25 (Spring):34–40.

Wagner, Helmut R., Kathryn Doyle, and Victor Fisher
1959   "Religious background and higher education." *American Sociological Review* 24 (December):853–856.

Walzer, Michael
1965   *The Revolution of the Saints*. Cambridge: Harvard University Press.

Warkov, Seymour, and Andrew M. Greeley
1966   "Parochial school origins and educational achievement." *American Sociological Review* 31 (June):406–414.

Warner, R. Stephen
1970   "The role of religious ideas and the use of models in Max Weber's comparative studies of non-capitalist societies." *Journal of Economic History* 30 (May):74–87.

Warren, Bruce L.
1970   "Socioeconomic achievement and religion: the American case." *Sociological Inquiry* 40 (Spring):130–155.

Wax, Murray
1972   "Commentary on Weber special issue." *Sociological Quarterly* 13 (Spring):278–279.

Weber, Max
1946   "The Protestant sects and the spirt of capitalism." In *From Max Weber: Essays in Sociology,* edited and translated by H. H. Gerth and C. Wright Mills. New York: Oxford University Press.
1947   *Gesammelte Aufsaetze zur Religionssoziologie.* Tuebingen: Mohr.
1951   *The Religion of China.* Translated by Hans H. Gerth. New York: Free Press.
1952   *Ancient Judaism.* Translated and edited by Hans H. Gerth and Don Martindale. New York: Free Press.
1958a *The Protestant Ethic and the Spirit of Capitalism.* Translated by Talcott Parsons. New York: Scribner.
1958b *The Religion of India.* Translated and edited by Hans H. Gerth and Don Martindale. New York: Free Press.

Weller, Neil J.
1960   "Religion and social mobility in industrial society." Ph.D. dissertation, University of Michigan, as reported in Lenski (1963).

White, Winston
1961   *Beyond Conformity.* New York: Free Press.

Whyte, William F.
1957   *The Organization Man.* Garden City, N.Y.: Doubleday.

Williams, Daniel Day
1968   *The Spirit and Forms of Love.* New York: Harper & Row.

Wrong, Dennis
1970   "Rationalization and the sociology of religion." In *Max Weber.* Englewood Cliffs, N.J.: Prentice-Hall.

Religious Creeds
and the Integration
of Advanced Industrial
Society

This chapter examines the role of religious creeds (religious beliefs and practices) in the processes that provide for the integration (unity and order) of advanced industrial societies, such as those in western Europe, the United States, Japan, and the USSR.[1] In such societies, as Durkheim (1964) recognized, societal integration results mainly from organic rather than mechanical solidarity, or, to use the modern idiom, from functional integration rather than from normative integration. Functional integration is the interdependence and coordination of the activities of differentiated components of society. Normative integration is the adherence to common cultural elements. Religious creeds are intimately connected with the processes of normative integration, for example, by supporting given values (see Chap. 2). Thus, the role of religious creeds in the integration of a society declines as the society becomes primarily integrated on functional rather than normative grounds. That is, religious creeds become less and less important in the integration of a society as it becomes less and less a single cultural or normative unit and more and more a single functional unit, as in the case of an advanced industrial society. "If there is one truth" the history of such societies "teaches us beyond doubt" Durkheim says (1964:169),

> it is that religion tends to embrace a smaller and smaller portion of social life. Originally, it pervades everything; everything social is religious. . . . Then, little by little, political, economic, scientific functions free themselves from the religious function, constitute themselves apart and take on a more and more acknowledged temporal character.

The process whereby the domination of religious institutions and symbols over the nonreligious declines has been called secularization by many sociologists of religion (e.g., Berger, 1967a:107; Wilson, 1966:xiv). Secularization has come to have many different and often conflicting meanings, as is made clear by Krausz (1971), Martin (1969), Schneider (1970), and Shiner (1967). In the interest of clarity, it would be best to use specific terms for each of the relevant processes. Following Shiner's suggestion (1967:213), this chapter adopts Parsons' practice (1962, 1963, 1966b) and uses the term *differentiation* rather than *secularization* to refer to the decline of religious institutions and symbols.[2] The influence of religious creeds in the integration of advanced industrial society is also diminished by what Weber (1958) has called the *disenchantment of the world*, a waning of beliefs and practices relative to the sacred. Such disenchantment results from increasing intellectualization and rationalization as manifested, perhaps best, in science and scientifically oriented technology, and also in modern bureaucracy. Disenchantment entails, as Weber notes (1958: 139), a belief that

> . . . there are no mysterious incalculable forces that come into play, but rather that one can, in principle, master all things by calculation. This means that the world is disenchanted. One need no longer have recourse to magical means in order to master or implore the spirits, as did the savage, for whom such mysterious powers existed. Technical means and calculation perform the service.

The process of disenchantment results in a world which is (Shiner, 1967:215) "gradually deprived of its sacred character as man and nature become the object of rational-causal explanation and manipulation." The culmination of such a process (Shiner, 1967:215) "would be a completely 'rational' world society in which the phenomenon of the supernatural or even of 'mystery' would play no part."

Durkheim, as well as Weber, recognized the possibility of a world disenchanted by the inroads of science (1965:479):

> Ever since the authority of science was established, it must be reckoned with. . . . From now on, the faith no longer exercises the same hegemony

as formerly over the system of ideas that we may call religion. A rival power [science] rises up before it which . . . submits it to its criticism and control. And everything makes us foresee that this control will constantly become more extended and efficient, while no limit can be assigned to its future influence.

Durkheim's observation notwithstanding, there are limits to the role and influence of the disenchantment of the world, even in an integrated, advanced, industrial society. The limits in question stem, in part, from the inability of science to solve moral or ethical issues. Science may help one master life technically (Weber, 1958:144), but "it leaves quite aside . . . whether we should and do wish to master life technically and whether it ultimately makes sense to do so."

Underlying both our examination of the impact of differentiation on the role of religious creeds in the integration of advanced industrial society and that of the impact of disenchantment, is a concern with the viability of Durkheim's contention (1965:474) that there is "something eternal in religion which is destined to survive all the particular symbols in which religious thought has successively enveloped itself." As Greenwald (1973) suggests, this contention may represent a shift in Durkheim's thinking about societal integration and may well contradict his earlier belief that the influence of religion inevitably declines in advanced industrial society. Nevertheless, the admonition that there is something eternal in religion is intriguing and should be given serious consideration.

To Durkheim (1965:474–475), the eternal something concerns the role religion plays in facilitating the efforts of a society to meet its "need of upholding and reaffirming at regular intervals the collective sentiments and the collective ideas which make [for] its unity." He came to believe that this need existed in all societies, however advanced industrially they may become. Accordingly, the eternal aspects of religion are (1965:62) the "beliefs and practices which unite into one single moral community . . . all those who adhere to them."[3] In other words, the eternal aspect is the role of religious creeds in the normative integration of a society, that is, in the processes which advance societal unity and order through adherence to common normative and cultural elements. Thus, whatever the changes in the specific *content* of religious creeds, regarded by Durkheim as "beliefs and practices relative to sacred things (see the Introduction), their *function*, their role in the normative integration of society, will persist.

This chapter discusses the impact of differentiation and disenchantment on the role of religion in the integration of advanced industrial societies. It does this with an eye toward determining the viability of the Durkheimian contention that the role of religious creeds in societal integration will persist and, even if diminished, not fade away completely.

Differentiation and the Role of Religious Creeds in Societal Integration

As indicated above, advanced industrial society is characterized by the differentiation of religious creeds from nonreligious creeds. The value systems, codes of behavior, and even the world view and epistemology of each differentiated sphere are applied to that sphere and are thought of as not necessarily applying to any other sphere. If religious principles are applied to another sphere it is because the internal dynamics or requirements of that sphere justify its application, not because the religious principles in question are accepted as intrinsically or preeminently worthwhile. For example, if business people decide to keep their word, and honor their contracts, it is understood to be because they find it to be good business, and not because religious considerations make it incumbent upon them to do so. The institutions of science and religion are similarly differentiated. They operate, as Hammond (1963:99) observes, in distinct spheres so that

> not for a long time has the church claimed to decide conflicts of a cognitive and *empirical* nature. The "right" way of building bridges and plotting planets has long since been institutionalized elsewhere [in theoretical and applied science]. . . . Religion no longer "informs" science. Conversely, the church's claim has not been questioned in matters of a cognitive and *non-empirical* nature. . . . Religion can and does inform . . . in matters of a cognitive and non-empirical nature [italics added].

As Berger notes (1967a:107), the nonreligious "sectors of society and culture are removed from the domination of religious institutions and symbols" which characterized preindustrial medieval societies. Religious and nonreligious institutions now operate in their separate, differentiated spheres. Common norms and a common culture no longer forge religious and nonreligious creeds into a single unity. The situation brought about by differentiation, according to Berger (1967a:133),

> represents a severe rupture of the traditional task of religion, which was precisely the establishment of an integrated set of definitions of reality that could serve as a common universe of meaning for the members of a society.

Moreover, the process of differentiation in advanced industrial society is not confined to the relationships between religious and nonreligious creeds. The various nonreligious institutions and their creeds are, in turn, each differentiated from one another. For example, the institutional creeds of the economy, politics, science, the family, and the arts are differentiated from one another. In other words (Luckmann, 1967:101), differentiation is a "process in which autonomous institutional 'ideologies' replaced within their own domain . . . an overarching and transcendent universe of norms" which had prevailed under the aegis of the medieval Church. In an advanced industrial society, the normative and cultural systems of one institutional sphere are not thought of as necessarily applying to those of another. There is no overarching set of norms or culture, no overarching creeds. While business is business, for example, and is run for private profit, government is presumably run for the public good. The standards used to judge a person's business behavior differ from those used to evaluate a civil servant's performance. What may be sauce for a person in business could well cook a civil servant's goose.

What is deemed proper in one institution in a differentiated society is apt to be deemed improper or undesirable in another. Parents ought to be emotionally involved with their children, but for scientists, emotional involvement with the subjects of their experiments would be improper. Each institutional sphere follows its own code of behavior, its own world view, its own creed. Each institution is shaped by its own history and its own internal dynamics. Common norms, a common culture or creed, do not forge the various institutions into a single moral community. There is, instead, a plurality of normative or cultural systems. They may be incompatible, yet none necessarily has to yield to another. Each is accepted as fully legitimate within its own domain.

As Berger and Luckmann have argued, the role of a religious creed in the life of an individual in a differentiated society is changed by the existence of a plurality of normative and cultural systems (Berger, 1967a, 1967b; Luckmann, 1967; Berger and Luckmann, 1963).[4] In their view, the religious creed becomes an essentially private or subjective matter rather than a public or objective one.[5] "More specifically," as Berger expresses it (1967a:151),

> the religious contents are "de-objectivated," that is, deprived of their status as taken-for-granted, objective reality in consciousness. They become "subjectivized" in a double sense: Their "reality" becomes a "private" affair of individuals, that is, loses the quality of self-evident intersubjective plausibility—thus one "cannot really talk" about religion any more. And their "reality" insofar as it is still maintained by the individual, is apprehended as being rooted within the consciousness of the individual rather than in any facilities of the external world. . . .

As a consequence of one's religious creed being a private affair, Luckmann (1967:99) observes, "the individual may choose from the assortment of 'ultimate' meanings as he sees fit—guided only by the preferences that are determined by his social biography." The individual is free to be a consumer in the marketplace of ideas and practices, free to choose between religious and nonreligious creeds or among religious creeds as he sees fit. Thus, a religious creed may serve to integrate, unify, and give order to the life of an individual or a group of individuals. Nevertheless, as Fenn notes (1972:31), while there are

> a number of symbolic systems which can be used to integrate individual biographies, or legitimate the claims of certain strata and institutions, these systems are inadequate to transform [differentiated] societies into a coherent normative order.[6]

Of course, as Fenn admits (1972:31), differentiation "does not drive religion from modern society." To the contrary, it "fosters a type of religion which has no major function for the *entire* society" (italics in original). That is, however relevant religious creeds may be to particular individuals and subgroups, they offer little that is relevant to the legitimation and integration of the total complex which is the social system of a differentiated advanced industrial society (see Hammond, 1963:99; Robertson, 1970:55–58; and Fenn, 1973:358).

The existence in society of organized or institutional religion that is "irrelevant in terms of moving forces" may appear paradoxical, Berger notes (1961:103).[7] He observes, however, that (1961:103)

> the paradox resolves itself in a simple proposition: The social irrelevance of the religious establishment is its functionality. . . . Organized religion . . . is functional precisely to the degree to which it is passive rather than active. . . . It is in this capacity that it is respected socially and supported politically . . . [and] meets many important psychological needs of the individual.

In this passive capacity, religion may serve as the basis for the integration of an individual's activities or identity,[8] and may also be used to commemorate significant events in one's life as when one is "hatched, matched, or dispatched," that is, at birth, marriage, or death. However, in this passive capacity, religion is not displaying the eternal something of which Durkheim spoke: its role in upholding and reaffirming, at regular intervals, the sentiments and ideas which help unify the lives not only of individuals or of subgroups, but of the total society. Hence, one must look further to find the something eternal in religion as manifested in modern societies, if indeed there is such a manifestation. It has been suggested that the so-called civil religion is that manifestation. We turn next to examine it.

The Civil Religion and the Limits
of Differentiation

Those who have sought to demonstrate that the something eternal in religion is the role of religious beliefs and practices in facilitating societal integration have generally based their efforts on a key Durkheimian assumption. Specifically, they assume, with Durkheim (1965: 475), that societal integration

> cannot be achieved except by the means of reunions, assemblies and meetings where the individuals, being closely united to one another, re-affirm in common their common sentiments; hence, come ceremonies which do not differ from religious ceremonies, either in their object, the result which they produce, or the processes employed to attain their results.

Consequently, the search for the eternal something in religion requires (1) the identification of appropriate common sentiments and (2) the identification of appropriate ceremonies. These ceremonies, like regular religious ceremonies, must have as their object sacred things, things set apart and forbidden. They must result in the upholding and reaffirmation of common sentiments. They must employ processes which invoke and manipulate sacred symbols.

Those who have taken these two steps have generally come to identify civil religion as manifesting the something eternal in religion in advanced industrial societies.[9] As Bellah (1967:5) acknowledges, the term *civil religion* comes, interestingly enough, from Rousseau not Durkheim. However, the relevant analyses of its content and function (e.g., Bellah, 1967; 1968; 1974; 1975) are clearly within the framework of Durkheim's discussion of the eternal aspects of religious creeds.[10] That is, civil religion is said to involve sentiments and ceremonies (beliefs and practices) which serve to integrate a society through the affirmation and manipulation of symbols sacred to that society.

The claim that the civil religion of an advanced industrial society plays a role in furthering societal integration is not a universally accepted one. Critics (e.g., Fenn, 1972) object that such a society is characterized by a high degree of differentiation and pluralism. Hence, they contend, its integration is not heavily dependent upon common sentiments or values. However, sociologists working within the Durkheimian framework do not necessarily argue that societal integration is heavily dependent upon a civil religion. At most they need only argue that the civil religion plays a necessary, even if small, role in societal integration. Moreover, those working in the Durkheimian tradition imply that however differentiated advanced industrial society may be, there is one institutional sphere which can be said to dominate or at least represent the society. The sphere they single out is the nation-state, the realm of politics and government.[11] That is, as Verba (1965:353) expresses it, they hold that "many of the functions that religion and religious symbols perform elsewhere in holding society together are performed in [an advanced industrial society] by the central political symbols." Thus, as Verba continues (1965:354), "political commitment . . . contains a prime component of primordial religious commitment" and "governmental institutions may have the significance of a religious kind" (1965:352).

In general terms, then, a civil religion may be defined, following Bellah (1967:8), as a collection of beliefs, symbols, and rituals with respect to sacred things which are institutionalized in a nation-state and its government and which, in turn, further the unity and order of the state and the society it represents.[12] Although aspects of a civil religion have been studied in England (see Shils and Young, 1953) and may well exist in other advanced industrial societies as well, the most extensive discussions of a civil religion refer to the American example, to which I now turn.[13]

The *American civil religion* is a "set of religious beliefs, symbols and rituals growing out of the American historical experience interpreted in the dimension of transcendence" (Bellah, 1968:389). The relevant historical interpretations draw upon popular themes in both Judaism and Christianity. For example, the American civil religion interprets the origins of American society in terms which refer to the biblical accounts of the Garden of Eden and the wandering of the people of Israel in the wilderness after the Exodus from Egypt (Bellah, 1975:3–16). American civil religion also makes frequent reference to God's special concern for a chosen people (Bellah, 1975:36–50). Indeed, it draws an analogy between Americans and the chosen people of Israel. Within this analogy (Bellah, 1967:8), "Europe is Egypt: America, the promised land. [And] God has led his people to establish a new sort of social order that shall be a light unto all nations."

Civil religion in America also celebrates the American Way of Life. Indeed, it is plausible to claim, as does Herberg (1974:79) that "the American Way of Life . . . is the civil religion of Americans." This way of life is most familiar in its political and economic aspects. Specifically, the American Way of Life "on its political side . . . means the Constitution. . . . On its economic side, it means 'free enterprise'" (Herberg, 1974:79). However, the American civil religion is not necessarily the worship of the American nation. It can be regarded as (Mead, 1967:477–478) "essentially prophetic" with its ideal and aspiration standing "in constant judgment over . . . the people, reminding them they are being judged and found wanting."[14] It includes (Bellah, 1967:12), "at its best . . . a genuine apprehension of universal and transcendent religious reality as seen in or, one could almost say, as revealed through, the experience of the American people."

The sacred objects in America's civil religion include the events of the American Revolution and the Civil War, as well as (Bellah, 1967:8) the "Declaration of Independence and the Constitution [as] the sacred scriptures." Moreover, as Hammond (1963:102) notes, the American civil religion raises "to hagiologic stature, the persons thought to have conceived and instituted the [American democratic] procedure: The Washingtons, Jeffersons and Lincolns." The civil religion also has (Herberg, 1974:62) "its sancta and shrines—think of Washington, D.C. and Hyde Park." Finally, in addition to its belief, symbols, and sacred objects, the American civil religion includes certain rituals or ceremonies. According to Warner (1953:2), these rituals comprise a

> ceremonial calendar which allow[s] Americans to express their common sentiments about themselves and share their feelings with others on set days pre-established by the society for this purpose. This calendar functions to draw all people together to emphasize their similarities and common heritage; to minimize their differences; and to contribute to their thinking, feeling and acting alike.

Memorial Day is, perhaps, the chief ceremony within the American civil religion (see Cherry, 1969; Bellah, 1967; Warner, 1953, 1961). Through the Memorial Day rites, Warner (1961:259) claims, the honored dead "become powerful sacred symbols which organize, direct, and constantly revive the collective ideals of the community and the nation." In addition to Memorial Day, the "annual ritual calendar for the civil religion" (see Bellah, 1967:11) includes the birthdays of Washington, and Lincoln, the Fourth of July, Veterans Day, and, of course, Thanksgiving.[15] Not all the important rituals and ceremonies of the American civil religion are celebrated annually. For example, one very central ceremony, the Presidential Inaugural, is scheduled on a quadrennial basis. Moreover, the occasion for certain crucial ceremonies is unpredictable. Chief among these (as recognized by Bellah, 1967; Cherry, 1969 and 1970, and especially Verba, 1965) are the funeral ceremonies for national figures, especially if they are important political leaders. In recent years, the funerals of John F. Kennedy, Martin Luther King, Jr., and Robert Kennedy have been occasions to reaffirm and uphold America's common values and are, as such, examples of the American civil religion in operation.

From a Durkheimian standpoint, the various ceremonies of the civil religion are clearly its most important aspect. Their importance stems from Durkheim's assumption (1965:475), noted at the beginning of this discussion, that the upholding and reaffirming of the collective sentiments and ideas which make for societal unity "cannot be achieved except by means of reunions, assemblies and meetings where the individuals, being closely united to one another reaffirm in common their common sentiments." In other words, as applied by students of the civil religion, the Durkheimian view is that (Shils and Young, 1953:80)

> a society is held together by the internal agreement about the sacredness of certain fundamental moral standards. . . . The central authority of an orderly society . . . is acknowledged to be the avenue of communication with the realm of the sacred values. . . . Intermittent rituals bring the society . . . into contact with [their] sacred values.

In short, the importance of the ceremonies of the civil religion stems from their role in facilitating the normative integration of the society, that is, in maintaining support for central normative and cultural elements. Furthermore, in light of both their function in furthering normative integration and their reference to sacred things, there is, in Durkheim's view (1965:475), no

> essential difference between the assembly of Christians celebrating the principal dates of the life of Christ, of Jews remembering the exodus from Egypt . . . and a reunion of citizens commemorating the promulgation of a new moral or legal system [as on July 4th] or some great event in the national life [such as a Presidential inaugural].

To a Durkheimian, all the ceremonies of the civil religion may properly be called religious. They all have a religious *content*, namely, reference to things sacred; and they all serve the religious *function*, namely, to further societal integration. Thus, the existence of a civil religion can be seen as demonstrating the persistence of religion even in an advanced industrial society. Moreover, the existence of a civil religion supports Durkheim's contention that there is something eternal in religion. Consequently, if the students of the civil religion are correct, even in advanced industrial society, the religious function is being performed with the aid of religious content, although that content has now enveloped itself more in political symbols and ceremonies than in traditional Judeo-Christian symbols and ceremonies.

Of course, the question of just how important the civil religion is in furthering societal integration remains an open empirical question.[16] It may well be that while there is something eternal in religion, it is no longer of very much importance in the integration of an advanced industrial society. Societal differentiation and pluralism may reduce even the civil religion to a greatly diminished role in societal integration. Thus, a civil religion may persist, playing a role in furthering normative integration, never completely fading away, while remaining on the periphery of a society whose integration is overwhelmingly functional in nature.[17] Sociologists of religion do not yet have the data to describe accurately just how important civil religion is to societal integration.

Disenchantment and Its Limits

As noted in the introduction to this chapter, disenchantment is a process whereby belief in the existence of incalculable mysterious or supernatural forces is undermined and replaced by the acceptance of the tenet that all things can, in principle, be mastered by intellectual or rational calculation. Disenchantment is, perhaps, best exemplified by science and by scientifically oriented technology. If disenchantment becomes total, nothing would be regarded as sacred, in the Durkheimian sense of the sacred being a "thing set apart and forbidden" (Durkheim, 1965:62). Beliefs and practices relative to the sacred would vanish in a world dominated by intellectual and rational pursuits.

Ironically, however, the very advance of science and scientifically oriented technology has illuminated possible limits to the process of disenchantment. That is, the advance of science and scientifically oriented technology have shown that it is likely that something of a sacred character will remain despite the inroads of intellectual and rational pursuits, that something will stand apart from, and even forbidden to the advances of rationality and disenchantment.

The possible limits of disenchantment are evident from two sources: (1) the application of the scientific perspective to the study of human endeavors in the development of the social sciences, and (2) experience with the processes which support the research and development of scientifically oriented technology. Both sources, social science and the development of technology, create doubt that a completely rational, intellectual, disenchanted society is possible.[18] To the contrary, they reveal the role of nonintellectual and nonrational processes in human affairs, even in the affairs of those in intellectual and rational pursuits.[19] Consequently, even as science and technology flourish, our era of disenchantment is increasingly characterized as much by a distrust of reason as it is by the use of reason (see Bendix, 1970; Lemert, 1974b). Even the era of disenchantment, it would appear, carries within it the seeds of, if not its own destruction, at least its own limitation.

Social science and the limits of disenchantment. The application of the scientific perspective to the study of human endeavors, especially in the works of Marx and Freud, leads to a questioning (Bendix, 1970:833) of the presumed "autonomy of knowledge and [an assertion] that knowledge is inseparable from its preconditions, whether these are called . . . class situation, or libidinal sublimation" or something else. Moreover (Bendix, 1970:825), the "classical writers of modern sociology . . . Durkheim, Weber, Pareto, Park, Thomas, Cooley, and Mead are discernible as a group by their common concern with the subjective presuppositions of thought." The work of these social scientists supports a position that subjective presuppositions are a precondition of knowledge. This position views the basic premises of science as just another set of subjective presuppositions.[20] Consequently, it is sensible to speak of a *myth* as being the basis of science, as Roszak does (1969:203–248) when he argues a "myth of objective consciousness" undergirds and legitimates scientific endeavor. In short, the application of the scientific perspective to the study of human endeavor leads to the realization that all human activity—even science, the epitome of rational, intellectual, disenchanted endeavor—is rooted in nonrational and nonintellectual elements; indeed, in a myth.

Of course, as Roszak recognizes (1969:209–210), there is an apparent contradiction in terms when one speaks of mythology in connection with science, since science "purports to be precisely that enterprise . . . which strips life of myths, substituting for fantasy and legend, a relationship to reality based, in William James' phrase, on 'irreducible and stubborn fact'." Admittedly, then, "there is no doubting the radical novelty of science in contrast to all earlier mythological world views" (Roszak, 1969:210). The scientific world view is not vulnerable to the kind of criticisms that pertain to temporal or physical mythology. The things with which science fills up time and space (e.g., electrons, gravitational fields, genes, and viruses) are clearly not the cultural equivalents of centaurs, Valhallas, and angels (see Roszak, 1969:212). Nevertheless, science does not reside "in the *world* the scientist beholds . . . but in his mode of viewing that world. A man is a scientist not because of what he sees, but because of how he *sees* it" (1969:213, italics in original). Thus, even though science does not locate its highest values "in mystic symbol or ritual or epic tales of faraway lands and times, but in a mode of consciousness, why should we hesitate to call it a myth?" (1969:214). After all, the crucial point is the "contention that objective consciousness is emphatically *not* some manner of definitive, transcultural development whose cogency derives from . . . [being] uniquely in touch with the truth" (1969:215, italics in original). To the contrary, the myth of objective consciousness, the legitimating myth of science, can be "gotten round and called into question by cultural movements which find meaning and value elsewhere" (1969:215).

Thus, the advance of the social sciences, especially the sociology of knowledge, as Baum (1970:185) notes, "uncovers the faith-orientation in all cultural processes" and reveals that "built into knowledge and the construction of the human world is an attitude toward reality." Moreover (Baum, 1970:185), the resulting "critique of science and its establishment may confront Western culture with the surprising realization that faith about life and people is built into the very construction of the rational, secular world." In other words, social science finds all knowledge, including scientific knowledge, to be relative,[21] specifically, knowledge is relative to subjective presuppositions. Moreover, all such presuppositions are equal, from the standpoint of science, inasmuch as there is no scientific, rational, or intellectual basis for choosing among them. There is, no scientific way to select a philosophy of life or a world view. Such matters involve questions of values and subjective preferences, questions which science per se seeks to avoid. Yet, such questions *cannot be* avoided. The use of intellect and reason, even in science itself, rests on factors that stand apart from intellect and reason in that they are subjective (nonintellectual and nonrational). Moreover, regardless of what the subjective presuppositions of knowledge are rooted in (libidinal sublimation, class situation, the collective conscience, an *Ethik*, a *Geist*, residues and sentiments, definitions of the situation and wishes, a primary group, or a generalized other) they are ineffable to a significant degree. They cannot all be put into words, certainly not the words of calm, unemotional, rational, intellectual prose. Consequently, with respect to science, these presuppositions bear what Smith (1968:587–588) calls "authentic marks of the sacred." They are "incomprehensible, in domitable, and important." They are incomprehensible to science because they are ultimately subjective and ineffable; they are indomitable because they resist complete analysis by science and cannot be mastered completely by purely technical means and calculations; yet they *are* important, since science cannot proceed without them.

As science advances into the study of human endeavors, it discovers what to itself is sacred or at least transcendent, namely, the subjective presuppositions upon which knowledge itself is based and upon which the order and unity (integration) of the scientific community is largely based. These presuppositions, while essential to rational and intellectual scientific endeavors are not themselves scientific; they are *in* science but not *of* science. They stand somewhat apart from science. Indeed, such presuppositions are forbidden to the advance of science, in that they are ultimately beyond the grasp of scientific manipulation. In short, the realm of subjective presuppositions —of values, ethics, ideology and epistemology, intuition and imagination—will remain no matter how disenchanted science makes the world. Indeed, in a world dominated by science, the realm of subjective presuppositions, namely, the mind and social relationships, may be regarded as sacred (see Smith, 1968:589, 591). Accordingly, even in a scientific age, it is not surprising that interest in mysticism, consciousness expansion, and encounter groups spreads.[22] That is, as Greeley (1970:206, 207), notes, many seek "to establish some sort of communion with the basic and primordial forces of the universe, even if they have to 'blow their minds' to do so," while "the group dynamics phenomenon seems to be, at least for many of its devotees, merely a somewhat different form of search for the transcendent." Such interest in the psyche and such phenomena as encounter groups reflect an understanding that mental and social processes, the *psyche* and the *socius*, are the ultimate resevoirs of the subjective presuppositions of knowledge—reservoirs that ultimately stand apart from and forbidden to the profane advance of science.

Technological research and development and the limits of disenchantment. The spread of scientifically oriented technology, like the advance of the social sciences, sets into play forces which highlight the role of subjective presuppositions in human endeavor, and thus tend to limit the disenchantment of the world. Interestingly, the spread of scientifically oriented technology results in limiting disenchantment more as a consequence of its ties to government and industry, which sponsor it, than from its own intrinsic qualities. Nevertheless, the spread of technology helps to undermine science's claim to immunity from domination by the vagaries of subjective presuppositions.

The support by federal agencies of various scientific research projects exerts, as Bendix (1970:840) observes, "a subtle but potent influence upon the direction which research . . . will take." Consequently, the "autonomy of science . . . is in doubt. . . . Public support of science . . . undermines the freedom of scientists from practical ends" (1970:840). A similar undermining of freedom from practical ends results from dependence on private industry for the support of scientific research and development.

The ends that research and development are to serve are decided by sponsors in government and industry not by scientists. Furthermore, government and industry decide which research projects to sponsor in terms of their own values and interests.[23] Thus, the dependence upon governmental and industrial support for the spread of scientifically oriented technology undermines science's claim to be free from practical ends. It shows science to be subservient, not to intellect and reason alone, but to the subjective presuppositions, the values and interests, of its sponsors. Once again, as with the development of the social sciences, the development of scientifically oriented technology sets in motion processes which reveal the intimate relationship between science and subjective presuppositions. Since, as noted above, such presuppositions are incomprehensible, indomitable, and important from the vantage point of science, continued dependence on them means that something of a sacred nature remains central to a world dominated by science, limiting its disenchantment.

Moreover, the undermining of science's claim to be free of the values and practical ends of government and industry leads to a realization that the judgment of technological advances is not itself a rational, intellectual, or scientific endeavor. Such judgment is more like the judgment of art, as described by Weber (1958:137–138), in which non-intellectual, nonrational, ethical, and even aesthetic standards are central. That is, in the judgment of technological advances, as in the judgment of art,

> it is not true that the work . . . or a period that has worked out new technical means . . . for instance, the laws of perspective, stands there-fore . . . higher than a work . . . devoid of all knowledge of those means and laws—if its form does justice to the material. . . . A work . . . which is a genuine "fulfillment" is never surpassed; . . . Individuals may differ in appreciating the personal significance of works . . . but no one will ever be able to say of such a work that it is "outstripped" by another work which is also a "fulfillment."

Similarly, it is not true that a *society* that has worked out new technical means, for instance, new laws of *science*, stands therefore higher than a *society* devoid of all knowledge of those means and laws—if its form does justice to its ideals. A *society* which is a genuine fulfillment of its ideals is also never surpassed. Individuals may differ in appreciating the personal significance of a society following these ideals, but no one can indisputably claim that such a society has been outstripped by another which is also a fulfillment. The judgment of technical advances is not a scientific judgment. As noted above (Weber, 1958:144), science itself "leaves quite aside . . . whether we should and do wish to master life technically and whether it ultimately makes sense to do so." Thus, while recourse to magical means and to imploring the spirits may decline, technical means and calculation will not suffice, not even in the judgment of technical advances. The technical advances of auto-motive engineering, which pollute the air, and of Auschwitz, which destroyed millions of human beings, cannot be judged by technical means and calculation alone. One's recourse must ultimately be to subjective presuppositions, to values and ethics, to one's world view and epistemology. Thus, even in a world dominated by science and scientifically oriented technology, there will be recourse to the myster-ious powers of the *psyche* and the *socius*, the ultimate reservoirs of subjective presuppositions, and thus, the ultimate guarantors of the meaning and legitimacy of science itself.

Finally, it should be noted that recourse to the mysterious powers of the *psyche* and the *socius*, such as in consciousness-expanding meditative exercises and encounter groups probing the wonders of love (*agape*), may well be called religious in Durkheim's sense (see 1965:62). They refer to transcendent or sacred things, things set apart and forbidden, which serve to integrate (unify and order) the activities of a given collectivity. Thus, references to the ultimate sources of meaning and legitimacy, whether or not such references are made in reunions, assemblies, or meetings representing the total society, may yet represent the eternal something in religion or at least the symbols in which religious thought can envelop itself and survive, however diminished and transformed, in an advanced industrial society. Durkheim's suggestion, based on his study of elementary forms of religion, that there may be something eternal in religion remains an intriguing one. However, as Hammond (1974:135) recognizes, "to expect . . . elementary forms to appear also in complex . . . plural societies is hardly in keeping with his [Durkheim's] argument." Rather, efforts should be made which, while remaining true to Durkheim's position, seek to discover "what some not-so-elementary forms might be." Such efforts will also serve to advance theoretical and empirical continuity in the sociology of religious creeds.

Summary

This chapter has examined the role of religious creeds, (religious beliefs and practices) in the processes which provide for the integration of advanced industrial societies. In such societies, integration results mainly from functional rather than normative factors. Consequently, given a close relationship between religious creeds and the processes of normative integration, the role of the former in the integration of an advanced industrial society declines as dependence on functional integration increases. The declining influence of religious creeds is further heightened by the process of differentiation and disenchantment. Nevertheless, it is possible, as Durkheim (1965:464) suggests, that there is "something eternal in religion which is destined to survive" even in advanced industrial societies. Thus, he believed that the processes of differentiation and disenchantment must ultimately be limited. The discussions of sociologists of religion as to the possibility that a civil religion might limit differentiation were examined. The possibility was also discussed that the development of the social sciences and of scientifically oriented technology have uncovered limits to the process of disenchantment by highlighting the role of the subjective presuppositions of knowledge. The existence of such presuppositions points to realms which may be regarded as sacred from the vantage point of science and thus as the possible source of something in religion which will survive even in advanced industrial societies.

FOOTNOTES

1. See Parsons' argument that religious creeds provide a basis for the integration of a modern society (1962, 1963, 1966a, 1966b, 1971). See Eister (1957), Porter (1973), and Fenn (1970) for a critique of Parsons' argument. See also Fenn's discussion of the variables which may affect the ability of religious creeds to facilitate the integration of modern differentiated society (1974).

2. Shiner (1967), in a comprehensive discussion of the various meanings of *secularization*, identifies the following processes: (1) decline of religion, wherein "previously accepted symbols, doctrines and institutions lose their prestige and influence"; (2) conformity with "this world," wherein a society turns its attention from the supernatural to become totally absorbed with pragmatic tasks; (3) transposition, wherein "arrangements which were once understood as grounded in divine power are transformed into phenomena of purely human creation and responsibility"; (4) movement from sacred to secular, wherein all decisions in society come to be based, increasingly, on rational and utilitarian grounds, and change is completely accepted as desirable; (5) desacralization, which is discussed in this chapter under the synonomous Weberian rubric "disenchantment of the world." For attempts to cut through the terminological confusion and provide a framework for research on secularization, see Fenn (1969), Porter (1973) and Westhues (1971).

3. Durkheim (1965:478) explicitly identifies the something eternal in religion as the "cult and the faith." These terms have changing, multiple, and often technical meanings and would, I believe, merely confuse the issue. Durkheim's use of the term *cult*, for example, renders it closer in meaning to *church*, as used by contemporary sociologists of religion. I have attempted to depict his true position accurately, in terms more understandable to the contemporary reader.

4. For discussions of the impact of differentiation on the content of religious creeds, especially on Christian theology, rather than on their role or function, see Berger (1967b:4–6), Lemert (1974a), and Parsons (1969:204–245). Luckmann (1967:104–114) also identifies what he calls "modern religious themes." See also McGuire (1972), who discusses the underground Church movement within the Roman Catholic Church as a reaction against the privatization of religion.

5. One consequence is a rise of religious individualism (Durkheim, 1965:62), that is, a condition in which religion consists "entirely in internal and subjective states, and which [is] constructed freely by each of us" (see the Introduction).

6. For a lively debate on Fenn's thesis, see comments by McFaul (1973), McNamara (1973), Newman (1973), Stauffer (1973), and Fenn's response (1973). See also Parsons (1971:99) who contends that modern societies, including America, "maintain strong moral commitments that have survived through, and have even been strengthened by, religious pluralism and secularization [differentiation]."

7. For a discussion of how religious organizations or congregations cope with their irrelevance, see Demerath (1974:22–28), Demerath and Hammond (1969:168–187), and Fackre (1966:275–297).

8. For a study of the role of religious beliefs and practices as a basis for integrating an individual's activities, see Schweiker (1969). The role of religion as a basis for personal identity is discussed in Part III in the context of Herberg's (1960) discussion of religious communities in America. See also Herberg (1962a, 1962b).

9. For an alternative approach within a Durkheimian framework to discussing the persistence of ritual in modern industrial societies, see Bocock (1970, 1974).

10. See, for example, Cherry (1969, 1970, 1971), Hammond (1963:102–103; 1968; 1974), Stauffer (1973), and Verba (1965). Various discussions of the concept of civil religion are reviewed by Jones and Richey (1974:3–18) and criticized by Lipsitz (1968) and J. F. Wilson (1971; 1974:115–137). An extensive bibliography of works pertaining to civil religion is found in Richey and Jones (1974:273–278).

11. Hammond (1974) in an insightful analysis, suggests that it is not the nation-state per se which dominates or integrates modern industrial society, but its legal institutions. He notes (1974:129) that in plural or differentiated societies, "legal institutions . . . are called upon not only to secure order but to give it a uniformly acceptable meaning as well. The result is a set of legal institutions with a decided religio-moral character." Hammond's views are tested and supported by Cole and Hammond (1974) in a broad sample of 115 contemporary nation-states. Thus, legal institutions may well be the source or focus of civil religion. However, Hammond adds that the legal institutions need not perform their task single-handedly, but may share it with the public schools. (See Hammond, 1968:383; 1974:134). Interestingly, as Wallace (1973) notes, Durkheim also discussed the important role of public education in transmitting the civil religion to the youth of a given society.

12. Here, as elsewhere in this section, I have tended to follow Bellah's earlier works (1967, 1968) on matters of definition and sociological analysis rather than his later works (1974, 1975). These later works are, as Bellah admits (1975: viii), exercises "in the analysis and interpretation of cultural meaning rather than in sociological explanation."

13. Curiously, despite Bellah's (1967:1) contention "that there actually exists . . . an elaborate and well-institutionalized civil religion in America," little, if any, direct sociological evidence for its existence has been offered. Moreover, Thomas and Flippen (1972:214) conclude their content analysis of editorials from 100 newspapers, seeking to document the existence of a civil religion in America, by commenting "a well defined . . . civil religion may be more the creation (and fantasy) of the liberal political intellectual elite than an active faith among the masses." On the other hand, Wimberly et al. (1974) found a distinct civil religious factor in their factor analysis of the responses of 115 persons who had attended a Billy Graham Crusade in Knoxville, Tennessee, during 1970.

14. Neuhaus (1970), for example, contends that the civil religion played a role in legitimating opposition to the Viet Nam war. However, Herberg (1974:76–88), Marty (1974:139–157) and Richardson (1974:161–184) describe tendencies within the American civil religion which are uncritically supportive of American culture and actions.

15. One can only wonder, in the absence of appropriate empirical studies, what the import is of the fact that the dates for celebrating most of the events on the so-called ritual calendar have been changed to various Mondays in the month of their occurrence. Whether or not this affects the presumed sacral character of the event in question is a matter for research to determine.

16. Some evidence of the integrative values of political ceremonies is found in Phillips and Feldman (1973). They find a drop in suicide rates near the July 4th holiday and interpret it, in terms of Durkheim's *Suicide* (1951), as indicative of temporarily increased societal integration.

17. It is also possible, as Bellah (1974, 1975) believes, that the content of the current civil religion in America is no longer as adequate to the task of facilitating societal integration as it once may have been.

18. The factors which support the principle of human interrelations of the managerial ideology prevalent in modern corporate bureaucracies also reveal the importance of nonintellective, nonrational elements even in the conduct of rationally defined corporate facts. (See chap. 2).

19. For alternative discussion of the limits of disenchantment in scientifically and technologically advanced societies, see Greeley (1972:251–257), McNamara (1973), Stauffer (1973:421–423) and especially Baum (1970).
20. For discussion of the role of presuppositions in the development of science in general, see Kuhn (1970). For a discussion of their role in the development of sociology in particular, see Friedrichs (1970, esp. chaps. 7–9) and Gouldner (1970, esp. chaps. 1, 2).
21. Lemert (1974b:95) discusses the development of a relativistic paradigm in the arts and theology, as well as in the physical and social sciences, which is "critical of traditional rationality . . . [and] suspicious of rationally generated 'systematic' explanations."
22. King (1970) and Back (1972) discuss, respectively, the spread of interest in mysticism and in encounter groups, albeit not from the perspective developed here. See Roszak (1973) and Baum (1970), who discuss the growth of interest in the nonrational and the nonintellective aspects of life from different perspectives. See also Greeley (1972, 1974).
23. Anderson (1974:207) reports that only about 15 percent of the funds spent on scientific research and development support basic research, that is, research serving the interests of advancing scientific knowledge per se. The remaining 85 percent supports applied research that is, research which seeks to create scientifically oriented technology of interest to government or industry.

REFERENCES

Anderson, Charles H.
1974 *Toward a New Sociology*, rev. ed. Homewood, Ill.: Dorsey Press.

Back, Kurt
1972 *Beyond Words*. New York: Russell Sage Foundation.

Baum, Gregory
1970 "Does the world remain disenchanted?" *Social Research* 37 (Summer): 153–202.

Bellah, Robert N.
1967 "Civil religion in America." *Daedalus* 96 (Winter):1–21.
1968 "Response." In *The Religious Situation: 1968*, edited by Donald Cutler. Boston: Beacon Press.
1974 "American civil religion in the 1970s." In *American Civil Religion*, edited by Russell E. Richey and Donald G. Jones. New York: Harper & Row.
1975 *The Broken Covenant: American Civil Religion in Time of Trial.* New York: Seabury Press.

Bendix, Reinhard
1970 "Sociology and the distrust of reason." *American Sociological Review* 35 (October):831–843.

Berger, Peter L.
1961 *The Noise of Solemn Assemblies.* Garden City, N.Y.: Doubleday.
1967a *The Sacred Canopy.* Garden City, N.Y.: Doubleday.
1967b "A sociological view of the secularization of theology." *Journal for the Scientific Study of Religion* 6 (Spring):3–16.

Berger, Peter L., and Thomas Luckmann
1963 "Sociology of religion and sociology of knowledge." *Sociology and Social Research* 47 (July):417–428.

Bocock, Robert J.
1970 "Ritual: civic and religious." *British Journal of Sociology* 21 (September):285–297.
1974 *Ritual in Industrial Society: A Sociological Analysis of Ritualism in Modern England.* London: Allen and Unwin.

Cherry, Conrad
1969 "Two American sacred ceremonies: their implications for the study of religion in America." *American Quarterly* 21 (Winter):739–754.
1970 "American sacred ceremonies." In *American Mosaic: Social Patterns of Religion in the United States,* edited by Phillip E. Hammond and Benton Johnson. New York: Random House.
1971 Editor, *God's New Israel: Religious Interpretations of American Destiny.* Englewood Cliffs, N.J.: Prentice-Hall.

Cole, William A., and Phillip E. Hammond
1974 "Religious pluralism, legal development and societal complexity: rudimentary forms of civil religion." *Journal for the Scientific Study of Religion* 13 (June):177–189.

Demerath, Nicholas J., III
1974 *A Tottering Transcendence: Civil vs. Cultic Aspects of the Sacred.* Indianapolis: Bobbs-Merrill.

Demerath, Nicholas J., III and Phillip E. Hammond
1969 *Religion in Social Context.* New York: Random House.

Durkheim, Emile
1951 *Suicide: A Study in Sociology.* Translated by John A. Spaulding and George Simpson. New York: Free Press.
1964 *The Division of Labor in Society.* Translated by George Simpson. New York: Free Press (paperback).
1965 *The Elementary Forms of the Religious Life.* Translated by Joseph W. Swain. New York: Free Press (paperback).

Eister, Alan W.
1957 "Religious institutions in complex societies: difficulties in the theoretic specification of functions." *American Sociological Review* 22 (August): 387–391.

Fackre, Gabriel
1966 "The crisis of the congregation: a debate." In *Voluntary Associations: A Study of Groups in Free Societies,* edited by D. B. Robertson. Richmond: John Knox Press.

Fenn, Richard K.
1969 "The secularization of values: an analytic framework for the study of secularization." *Journal for the Scientific Study of Religion* 8 (Spring): 112–124.
1970 "The process of secularization: a post-Parsonian view." *Journal for the Scientific Study of Religion* 9 (Summer):117–136.
1972 "Toward a new sociology of religion." *Journal for the Scientific Study of Religion* 11 (March):16–32.
1973 "Talking past one another: notes on the debate." *Journal for the Scientific Study of Religion* 12 (September):353–359.
1974 "Religion and the legitimation of social systems." In *Changing Perspectives in the Scientific Study of Religion,* edited by Alan W. Eister. New York: Wiley.

Friedrichs, Robert W.
1970   *A Sociology of Sociology.* New York: Free Press.

Gouldner, Alvin
1970   *The Coming Crisis of Western Sociology.* New York: Basic Books.

Greeley, Andrew M.
1970   "Superstition, ecstasy and tribal consciousness." *Social Research* 37 (Summer):203–211.
1972   *Unsecular Man: The Persistence of Religion.* New York: Schocken Books.
1974   *Ecstasy: A Way of Knowing.* Englewood Cliffs, N.J.: Prentice-Hall.

Greenwald, David E.
1973   "Durkheim on society, thought and ritual." *Sociological Analysis* 34 (Fall):157–168.

Hammond, Phillip E.
1963   "Religion and the 'informing' of culture." *Journal for the Scientific Study of Religion* 3 (Fall):97–106.
1968   "Commentary on 'Civil Religion in America'." In *The Religious Situation: 1968*, edited by Donald R. Cutler. Boston: Beacon Press.
1974   "Religious pluralism and Durkheim's integration thesis." In *Changing Persepectives in the Scientific Study of Religion*, edited by Alan W. Eister. New York: Wiley.

Herberg, Will
1960   *Protestant—Catholic—Jew.* Garden City, N.Y.: Doubleday (Anchor Books).
1962a "Religion in a secularized society: the new shape of religion in America." *Review of Religious Research* 3 (Spring):145–158.
1962b "Religion in a secularized society: some aspects of America's three-religion pluralism." *Review of Religious Research* 4 (Fall):33–45.
1974   "America's civil religion: what it is and whence it comes." In *American Civil Religion*, edited by Russell E. Richey and Donald G. Jones. New York: Harper & Row.

Jones, Donald G., and Russell E. Richey
1974   "The civil religion debate." In *American Civil Religion.* New York: Harper & Row.

King, Winston L.
1970   "Eastern religions: a new interest and influence." *Annals of the American Academy of Political and Social Science* 387 (January):66–76.

Krausz, Ernest
1971   "Religion and secularization: matters of definition." *Social Compass* 18 (2):203–212.

Kuhn, Thomas S.
1970   *The Structure of Scientific Revolutions*, 2nd ed. University of Chicago Press.

Lemert, Charles
1974a "Cultural multiplexity and religious polytheism." *Social Compass* 21 (3):241–254.
1974b "Sociological theory and the relativistic paradigm." *Sociological Inquiry* 44 (2):93–104.

Lipsitz, Lewis
1968   "If as Verba says, the state functions as a religion, what are we to do to save our souls." *American Political Science Review* 62 (June):527–535.

Luckmann, Thomas
1967   *The Invisible Religion*. New York: Macmillan.

Martin, David
1969   *The Religious and the Secular*. New York: Schocken Books.

Marty, Martin E.
1974   "Two kinds of two kinds of civil religion." In *American Civil Religion*, edited by Russell E. Richey and Donald G. Jones. New York: Harper & Row.

McFaul, Thomas R.
1973   "Which way the future? a critique of Glock's 'Images of God' and Fenn's 'New Sociology of Religion.'" *Journal for the Scientific Study of Religion* 12 (June):231–235.

McGuire, Meredith B.
1972   "Toward a sociological interpretation of the 'Underground Church' movement." *Review of Religious Research* 14 (Fall):41–47.

McNamara, Patrick H.
1973   "Comment on Fenn's 'Toward a New Sociology of Religion.'" *Journal for the Scientific Study of Religion* 12 (June): 237–239.

Mead, Sidney E.
1967   "The nation with the soul of a church." *Church History* 36 (September): 262–282.

Neuhaus, Richard John
1970   "The war, the churches and civil religion." *Annals of the American Academy of Political and Social Science* 387 (January):128–140.

Newman, William M.
1973   "Which Durkheimian assumption? a contribution to the Fenn-McNamara-McFaul colloquy." *Journal for the Scientific Study of Religion* 12 (September):361–363.

Parsons, Talcott
1962   "The cultural background of American religious organization." In *Ethics and Bigness*, edited by H. Cleveland and H. D. Lasswell. New York: Harper & Row.
1963   "Christianity and modern industrial society." In *Sociological Theory, Values and Sociocultural Change*, edited by E. A. Tiryakin. New York: Free Press.
1966a   "Religion in a modern pluralistic society." *Review of Religious Research* 7 (Spring):125–146.
1966b   *Societies: Evolutionary and Comparative Perspectives*. Englewood Cliffs, N.J.: Prentice-Hall.
1968   "On the concept of value-commitments." *Sociological Inquiry* 38 (Spring):135–160.
1969   "Belief, unbelief and disbelief." In *The Culture of Unbelief: Studies and Proceedings from the First International Symposium on Belief Held at Rome*, edited by Rocco Caporale and Antonio Grumelli. University of California Press.
1971   *The System of Modern Societies*. Englewood Cliffs, N.J.: Prentice-Hall.

Phillips, David P., and Kenneth A. Feldman
1973 "A dip in deaths before ceremonial occasions: some new relationships between social integration and morality." *American Sociological Review* 38 (December):678–696.

Porter, Judith R.
1973 "Secularization, differentiation, and the function of religious value orientations." *Sociological Inquiry* 43 (1):67–74.

Richardson, Herbert
1974 "Civil religion in theological perspective." In *American Civil Religion,* edited by Russell E. Richey and Donald G. Jones. New York: Harper & Row.

Richey, Russell E., and Donald G. Jones
1974 Editors, *American Civil Religion.* New York: Harper & Row.

Robertson, Roland
1970 *The Sociological Interpretation of Religion.* New York: Schocken Books.

Roszak, Theodore
1969 *The Making of a Counterculture.* Garden City, N.Y.: Doubleday (Anchor Books).
1973 *Where the Wasteland Ends.* Garden City, N.Y.: Doubleday (Anchor Books).

Schneider, Louis
1970 "Drift in religion and society: toward the future." In *Sociological Approach to Religion.* New York: Wiley.

Schweiker, William F.
1969 "Religion as a superordinate meaning system and socio-psychological integration." *Journal for the Scientific Study of Religion* 8 (Fall):300–307.

Shils, Edward, and M. Michael Young
1953 "The meaning of the Coronation." *Sociological Review* 1 (December): 63–81.

Shiner, Larry
1967 "The concept of secularization in empirical research." *Journal for the Scientific Study of Religion* 6 (Fall):207–220.

Smith, Huston
1968 "Secularization and the sacred: the contemporary scene." In *The Religious Situation: 1968,* edited by Donald Cutler. Boston: Beacon Press.

Stauffer, Robert E.
1973 "Civil religion, technocracy, and the private sphere: further comments on cultural integration in advanced societies." *Journal for the Scientific Study of Religion* 12 (December):415–426.

Thomas, Michael C., and Charles C. Flippen
1972 "American civil religion: an empirical study." *Social Forces* 51 (December):218–225.

Verba, Sidney
1965 "The Kennedy assassination and the nature of political commitment." In *The Kennedy Assassination and the American Public,* edited by Bradley S. Greenberg and Edwin B. Parker. Calif.: Stanford University Press.

Wallace, Ruth
1973   "The secular ethic and the spirit of patriotism." *Sociological Analysis* 34 (Spring):3–11.

Warner, W. Lloyd
1953   *American Life: Dream and Reality.* University of Chicago Press.
1961   *The Family of God: A Symbolic Study of Christian Life in America.* New Haven: Yale University Press.

Weber, Max
1958   "Science as a vocation." In *From Max Weber: Essays in Sociology,* edited and translated by H. H. Gerth and C. Wright Mills. New York: Oxford University Press.

Westhues, Kenneth
1971   "An elaboration and test of a secularization hypothesis in terms of open-systems theory of organization." *Social Forces* 49 (March):460–469.

Wilson, Bryan R.
1966   *Religion in Secular Society.* London: C. A. Watts & Co.

Wilson, John F.
1971   "The status of 'civil religion' in America." In *The Religion of the Republic,* edited by Elwyn A. Smith. Philadelphia: Fortress Press.
1974   "A historical approach to civil religion." In *American Civil Religion,* edited by Russell E. Richey and Donald G. Jones. New York: Harper & Row.

Wimberley, Ronald C., C. M. Lipsey, Donald A. Clelland, and Thomas C. Hood
1974   "The civil religion dimension." Paper delivered at the American Sociological Association meetings, Montreal.

II

the sociology of religious congregations

Choice-Points in Religious Congregations:
The sect-church legacy and beyond

The sociology of religious congregations, that is, the sociological study of social organizations or associations in which people seek desired relationships with the sacred, in general, or the supernatural or divine, in particular, has been dominated for over six decades by Ernst Troeltsch's classic work, *The Social Teachings of the Christian Churches* (which was first published in Germany in 1912).[1] Virtually every sociological discussion of religious congregations has referred, in one way or another, to the distinction which Troeltsch made between the sect and the church (see esp. 1931:331–343; 991–1013).[2]

Troeltsch himself, however, while distinguishing between the sect and the church contended (1931:340–341) that the "all-important point" to remember was that "both types are a logical result of the Gospel and only conjointly do they exhaust the whole range of its . . . social results, which," he added, "are always connected with the religious organization." In other words, Troeltsch regarded the sect and the church as legitimate expressions of different aspects of Christian religious creeds. Troeltsch described the different organizational expressions which were the sect and the church in some detail; however, he never explicitly identified nor systematically discussed the dimensions along which they differed.

According to Troeltsch, the sect type expression of the Christian Gospel is chiefly characterized by religious congregations described as follows: (1) Their "members join of their own free will," that is, "an individual is not born into a sect; he enters on the basis of conscious conversion" (1931:339); (2) They "aim at a direct personal fellowship between the members of each group." (1931:331); (3) They "renounce the idea of dominating the world," that is, "their attitude towards the world, the State and society may be indifferent, tolerant or hostile" (1931:331); (4) They "are connected with the lower classes, or at least with those elements in Society which are opposed to the State and to Society" (1931:331).

The church type of expression of the Christian Gospel, on the other hand, is chiefly characterized by religious congregations (1) whose membership "is born into it, and through infant baptism . . . comes under its . . . influence" (1931:338); (2) which have both a priesthood and a hierarchy (1931:338); (3) which "dominate Society, compelling all the members of Society to come under its sphere and influence" (1931:338), and work for its ends "only by a process of adaptation and compromise" (1931:339); and (4) which are "dependent upon the upper classes, and upon their development" (1931:331).

There have been three main lines of development in the use of the sect-church distinction or typology since Troeltsch presented it.[3] One line of development entails attempts to provide greater flexibility in dealing with the enormous variety of religious congregations than is found in Troeltsch's dichotomy. A second line of development has been to modify the dichotomy and apply it to the study of the relationships of individual members to the religious congregation, especially as those relationships are affected by socioeconomic status. A third line of development has been to adapt Troeltsch's discussions to the study of the origin and development of religious congregations. The first two of these three lines of development are discussed in this chapter, the third in Chapter 5.

Interestingly, most of the work within the first line of development in the use of the sect-church typology proceeds from Troeltsch's own observation (1931:1009) that the "Protestant Church-type no longer represents the pure Church-type." Such work has generally proceeded in one of two different directions, despite their common link to Troeltsch's work. Specifically, some sociologists of religion have sought to increase the descriptive power of Troeltsch's original insights and suggestions, while others have sought to increase its explanatory power.

Attempts to improve the descriptive power of Troeltsch's original work have generally resulted either in the definition of one or more new types thought to differ from the original pair in some significant way or to a more systematic and explicit discussion than is found in Troeltsch of the dimensions along which all types of religious congregations are said to vary. The discussions of the denomination as a type of religious congregation or organization by Becker (1932:646), Martin (1962), Niebuhr (1929:12–21) illustrate efforts to describe additional types, as does Becker's discussion of the cult (1932:627). The *denomination* is introduced as a type to refer to those congregations or organizations which claim a broad membership but yet do not seek, as does the church, to compel all in a given society to be under its influence. The *cult* is described by Becker (1932:847) as a "very amorphous, loose-textured, uncondensed type of social structure" whose goal "is not the maintenance of the structure itself, as is the case of the church and sect, but is that of purely personal ecstatic experience, salvation, comfort, and mental or physical healing."

Robertson (1970:113–149) and Yinger (1970:251–281) illustrate efforts to more systematically and explicitly discuss the dimensions which are thought to underlie differences among the vast variety of religious congregations or organizations. Robertson identifies two underlying dimensions: one is whether the effective leaders of the organization perceive it to have a unique claim on religious legitimacy or whether other groups are regarded as equally legitimate, and the second is whether the operative principle of membership is inclusive or exclusive. Yinger, on the other hand, identifies three dimensions. The first, like Robertson's second, refers to the inclusiveness or exclusiveness of the membership; the second is the degree of acceptance or rejection of secular values and secular institutions; and the third, the degree of development of an integrated organization with a professional staff and a bureaucratic structure.

Efforts to improve the explanatory power of Troeltsch's original insights and suggestions have generally, like Troeltsch, sought to understand religious congregations as an expression or implementation of ideological or creedal elements. Berger (1954), Johnson (1957), and Gustafson (1967) believe, as did Troeltsch, that the explanatory elements were aspects of a given religious creed. Thus, Berger (1954) argued that variations among religious organizations could be best understood in light of doctrinal differences as to whether access to grace is regarded as based in objective rather than subjective means. Johnson (1957) argued that the crucial element was the sacramental system used to help attain "justification" or salvation. For Gustafson (1967:67) there were two key elements: one, which like Berger's, points to belief in objective rather than subjective means as basic to the attainment of grace; and one which refers to whether emphasis is placed on "the salvation of individuals and their protection from sin" or on efforts to "make Christianity a universal phenomenon." More recently, Johnson (1963, 1971) has offered the view that the explanatory element is not an aspect of a religious creed per se, but the extent to which the organization accepts or rejects the dominant secular values of the society in which it exists. Snook (1974) has also suggested that the key to explaining variations among religious congregations is not an aspect of its creed, but is how the authority is structured within the group, that is, the kind or degree of authority exercised within the organization.

Recently, sociologists of religion have come to question the sect-church typology, more than half a century old, and to eschew attempts to define additional types or focus on some key dimension of the sect or church in hopes of explaining variations in other dimensions. Some sociologists of religion have called for an end to use of the sect-church distinction. Goode (1967a:77), for example, contends that the distinction between church and sect "has no power to explain or elucidate" and adds that "unless it undergoes a radical revision . . . church-sect must be seen as a dead concept, obsolete, sterile and archaic." Coleman (1968:59) believes that "the literature on church-sect leaves the reader lost in a morass of conflicting and arbitrary definitions," but stops short of calling for abandoning the distinction altogether. Eister (1967:85) calls for a challenge to the assumption that "there is, somehow *a* dimension of 'church-sectness' that has, or could have, some conceptual soundness about it." Even Demerath (1967a:82–83), who believes that the sect-church "concept has had its value . . . and . . . ability to bring together—if not unify—a host of specific considerations and variables," ultimately calls for the abandonment of the sect-church distinction, which applies only to religious congregations or organizations, in favor of concepts that apply "across the institutional spectrum." The use of such concepts, as Demerath and Hammond (1969:162) recognize, would provide analyses of religious congregations with "insights to be had from analyses of other forms of organization," that is, it would contribute to substantive continuity, the continuity between the sociology of religion and other branches of sociology. Demerath and Hammond (1969:163–196) analyze religious organizations in terms of the well-known Parsonian concepts of adaptation, goal attainment, integration, and latency (pattern maintenance and tension management) as is also done by Metz (1967). The interests of substantive continuity are also served by the efforts of Benson and Dorsett to replace the sect-church typology with a theory of religious organization based on the concepts of bureaucratization, professionalization, secularization, and integration. They argue (1971:138) that such a theory contributes to "the linkage of religious organization studies with the more general field of formal organization studies," as is the case in a study by Scalf, Miller, and Thomas (1973).

The approach of this chapter does not depart as radically as those of Demerath and Hammond (1969) and Benson and Dorsett (1971) from the legacy of the sect-church distinction. That is, it does not seek to import concepts from other more general branches of sociology to the study of religious organizations. To do so, would, I believe, unnecessarily break the empirical and theretical continuity which stems, as Demerath and Hammond recognize (1969:157), from the great volume of work that has been invested in the sect-church distinction. Thus, some, but by no means all, substantive continuity is sacrificed here in the interest of greater theoretical and empirical continuity.

Continuity with previous work must be maintained without perpetuating its shortcomings, the chief of which are two. The first is the inability of any list of relatively few types to match the enormous variety of religious organizations (see Nelson, 1969; Warburton, 1969; Wilson, 1961:325–327)—a difficulty which persists even if use of the types is restricted to studies of Christian organizations, as Troeltsch originally intended, and not extended to studies of non-Christian religious organizations. Secondly, the use of a typology tends to imply that the appearance of various characteristics which define a type are empirically correlated, that is, that each of the defining traits tends to appear whenever any of the others appear. As Goode (1967a: 1967b) notes, however, the evidence for the co-appearance of the various defining characteristics of the sect or church is not convincing. Indeed, as Johnson observes (1963:540, 1971:132), the Roman Catholic Church, the prototype of churchlike organization, often evinces a sectlike lack of accommodation to modern society.[4] The mixture of sectlike and churchlike characteristics within the prototypical churchlike organization is also evident in the observations of Demerath and Hammond (1969:75–76).

> On the one hand, Catholicism is blatantly churchlike in its organizational structure, its rigid ritualism, and in its willingness to act within society. . . . On the other hand, . . . Catholicism has retained much . . . sectlike flavor. Its doctrine remains other worldly. . . . It retains a charisma of office . . . continues to advance a total ideology that seeks to penetrate every nook and cranny of the parishioner's life; and, finally . . . has retained substantial lower-class membership. . . .

In short, the major shortcoming of the sect-church legacy is twofold: not every organization fits into the types provided, and

109

some organizations fit more than one. The legacy has not provided types which are mutually exhaustive and mutually exclusive, as a sound scientific typology must. Furthermore, the types do not provide the flexibility needed to deal with the great variety of religious organizations created by the failure of the defining traits of the given types to co-vary uniformly.

The resolution of the dilemma of one seeking, as I do, to remain within the legacy of the sect-church distinction while avoiding its shortcomings entails a two-step process. First, it is necessary, as Eister (1967:86) suggests, "to 'break down' the multi-dimensional conglomerates which presently pass for 'sect' or for 'church' entirely into their component variables or attributes." This involves, as O'Dea recognizes (1968:134), "replacing the global concepts with a number of *choice points* which give rise to one kind of organizational tendency rather than another" (italics added). Secondly, the nature of the covariation among the attributes of religious organization and between them and external factors must be examined empirically.

The twofold approach of first identifying attributes or dimensions rather than types of religious congregations and then studying the pattern of their empirical relationships, rather than positing them a priori, avoids the prime shortcomings of the sect-church legacy. It provides the flexibility needed to deal with the great variety of religious congregations and the many variations in the appearance of any given set of attributes. Moreover, since the attributes or dimensions studied come out of the sect-church legacy, the valued theoretical and empirical continuity is maintained. In addition, since the dimensions of a religious organization are, presumably, not entirely unlike those of other forms of organizations, it should prove possible to link studies of them with those of nonreligious organizations, thus preserving some substantive continuity as well.

The major dimensions or choice-points facing religious congregations are those which have been central in the long history of the sect-church distinction. In identifying and discussing these choice-points or dimensions, this chapter develops an approach, which it calls the *choice-point approach*, to the study of religious congregations which provides the flexibility sought by the sociologists of religion who established the first line of development of the sect-church legacy. The use of the choice-point approach is illustrated by applying it to the second line of development in the sect-church legacy. This line entails modifying the dichotomy and applying it to the study of the relationships of individual members to their respective religious congregations, especially as those relationships are affected by their socioeconomic status. The second line of development has led to the positioning of what shall be called the socioeconomic status, or SES, hypothesis. This chapter discusses the SES hypothesis using the choice-point approach. In Chapter 5, the choice-point approach is used to discuss the third main line of development within the sect-church legacy, the adaptation of Troeltsch's work (1931) to the study of the origins and development of religious congregations.

Choice-Points in Religious Congregations

The sociological study of religious congregation can be advanced if attention is focussed on the various choice-points or issues facing them rather than on an attempt to construct conglomerates of attributes comprising ideal types. The choice-points facing religious congregations may be categorized, following Demerath and Hammond (1969:70), as pertaining either to the organization's internal characteristics or to its external relations with the surrounding social context. For each choice or issue, it is possible to identify a sectlike and a churchlike response (see Table 1). However, in so identifying choices, it should be clear there is *no* implication that there is any underlying "sectness" or "churchness." An organization may be sectlike in some respects and churchlike in others. In short, *no* attempt will be made to recon-

Table 1 CHOICE-POINTS IN RELIGIOUS CONGREGATIONS

	Sectlike Choice	Churchlike Choice
1. Internal Characteristics		
a. Criterion of membership	A test	Birth
b. Extent and character of member's involvement	High and personal	Low and impersonal
c. Leadership	Informally trained; non-hierarchical	Formally trained; hierarchical
2. External Relations		
a. View on status quo	Tolerant, indifferent, or hostile	Accepting
b. Audience	Deprived elements	Universal in principle; middle or upper class in practice

struct the sect type, or the church type. The identification of sectlike and churchlike choices serves primarily to facilitate the correlation between the choice-point approach to the study of religious congregations and the work that was done within the tradition of the sect-church legacy for more than half a century. In the discussion below, the particular issues or choices facing religious organizations are selected, in part, because they are most like those facing nonreligious organizations. Such selection facilitates the use of work in other branches of sociology. As a consequence, some of the more specifically religious issues often raised in discussions of sect and church, such as choice of doctrine and form of worship, are not treated here.

Internal characteristics. With respect to their internal characteristics, religious congregations may be said to face three central issues or choice-points: (1) what the criteria of membership are to be, (2) what the extent and character of the members' involvement with the organization is to be, and (3) what the composition of the leadership is to be. Any attempt to resolve these three issues obviously presupposes that there is to be a religious organization. However, it must be noted that not all expressions of religion are organized. Troeltsch (1931:376–382; 729–753; 993–994) and, more recently, Luckmann (1967) recognize that many religious individuals eschew organized religion in favor of more individualized modes of expression. Troeltsch and Luckmann agree that such non-organized, individualized forms of religion could well become the modal pattern among the more educated elements of society.[5] As Troeltsch (1931:381) puts it, in addition to the church and sect, there is

> a third type—that of religious individualsm which has no external organization, and which has a very independent attitude, with widely differing views of the central truths of Christianity. . . . Gradually, in the modern world of educated people, the third type has come to predominate. This means that all that is left is voluntary association with like-minded people, which is equally remote both from Church and sect.

Nevertheless, both writers agree that the various forms of religious organization will persist for some time to come.

One of the more difficult issues facing any religious congregation is that of determining what the criteria for membership are to be. On the one hand, membership may be open to all who are born into the organization, that is, the children of current members. Such is the churchlike choice. On the other hand, membership may be restricted to those who volunteer for membership and who pass some sort of test. Such is the sectlike choice. The test itself may be something as difficult to assess as whether or not one has had an experience of sanctification so subjective as to defy specification of its external manifestations, as Holiness groups require, or something more overt such as glossolalia (ability to speak in tongues), required by Pentacostalists (see Warburton, 1969:131–132). Obviously, the major faith groups in America are characterized primarily by the churchlike choice of relying on a membership which is for all intents and purposes born into the group. However, all the major groups also include many members who join voluntarily as a result of conversion. That is, the major faith groups employ both the churchlike option of a membership by birth and the sectlike option of a membership by choice.

The second major issue facing religious organizations is that of specifying the extent and character of their members' involvement in the organization. This issue arises with respect to two different components of the organization, the formal and the informal (see Demerath, 1965:63–72). The formal aspects of the organization are those instrumental in the attainment of the organization's goals and purposes or its maintenance. Formal activities may range from church services which "bring one closer to God" to the supervision of finances, house, and grounds, which is necessary if there is to be a place in which to hold services. The informal aspects of an organization are primarily the functions which provide personal fellowship and friendship. In either case, formal or informal, the expectation and obligation for a deep involvement is the sectlike choice, while the churchlike choice permits minimal involvement. The enormous variety in the degree of involvement ranges from the virtually total commitment of the monastic life to that of the isolated religious communities of the Hutterites and the Amish; from the deep commitment of the evangelic Jehovah Witness or the Mormon missionary to the somewhat lesser, segmented involvement of the frequent church attender and the minimal commitment of those who only attend services on the key holidays of Christmas, Easter, or the Jewish High Holidays. Similarly, there is great variation of involvement in the informal aspects of the religious organization. In some cases, there is a deep and personal fellowship, in which the members truly regard each other as brothers and sisters and have few, if any, social contacts outside their immediate religious circle. In other cases, many members, even in the same local congregation, are merely passing acquaintances, who barely recognize each other on sight and whose close friends are outside their religious circles. Of course, there are instances of all the degrees in between.

The third issue whose resolution differentiates the internal characteristics of one religious congregation from those of another is that of the composition of the leadership. Here the sect-church legacy highlights two subissues: (1) what the degree of the leadership's formal training is to be, if any, and (2) how authority is to be shared by the leadership and the membership. With respect to formal training, the sectlike choice is to require little, if any. Indeed, literacy is not necessarily required and leadership may be based solely on demonstration of special gifts of the Spirit. On the other hand, the churchlike choice is to require many years of special, formal training in both religious and secular matters. With respect to the sharing of authority, the churchlike choice is to vest authority in the organization's officers, the priests, who are, in turn, organized hierarchically. Authority is said to flow down from the highest offices of the organization to the lower levels of the priesthood and eventually to the membership at large. Thus, members have only a small share of the authority of the churchlike organization. Major decisions are made by the highest levels of the hierarchically ordered priesthood. On the contrary, the sectlike choice calls for democratic or egalitarian modes of decision making with the priest or minister sharing authority with the membership. Congregations taking the sectlike option, view authority as flowing from the members to their leaders. There is a third option which stands between the extremes of the sectlike and churchlike choices. The third option vests authority in a level between the general membership and the higher levels of a hierarchy of priests. It views authority as flowing from this middle level both upward through a hierarchy and downward to the membership at large. This third option is characteristic of the various branches of Presbyterianism, while Episcopalians and Roman Catholics are organized in a churchlike manner, and Baptists and other locally oriented bodies are more sectlike.

External Relations. In addition to their differences with respect to internal characteristics, religious congregations vary with respect to their external relations with the surrounding social context. Specifically, the sect-church legacy highlights two aspects of the external relations of a given congregation: (1) its attitude toward the secular status quo, and (2) the audience to which it addresses its message and from which it draws adherents.

The churchlike attitude towards the secular status quo is clearly described by Troeltsch (1931:331): "The church . . . is overwhelmingly conservative [and] to a certain extent accepts the secular order. . . . The church both stabilizes and determines the social order." The churchlike attitude toward the secular status quo is one of identification and support. It seeks to legitimate the secular order. However, the churchlike response of acceptance of the secular order is not necessarily one of complete subservience, for the churchlike organization seeks ultimately to dominate the secular order. It seeks to educate or influence the secular order in hopes of moving secular practices closer to the congregation's basic values. As Troeltsch (1931:339) puts it,

> the Church is the great educator . . . and like all educators she knows how to allow for various degrees of capacity and maturity, and how to attain her ends only by a process of adaptation and compromise.

In other words, the churchlike response is to accept the status quo for what it is, to take it on its own terms, and then seek to influence the secular order slowly through a process of adaptation and compromise, a two-way process calling for changes in both the churchlike congregation and the secular order.

The sectlike response to the secular order, on the other hand, is to (Troeltsch, 1931:331) "renounce the idea of dominating the world." Their attitude toward "the world, the State and society may be indifferent, tolerant or hostile." The sectlike response is uncompromising; it does not call for the domination of the secular order, rather the sectlike response is to gather a select group and either to withdraw them from the world or to place them in sharp opposition to it.

Some of the variations in the sectlike attitude towards the secular order are described by Wilson (1959:5–7). He speaks of four types of sectlike responses, the Conversionist, the Adventist, the Introversionist and the Gnostic.[6] The Conversionist response, typically found among orthodox fundamentalist or Pentecostalist groups, is opposed to modern science and holds the cultural and artistic values of the wider society in disdain. The Adventists, such as the Jehovah Witnesses, and the Christadelphians, are "hostile toward the wider society and look forward to its overthrow." The Introversionist or pietistic groups seek to direct the attention of their members away from the world. However, such groups may permit some of their members to be active in the world if their conscience demands it and if they remain at the periphery of social concerns. The Gnostics, such as the Christian Scientists, tolerate the cultural standards of the wider society and seek their own advancement in the world, or that of the movement.

Religious congregations vary with respect to the audiences to which they address themselves and from which they draw adherents. The audience sought by the organizations taking the churchlike choice is, in principle, universal, all are welcome as members. In practice, however, the churchlike organization usually draws its audience and adherents from the middle and upper classes and from other people identified with the established secular order. The sectlike choice, as Troeltsch (1931:331) noted, is to be "connected with the lower classes, or at least those elements in Society which are opposed to the State and to Society." Such elements generally include those who suffer

115

from deprivation of some sort, that is, those who suffer, in Barber's (1941:164) words, "the despair caused by inability to obtain what the culture has defined as the ordinary satisfaction of life." Or who, as Glock and Stark put it (1965:246), "feel disadvantaged in comparison either to other individuals or groups or to an internalized set of standards." It should be stressed that the deprivation suffered by those to whom a sectlike congregation addresses itself is relative and not absolute. Aberle (1965:538) writes:

> The discovery of what constitutes a serious deprivation for particular groups or individuals . . . requires careful attention to the reference points that people employ to judge their legitimate expectations as well as their actual circumstances. Among the obvious reference points that can be, and are used . . . are: (1) one's past versus one's present circumstances; (2) one's present circumstances versus one's future circumstances; (3) one's own versus someone else's present circumstances.

The deprivation may be one or more of five types identified by Glock and Stark (1965:246–249): economic, social, ethical, psychic, and organismic. Economic deprivation is characterized by a limited income and limited access to the necessities and luxuries of life. Social deprivation is a lack of power, prestige, or opportunities for social participation. Such lack may exist at all income levels, for example, middle-class blacks or women of wealth may find their paths to political power blocked despite the absence of poverty. Ethical deprivation is characterized by the inability to lead one's life according to one's own values and the feeling of being forced to follow values one rejects. For example, an artist might have to abandon his own standards in order to be popular and a rugged individualist might find it necessary to work on the corporate team. Psychic deprivation is the lack of any meaningful value system with which to order and interpret one's life, a condition many alienated and uncommitted youth find themselves in (see Keniston, 1965). Organismic deprivation involves a physical or mental deformity, ill health, or other such stigmatizing or disabling traits.

In sum, then, it is suggested here that future studies of religious congregations, while *not* attempting to reconstruct conglomerates of attributes comprising specific types, should remain within the traditions of the sect-church legacy. They may do so by using the choice-point approach. This approach focusses attention upon internal characteristics such as membership criteria, the extent and character of members' involvement, and the composition of the leadership, as well as upon external relations with the surrounding social context. Studies of the latter could include examination of the congregation's attitude towards the secular status quo and of the audience to which the organization addresses itself and from which it draws adherents.

116

Applying the Choice-Point Approach
to the SES Hypothesis

As was indicated above, sociologists of religion working within the tradition stemming from Troeltsch's (1931) insights into the differences between sectlike and churchlike religious congregations have posited and sought to test the socioeconomic hypothesis dealing with the involvement of individual members to their respective congregations. The SES hypothesis holds that regardless of the characteristics of the congregation itself, the degree and kind of involvement in it on the part of individual members of low socioeconomic status is more sectlike and less churchlike than the involvement of members of middle or high socioeconomic status. The differences predicted by the SES hypothesis in the way individuals relate to their respective congregations are said to hold regardless of the characteristics of the congregation with which they are affiliated and in which they practice their religion. For example, the SES hypothesis predicts that individuals of low socioeconomic status exhibit a sectlike involvement in a given congregation even if they have joined a churchlike organization. The background or roots of the SES hypothesis and evidence pertaining to it are discussed next, with an eye towards highlighting the value of the choice-point approach just developed.

The roots of the hypothesis.   The roots of the SES hypothesis lie in two classic works within the legacy of the sociological study of the differences between sectlike and churchlike congregations: *The Social Teachings of the Christian Churches* (1931), by Troeltsch, first published in Germany in 1912, and *The Social Sources of Denominationalism* (1929), Niebuhr's landmark investigation. The hypothesis is rooted in one of Troeltsch's central observations and one of Niebuhr's basic themes concerning differences among religious organizations. The framing of the SES hypothesis involves the application of their insights (which focussed on religious congregations per se) to the study of the involvement of individuals with religious congregations.[7]
 Troeltsch, it may be recalled, observed that "the church . . . becomes dependent upon the upper classes," while "the sects . . . are connected with the lower classes" (1931:331). That is, in the terms of the choice-points facing religious organizations (discussed above), Troeltsch's observation implies that the audiences associated with the religiosity of churches differ from those associated with the religiosity of sects. Churchlike religiosity draws its audience from the upper class, while sectlike religiosity draws its audience from the lower classes. Moreover, Troeltsch's observation forms one basis for a main

117

theme in Niebuhr's work, which is that the division of Christianity into various denominations "closely follows the division of men into . . . economic groups" (1929:6).

Niebuhr expands upon his theme by noting some of the specific characteristics which distinguish the religion of what he called "the economically disenfranchised classes" from that of the middle classes. The religion of people of lower socioeconomic status, the economically disenfranchised, according to Niebuhr (1929:30–31), includes such features as "emotional fervor"; "a marked propensity toward millenarianism," with its concern for a collective, not merely personal salvation; and an "appreciation of the religious worth of solidarity and equality, of sympathy and mutual aid." The religion of the middle class, on the other hand, is characterized, among other features, by a calm, "practical rationalism," (1929:83), rather than by emotional fervor; by an interest in individual or personal salvation, (1929:82), rather than in social or collective redemption in a millennial age; and by a lack of "regard for the neighbor" (1929:89), that is, it is not particularly concerned with sympathy or mutual aid.

Leaving aside the doctrinal issues surrounding the matter of one's relationship to the possible coming of a millennial age, the issues discussed by Niebuhr may be said to pertain to two of the choice-points facing religious congregations discussed above. One involves external relationships, the audience to which the congregation addresses itself and from which it draws its adherents. The other involves internal relationships, the extent and character of the members' involvement with the congregation. Thus, Niebuhr's discussion, as well as Troeltsch's, may be interpreted as suggesting that congregations which make the sectlike choice of appealing to members of the lower socioeconomic status will also choose the sectlike option of expecting a personal involvement on the part of their members. Personal involvement means that one's emotions are involved and that one participates in a network of fellowship and personal friendships, the informal aspects of the organization. Analogously, the discussions of Niebuhr and Troeltsch may be interpreted as suggesting that congregations which make the churchlike choice of appealing to people of the middle or upper socioeconomic status will also choose the churchlike option of stressing impersonal involvement on the part of their members. Impersonal involvement entails calm, practical, even calculating, rational thought, not emotions, and does not require participation in an informal network of fellowship and friendship, although participation in the formal network of committees and meetings which deal with the "business" of the congregation may be valued.

Obviously, such an interpretation of the observation made by

118

Troeltsch and the theme stressed by Niebuhr highlights the implications for the study of the structure of religious congregations *per se* rather than for the study of the involvement of individuals in the congregation as called for in the SES hypothesis. Moreover, such was the prevailing interpretation of the work of Troeltsch and Niebuhr for a considerable period among sociologists of religion. One reason for the prevalence of a congregation-oriented interpretation is, of course, that the remarks made by Troeltsch and Niebuhr concerning social class and religion were made within the context of their broader examination of the sect-church distinction. As noted above, the primary focus of that distinction is on characteristics of religious congregations, not on differences among religious individuals. Thus, the implication of what Troeltsch and Niebuhr had said for the study of differences in how individuals related to the congregation was overlooked in efforts concentrated on the study of the congregation itself. Furthermore, within the sect-church legacy, with its use of ideal types, attention is drawn away from interest in the possibility of differences within a given congregation, as posited by the SES hypothesis. As Demerath (1965:43) notes, "one of the criteria of the ideal church and the ideal sect is that the members of each will be similar." Thus, within the sect-church legacy, and especially when reliance on the use of ideal types is strong, there is little, if any, impetus for the study of individual differences. The legacy focusses attention upon the congregation itself, not on its members, and tends to assume homogeneity within these congregations, rather than suggesting an examination of the degree of heterogeneity, or differences, among the membership. Given the lack of impetus, it is not surprising that it was over four decades after Troeltsch's original work and nearly three decades after Niebuhr's, that the first attempts were made to apply the insights of the sect-church legacy to the study of differences among members of religious congregations rather than to the study of the congregation itself.

The first attempts to apply the insights of the sect-church legacy to the study of members of religious congregations were made by Dynes (1955, 1957) and were followed shortly by those of Demerath (1961, 1965). It is on the basis of their work that the SES hypothesis was given specific form. Attention was turned to the hypothesis that regardless of the emphasis of the given religious congregation with which one is formally affiliated, the involvement in the given congregation on the part of an individual of low socioeconomic status is more sectlike and less churchlike than that of an individual with middle or high socioeconomic status, while that of individuals of the latter statuses are more churchlike and less sectlike.[8] More specifically, the SES hypothesis holds that regardless of the emphasis of the

119

congregation with which one is formally affiliated, the involvement of those of low socioeconomic status will be more personal and more focussed on informal networks than that of those of middle or high socioeconomic status, while the involvement of the latter status will be more impersonal and more focussed on formal networks within the congregation. Various aspects of the hypothesis have also been tested in the works of Goode (1966, 1968) and of Estus and Overington (1970).

The empirical evidence. Dynes (1955), in a study of a sample of 360 members of the Protestant population in the metropolitan area of Columbus, Ohio, constructed a scale on which low scores indicated "the acceptance of the Sect type of religious organization and high scores . . . the acceptance of the Church type" (1955:557). He correlated the scale scores of individuals with their socioeconomic status; the latter was assessed by three different measures: educational attainment, census occupational classifications, and the North-Hatt scale of occupational prestige (see North and Hatt, 1947). The results with each of the three measures of socioeconomic status indicate that for the population as a whole "Churchness is associated with high socioeconomic status and, conversely, that Sectness is associated with low socio-economic status" (Dynes, 1955:559). However, the SES hypothesis does not speak merely of a relationship between socioeconomic status and differences in individual religiosity for a population as a whole, it makes the more specific prediction that the relationship will hold even within a given congregation. Thus, further empirical testing probing the relationship between socioeconomic status and one's involvement in a given congregation is called for by the SES hypothesis. Fortunately, Dynes did such further testing. He found that within each of the two denominational groups in his sample large enough to permit meaningful statistical analysis, namely, Methodists and Presbyterians, the relationship between socioeconomic status and scores on the sect-church scale held. That is, as Dynes notes (1955:560), "holding denominational affiliation constant, then, the difference in the degree of Churchness and Sectness is still associated with socio-economic status." Dynes' study would, then, appear to lend support to the SES hypothesis. However, the ultimate strength of that support rests not only in the direction of the findings, but also in the content of the measurement, the operational definitions of how churchlike or sectlike one's involvement with the congregation is. Here, unfortunately, Dynes' study falls short, thus leaving its ultimate relevance to the SES hypothesis more that of suggesting its content than of actually providing empirical support for it. That is, from the standpoint of this chapter, Dynes' work is noteworthy more because it is the first to suggest that the insights of the sect-church legacy be applied, in the form of the SES hypothesis, to the study of differences in the involvement of individuals in their respective congregations than it is as the first to test that hypothesis.

From the standpoint of the SES hypothesis, the defect in the scale constructed by Dynes is that while some of its items pertain to variables relevant to the hypothesis, most of its items deal with extraneous variables. That is, Dynes' operational definition of "sectness" and "churchness" is not that specifically called for by the SES hypothesis in that Dynes' measure does not concentrate on the specific choice-points relevant to the SES hypothesis. For example, Dynes' scale includes items which pertain to doctrinal matters, such as, how literally one should interpret the Bible and how otherworldly one ought to be. Unfortunately, doctrinal matters are not pertinent to the SES hypothesis as stated above. The scale also refers to aspects of congregational involvement not mentioned in the SES hypothesis as it is framed above, such as the degree of professionalism among the clergy that one prefers. On the other hand, the scale does include at least some items of direct relevance to the SES hypothesis, such as those dealing with a preference for emotional fervor in religious observances and those which stress the sense of community among fellow believers. Unfortunately, it is not possible to discern from Dynes' report the extent to which the relationship he found between SES and his scale of "sectness" and "churchness" results from items relevant to the SES hypothesis as stated here and to what extent it is due to other items.

Dynes' (1957) second study, which uses the same scale and sample population as the first, is, like the first, more significant for our purposes for having suggested that the insights of the sect-church legacy be applied to the study of differences in the involvement of individuals in religious organizations than for the specific results which it contains. However, the results do indicate (1957:334) that the more someone accepts the secttype of congregation as opposed to the churchtype, the more likely it is that for such a person

> . . . the religious group appears to be the most meaningful association and source of friendship. This was indicated by the fact that he . . . belongs to more subgroups within an undifferentiated organization, states . . . that he derives more satisfaction from these religious associations as contrasted with "secular" groups, and draws most of his close friends from within his religious group.

The scores on Dynes' scale are related to the degree to which an individual is involved in a personal way in the informal or friendship networks within a congregation. Given the previous finding (Dynes, 1955) that the degree of acceptance of the secttype as opposed to the churchtype of congregation is greater among those of lower socioeconomic status than among those of middle or high socioeconomic status, the results of the second study suggest, but by no means prove, the validity of the SES hypothesis. For example, the results suggest that since both low socioeconomic status and a high level of personal involvement in the informal networks within a religious organization are related to scores on Dynes' scale, low SES and such involvement may be related to each other. In short, two variables, involvement and socioeconomic status, each of which is related to a third, the scale scores, may be related to each other. However, evidence directly testing the possibility of such a relationship is not found in either study by Dynes. Dynes' studies (1955, 1957) suggest that the insights of the sect-church legacy be applied to the study of the involvement of individuals in their respective congregations, and support the plausibility of the SES hypothesis. However, they do not provide evidence directly bearing on the hypothesis. Such direct evidence is, however, provided by a pair of studies by Demerath (1961, 1965).

In the first of his pair of studies, Demerath examines the relevant responses of some 2720 Lutherans to a questionnaire distributed in 1956 by the National Lutheran Council to members of congregations in large cities throughout the United States. His analysis focusses upon three forms of participation in or involvement with one's congregation: (1) ritual observance, measured by the number of times the individual attends Sunday services, (2) organizational participation, measured by the number of formal church organizations to which the individual belongs, and (3) communal attachment, measured by how many of an individual's five closest friends are members of the congregation. Each of the forms of involvement is positively correlated with the other two, that is, each increases as each of the others increases, and decreases as each of the others decreases. However, while ritual observance and communal attachment are only weakly associated, the relationship between ritual observance and organizational participation is particularly strong. In view of the strength of this latter relationship, Demerath chose to use only one of the measures, ritual observance, in the more detailed analyses of his study and to omit the measure of formal participation. From the standpoint of the SES hypothesis this omission is unfortunate since ritual observance is not necessarily a direct measure of churchlike involvement as defined by the hypothesis. For example, church attendance does not necessarily reflect participation in the formal or impersonal aspects of a congregation since the degree to which such attendance is a formal obligation of membership varies from faith to faith, as does the degree to which the services themselves are formal and reserved (as they are in the Lutheran congregation Demerath studied) rather than characterized by emotional fervor. In any case, communal attachment is clearly a measure of a sectlike involvement as defined by the SES hypothesis. Thus, the SES hypothesis, as applied to Demerath's study, predicts that ritual observance will increase with increasing socioeconomic status, while communal attachment will decrease. The data, using an index of socioeconomic status which combines education, family income, and occupational prestige, generally confirm the SES hypothesis. Moreover, the hypothesis is supported, Demerath notes (1961:152), even though "our data refer only to Lutherans and not members of a sect." That is, the data are from a rather restricted range of respondents (all within a churchlike congregation), one less likely than a wider range to evince sectlike tendencies.

In a further test of an aspect of the SES hypothesis, Demerath examined the relationship between one's socioeconomic status and the degree to which one finds religion personally rewarding or helpful. Specifically, respondents were asked to indicate how much help the church was to them in a number of areas of their lives. These areas ranged from "helping me to know of God's care and love for me" to "helping me to meet friends." The degree to which individuals believe they receive help in given areas of life may be interpreted as a measure of the degree of personal involvement in the church— personal in the sense that one is personally rewarded or personally helped. The results again confirm the SES hypothesis; that is, "with declining status, there is an increasing propensity to experience a material or psychological reward from one's contact with the church" (Demerath, 1961:154).

The results of Demerath's first study, though restricted to members of one denomination, "suggest that status is differently related to religious involvement depending upon what kind of indicator of involvement is used" (1961:154). More specifically (1961:154), the

> . . . findings indicate that . . . compared with middle- and upper-class propensities to engage in the more impersonal forms of [Lutheran] ritual and organizational activity, the lower classes tend to be more personally involved in the church as a community. In addition, the lower-status groups appear to be more [personally] rewarded by religion in their everyday life.

However, it should be recalled that the findings are from only one denomination. Additional study involving a wider range of religious organizations is found, fortunately, in Demerath's later work (1965),

123

which examines the relationship between socioeconomic status and involvement among individuals across a wider, although admittedly still limited, range.

Demerath's later study examines questionnaire responses from approximately 9000 members of five denominations: the National Lutheran Council, The American Baptist Convention, the Congregationalists (before the merger with the Evangelical and Reformed Churches), the Disciples of Christ, and northern Presbyterians. The study itself is a secondary analysis of data collected in 1957 in a study sponsored by the National Council of Churches. The purposes of the original study restricted the study population to members of congregations outside the American South (1965:xxiv).

Demerath prepared for his analyses by constructing two separate scales of an individual's involvement with his congregation: the Index of Churchlike Religiosity (1965:78) and the Index of Sectlike Religiosity (1965:79). Each scale consisted of three items. The Index of Churchlike Religiosity measured (1) frequency of attendance at Sunday services; (2) participation in the formal organization of the congregation (e.g., on committees dealing with the congregation's finances, Sunday school, choir, or buildings, and grounds); and (3) participation in nonchurch organizations (e.g., the Rotary Club, parent-teacher groups, political groups, volunteer community organizations, the Scouts).

From the standpoint of the SES hypothesis within the framework of the choice-point approach, only the second item is obviously or directly related to the variables mentioned in the hypothesis. That is, only participation in congregational committees is obviously or directly related to the degree to which one's involvement in a congregation is impersonal and formal. The relevance of the measure of attendance at Sunday services is questionable, as noted above. That is, the measure of attendance may or may not be appropriate for measuring a churchlike involvement with respect to the specific dimension or choice-point involved in the SES hypothesis. The relevance of the third item may also be open to question. However, its inclusion is defensible since it is designed to reflect the degree to which one's involvement is segmented, that is, shared with other organizations. If one's involvement is segmented and one's commitments and involvements are divided between church and nonchurch activities, then they may be said to be less personal, or more impersonal, than those which are not divided and which involve more of one's total person. Consequently, the extent of involvement in nonchurch activities may be seen as pertinent to an attempt to assess the degree to which one's involvement is personal or impersonal, and thus relevant to the particular choice-point which the SES hypothesis seeks to apply to the study of variations among the religious involvement of individuals.

The three items of Demerath's Index of Sectlike Religiosity measure (1) the number of close friends in the congregation, (2) the extent to which religion is found to be personally helpful or rewarding, using measures discussed above from the earlier study (1961), and (3) the extent of disapproval of a minister's participation in community affairs and controversy. As noted above, the first two measures seek to assess the degree to which one's relationship to a congregation is a personal one involving the informal network of the organization. The relevance of the third item to such an assessment is not obvious. However, as Demerath claims (1965:76), it may reflect "a strategy of insulating members . . . to protect the intimacy of the . . . community" of believers. If disapproval is indeed part of such a strategy, it would be part of a general relationship which is intimate or personal, involving the informal network within the religious organization. As such, it would be pertinent to the choice-point referred to by the SES hypothesis.

Demerath's analysis of the relationship between socioeconomic status (measured by an index combining items on education, income, and occupational prestige) and each of his indexes of religiosity was performed in two parts. The first part is an extension and replication of his earlier study and deals only with Lutherans. The second part used respondents from the four non-Lutheran denominations in his study population. The results of the first part of the analysis support the SES hypothesis, as it has been developed in this chapter. That is, as Demerath (1965:94) notes, "Every table and every comparison within them supports the thesis that religiosity has churchlike and sectlike components which have opposite associations with social status." More specifically, low socioeconomic status is associated with a sectlike religiosity stressing a personal involvement in the informal network of a congregation, while middle or upper socioeconomic status is associated with a churchlike involvement stressing a less personal, segmented involvement with the congregation's formal network. Demerath also found that among the Lutherans he studied, age, sex, and subjective social class, while each important in its own right, did not override the relationship between socioeconomic status and differences in individual involvement (1965:94–103). More importantly, in the second portion of his analysis, which used data from the four other denominations (Congregationalists, Presbyterians, Disciples of Christ, and Baptists), Demerath found (1965:122), that "the original relations between individual status and the types of individual religiosity persist, regardless of the . . . denominational context." In sum, Demerath (1965:123) found that regardless of denomination, "the incidence of churchlike religiosity is positively related to individual status, and the incidence of sectlike religiosity is negatively related." These findings are supportive of the SES hypothesis.

125

Demerath's second study, despite its range of denominations, does share a defect with the studies of Dynes (1955, 1957) relative to the SES hypothesis.[9] As suggested above, there is some question as to the relevance of the measure of religious involvement to the variables specified in the SES hypothesis. That is, while the scales refer to churchlike and sectlike involvement, they may introduce elements extraneous to the specific choice-points alluded to by the hypothesis. Since *church* and *sect* are generally used as global terms, it is important to be specific as to just which choice-points are pertinent to a given use of the terms. Such specificity in the use of Demerath's findings is possible if the relationship between socioeconomic status and each item of his two religiosity scales is known. Unlike Dynes, Demerath does provide the desired item by item analysis (1965:205–208). "Clearly all three of the items of the sectlike measures confirm the hypothesis," he writes (1965:205), "the upper status group has the lower score on each; the low-status parishioners have by far the highest." The results for the individual items which comprise the Index of Churchlike Religiosity are not as consistent. Demerath reports (1965:205) that results involving two of the items, participation in the formal activities of the congregation and participation in nonchurch organizations, are consistent with the SES hypothesis. However, results involving the third item in the index, church attendance, do not support the SES hypothesis; no relationship was found between socioeconomic status and church attendance. He (1965:207–208) offers several possible explanations for the lack of a relationship. Generally, his explanations are tantamount to arguing that the failure is an artifact of the idiosyncracies of the composition of his study population. Obviously, further research is needed to determine just what the relationship between church attendance and socioeconomic status is. There is also a need for a more careful understanding of the meaning of church attendance, so that it may be determined if its measurement is indeed relevant to the choice between impersonal and formal relationships to a religious organization and personal and informal ones. Clearly, the application of the sect-church distinction to individual involvement with the organization rather than to the organization itself, under the guidelines of the choice-point approach to the study of such differences, calls for such determination.

Studies by Goode (1966) and by Estus and Overington (1970) delve further into the relationship between church attendance and socioeconomic status with an eye toward understanding the meaning or significance of such attendance. Goode's study consists of secondary analyses of data collected in two studies. One of the original studies, done in 1959, was an attitude survey of residents of the southern

Appalachian region of the United States. The final sample of just over one thousand individuals was composed almost entirely of whites and Protestants, largely from rural areas, and most were blue-collar workers, manual laborers, or farmers. The design of the original study resulted in a study population which was one-third church leaders, one-third church members who were not leaders, and one-third nonmembers. The study population in the other study, done in 1957, consisted of nearly five thousand respondents, all members of the Congregationalist church. Moreover, the sample in the second study contained a high proportion of white-collar workers, college-educated persons, and people with high incomes, all from metropolitan areas. Thus, as Goode notes, "this sample neatly complements the sample . . . included in the Appalachian study" with its large number of rural blue-collar workers (1966:107). More importantly, the results of the analyses of data from the two different study populations agree.

For the purposes of this chapter, Goode's results fall into two categories. The first set of results merely confirms the suggestions from Dynes' studies (1955, 1957) and the earlier work by Demerath (1961, 1965).[10] These results consist of the findings that (1) church attendance and participation on church committees or organizations are each positively related to socioeconomic status; (2) participation in nonchurch organizations is also positively related to socioeconomic status; and (3) participation in church organizations and nonchurch organizations are positively related to each other. Moreover, in a brief note amplifying his results, Goode (1967b) reports that the relationship between socioeconomic status and church attendance holds whether one belongs to a fundamentalist denomination, a conservative denomination, or a more liberal denomination. In sum, Goode's first set of findings support the SES hypothesis in that they show that the pattern of individual involvement as reflected in church attendance for individuals of low socioeconomic status differs from the pattern among individuals of middle or upper socioeconomic status, regardless of one's formal denominational affiliation. However, as noted above, there is some question as to whether church attendance is an appropriate measure of differences along the particular dimension or choice-point of relevance to the SES hypothesis. Goode's second set of results helps clarify the meaning of such attendance and, thus, the relevance of such attendance to the SES hypothesis, as stated here within the framework of the choice-point approach to the study of differences between churchlike and sectlike involvements.

Specifically, Goode's second set of results indicate that whether socioeconomic status is measured by occupation or education, controlling for the degree of participation in nonchurch formal organizations greatly attenuates, or reduces, the original uncontrolled relationship between socioeconomic status and church attendance. That is, among individuals whose degree of participation in nonchurch organizations is similar, the relationship between their socioeconomic status and participation in church activities is slight, and much less than it is in the study population as a whole. In other words, although status differences in church activity persist with nonchurch activity controlled, they are "reduced significantly" (Goode, 1966:110). Much, if not all, of the original, uncontrolled relationship between socioeconomic status and church attendance may be due to a relationship between status and some general propensity for participation in organizations of all sorts, religious and secular. That is, as Goode (1966:111) observes, his

> . . . findings strongly suggest that church activity, such as attendance at church ritual, cannot be seen as an unambiguous reflection of religiosity. . . . It appears that church activity . . . can be subsumed, at least partially, under general associational activity.

A measure of church attendance, as Goode goes on to say (1966:111) "is not a measure that can be considered specifically religious in character"; indeed, "it cannot be said to measure a purely religious variable; secular variables are intertwined with it." Goode's study suggests that church attendance not be used as a measure of individual religiosity. Consequently, the failure of church attendance to relate to socioeconomic status, as predicted by the SES hypothesis, may not be damaging to that hypothesis, since the hypothesis refers to religious involvement, and church attendance, ironically, may be a poor indicator of religious involvement per se.[11]

The search for measures which are appropriate to the task of determining whether or not socioeconomic status and differences in individual involvement in the congregation are related as predicted by the SES hypothesis is continued in the work of Estus and Overington (1970).[12] That is, their study continues the empirical investigation into the validity of the prediction that involvement is more likely to be reflected in personal relationships centering on the informal network of a congregation for persons of low rather than middle or high socioeconomic status, while impersonal or segmented involvement (which concentrates on the formal structure of a congregation) is more likely for persons of middle or high rather than low status.

The Estus and Overington study (1970) consists of a secondary analysis of data collected from a national sample of church members from nine major Protestant denominations gathered for the National Council of Churches in 1957. In all just over 13,000 questionnaires were collected from laymen in 52 churches in 23 urban centers across the United States. Interestingly, the study population examined by Estus and Overington is the larger population from which are drawn Demerath's more limited study of Lutherans (1961), Goode's study of Congregationalists (1966), and Demerath's wider study of five denominations (1965). Thus, Estus and Overington are in a position to attempt to replicate the earlier studies using the entire study population, rather than just subparts of it.

In their attempt to extend and replicate the earlier studies, Estus and Overington examine the relationships among the four variables central to the earlier studies: (1) socioeconomic status, which they measure both by education and occupation; (2) participation in the formal network of the congregation, which they measure by attendance at church services, financial contributions to the congregation, and the holding of leadership positions in organizations within the congregation; (3) participation in formal organizations outside the congregation, which is measured by the number of such memberships; and (4) participation in the informal network of the congregation. This last variable is measured by a three-item scale called the Integration Scale, (1970:767), which asks how good a job the congregation is doing, how many members one knows by name, and how many of one's five best friends are members.

As was the case in the Demerath (1961, 1965) and Goode (1966) studies, Estus and Overington find that socioeconomic status is positively related to participation in the formal structure of a congregation. That is, the higher one's status, the more likely one is to be involved with the congregation's formal structure. Participation in the formal organizations outside the congregation is similarly positively related to socioeconomic status. However, while contributing financially to a congregation and holding office within it, two measures of participation in the congregation's formal structure, are each positively related to participation in noncongregational formal organizations, church attendance is not related to noncongregational activity at all. Consequently, if there is a general associational factor, as suggested by Goode (1966), church attendance appears not to be part of it. Doubt that church attendance is part of a general tendency toward organizational participation is also raised by the failure of Estus and Overington to find any significant attenuation or weakening of the relationship between church attendance and socioeconomic status when noncongregational activity is controlled, although such a control does weaken the relationship between status and other measures of formal congregational activity. In short, the measure of church attendance does not behave like other measures which more obviously assess participation in the formal structure of a congregation. Since a scale of church attendance does not relate to other variables as would more obvious measures of participation in the congregation's formal structure, its use as a measure of such participation is called into question. Attendance at church services does not appear to be a simple or clear indicator of the character of one's involvement in a congregation. The meaning of such attendance remains unclear despite the studies by Demerath, Goode, and Estus and Overington. It would be wise not to look at church attendance as a measure of the extent to which one's religious involvement is formal and impersonal as opposed to personal and informal. The studies just discussed indicate that measures of financial contributions and of holding office in congregational committees, such as those used by Estus and Overington, are better measures of the formal and impersonal mode of involvement, while measures of how many acquaintances and friends one has within the congregation more aptly reflect the personal and informal mode of involvement.

When Estus and Overington do use their Integration Scale, which includes measures of the number of one's friends and acquaintances in one's congregation, they find it has a curvilinear relationship with socioeconomic status. They find (1970:768) that one's chances of being highly integrated in a congregation's informal network are highest if one has a low status, next highest if one is from the upper status, and least if one is of the middle status. These results do not, of course, contradict the SES hypothesis as stated above, although they do amplify or modify it. It still appears that those of low socioeconomic status are more apt to be involved in a congregation's informal structure than those of middle or upper status, whatever the relative level of involvement between the two higher statuses.

The results of the various analyses just reviewed are all compatible with the SES hypothesis as it has been developed here within the framework of the choice-point approach to differences between churchlike and sectlike congregations and then applied to the study of differences in the involvement of individuals in their respective congregations (Dynes, 1955, 1957; Demerath, 1961, 1965; Goode, 1966, 1967b, 1968; Estus and Overington, 1970). The difficulties and inconsistencies encountered when examining results involving measures of church attendance highlight the need to pay careful attention to the conceptual and operational definition of *church* and *sect* in any given study.[13] Such definitions should avoid any assumption, tacit or otherwise, that church and sect can be properly used as global concepts referring to a proven complex of relationships among a number of measures of various differences between churchlike and sectlike congregations. Nor can church and sect properly refer to any single dimension of "churchness" or "sectness." None is well understood or well documented. To use church and sect as global concepts, or to refer to a single dimension is to misrepresent the facts, as known, and inhibit the theoretical discussions and empirical investigations which will be needed to advance understanding by sociologists of religion of issues raised by the tradition of the study of differing expressions of religiosity begun by Troeltsch, nurtured by Niebuhr, and expressed in the SES hypothesis.

Summary

This chapter first identified two main lines of development in the more than half-century of discussion of Troeltsch's (1931) seminal treatment of the secttype and churchtype of religious congregation. It was noted that contemporary sociologists of religion have grown increasingly disillusioned with the original typology and have sought ways to link the discussion of religious organization more closely with the more general study of formal organizations. An approach was presented which, while remaining within the sect-church tradition, provided for a link with the general study of formal organizations. The approach involves identifying several crucial choice-points or issues facing religious congregations rather than attempting to construct conglomerates of attributes comprising ideal types.

Two sets of choice-points or issues were identified. The first set pertains to the internal characteristics of religious congregations. It includes such matters as the criteria for membership, the extent and character of member involvement, and the composition of the leadership. The second set of choice-points involves the external relations of the congregation with the surrounding social context. This set of choices involves the questions of what attitude to take toward the secular status quo and what audience should be addressed and looked upon as the primary source of adherents.

The remainder of the chapter applied the choice-point approach to the examination of studies of differences in how individuals relate to their respective congregations. The studies under examination all helped either to formulate or test the SES hypothesis. The SES hypothesis holds that regardless of the characteristics of the congregation itself, the degree and kind of involvement on the part of individual members is affected by their respective socioeconomic status. Specifically, the SES hypothesis holds that in all congregations, members of low socioeconomic status have a more sectlike and less churchlike involvement than do members of middle or high socioeconomic status. The choice-point approach was found to be useful in helping to interpret the empirical results and in pointing to the need for more appropriate measures of involvement.

FOOTNOTES

1. The term *congregation* is used here as a generic term to refer to all forms of organizations in which people seek desired relationships with the sacred. Thus, the term is not restricted, as used here, to reference to single, local bodies, but includes organizations of two or more local bodies as well.
2. For comments on the entire body of Troeltsch's work, and not just his discussion of the distinction between church and sect, see Adams (1961), Little (1961) and Reist (1966).
3. The distinction between church and sect did not originate with Troeltsch. He developed a distinction made by his teacher, Max Weber (1946: 302–322; 1958: 144–154). See also Weber (1973) and for further discussion of antecedents of Troeltsch's distinction, see Hill (1973:47–51).
4. Westhues (1971, 1973) identifies some of the factors which induce or inhibit the sectlike lack of accommodation by the Roman Catholic Church to its host society.
5. These forms also constitute the pattern of religious individualism, which, as noted in the Introduction, Durkheim (1965:62) recognized as a possible religious form of the future. Luckmann's views are discussed in Chapter 3.
6. Wilson (1970, 1973) identifies as many as nine sectlike responses to the standards of the secular world. The four discussed here, are the major ones and suffice to indicate that there is a variety of sectlike responses. They are referred to again in Chapter 5 in the discussion of the development of sectlike congregations.
7. The suggestion that different socioeconomic strata are associated with different religious outlooks may also be found in Weber (1963: 80–117). However, Weber's discussion is mainly concerned with differences in doctrine, rather than in styles of organizational involvement, and thus is not directly pertinent to the issues raised by the SES hypothesis as stated here.
8. Dillingham reviews earlier studies of the relationship between socioeconomic status and religion done by Allinsmith (1948), Bultena (1949), Burchinal (1959), Cantril (1943), Hollingshead (1949), Lenski (1953), and Lazerwitz (1961). The relevance of these earlier studies to the SES hypothesis is limited by two factors: (1) The studies rely heavily on measures of church attendance, which are of questionable value in assessing religious involvement as defined by the SES hypothesis. (2) The studies generally aim at ranking various denominations and thus look at gross differences between groups rather than at the individual differences within the group relevant to the SES hypothesis. For further comment on early studies and their relevance to the SES hypothesis, see Demerath (1965: 1–26).
9. For further comment on the relevance of work by Dynes and Demerath to the sect-church legacy, see Goode (1967a), whose focus is on the legacy as a whole and not just on the SES hypothesis, as intended here. See also Demerath's response to Goode (1967a) and their subsequent exchange (Demerath, 1967b; Goode, 1967b).
10. In another, later study, Goode (1968) offers a further finding which confirms the suggestions from the work of Dynes (1955, 1957) and Demerath (1961, 1965), that the degree to which one finds religion or church membership helpful is inversely related to one's socioeconomic status. The data in this later

study consist of responses from the members of the Congregationalist churches who comprise one of the study populations used in his earlier study (1966).

11. Support for the view that church attendance measures something other than the forms of involvement with one's congregation relevant to the SES hypothesis is found in the factor analytic study of King and Hunt (1975). They find that the factor constituted by measures of church attendance is separate from a factor constituted by measures of organizational activity within the congregation and one, by measures of financial support of the congregation.

12. Goode (1970: 780) offers his own comments on the work of Estus and Overington. He regards their work, as I do, as an extension of his own.

13. Estus and Overington (1970:771–777) proffer an interesting theory of the meaning of church attendance which, while attempting to explain the differences in attendance on the part of individuals of differing socioeconomic status, lies largely outside the sect-church legacy. Thus, it is not examined here. For other approaches, outside the sect-church legacy, to the study of individuals' involvement in their respective congregations, see Schweiker (1969) and Roof (1974).

REFERENCES

Aberle, David
1965 "A note on relative deprivation theory as applied to millenarian and other cult movements." In *Reader in Comparative Religion*, 2nd ed., edited by William A. Lessa and E. Z. Vogt. New York: Harper & Row.

Adams, James Luther
1961 "Ernst Troeltsch as analyst of religion." *Journal for the Scientific Study of Religion* 1 (October):98–109.

Allinsmith, Wesley
1948 "Social-economic status and outlook of religious groups in America." *Information Services* 27 (May 15):no. 20, pt. 2.

Barber, Bernard
1941 "Acculturation and messianic movements." *American Sociological Review* 6 (October):163–169.

Becker, Howard
1932 *Systematic Sociology: On the Basis of the "Beziehunglehre" and "Gebildelehre" of Leopold von Wiese.* New York: Wiley.

Benson, J. Kenneth, and Jane H. Dorsett
1971 "Toward a theory of religious organization." *Journal for the Scientific Study of Religion* 10 (Summer):130–151.

Berger, Peter L.
1954 "The sociological study of sectarianism." *Social Research* 21 (Winter): 473–476.

Bultena, Louis
1949 "Church membership and church attendance in Madison, Wisconsin." *American Sociological Review* 14 (June):384–389.

Burchinal, Leo G.
1959 "Some social status criteria and church membership and church attendance." *Journal of Social Psychology* 49 (February):53–64.

the sociology of religious congregations

Cantril, Hadley
1943 "Educational and economic composition of religious groups." *American Journal of Sociology* 48 (March):574–579.

Coleman, John A., S.J.
1968 "Church-sect typology and organizational precariousness." *Sociological Analysis* 29 (Summer):55–66.

Demerath, Nicholas J., III
1961 "Social stratification and church involvement: the church-sect distinction applied in individual participation." *Review of Religious Research* 2 (Spring):146–154.
1965 *Social Class in American Protestantism.* Skokie, Ill.: Rand McNally.
1967a "In a sow's ear: a reply to Goode." *Journal for the Scientific Study of Religion* 6 (Spring):77–84.
1967b "Son of a sow's ear." *Journal for the Scientific Study of Religion* 6 (Fall):275–277.

Demerath, Nicholas J., III, and Phillip E. Hammond
1969 *Religion in Social Context.* New York: Random House.

Dillingham, Harry C.
1965 "Protestant religion and social status." *American Journal of Sociology* 70 (January):416–422.

Durkheim, Emile
1965 *The Elementary Forms of the Religious Life.* Translated by Joseph W. Swain. New York: Free Press (paperback).

Dynes, Russell R.
1955 "Church-sect typology and socio-economic status." *American Sociological Review* 20 (October):555–560.
1957 "The consequences of sectarianism for social participation." *Social Forces* 35 (May):331–334.

Eister, Allan W.
1967 "Toward a radical critique of church-sect typologizing: comments on 'some critical observations on the church-sect dimension.'" *Journal for the Scientific Study of Religion* 6 (Spring):85–90.

Estus, Charles, and Michael A. Overington
1970 "The meaning and end of religiosity." *American Journal of Sociology* 75 (March):760–778.

Glock, Charles Y., and Rodney Stark
1965 *Religion and Society in Tension.* Skokie, Ill.: Rand McNally.

Goode, Erich
1966 "Social class and church participation." *American Journal of Sociology* 72 (July):102–111.
1967a "Some critical observations on the church-sect dimension." *Journal for the Scientific Study of Religion* 6 (Spring):69–77.
1967b "Further reflections on the church-sect dimension." *Journal for the Scientific Study of Religion* 6 (Fall):272–273.
1968 "Class styles of religious sociation." *British Journal of Sociology* 19 (March):1–16.
1970 "Another look at social class and church participation: reply to Estus and Overington." *American Journal of Sociology* 75 (March):779–781.

Gustafson, Paul
1967   "UO-US-PS-PO: a restatement of Troeltsch's church-sect typology."
       Journal for the Scientific Study of Religion 6 (Spring):64–68.

Hill, Michael
1973   *A Sociology of Religion.* New York: Basic Books.

Hollingshead, August
1949   *Elmtown's Youth.* New York: Wiley.

Johnson, Benton
1957   "A critical appraisal of the church-sect typology." *American Sociological
       Review* 22 (February):88–92.
1963   "On church and sect." *American Sociological Review* 28 (August):539–
       549.
1971   "Church and sect revisited." *Journal for the Scientific Study of Reli-
       gion* 10 (Summer):124–137.

Keniston, Kenneth
1965   *The Uncommitted: Alienated Youth in American Society.* New York:
       Dell.

King, Morton B., and Richard A. Hunt
1975   "Measuring the religious variable: national replication." *Journal for
       the Scientific Study of Religion* 14 (March):13–22.

Lazerwitz, Bernard
1961   "Variations in church attendance." *Social Forces* 39 (May):301–309.

Lenski, Gerhard
1953   "Social correlates of religious interest." *American Sociological Review*
       18 (October):533–544.

Little, David
1961   "Religion and social analysis in the thought of Ernst Troeltsch." *Journal
       for the Scientific Study of Religion* 1 (October):114–117.

Luckmann, Thomas
1967   *The Invisible Religion.* New York: Macmillan.

Martin, David
1962   "The denomination." *British Journal of Sociology* 13 (March):1–14.

Metz, Donald L.
1967   *New Congregations: Security and Mission in Conflict.* Philadelphia:
       Westminster Press.

Nelson, Geoffrey K.
1969   "The spiritualist movement: a need for a redefinition of the concept
       of cult." *Journal for the Scientific Study of Religion* 8 (Spring):152–160.

Niebuhr, H. Richard
1929   *The Social Sources of Denominationalism.* New York: Holt, Rinehart
       and Winston.

North, Cecil C., and Paul K. Hatt
1947   "Jobs and occupations: a popular evaluation." *Public Opinion News* 9
       (September):3–13.

O'Dea, Thomas
1968 "Sects and cults." *International Encyclopedia of the Social Sciences* 14:130–136.

Reist, Benjamin A.
1966 *Toward a Theology of Involvement: The Thought of Ernst Troeltsch.* Philadelphia: Westminster Press.

Robertson, Roland
1970 "Religious collectivities," In *The Sociological Interpretation of Religion.* New York: Schocken Books.

Roof, W. Clark
1974 "Explaining traditional religion in contemporary society." In *Changing Perspectives in the Scientific Study of Religion,* edited by Allan W. Eister. New York: Wiley.

Scalf, John H., Michael J. Miller, and Charles W. Thomas
1973 "Goal specificity, organizational structure and participant commitment in churches." *Sociological Analysis* 34 (Fall):169–184.

Schweiker, William F.
1969 "Religion as a superordinate meaning system and socio-psychological integration." *Journal for the Scientific Study of Religion* 8 (Fall):300–307.

Snook, John B.
1974 "An alternative to church-sect." *Journal for the Scientific Study of Religion* 13 (June):191–204.

Troeltsch, Ernst
1931 *The Social Teachings of the Christian Churches,* 2 vols. Translated by Olive Wyon. New York: Macmillan.

Warburton, T. Rennie
1969 "Holiness religion: an anomaly of sectarian typologies." *Journal for the Scientific Study of Religion* 8 (Spring):130–139.

Weber, Max
1946 "The Protestant sects and the spirit of capitalism." In *From Max Weber: Essays in Sociology.* Translated and edited by H. H. Gerth and C. Wright Mills. New York: Oxford University Press.
1958 *The Protestant Ethic and the Spirit of Capitalism.* Translated by Talcott Parsons. New York: Scribner.
1963 *The Sociology of Religion.* Translated by Ephraim Fischoff. Boston: Beacon Press.
1973 "On church, sect and mysticism." Translated by Jerome L. Gittleman and edited by Benjamin Nelson. *Sociological Analysis* 34 (Summer): 140–149.

Westhues, Kenneth
1971 "An elaboration and test of a secularization hypothesis in terms of open systems theory of organization." *Social Forces* 49 (March):460–469.
1973 "The established church as an agent of change." *Sociological Analysis* 34 (Summer):106–127.

Wilson, Bryan R.
1959 "An analysis of sect development." *American Sociological Review* 24 (February):3–15.

1961   *Sects and Society*. University of California Press.
1970   *Religious Sects*. New York: McGraw-Hill.
1973   *Magic and the Millenium*. New York: Harper & Row.

Yinger, J. Milton
1970   "Types of religious organizations." In *The Scientific Study of Religion*. New York: Macmillan.

BERNSTEIN, EDITORIAL PHOTOCOLOR ARCHIVES

Applying the
Choice-Point Approach:
The rise of sects
and the sect-to-church
hypothesis

One of the main lines of development in the long history of the sect-church distinction has led to the positing of two important hypotheses, one dealing with the rise of sectlike organizations and the other with the processes of organizational change and development within religious bodies. The former hypothesis is here called the *compensatory substitution hypothesis*, and the latter is best known as the *sect-to-church hypothesis*. The aim of this chapter is to discuss both hypotheses within the framework provided by the choice-point approach to the study of religious congregations (see Chap. 4). These discussions help further demonstrate the value of the choice-point approach for improving upon the legacy of the sect-church distinction without destroying the desired continuity with that legacy.

The Rise of Sectlike Organizations

Since Niebuhr's historical study of the rise of various Protestant sects (1929) and the early case studies by Boisen (1939), Holt (1940), and Pope (1942), the central question in the sociological study of the rise of sectlike congregations has been why do religious organizations which are sectlike in that they adopt a noncomprising posture toward the secular world, have stringent requirements for membership, and demand a high degree of personal involvement from their members attract persons who suffer from deprivations of one sort or another? In other words, why do congregations which adopt sectlike positions, with respect to their external relations with the secular status quo, internal characteristics of membership criteria, and extent and character of membership involvement, attract a sectlike audience of deprived persons?

The essential answer to the question just posed is contained in an hypothesis concerning the rise of sectlike congregations which I call the compensatory substitution hypothesis. The hypothesis stems from the early studies of Niebuhr, Boisen, Holt, and Pope, just mentioned, which focus on the development of sectlike congregations among modern Protestants, as well as from studies, such as those summarized by Talmon (1965), Cohn (1961, 1964), and Lanternari (1965), and those recently conducted by Carroll (1975) and Flora (1973), of movements which have taken a noncompromising stance toward the secular status quo in nonindustrial societies and which have stringent requirements for those who wish to join their deeply involved membership.

The underlying assumption of the comprensatory substitution hypothesis is, as Pope puts it (1942:137), that the "sects substitute religious status for social status." The hypothesis holds that membership in a sectlike congregation enables people to replace or *substitute* religious standards relative to which they are not deprived but privileged for the secular standards relative to which they are deprived. Thus, membership in a sectlike congregation helps one overcome or *compensate* for a feeling of relative deprivation or failure. It offers the possibility of alleviating or compensating for the despair caused by an inability to obtain what one's culture defines as the ordinary satisfactions of life, and for the feeling of being disadvantaged in comparison to others or to an internalized standard. It does so by supplying standards in terms of which one receives the ordinary satisfaction of life and is not disadvantaged. As Yinger (1970:308) says, "sectarian beliefs and practices among the deprived members of a society relieve the 'pain' that many people feel as a result of their highly disprivileged position."

The compensatory substitution hypothesis of the rise of sectlike congregations also specifies the process by which the standards of sectlike congregations come to provide compensatory substitution for the relative deprivation of their members; that is, it does not merely assert that the process of compensatory substitution takes place, it seeks to explain how it occurs.

According to the hypothesis, the key to understanding how compensatory substitution is provided by membership in a sectlike congregation (with its noncompromising stance toward the secular world, stringent membership requirements, and demands for a high degree of personal involvement) lies in understanding the theology or ideology which supports its posture toward the secular world. That is, the focus of compensatory substitution hypothesis is on the relationship between the organization's theology or ideology and the felt deprivations of its members.[1] The hypothesis seeks to understand how the ideology can provide a basis for standards which both substitute for the established standards, in terms of which members are deprived, and compensate for their felt deprivations. The hypothesis regards theological factors as of primary importance in the process of providing compensatory substitution. The other aspects of the organization in question, its stance toward the secular world, its membership criteria, and its demands for deep personal involvement, are seen as of derivative importance; that is, they derive their importance from the role they play in gaining members' initial acceptance of, and long-term commitment to, the group's theology.

The process whereby sectlike congregations provide their members with substitutes for established standards which compensate for felt deprivations is a process by which members are weaned away from the established standards and converted or resocialized into a new set of standards in terms of which members do not feel deprived, but privileged (see Lofland, 1966; Lofland and Stark, 1965). Status in the congregation and status with respect to its standards are *substituted* for those related to the established order and its standards. Since the new status is one of privilege, or at least nondeprivation, the old feelings of deprivation are *compensated* for, or counterbalanced by, new feelings of worth with respect to the new (substitute) standards.

In general, sectlike congregations employ two tactics in the process of providing compensatory substitution. First, they facilitate transvaluation, the redefinition of earthly values as relatively unimportant, by comparing earthly values with their own more important supernaturally sanctioned values. Secondly, heavenly or spiritual rewards are contrasted with the transient pleasures of the secular world. Such a contrast emphasizes the insignificance of secular well-being when compared to spiritual well-being or well-being in the afterlife.

Whatever the specific means by which compensatory substitution is eventually provided, the first step in the process of weaning prospective members of a sectlike congregation away from established standards is to provide them with a vehicle for expressing their resentment against society and its standards. Such a vehicle may be found in the uncompromising stance of the group with respect to the secular order.

141

As Glock and Stark (1965:250) note, "latent resentment against society tends to be expressed in an ideology which rejects and radically devalues the society." Such resentment is expressed in the theology of many sectlike congregations. According to compensatory substitution hypothesis, the pleasure of expressing such resentment is a reward which binds one, or at least attracts one, to the organization whose ideology permits the expression. The first step, then, is one in which the prospective members say, in effect, "I want to know more about your congregation because I like what you're saying. It makes me feel good to hear it."

The second and third steps come after a prospective member has become an actual new member. In the first place, the stringent membership requirements mean that a new member has *paid* a good deal to join, in psychological or personal terms. For example, new members may be required to confess openly the sins of their past, to denounce thoroughly and publicly their prior behavior. The price paid for membership is the embarrassment and self-degradation that is involved. A new member may be required to adopt an unusual dress or hair style, such as the saffron robes and shaved head of the Hare Krishna movement, the uniform of the Salvation Army, or the "straight" hair style of the Jesus People, which are apt to bring derision and ridicule from the "outside" world. In addition, merely associating with people whom others think are odd may involve some psychological or personal costs. In any case, as a dissonance theorist would argue (see Festinger, 1957), the more one pays to join a group the more inclined he is to think it worthwhile, (to be worth what he paid to get in it would have to be good). Since one is inclined to remain a member of a group he thinks is worthwhile, the stringent membership requirements tend to induce continued membership and to minimize the tendency to drop out. Continued membership in the group results in continued exposure to its ideology or theology. Continued exposure increases the chances of continued acceptance.

Once in the group, the demands for deep and personal involvement in the group's activities also work to enhance continued membership in the group. Such involvement leaves little time and energy to consider alternatives. Moreover, the involvement itself is apt to be rewarding, so one does not want to consider alternatives, even if one had the time and energy.

In sum, then, the stringent membership requirements, demands for deep and personal involvement, and noncompromising stance on the secular world all work to enhance acceptance of the group's theology. However, the compensatory substitution hypothesis does not regard allegiance to the theology of a sectlike congregation as merely a side effect of its posture towards the world and of its internal characteristics.

The main basis of the allegiance is the elective affinity (see p. 45) between the theology and the felt deprivations of members prior to joining.[2] That is, ultimately compensatory substitution is provided not as a side effect, but as a result of the power of the theology to provide means with which members of the deprived segments of society can deal with their basic existential problem, namely, their sense of deprivation. An illustration of how an elective affinity between the theology of a sectlike congregation provides compensatory substitution is provided by Robbins (1969), Robbins and Anthony (1972), and Anthony and Robbins (1974:479–511) in case studies of the appeal of the teachings of Meher Baba to a segment of contemporary youth.[3]

Meher Baba is, as Anthony and Robbins (1974:486) note, "a recently deceased (January 31, 1969) Indian spiritual master who claimed to be the most recent manifestation of the avataric tradition." Baba taught that Zoroaster, Rama, Krishna, Buddha, Christ, and Mohammed were all human manifestations of the same divine being and that Baba himself was the last manifestation of this being. Baba's appearance closes the cycle. The essence of Meher Baba's universal message is love. Baba himself is held to be an infinitely loving master, the essence and embodiment of affection and expressiveness (Robbins and Anthony, 1972:132–133). These teachings are accompanied by an "emphasis on meditation and inner realization" (Robbins, 1969:312).

The youths who are attracted to the teachings of Meher Baba may be said to evince ethical deprivation; that is, they are unable to live according to their own values and feel forced to follow values they reject (see p. 116 and Glock and Stark, 1965). The ethical values which the youths wish to implement are basically humanistic and personalistic, that is, they stress roles and relationships which are loving. These relationships are diffuse and affective; they treat the individual as an end, not a means, and value people for what they are more than for what they do or accomplish. Such an ethic is difficult to live by since humanistic and personalistic tenets are difficult, if not impossible, to accommodate to the instrumental processes of the adult occupational world. The latter world is materialistic more than humanistic, impersonal more than personal. It stresses functionally specific roles and relationships which are affectively neutral; roles and relationships in which people are often treated as means, not ends, and not merely for what they are, but valued, for what they do and have accomplished.

Many youths attracted to the teachings of Meher Baba first sought to deal with their ethical deprivation by joining the drug subculture. However, their attempt failed, in part, because of the tendency of drug use to lead to behavior which was not loving. Anthony and Robbins (1974:498) find:

143

1. Drug dependency often involves the proliferation of highly instrumental relationships with peers, which are treated not as ends in themselves but as means for obtaining drugs. 2. . . . The need for drugs instigates dishonesty—people are "burned" . . . and "ripped off" . . . all of which falls short of "love." 3. The illegal status of "drug abuse" tends to breed "paranoia" over the ever-present threat of a "bust."

The initial appeal of the teachings of Baba lies in easy accommodation between drug use and the Eastern mysticism within his teachings. As Robbins notes (1969:312):

> For both the psychedelic enthusiast and the oriental mystic, getting the most out of life involves the enhancement of intrapsychic consciousness and the probing of inner depths rather than action in the phenomenal world.

However, the more enduring basis of attraction is the ability of the teachings of Meher Baba to help followers overcome ethical deprivation; to find a means of living according to their love-oriented, expressive ethic while operating in "straight" society at a "straight" job.

Thus the Baba movement, through its teachings, "ameliorates the problem of 'loveless' work roles in adult instrumental milieux by 'deriving' instrumental role-orientations (qua 'selfless service') from expressive ones" (Anthony and Robbins, 1974:510). Meher Baba urges followers to demonstrate the social relevance and universality of his teaching by acting lovingly in the world. It encourages them to take jobs in the straight world as long as the work involved is in the selfless service of others. One may be a social worker, teacher, or nurse, indeed, even a construction worker or salesperson if the work is defined as providing a needed service to others and not just a means of making money for oneself or the employer. The ethic of selfless service derived from Baba's teachings synthesizes the expressive role orientations of the formerly ethically deprived youth into the instrumental role orientations of the secular status quo. Baba's "ethic incorporates the instrumental values . . . within the larger society, while maintaining the expressive emphasis which gave it birth" (Robbins and Anthony, 1972:139). Thus, Baba's teachings help youths overcome and compensate for their sense of ethical deprivation by making it possible to live according to their humanistic and personalistic values within a materialistic and impersonal society.[4] The teachings help them cope with their most central existential problem (their felt sense of deprivation) and thereby create a basis for an elective affinity between the youths and the teachings. The teachings of Baba are *substituted* for the standards of the secular world, that is, the ideology or theology provides a compensatory substitution for the felt sense of ethical deprivation. The followers of Baba are not ethically deprived in terms of the standards of Baba's teachings; quite the contrary, they are privileged to lead a life in accordance with those standards.

To explain *how* compensatory substitution occurs is not to explain *why* it occurs. The need to explain why religious means of coping with felt deprivations are used rather than other means has long been noted in the sociological study of the rise of sectlike organizations. The use of religious means in dealing with felt deprivation is but one of several possible responses. Other responses include retreat into addiction or mental illness, the use of illegal means to attain whatever one is deprived of, and social protest or rebellion. Boisen (1939), for example, noted some similarities between the world-view of the psychotic and that of the members of the sectlike organizations he studied. Holt, who studied similar groups before World War II, observed (1940:747) that

> . . . it would be interesting to determine whether the distribution and growth of Pentecostal and Holiness religion is functionally related to the distribution and strength of the labor union movement, since the later might be another type of adjustment to the urban situation by workers in the lower income brackets.

Stark (1964) and Marx (1967) have studied the possible interchangeability of religious movements and social protest as a response to deprivation. Lofland and Stark, in more general terms (1965:867), identify three classes of attempted solutions to the problem of felt deprivation—the psychiatric, the political, and the religious.

> In the first, the origin of problems is typically traced to the psyche, and manipulation of the self is advocated as a solution. Political solutions, mainly radical, locate the sources of problems in the social structure and advocate reorganization of the system as a solution. The religious perspective tends to see both sources and solutions as emanating from an unseen and, in principle, unseeable realm.

In still more general terms, Talmon (1965:530) relates the rise of religious movements among deprived groups to "uneven relations between expectations and the means of their satisfaction" and to "incongruities in the realm of regulation of ends" (1965:531). In other words, he relates it to the conditions of anomie which have long been regarded (see Merton, 1957) as the social structural sources of retreatism, crime, and social protest.

In short, the general conditions which lead some to cope with their felt deprivations through religious means may well lead others to nonreligious means. There is no necessary one-to-one relationship between felt deprivation and joining a sectlike congregation within which to deal with that deprivation. As Lofland and Stark (1965:868) note, even among those with

> . . . a general propensity to impose religious meaning on events . . . a number of alternative responses still remain. First, people can persist in stressful situations with little or no relief. Second, persons often take specifically problem-directed action to change troublesome portions of their lives, without adopting a different world [as in a sect] to interpret them. . . . Third, a number of maneuvers exist to "put the problem out of mind." In general, these are compensations for or distractions from problems in living, e.g., addictive consumption of mass media, preoccupation with child-rearing, or immersion in work. More spectacular examples include alcoholism, suicide, promiscuity and so on.

There are, then, intervening variables between the existence of felt deprivation and the joining of a sectlike congregation. These intervening variables must be specified if the compensatory substitution hypothesis is to be an adequate sociological explanation. Doing so will help specify not only *how* compensatory substitution occurs in a religious context, but *why* it takes place in that context rather than in some other. Although there is no general explanation of why religious means rather than other means are used in coping with deprivation, there are some leads as to how to proceed.[5] These leads deal with two sets of factors, predisposing conditions and situational contingencies (Lofland and Stark, 1965:864).

In Cohn's discussion (1964) of millenarian movements, he implies that there may be cross-cultural differences in the conditions predisposing one to use religious means in dealing with deprivation. He suggests that Judeo-Christian theology is more supportive of the use of such means than are the religious traditions of the Orient. Persons highly conversant with the relevant aspects of Judeo-Christian theology would be more apt to use religious means to cope with deprivation than would those not conversant with that tradition. Malalgoda (1970) observes, however, that sectlike organizations do develop in the Orient to deal with felt deprivation even in the absence of strong theological support. While theological traditions may play a part in determining responses to deprivation, as Cohn suggests, they may not, as Malalgoda suggests, be the only factors.

According to Lofland and Stark (1965) demographic factors may establish conditions predisposing one to use a religious rather than a psychiatric or political perspective in dealing with deprivation. They suggest (1965:867) that persons from small towns and rural communities may be more accustomed than urbanites to defining the world in religious terms. Holt (1940) suggests that a propensity to use a religious perspective varies across regions in the United States and is highest in the South. Turning to a sectlike congregation rather than to a political movement, for example, would be more natural to a deprived small-towner or Southerner than to an urbanite or non-southerner with similar problems.

Boisen (1939) suggests that people are more predisposed to seek a religious solution to their problems rather than the privatized response of mental illness if they recognize that their problems are widespread and not idiosyncratic to them. He suggests (1939:192) that

> the fact that people suffer together through no particular fault of their own leads them, at least in many cases, to seek for some common solution, some common hope, and to find this in religious faith.

Aberle (1965) suggests that resort to the supernaturalism of a sectlike congregation rather than to political action is more likely where the latter is seen as inaccessible or futile, such as it is to those who perceive themselves as lacking financial and other resources needed to mount a political protest or when no alternatives to the current social order are presented which would reconstitute it so as to yield the desired satisfaction. In short, one may turn to a sectlike congregation to cope with felt deprivation either when one can conceive of no secular alternative to the status quo or when one believes political means for a change are beyond one's reach.

In addition to the role played by such predisposing factors as tradition, demography, how widespread the problems are, and the availability of secular solutions, whether or not one joins a sectlike congregation may well depend upon any number of situational contingencies. Lofland and Stark (1965:870) for example, stress the importance of "turning points" in facilitating conversion to a sectlike view. A turning point is defined (1965:870) as

> . . . a moment when old lines of action [are] complete, [have] failed or been disrupted, or [are] about to be so, and where [one faces] the opportunity (or necessity), and possibly the burden, of doing something different with [one's life].

Such turning points may result from recent migration to a new area, loss of employment, business failure, dissolution of a marriage, and school situations such as failure, withdrawal, or graduation. As Lofland and Stark note (1965:870),

> the significance of these various turning points is that they increased the pre-convert's awareness of and desire to take some action about his problems, *at the same time giving him a new opportunity to do so.* Turning points [are] situations in which old obligations and lines of action were diminished and new involvements become desirable and possible [italics in original].

Joining a sectlike congregation and adopting its worldview may be among the involvements which are desirable and possible. However, since sectlike congregations are often small and relatively obscure, mere exposure to it, let alone joining it, is subject to the various contingencies which influence whether or not one comes in contact with it. For example, Harrison (1974:56), in a study of recruitment to Catholic Pentecostalism, notes that "since Catholic Pentecostalism receives only limited coverage in the mass media, most people first encounter it through contacts with friends or acquaintances."[6] He goes on to say (1974:56–57) that such early encounters aid recruitment in four ways: (1) they impress the newcomer with the "warmth and friendliness of members and their ability to express their religious feelings"; (2) they lead to pressures to participate; (3) they often begin the socialization of newcomers into the group; and (4) they help newcomers to resolve doubts about the claims of the movement. Whatever the specific value of such encounters, one is more likely to be exposed to a sectlike congregation if one has friends in it than otherwise. If one's friends and acquaintances are more politically inclined or "into drugs," one may respond to the turning point in one's life by trying politics or drugs, rather than religion, as a solution to the problem of his felt deprivations. Thus, in addition to the predisposing factors cited above, such situational contingencies as turning points and those affecting exposure to it play a role in explaining why one joins sectlike congregations.[7] The compensatory substitution hypothesis will not be a complete explanation of the rise of sectlike congregations until it can systematically take into account both the predisposing and situational factors which affect membership in a sectlike congregation and conversion to its worldview. That is, an explanation will not be complete until it has explained not only *how* compensatory substitution occurs within a religious context, but *why* it occurs in such a context rather than, for example, in a psychiatric or political context.

Change and Development Within Congregations

The study of development or change on the part of congregations has been dominated by two works, first and foremost, Niebuhr's classic study (1929), *The Social Sources of Denominationalism*, and, second, Pope's "Patterns of Denominational Development: Churches and Sects," in his study, *Millhands and Preachers* (1942: 117–140). Just as until very recently virtually every sociological discussion of the structure of religious congregations sought to develop or apply ideas found in Troeltsch's work, virtually every sociological study of the processes of change or development on the part of religious congregations has sought, until quite recently, to develop or test hypotheses first formulated by Niebuhr and then elaborated by Pope.

The Niebuhr-Pope position on the development of religious congregations is embodied in the so-called sect-to-church hypothesis, and is discussed here using the choice-point approach to the study of congregations. Modifications in the Niebuhr-Pope formulations will be suggested, based on use of the approach. Use of the choice-point approach (developed in Chap. 4) to summarize the Niebuhr-Pope position, and to suggest modifications in it, further demonstrates the approach's heuristic value.

The Niebuhr-Pope sect-to-church hypothesis. Niebuhr's general position on how best to approach the study of the development of religious congregations is quite clear: one should begin with the creation of a sectlike body.[8] However, he quickly adds (1929:19) the claim that the "sociological character of sectarianism . . . is almost always modified in the course of time. . . . By its very nature the sectarian type of organization is valid for only one generation." The direction of change in what he regards as inherently unstable secttypes of congregations, is simple and obvious to Niebuhr (1929:20): "the sect becomes a church."[9] Moreover, the transformation from sect to church involves the interrelated modification of virtually all aspects of a religious congregation, changing as a more or less undifferentiated whole. To his credit, Niebuhr does identify some specific components of the sociological character, the organization, of sectlike bodies which he believes to be "almost always modified in the course of time" by a natural process which transforms the congregation into a churchlike body. The choice-point approach to the study of religious congregations is used here first to discuss Niebuhr's formulation of the sect-to-church hypothesis; attention is then turned to Pope's elaboration of Niebuhr's original formulations.

The modifications which Niebuhr contended marked the transition from the organization or structure of a sectlike body to that of a churchlike body may be categorized in terms of four of the choice-points facing all congregations: (1) the criteria of membership, (2) the character of the involvement of members, (3) the composition of the leadership, and (4) attitudes toward the secular status quo. The first three refer to the internal structure or relations of the congregation in question, the fourth, to its external relations.

The first, and perhaps the most basic, change is the shift from criteria of membership which stress convictions voluntarily "fashioned . . . in the heat of conflict . . ." (1929:20) to those which accept a child of a member who may only "hold the convictions it has inherited"

(1929:20). That is, one crucial difference between sect and church is that "members are born into a church while they must join a sect" (1929:17). Thus, one sign of the transition of a congregation from a sectlike to a churchlike social structure is the transition from an association based on the voluntary membership of adults who have passed some test of their faith to a group which accepts the children of its members by right of birth. These children, or birthright members, may, of course, come to accept the beliefs and practices of the group through the processes of education and discipline, through socialization and social control. Nevertheless, a membership composed of individuals who come to their beliefs through education and discipline imposed by others, as opposed to a membership who come to the group of their own volition is, in Niebuhr's view, the membership of a church, not that of a sect. When "children are born into the group and infant baptism or dedication becomes once more a means of grace . . . the sect becomes a church," he concludes (1929:20).

In addition to the rise of birthright membership, Niebuhr identifies two other modifications in the internal relations of a congregation which mark the transition from sect to church. One is a decline in the fervor or enthusiasm of the membership. The character of the members' involvement becomes somewhat less emotional and, in that sense, less personal. Niebuhr does not go as far as to claim that fervor or enthusiasm is totally lost; he merely observes that it is no longer equal to that of the original sect members and that (1929:20) "easily imparted creeds are substituted for the difficult enthusiasm of the pioneers."

The last of the changes in internal structure discussed by Niebuhr is a change in the composition of the leadership. "An official clergy, theologically educated and schooled in the refinements of ritual, takes the place of lay leadership," he claims (1929:20).[10]

In his discussion of the transition from sect to church, Niebuhr also comments upon the external relations of the congregation. He discusses attitudes towards the secular status quo and is especially concerned with the degree of willingness or resistance to compromise Christian ethical principles to meet the prevailing secular demands. Such compromise is inevitable, he believes (see 1929:5).[11] Yet, the sectlike congregation is characterized by a great unwillingness and strong resistance to making such compromises. However, even in a sect, Niebuhr hypothesizes (1929:20) that "as generation succeeds generation, . . . isolation . . . from the world becomes more difficult." Inevitably, "compromise begins and the ethics of the sect approach the churchly type of morals" (Niebuhr, 1929:20). Churchly morals entail "a compromise made far too lightly between Christianity and the world" (Niebuhr, 1929:6). As generations pass, then the sect's ethic, that is, its attitude towards the secular status quo increases in its acceptance and accomodation until a point is reached where its ethic is more characteristic of that of a church than that of a sect.[12] Furthermore, according to Niebuhr (1929:20), "as with the ethics, so with the doctrine [of membership and involvement], so also with the administration of religion. . . . So the sect *becomes* a church" (italics mine). In other words, sectlike options are replaced by churchlike options at each of the choice-points discussed.

The view that sectlike bodies eventually become churchlike bodies is similarly found in Pope's discussion (1942:117–140) of the patterns of denominational development. Pope formulates (1942:118) the sect-to-church hypothesis as follows: "The sect arises as a schism from a parent ecclesiastical body. . . . It then becomes a distinct and independent . . . religious organization, but moves, if it survives, increasingly toward the Church type." Making explicit what is only implicit in Niebuhr's discussion, Pope adds (1942:120) that "movement on the scale between sect and Church is, with minor exception, in one direction only." That is, the movement from sect to church is essentially unidirectional; churches rarely, if ever, develop the attributes of a sect. Pope also elaborates on what Niebuhr says about the specific changes which occur as a given sectlike body is transformed into a churchlike body. That is, without contesting the general accuracy of Niebuhr's description of the process of sect-to-church development, Pope specifies some changes, not mentioned by Niebuhr, which mark that process.

In all, Pope identifies some twenty-one of what he calls (1942:122) "the specific aspects of the movement along the scale from sect to Church."[13] He tacitly assumes that all twenty-one aspects are interrelated and that all move apiece along the "scale from sect to Church." Like Niebuhr, Pope cites changes pertaining to (1) the criteria of membership, (2) the character of the involvement of members, (3) the composition of the leadership, and (4) attitudes toward the secular status quo. In addition, Pope identifies a change in the audience from which the congregation draws its membership.

Pope asserts (1942:123), as did Niebuhr before him, that as a religious body moves from a sectlike to a churchlike congregation, the criteria of membership shift from "voluntary, confessional bases . . . to . . . membership . . . [based on] an educational process"; in other words, "from emphasis on evangelism and conversion, to emphasis on religious education." The criteria of membership also involve a change "from principal concern with adult members to equal concern for children of members" (1942:123), and from "excluding unworthy members to . . . embracing all who are socially compatible." That is, a test of one's religious worth is replaced by a test of one's friendliness or social compatibility with present members.

151

The changes in the nature of the involvement of the congregation's members as the transition from sect to church occurs are discussed in more detail by Pope than by Niebuhr. Niebuhr merely refers to a diminishing fervor. Pope agrees, but seems to see it as part of a general pattern of the transition from an emotional and personal involvement, which calls for great expenditures of time and effort in religious activities, to a less emotional more impersonal involvement, which does not require a great deal of time or effort. Specifically, Pope describes the transition from sect to church as' one marked by changes in the content of religious services. These changes evidence a decline in the emotional and personal involvement called for on the part of worshipers. For example, worship services marked by emotional fervor, spontaneity, and hymns based on lively folk music are replaced by restrained services characterized by a fixed order of worship and by the use of "slower, more stately hymns" (1942:123–124). There is also a decline of interest and concern with members' personal religious experiences. The decline in the demand on members' time and effort is reflected in the declining frequency of special religious services and in the movement from "a high degree of congregational participation in the services and administration of the religious group to delegation of responsibility to a comparatively small percentage of the membership" (1942:123).

The internal structure of the congregation is changed not only by a decline in the number of laymen involved in its administration, but, Pope notes (1942:123), by the change from "an unspecialized, unprofessionalized, part-time ministry to a specialized, professional, full-time ministry." The external relationships of the congregation change as well. For example, "renunciation of prevailing culture and social organization or indifference to it" is replaced by "affirmation" (Pope, 1942:122). The process of affirming prevailing cultural standards may even go so far as to involve, in Pope's view (1942:123), an acceptance of "general cultural standards as a practical definition of religious obligation" and a growing rejection of "strict Biblical standards, such as tithing," with which a sect typically begins. In addition to these changes in attitudes toward the secular status quo, there is, according to Pope (1942:122), a change in the audience from which the congregation draws its membership. Specifically, there is a movement "from membership composed chiefly of the propertyless to membership composed of property owners."

In sum then, the Niebuhr-Pope formulation of the sect-to-church hypothesis holds that the internal characteristics and the external relations of sectlike congregations necessarily become churchlike. Moreover, all the various aspects or dimensions of a sectlike congregation, all the various choice-points facing it, are assumed to be so interrelated that a change in one necessarily involves a change in the other. From the standpoint of the choice-point approach to the study of religious congregations (see pp. 111–116), such a formulation requires two modifications if it is to be the basis for an adequate sociological view of the processes of change and development within religious congregations. First, some explanation must be provided as to how and why changes in various aspects of a sectlike congregation are related, that is, how the actions taken with respect to one choice-point affect action relevent to another. Secondly, some explanation must be provided for the failure of one or more aspects of a sectlike congregation to become churchlike. That is, even if "movement on the scale between sect and Church is . . . in one direction only," as Pope claimed, the movement may be absent in some aspects, minor or moderate in others, and only considerable in a relatively few.[14]

The sect-to-church hypothesis and sect development.   The choice-point approach to the study of religious congregations does not challenge the Niebuhr-Pope formulation of the sect-to-church hypothesis itself. That is, the question of whether or not sectlike congregations almost always develop into churchlike congregations is an empirical possibility which the choice-point approach cannot deny. It would merely call, as does the hypothesis itself, for empirical investigations into the question of how frequently such development does in fact take place, and under what conditions. That is, both the sect-to-church hypothesis and the choice-point approach call for studies describing the development of sectlike congregations, such as Niebuhr's own broad historical overview (1929:26–105) of Calvinism, Methodism, and various Baptist, Anabaptist, and Pietistic groups; Pope's more limited account of the history of congregations in Gaston County, North Carolina (1942: 117–140); and Boisen's similar early study (1940) of Monroe County, Indiana. However, these studies, and subsequent works which describe the transformation of sectlike bodies to churchlike bodies, (Brewer, 1952; Clear, 1961; Eister, 1949; Isichei, 1964; Muelder, 1957; Pfautz, 1955 and 1956; Whitley, 1955 and 1959; and Young, 1960), did not seek to explain how or why the transformation takes place. They concentrated on depicting the details of the change. Even studies which document some aspect of the arrest of the movement from sect to church typically fail to offer a general explanation of the process (e.g., Benson and Hassenger, 1972; Francis, 1948; Gerlach and Hine, 1968; O'Dea, 1954; Redekop, 1974; Robertson, 1967; Warburton, 1967; and Wilson, 1967b).[15] It is clear, from the standpoint of the choice-point approach at least, that an explanation is needed,[16] not only to account for any arrest of the movement from sect to church, but to account for the very occurrence of that movement. That is, the choice-point approach views each of the various aspects of a congregation, each of the choice-points facing it, as more or less independent of each other. There is no assumption that a given religious organization must eventually make only churchlike or, for that matter, only sectlike choices. The various aspects or choice-points of a given congregation do not necessarily move apiece. They are thought of as being independent of one another, so that change may occur with respect to one, but not another. If change does occur with respect to more than one choice-point, the interrelatedness of these changes must be explained.

Interestingly, Niebuhr and Pope each offers an explanation of sorts of the processes which transform a sectlike body into a churchlike body. However, as is shown below, Niebuhr's explanation fails to account for (1) why the internal characteristics and external relations of a sectlike body both change in a churchlike direction and (2) how the transformation might be impeded. Pope's explanation provides a mechanism to explain contemporaneous change in internal characteristics and external relations but fails to specify any possible impediments to the process. Their explanations of the transformation of a sect into a church are related in much the same way as their descriptions of the transformation are related: Pope's explanation is an elaboration and modification of that originally proposed by Niebuhr. Niebuhr's explanation (1929:19–20) of why the process by which the sect becomes a church occurs contains two essential elements involving references to, first, the "natural processes of birth and death" and second, "an increase in wealth." The first, is used to explain changes in the internal characteristics or structure of a sectlike body; the second, to explain changes in external relations.

Niebuhr views the processes of birth and death as naturally resulting in the transformation of the internal structures of a congregation from that of a sectlike body into that of a churchlike body. The transformation begins, in his view (1929:19), with the "children born to the voluntary members of the first generation" who proceed "to make the sect a church long before they have arrived at the years of discretion." The process of transformation starts with the birth of the children because, claims Niebuhr (1929:19–20), "the sect must take on the character of an educational and disciplinary institution, with the purpose of bringing the new generation into conformity with ideals and customs" adopted by the original (first-generation) sect members. The birth of a second generation which is to be educated and disciplined undermines the principle of voluntary membership, which Niebuhr believes characterizes a sect. "Rarely," Niebuhr writes (1929:20), "does a second generation hold the convictions it has inherited with a fervor equal to that of its fathers." The reason, Niebuhr implies, is that convictions held as a result of socialization and social control, education and discipline, cannot be as strong as those presumably "fashioned . . . in the heat of conflict and at the risk of martyrdom" by the founders of the sect (1929:20). With the death of the first generation of members, the congregation comes to be dominated by the second generation, with consequent changes: the criteria for membership change from voluntarism to birthright, and the involvement of members is characterized by less fervor. "By its very nature," Niebuhr asserts (1929:19), "the sectarian type of organization is valid for one generation"; that is, for the first generation, whose members join the group voluntarily, with great fervor for its ideals and practices.[17]

The change in the character of the membership is accompanied, according to Niebuhr, by a change in the leadership. Specifically, as noted above, a lay leadership is replaced by an official, theologically educated clergy. Unfortunately, Niebuhr does not explain why the change in the membership necessitates a change in leadership. However, a reason that would be consistent with his view is that with the decline of fervor among birthright members, there is a decline among the laity in the willingness to volunteer for the responsibilities of leadership. Consequently, if leadership is to be provided, leaders must be official, or paid. Thus, the processes of birth and death, combined with a decline in fervor can be seen as leading to a transformation of the internal characteristics of a sectlike body into those of a churchlike body.

Niebuhr's explanation of the transformation of the external relations of a congregation from a sectlike rejection of or indifference to the ways of the secular status quo to a churchlike accommodation to them, like his explanation of the changes in internal characteristics, views the process as a natural one which is rarely, if ever, successfully blocked. Internal relations are transformed by the processes of birth and death, and external relations are transformed as a "natural" result of "an increase in wealth," which results, Niebuhr asserts (1929:20), "when the sect subjects itself to the discipline of asceticism in work and expenditure." Furthermore, in Niebuhr's view (1929:20), "with the increase in wealth the possibilities for culture become more numerous and involvement in the economic life of the nation as a whole can less easily be limited." A process of compromise with the values and practices of the secular status quo, its culture, and its economic system, begins. Soon, according to Niebuhr, the sectlike attitude of indifference or hostility to the secular world is replaced by an attitude which stresses accommodation and acceptance.

Thus, for Niebuhr, both the internal characteristics and the external relations of a sectlike congregation are transformed naturally and become churchlike. The natural process by which first-generation members are replaced by their descendants transforms the internal characteristics of the congregation, while the inevitability of compromise with the secular world as wealth increases transforms its external relations. Unfortunately, Niebuhr fails to explain how the two processes are related. He does not explain how a decline in fervor and the rise of birthright membership might affect the external relations of a sectlike body; nor how an increase in wealth and a willingness to compromise with secular forces might affect its internal characteristics. Of course, the decline in fervor and a rise in birthright membership, on the one hand, and an increase in wealth and a greater willingness to compromise, on the other, all affect members of the same population, namely, the descendants of the organization's founders. That is, both membership and wealth may be "inherited." Nevertheless, such a dual inheritance would not explain the dual transformation of the congregation's internal characteristics and external relations.

Two reasons may be proffered for the inability of the dual inheritance of membership and wealth to explain a contemporaneous change in the internal characteristics and external relations of a sectlike congregation. First, organizational properties do not bear any necessary one-to-one relationship with changes among its individual members. That is, changes in individual members do not necessarily bring about concomitant changes in the organization to which they belong. Thus, even though the fervor of individual birthright members declines and their willingness to compromise increases along with their wealth, the congregation may, nonetheless, manage to maintain its standards of membership and/or its attitudes toward the secular world. Changes which affect individual members may be resisted at the organizational level. For example, new members may be found who have a high level of enthusiasm and commitment; an authoritarian leadership can insulate itself against the demands of the membership and perpetuate norms not widely accepted by the membership. In short, even if the dual inheritance to which Niebuhr refers were widespread, it would not necessarily explain why the transformation of the internal characteristics and external relations of a sect are transformed contemporaneously into the characteristics of a church.

A second reason for rejecting Niebuhr's explanation is that the presumed dual inheritance is not apt to be widespread. Indeed, the presumed increase in the wealth of individual members is apt to be uncommon. Niebuhr believes wealth will increase, as noted above, as a result of submission to the "disciplines of asceticism." However, as was shown in the discussion of the Weber Thesis (see p. 53), there is no evidence that adherence to Protestant asceticism brings individual wealth. The lack of a necessary link between asceticism and wealth is also noted by Pope, whose study (1942:119) indicated that "sectarian ascetism [sic] and moral discipline have not caused a majority of the members of any religious sect . . . to ascend appreciably in the economic scale." Pope, then, rejects Niebuhr's notion that all, or even most, sect members experience an increase in wealth. Consequently, Pope begins his explanation of the transformation of the sect into a church by modifying somewhat Niebuhr's original explanation insofar as it refers to an increase in wealth. Pope also modifies and then elaborates upon Niebuhr's reference to the influence of the natural processes of birth and death. Interestingly, this latter modification ultimately leads Pope to a formulation which is more compatible with the choice-point approach than either his or Niebuhr's original description of the process of sect-to-church transformation.

Pope begins his explanation of the processes which change the sect into a church by noting (1942:119) that contrary to what Niebuhr implies, "The change does not follow an improvement of economic status in its membership as a whole, but is consequent on the growing opulence of a small minority of its membership." The small minority of opulent members, whom Pope describes (1942:119) as "becoming more affluent and 'responsible,' " are "able to influence the life of [a sect] after they have attained comparative economic wealth because a struggling sectarian group stands in need of many things money can buy" (1942:120).[18] The influence of the more affluent and responsible members is used, Pope implies, to move the group from hostility and indifference regarding the standards of the secular world to a position in support of those standards. As Pope puts it (1942:120), the sect is inclined "to settle down with its few leaders who become community leaders also." In short, the influence of a few affluent members induces the sectlike congregation to compromise its hostility or indifference toward secular standards and to alter its external relations in the direction of accommodation with and acceptance of those standards.

The internal characteristics of the sect also change, in Pope's view (1942:120) as "more extensive contact with society is forced upon it . . . by the very necessities of institutional existence." These necessities include, but are not confined to, the need to define the relationships of "children . . . born to members of the sect . . . to the religious contract" (1942:120), a need stressed by Niebuhr; and the need to care for "relatives—careless husbands, aged mothers—who are not signatories to the contract, but for whose religious welfare (especially if a funeral must be held) the new sect has a derived, but inescapable, responsibility" (1942:121). That is, Pope argues (1942:121), "wider social bonds intersect and relax the tautness of religious bonds," and the standards of membership and involvement are changed.

Further pressure to change stems from the existence of "social pressure . . . against immoderate deviation from conventional religious patterns," which causes "members of a sect . . . [to] lose ardor under its restraining influence" (1942:121). As ardor diminishes, and with it, presumably, members' involvement, an official hierarchy develops, charged with the responsibility of administering the group's programs, for example, arranging a place for nightly prayer meetings and buying songbooks.[19] The hierarchy (the leaders) develop an interest in building up the church. They begin, Pope asserts (1942:121), to compare their group "with other religious groups, and to regard others as rivals."[20] As the

> rivalry between sects ensues, and each seeks to outdistance the others—no longer simply in religious possessions [e.g., church buildings], but in terms that the entire society accepts and can understand, which are, by definition, qualities that characterize a Church rather than a sect (1942: 121–122).

In sum, then, Pope explains the transformation of the internal characteristics of the sect into those of a church as being the result of a combination of three forces: (1) social bonds, especially family ties, which relax the hold of the religious group on its members; (2) social pressures against unconventional religion which weaken the ardor of the membership; and (3) a desire to outdistance other groups in terms accepted by the entire society, a desire fed by the interests of the leadership. Interestingly, reference to these last two forces provides a mechanism which could explain the contemporaneous change in the internal characteristics and external relations of a sectlike organization into those of a churchlike body. Specifically, the internal characteristics of the organization can now be said to change as a result of a process of accommodating to the standards of nonsect members, that is, of the larger society. In other words, the internal characteristics of the organization are changed to meet the approval, or at least ease the disapproval, of the larger society. Thus, the transformation of its internal characteristics are seen as part of the process or strategy by which the sectlike congregation gains the tolerance and acceptance of the larger society. Such a view does indeed provide a mechanism which links changes in external relations (growing acceptance and accommodation to the demands and standards of the larger society) to changes in internal characteristics. The internal characteristics change, according to Pope (1942:122), to "qualities that characterize a Church rather than a sect" because only then will the entire society accept and understand the members of the sect and their organization.

Interestingly, however, the specifications of *social pressure* and *terms that the entire society accepts and can understand* transform the sect-to-church hypothesis itself. It is no longer an hypothesis which views the transformation of a sect into a church as a process of the natural development of factors inherent in the sectlike congregation itself, factors such as the need to educate and motivate birthright members stressed by Niebuhr. The dynamic agents of the transformation process are now located in the environment of the sectlike congregation, not in the congregation itself. The process of transformation itself is now seen as one basically reflecting a tendency for sects to change from a position of social rejection to one of social acceptance. Such a change may, as Fallding comments (1974:153), indicate that "there is a definite tendency for sects to mellow." Moreover, such a tendency makes the process by which sects become churches one in which the movement "to acceptance of general cultural standards as a practical definition of religious obligations" is the central core of the process of transformation (Pope, 1942:123). However, it is a tendency which draws its impetus from factors external to the sectlike congregation itself. The impetus originates in the congregation's environment. Like all environmental forces, under given conditions it may be blunted, and its effects avoided. That is, sects need not *always* become churches. Even if, as Niebuhr claimed, they almost *always* do, there are exceptions to the general movement from sect to church.[21] A complete statement of the sect-to-church hypothesis, according to the requirements of the choice-point approach, must both explain the successful completion of the transformation, and specify the conditions under which the process of transformation is impeded or blocked. The task of amplifying the sect-to-church hypothesis requires identifying some factors which might impede the development of a given sectlike congregation into a churchlike congregation by enabling it to resist the pressure on it to accept the prevailing standards and definition of one's religious obligations. That is, there is a need to identify protective mechanisms which a sectlike congregation may develop to isolate and insulate itself, protecting itself from the influences of external social pressures.[22] Such protective mechanisms would facilitate the sect's efforts to keep "itself 'unspotted from the world' " (Wilson, 1959a:10). The protective mechanisms employed by a sectlike congregation to blunt or reduce the influence of external social pressures to conform to the standards of the larger society may be mechanisms of isolation or of insulation. Mechanisms of isolation are designed to reduce the influence of the external world by reducing the level of social contact between members and nonmembers, including the actual physical or geographic separation of the sect from the outside world. For example, the group may live in a self-contained, essentially self-sufficient community of members as do the Amish or the Pennsylvania Dutch. However, social contact may be reduced without physical separation. As Wilson (1959a:11) notes, "isolation may also be linguistic, a condition illustrated by the various bodies of Mennonites, Hutterites and Dukhobors." That is, a language barrier may be as effective a mechanism of isolation as is physical separation. Isolation may also result (Wilson, 1959*a*:11), from an "injunction to maintain social separateness from the alien," that is, to stick to one's own kind and avoid contact with the heathen and the unbeliever. Such social isolation may be facilitated by a practice of following a distinctive dress code, such as was characteristic of the early Quakers and is now characteristic of such diverse groups as the Salvation Army, the Hare Krishna movement, and even the "Jesus freaks" who wear "straight" hair styles. The wearing of any distinctive visible sign, such as a large religious symbol, would suffice to permit members to identify each other readily and thus facilitate a practice of confining their social contacts to each other. Such signs, especially where they are objects of derision and ridicule, might suffice to warn nonmembers to avoid interaction with members, thus reducing the level of social contact between the two. Thus, the practice of following a distinctive dress code is a doubly effective mechanism of isolation since it enables members to seek each other out and enables a nonmember to avoid them. Either way the mechanism of isolation is successful, and the potential influence of external social pressures is blunted by reducing the level of social contact between members and nonmembers.

The use of mechanisms of isolation, with their emphasis on social separation, may come into conflict with other sectlike values, however. As Wilson notes (1959*a*:11), "tension between the demand for separateness and other sect values arises in the injunction, accepted by many sects, to go out and preach the gospel." Going out and preaching the gospel could well involve a sect member in extensive social contact with nonmembers. Evangelism involves exposure to the world and the risk of being influenced by the social pressure it exerts. Since not all sectlike congregations practice evangelism in the same way or to the same degree, some remain more isolated than others. Introversionist or pietistic sects (e.g., the Quakers or some Holiness movements), which emphasize a member's possession of the Spirit, and Gnostic sects (e.g., Christian Science), which stress acceptance of a new, special body of esoteric knowledge, do not, in Wilson's judgment, generally evangelize, or do so only by formalized procedures. These procedures presumably minimize the opportunity for nonsect members to exert pressures on the evangelizing sect members toward conformity to the general standards. Thus, the mechanisms of isolation employed by Introversionist and Gnostic sects are not greatly challenged by an injunction to go out and preach the gospel.[23]

Adventist and Conversionist sects, on the other hand, often face the challenge of the tension between separation and evangelism. If they are to maintain their separation, they need protective mechanisms beyond those of isolation; they need mechanisms of insulation, mechanisms which seek, as Wilson says (1959a:11), to "protect sect values by reducing the influence of the external world *when contact necessarily occurs*" (emphasis added). One such mechanism is to combine a distinctive doctrine with an insistence on strict standards of doctrinal understanding. The combination strengthens the members' belief and insulates them against a temptation to abandon group values. Wilson implies that such a mechanism is better provided by Adventist sects, such as the Jehovah Witnesses, which direct their attention to the more or less imminent end of the present world order, than by Conversionist sects, such as the Salvation Army or the various Pentecostal groups, which stress fundamentalist Christian orthodoxy and the individual's coming to Christ. An Adventist sect is typically better insulated or protected, since (1959a:11) "it sends its evangelizing agents into the world only after their doctrinal understanding has been thoroughly tested and their allegiance well tried." Furthermore, Wilson adds (1959a:11), an Adventist sect typically "subjects those who wish to join the movement to examination of their doctrinal knowledge." The examination very likely lowers the possibility that would-be members will seek to exert pressures on the movement to conform to the standards of the outside world, which they now also reject. Conversionist sects, on the other hand, (Wilson, 1959a:11) experience great tension between the injunction to be separate and the injunction to evangelize and "have evolved least protection for themselves on these vulnerable points." They tend to use young evangelizing agents, whose commitments are presumably not yet well tried, their doctrine is often more difficult to distinguish from that of churchlike congregations, and their tests of the faith of converts is inadequate and subordinated to Conversionist enthusiasm.

Thus, the protective mechanisms which a sectlike congregation employs to maintain its aloofness from the values of the world include mechanisms of insulation as well as of isolation. Perhaps the best mechanisms of insulation, as Wilson implies, are those which increase the level of a member's commitment to a point where external influences can no longer outweigh or overwhelm him. Although sociologists of religion have not systematically studied such mechanisms,[24] Kanter's insightful study (1968) of commitment mechanisms in Utopian communities provides some suggestions as to what they might be. In all, she identifies six mechanisms which increase commitment and, thus, "the willingness of social actors to give their energy and loyalty" to a given organization (1968:499). Sectlike congregations which develop functional equivalents of these mechanisms would have members whose commitment to sect values are not easily, if at all, shaken by or transferred to the values of the larger society.

The first pair of the six mechanisms which Kanter identifies, *sacrifice* and *investment*, involves a member's cognitive orientations "inducing the individual to cognize participation in the organization as profitable in terms of rewards and costs" (1968:504). Sacrifice "involves the giving up of something valuable or pleasurable in order to belong to the organization" (1968:504). Investment, on the other hand, is a process whereby the individual commits current and future profits to the organization "so that he must continue to participate if he is going to realize them" (1968:505). Neither sacrifice nor investment is confined to tangible or material goods. The sacrifice may involve agreeing to abstain from such oral gratifications as tobacco, alcohol, or meat; from such personal indulgences as reading or dancing; or from promiscuous sexual relations. Such sacrifices are often called for by sectlike organizations. Investments, like sacrifices, may involve intangibles, such as time and energy, as well as tangibles, such as money or personal possessions. The irreversibility of such investment may be made clear by a failure to keep records of gifts, money, or property and a strict policy of no refunds to defectors.

The second pair of mechanisms identified by Kanter is *renunciation* and *communion*. Each of these mechanisms involves "the attachment of an individual's fund of affectivity and emotion to the group" (1968:507) and the emotional gratification which comes from participating in and identifying with the members of a close-knit group. Renunciation involves the cutting off of previous emotional ties to nonmembers; communion, the enhancement of the feeling of oneness with the group and the growth of a "we-feeling." Renunciation may go so far as to require severing family ties, denying obligations to relatives, spouse and parents alike. Such obligations may, as noted above, weaken one's commitment to a sectlike congregation. In any case, communion is enhanced by group ritual, such as community singing, or by any ritual which "involves collective participation in ceremonies or recurring events of symbolic importance" (1968:510). Religious services could also serve to enhance communion.

Wilson (1959a:14) makes the point that sectlike congregations differ in the degree to which they stress communion. In types such as the Introversionist and Adventist sects, stress on communion is high (1959a:14):

> Fellowship is an important value for all members: fellow-members are "brethren"; relationships as far as possible are primary; the local meeting is a face-to-face group. The individual is a sect-member before he is anything else, he is expected to find his friends within the group. . . .

A Conversionist sect, on the other hand, stresses communion only partially. As Wilson (1959a:14) observes, "its concept of brotherhood extends beyond sect boundaries and its standards are less rigorous. It accepts individuals more lightly, socializes them less intensely." A Gnostic sect places little stress on communion. As Wilson expresses it (1959a:14), the Gnostic sect is "more frankly a Gesellschaft: the individual's relationships to other devotees are secondary. . . . Brotherhood is an alien concept. . . . The impersonality of relationships may even be regarded as ideal."

The third and last pair of mechanisms discussed by Kanter are *mortification* and *surrender*. Both involve a commitment to group norms and an acceptance of obedience to the authority of the group as a moral necessity. Mortification involves the individual's coming to regard himself as small before the greatness of the organization and a reduction in the sense of autonomous identity. The result of mortification is that one "can have no self-esteem unless he commits himself to the norms of the group, evaluating its demands as just and morally necessary" (1968:512). Mortification often occurs in its less extreme and less coercive forms in religious groups which "attempt to erase the 'sin of pride,' the sin of being too independent or self-sufficient, substituting instead a self which is subject to the influence of the collectivity," that is, of the sect (1968:512). Mortification may also involve nothing more than the practice of confession or self-criticism common at many revival meetings. Surrender involves the ceding of one's decision-making prerogatives to a greater power,[25] such as is commonly done, Kanter implies, when one defines another person as a charismatic leader. Widespread acceptance of someone as a charismatic leader is often the first step in the creation of a sectlike organization. Surrender may also be enhanced by what Kanter (1968:514) calls *institutionalized awe*, that is, ideological systems and structural arrangements which not only give order and meaning to one's life, but which provide "a sense of rightness, certainty, and conviction." Such institutionalized awe may clearly (1968:514), be provided by "reference to a higher order principle, e.g., . . . the will of God." It may also be provided by the imputation of special or magical powers to members by virtue of their belonging, and by linking these powers to "great figures of historical importance," (Kanter, 1968:514), such as Jesus, presumably.

It would appear, then, that forms of mortification and surrender are found in various sectlike congregations. Moreover, such a view is shared by Wilson when he observes (1959a:13) that "at some level the individual member's commitment to the sect must be total. This may mean . . . a commitment to regulate all social and moral affairs entirely as the sect directs." He adds, however, that not all sectlike congregations demand a commitment to regulate one's affairs as the sect directs. Such a commitment is most common among Introversionist and Adventist sects. Conversionist sects also value moral rectitude, but are less stringent and demanding in implementing the value than

163

are the Adventists and the Introversionists. Gnostic sects, on the other hand, do not stress the moral correlates of their ideological positions.

In sum, there are a number of mechanisms of both isolation and insulation which sectlike congregations may employ in their efforts to protect themselves from pressures to conform. Sectlike congregations may find ways to survive and thrive which do not involve their becoming churchlike. Despite the Niebuhr-Pope position that new sects steadily become old churches, some sects persist as sects, continuing, as Wilson (1970:233) observes, "to assert a strong contracultural position, demanding exacting tests even of their own young people before admitting them, and holding themselves aloof from the wider society."

Summary

This chapter applied the choice-point approach to the study of religious congregations to two hypotheses developed within the framework of the sect-church legacy. One hypothesis, the compensatory substitution hypothesis, deals with the rise of sectlike congregations; the other, the sect-to-church hypothesis, with the processes of change and development on the part of sectlike congregations.

The compensatory substitution hypothesis seeks to explain *how* congregations which are sectlike, in terms of their internal characteristics and relations to the status quo, attract adherents from among the deprived or disadvantaged elements of a society. It is still not clear *why* religious rather than secular organizations come to be elected by deprived individuals as a vehicle for dealing with their deprivation. That is, it was noted that membership in a religious congregation and in certain secular organizations may be regarded as functional equivalents. While no firm explanation can be given of why the religious alternative is chosen, the importance of predisposing factors and certain situational contingencies was noted.

The sect-to-church hypothesis, as stated by Niebuhr (1929) and Pope (1942), was reformulated so as to highlight changes in each of the relevant choice-points. Two modifications in the hypothesis were suggested: (1) to replace the assumption that all aspects of a congregation change apiece with an explanation of just how change with respect to one choice-point is related to that in another; and (2) to replace the assumption that the transformation from sect to church is inevitable with an explanation of how it can be impeded. The former modification leads to a realization of the importance of environmental factors in the transformation of sectlike bodies into churchlike ones. The latter modification leads to a realization of the importance of isolating and insulating mechanisms in impeding the transformation from sect to church.

FOOTNOTES

1. This relationship is questioned in empirical studies by Hine (1974) and Nelsen (1972), but not definitively so.
2. Such affinities are studied further by Schwartz (1970) in his examination of Pentecostal and Seventh Day Adventist belief systems and their appeal to the economically disadvantaged.
3. For a general overview of religious movements, such as Meher Baba, which appeal to contemporary youth, see Snelling and Whitley (1974:315–334), Wuthnow and Glock (1973), and especially Robbins, Anthony, and Curtiss (1975). The Jesus People movement is discussed by Balswick (1974). Ellwood (1973), Richardson, Harder, and Simmonds (1972), Simmonds, Richardson, and Harder (1974), and Petersen and Mauss (1973:261–279). Judah (1974a; 1974b:463–478) examines the Hare Krishna movement.
4. Of course, as Robbins, Anthony, and Curtiss (1975:56) recognize, not all sect-like congregations serve to facilitate the assimilation of their members into conventional society. Some, which they call "marginal movements," serve instead to remove their members from conventional pursuits and to lock them into positions of social marginality. Whether assimilation or marginality results, the individual may experience compensatory substitution with respect to his previous felt deprivations.
5. Allen (1974) offers an alternative approach to explaining the choice of religious means which is also cognizant of the role of predisposing and situational factors.
6. For other studies of Catholic Pentecostals, see Fichter (1974, 1975), McGuire (1974, 1975), Harper (1974), and Harrison (1975).
7. Segger and Kunz are critical of the Lofland-Stark model of the steps to joining a sectlike congregation adapted here. Their study of 77 Mormon converts lends little support to the model. However, as they note (1972:184), the converts in their study "were sought, they were not seekers." The model is designed to apply to seekers. Moreover, an earlier study of the same converts (Segger and Blake, 1970) reveals that one-third (29/77) are no longer active Mormons, more than the proportion (27/77) of those who are very active Mormons. Perhaps, concentration on the very active converts would lend more support to the model.
8. As Glock and Stark (1965:242–260) and Steinberg (1965) point out, however, not all new congregations begin as sectlike bodies. Some, such as the Reform Judaism movement studied by Steinberg, may begin as churchlikes bodies, at least insofar as their willingness to accept the general values of the secular status quo is concerned.
9. Ironically, while Niebuhr's discussion of the transformation of a sect into a church makes use of Troeltsch's typology, it is likely that Troeltsch himself would have rejected Niebuhr's argument, or at least, one of its possible implications. Specifically, Troeltsch would have rejected any implication that one of the two forms of religious congregation, (sect and church) is somehow more original and, thus, truer to the roots and traditions of Christianity. Such an implication would have been rejected because it is alien to Troeltsch's basic tenet (see p. 106) that sect and church refer to two equally legitimate patterns of Christian religious organization. Niebuhr, on the other hand, clearly regarded sects as more religiously pure, less compromised, than churches. Thus, it is implicit in Niebuhr's view that the process of sect-to-church development is one of the devolution of a more pure into a less pure form of organization. While admitting that compromise is inevitable, he contends (1929:5) that

"the fact that compromise is inevitable does not make it less an evil." Thus, Niebuhr's view of sect and church differs from that of Troeltsch, who, as Eister (1973:363) notes, viewed each as "governed by its own conception of Christian imperatives; [as] 'legitimately Christian' . . . alternatives not necessarily developmentally related in the sense in which Niebuhr saw the 'church' as an 'outgrowth' of the sect."

For an early reformulation of Niebuhr's views accepting the inevitability of compromise between religious values and the demands of the secular world but making no moral judgment on the various forms of religious congregations, see Becker (1932:614–632).

10. Wilson (1959b) described some of the role conflicts and status contradictions which beset the clergy of at least one Pentecostalist movement as the process of transition to an official clergy takes place.

11. The importance of Niebuhr's views on the inevitability of compromise as they relate to his formulation of what is here called the sect-to-church hypothesis is discussed by Eister (1973).

12. Johnson (1971) is critical of Niebuhr's claim that interaction with the world inevitably compromises the sect. He notes (1971:129) that while "the world may compromise the sect, . . . some sects are able to compromise the world by having an impact on it." He also argues (1971:131–132) that the church is not necessarily compromised.

13. Of the twenty-one aspects mentioned by Pope (1942:122–124), only four cannot readily be categorized in terms of the choice-point approach (see Chap. 4). One deals with a doctrinal matter, two deal with relations to other religious bodies, and one refers to an increase in the corporate wealth of the congregation (i.e., not the wealth of individual members).

14. A third modification may also be called for which would attempt to explain change and development in churchlike congregations. Such congregations need not be regarded, as the sect-to-church hypothesis implicitly regards them, as fully developed finished products no longer facing significant choices or possibilities for change. One basis for such an attempt may be found in Thompson's sociohistorical study (1970) of the responses of the Church of England to the social changes which marked the period from 1800 to 1965, a period which, he describes (1970:2) as one in which "the Church was to survive as an Established Church, it would have to adapt its organization to the changed circumstances." In addition, Harrison (1959) and Takayama (1975) have studied the development of the authority structures of churchlike bodies, and Hoge and Faue (1973) have applied the sect-church typology to the study of conflict within Protestant churches. It might also be hoped some studies will be undertaken into the conditions under which churchlike bodies do or do not give rise to schisms which result in the formation of sectlike congregations.

15. The failure to offer any general explanation is probably more true of those who wrote before Wilson did (1959a). He offered an alternative to the Niebuhr-Pope formulation which allowed for the persistence of sectlike congregations as *sects*, and sought to explain how and why they changed, if at all. Still, even the later pieces are largely concerned with explaining the history or development of a specific organization and are usually reluctant to generalize.

16. An effort to move toward such an explanation is made by Coleman (1968). It uses an approach based on O'Dea's discussion (1966:90–97) of institutional dilemmas facing religious organizations, not the choice-point approach. Nelson (1971) suggests that the sect-church distinction be replaced, in the study of congregational change, by one which distinguishes between what he calls *associational* and *communal* forms of religious congregation. As he uses it, the distinction involves only one of the many choices facing a given congregation, namely, that pertaining to the degree and kind of member involvement. Mol's discussion (1970) of the degree to which congregations in Australia and New Zealand compromise with the secular values of the larger society introduces the concept of *cohesion*.

166

17. Wilson (1959a:11–12) challenges Niebuhr's position: "It is an oversimplification to say . . . that the second generation makes the sect into a denomination." According to Wilson, the difficulty in winning the allegiance of the second generation varies from one type of sectlike congregation to another. Introversionist and Adventist sects are "apt to hold their second generation without damage to sect identity" (1959a: 12). Gnostic sects have somewhat more difficulty in winning the allegiance of their second generation; while Conversionist sects have the most difficulty.

18. Metz (1967) finds an analogous process at work in the development of the new churchlike congregations he studies. He finds (1967:80) that the undertaking of a building program brings into prominence those who have "been of great help in handling loans, in arranging for contractors, and in securing insurance." That is, the leadership is chosen on the basis of business skills, not religious understanding. One result is a movement of the congregation toward a concern with financial matters which outweighs its concern for implementing the religious creed of the group.

19. Wilson (1967a:14–15) lists some eight tasks or procedures which sectlike congregations must deal with and which involve at least a minimal hierarchy. These tasks range from arranging the time and place for meetings, through procedures for establishing a minimal basis of doctrinal consensus and dealing with new members, to the regulation of the group's involvement with external authorities. Nevertheless, these matters may be handled by very rudimentary organization. They do not, in Wilson's view, necessarily move the congregation significantly in a churchlike direction.

20. Wilson (1959a:12–13) argues that not all sectlike congregations are equally susceptible to the tendency to evaluate themselves on terms provided by the larger society. He does acknowledge (1959a:13) that there is often a conflict "between genuine separateness from the world and the desire for social respectability." However, he notes that only the Conversionist sects are very susceptible to transformation in a churchlike direction because of such conflicts. Adventist, Introversionist, and Gnostic sects are generally able to resist the pressure such conflict exerts on the maintenance of sectlike qualities.

21. Wilson (1970:234) believes that the evidence which Niebuhr and Pope found in their own studies is biased by being derived "from evidence of American society, where sects are somewhat lightly transformed into denominations," and by a preponderance of Conversionist sects, which he believes are most apt to be transformed into churches. He discusses (1970:236–242) various patterns of development found among non-Conversionist sects.

22. Johnson (1971) and Redekop (1974) suggest that in addition to the influence of any protective mechanisms, the nature and extent of the external pressures themselves play a role in whether or not a sectlike congregation changes in a churchlike direction. In his study of factors which enabled Old-Colony Mennonites and Mormons to remain relatively sectlike, Redekop (1974:346) cites the differential ability of societies to "tolerate and integrate radical protests." Pluralistic societies, he implies, are better able to tolerate radical protests and to permit the persistence of a sectlike body as a sect. He notes that even the tolerance of a pluralistic society may vary with the extent to which central and sacred values are challenged by the sect.

23. For a discussion of some of the organizational aspects of evangelism, see Bibby and Brinkerhoff (1974).

24. Discussions of the problem of maintaining some very specific belief, for example, that the world will soon end, may be found in Bittner (1963), Lofland (1966:191–255), and Zygmunt (1970).

25. In a later version of her views, Kanter (1972:74) refers to the "process whereby an individual attaches his decision-making prerogatives to a power greater than himself" as *transcendence* rather than as *surrender* and discusses it at length (1972:111–125). The change in terminology does not affect the use made of her discussion here.

REFERENCES

Aberle, David
1965 "A note on relative deprivation theory as applied to millenarian and other cult movements." In *Reader in Comparative Religion*, 2nd ed., edited by William A. Lessa and E. Z. Vogt. New York: Harper & Row.

Allen, Graham
1974 "A theory of millennialism: the Irvingite movement as an illustration." *British Journal of Sociology* 25 (September):296–311.

Anthony, Dick, and Thomas R. Robbins
1974 "The Meher Baba movement: its effect on post-adolescent youthful alienation." In *Religious Movements in Contemporary America*, edited by Irving Zaretsky and Mark Leone. Princeton University Press.

Balswick, Jack
1974 "The Jesus people movement: a sociological analysis." In *Religion American Style*, edited by Patrick McNamara. New York: Harper & Row.

Becker, Howard
1932 *Systematic Sociology: On the Basis of the Beziehungslehre and Gebilde-lehle of Leopold von Wiese*. New York: Wiley.

Benson, J. Kenneth, and Edward W. Hassinger
1972 "Organization set and resources as determinants of formalization in religious organizations." *Review of Religious Research* 14 (Fall):30–36.

Bibby, Reginald W., and Merlin B. Brinkerhoff
1974 "When proselytizing fails: an organizational analysis." *Sociological Analysis* 35 (Autumn):189–200.

Bittner, Egon
1963 "Radicalism and the organization of radical movements." *American Sociological Review* 28 (December):928–940.

Boisen, Anton T.
1939 "Economic distress and religious experience." *Psychiatry* 2 (May):185–195.
1940 "Divided Protestantism in a midwest county: a study in the natural history of organized religion." *Journal of Religion* 20 (October):359–381.

Brewer, Earl
1952 "Sect and church in Methodism." *Social Forces* 30 (May):400–408.

Carroll, Michael P.
1975 "Revitalization movements and social structure: some quantitative tests." *American Sociological Review* 40 (June):389–401.

Clear, Val
1961 "The Church of God: a study in social adaptation." *Review of Religious Research* 2 (Winter):129–133.

Cohn, Norman
1961 *The Pursuit of the Millennium*. New York: Harper & Row.
1964 "Medieval millenarianism: its bearing on the comparative study of millenarian movements." In *Religion, Culture and Society*, edited by Louis Schneider. New York: Wiley.

168

Coleman, John A., S. J.
1968 "Church-sect typology and organizational precariousness." *Sociological Analysis* 29 (Summer):55–66.

Eister, Allan W.
1949 "The Oxford Movement: a typological analysis." *Sociology and Social Research* 34 (November):116–124.
1973 "H. Richard Niebuhr and the paradox of religious organization: a radical critique." In *Beyond the Classics? Essays in the Scientific Study of Religion*, edited by Charles Y. Glock and Phillip E. Hammond. New York: Harper & Row.

Ellwood, Robert S., Jr.
1973 *One-way: The Jesus Movement and Its Meaning.* Englewood Cliffs, N.J.: Prentice-Hall.

Fallding, Harold
1974 *The Sociology of Religion.* Toronto: McGraw-Hill Ryerson.

Festinger, Leon
1957 *A Theory of Cognitive Dissonance.* New York: Harper & Row.

Fichter, Joseph H.
1974 "Liberal and conservative Catholic-pentecostals." *Social Compass* 21 (3):303–310.
1975 *The Catholic Cult of the Paraclete.* New York: Sheed and Ward.

Flora, Cornelia Butler
1973 "Social dislocation and Pentecostalism: a multivariate analysis." *Sociological Analysis* 34 (Winter):296–304.

Francis, E. K.
1948 "The Russian Mennonites: from religion to ethnic group." *American Journal of Sociology* 54 (September):101–107.

Gerlach, Luther P., and Virginia H. Hine
1968 "Five factors crucial to the growth and spread of a modern religious movement." *Journal for the Scientific Study of Religion* 7 (Spring):22–40.

Glock, Charles Y., and Rodney Stark
1965 Editors, *Religion and Society in Tension.* Skokie, Ill.: Rand McNally.

Harper, Charles L.
1974 "Spirit-filled Catholics: some biographical comparisons." *Social Compass* 21 (3):311–324.

Harrison, Michael
1974 "Sources of recruitment to Catholic Pentecostalism." *Journal for the Scientific Study of Religion* 13 (March):49–64.
1975 "The maintenance of enthusiasm: involvement in a new religious movement." *Sociological Analysis* 36 (Summer):150–160.

Harrison, Paul M.
1959 *Authority and Power in the Free Church Tradition: A Social Case Study of the American Baptist Convention.* Princeton University Press.

Hine, Virginia H.
1974 "The deprivation and disorganization theories of social movements." In *Religious Movements in America*, edited by Irving L. Zaretsky and Mark P. Leone. Princeton University Press.

Hoge, Dean R., and Jeffrey L. Faue
1973 "Sources of conflict over priorities of the Protestant Church." *Social Forces* 52 (December):178–194.

Holt, John B.
1940 "Holiness religion: cultural shock and social reorganization." *American Sociological Review* 5 (October):740–747.

Isichei, Elizabeth Allo
1964 "From sect to denomination among English Quakers." *British Journal of Sociology* 15 (September):207–222.

Johnson, Benton
1971 "Church and sect revisited." *Journal for the Scientific Study of Religion* 10 (Summer):124–137.

Judah, J. Stillson
1974a *Hare Krishna and the Counterculture.* New York: Wiley.
1974b "The Hare Krishna movement." In *Religious Movements in Contemporary America*, edited by Irving L. Zaretsky and Mark P. Leone. Princeton University Press.

Kanter, Rosabeth Moss
1968 "Commitment and social organization: a study of commitment mechanisms in utopian communities." *American Sociological Review* 33 (August):499–517.
1972 *Commitment and Community: Communes and Utopias in Sociological Perspective.* Cambridge: Harvard University Press.

Lanternari, Vittorio
1965 *The Religions of the Oppressed: A Study of Modern Messianic Cults.* New York: New American Library (Mentor Books).

Lofland, John
1966 *Doomsday Cult.* Englewood Cliffs, N.J.: Prentice-Hall.

Lofland, John, and Rodney Stark
1965 "Becoming a world-saver: a theory of conversion to a deviant perspective." *American Sociological Review* 30 (December):862–875.

Malalgoda, Kitsiti
1970 "Millennialism in relation to Buddhism." *Comparative Studies in Society and History* 12 (October):424–441.

Marx, Gary T.
1967 "Religion: opiate or inspiration of civil rights militancy among Negroes." *American Sociological Review* 32 (February):64–73.

McGuire, Meredith B.
1974 "An interpretive comparison of elements of the Pentecostal and underground church movements in American Catholicism." *Sociological Analysis* 35 (Spring):57–65.
1975 "Toward a sociological interpretation of the Catholic Pentecostal movement." *Review of Religious Research* 16 (Winter):94–104.

Merton, Robert K.
1957 "Social structure and anomie." In *Social Theory and Social Structure*, rev. ed. New York: Free Press.

Metz, Donald
1967 *New Congregations: Security and Mission in Conflict.* Philadelphia: Westminster Press.

Mol, J. J.
1970   "Secularization and cohesion." *Review of Religious Research* 11 (Spring):183–191.

Muelder, Walter
1957   "From sect to church." In *Religion, Society and the Individual*, edited by J. Milton Yinger. New York: Macmillan.

Nelsen, Hart M.
1972   "Sectarianism, world view, and anomie." *Social Forces* 51 (December): 226–233.

Nelson, Geoffrey K.
1971   "Communal and associational churches." *Review of Religious Research* 12 (Winter):102–110.

Niebuhr, H. Richard
1929   *The Social Sources of Denominationalism.* New York: Holt, Rinehart and Winston.

O'Dea, Thomas
1954   "Mormonism and the avoidance of sectarian stagnation: a study of church, sect and incipient nationality." *American Journal of Sociology* 60 (November):285–293.
1966   *The Sociology of Religion.* Englewood Cliffs, N.J.: Prentice-Hall.

Petersen, Donald W., and Armand L. Mauss
1973   "The cross and the commune: an interpretation of the Jesus people." In *Religion in Sociological Perspective: Essays in the Empirical Study of Religion*, edited by Charles Y. Glock. Belmont, Calif.: Wadsworth.

Pfautz, Harold W.
1955   "The sociology of secularization: religious groups." *American Journal of Sociology* 61 (September):121–128.
1956   "Christian Science: a case study of the social psychological aspect of secularization." *Social Forces* 34 (March):246–251.

Pope, Liston
1942   *Millhands and Preachers.* New Haven: Yale University Press.

Redekop, Calvin
1974   "A new look at sect development." *Journal for the Scientific Study of Religion* 13 (September):345–352.

Richardson, James, Mary W. Harder, and Robert B. Simmonds
1972   "Thought reform and the Jesus movement." *Youth and Society* 4 (2): 185–200.

Robbins, Thomas
1969   "Eastern mysticism and resocialization of drug users." *Journal for the Scientific Study of Religion* 8 (Fall):308–317.

Robbins, Thomas, and Dick Anthony
1972   "Getting straight with Meher Baba: a study of mysticism, drug rehabilitation and post-adolescent role-conflict. *Journal for the Scientific Study of Religion* 11 (June):122–140.

Robbins, Thomas, Dick Anthony, and Thomas Curtiss
1975   "Youth culture religious movements: evaluating the integrative hypothesis." *Sociological Quarterly* 16 (Winter):48–64.

Robertson, Roland
1967   "The Salvation Army: the persistence of sectarianism." In *Patterns of Sectarianism*, edited by Bryan R. Wilson. London: Heinemann.

171

Schwartz, Gary
1970 *Sect Ideologies and Social Status.* University of Chicago Press.

Seggar, John F., and Reed H. Blake
1970 "Post-joining participation: an exploratory study of convert inactivity." *Review of Religious Research* 11 (Spring):204–209.

Seggar, John, and Phillip R. Kunz
1972 "Conversion: evaluation of a step-like process for problem-solving." *Review of Religious Research* 13 (Spring):178–184.

Simmonds, Robert B., James T. Richardson, and Mary W. Harder
1974 "Organizational aspects of a Jesus movement community." *Social Compass* 21 (3):269–282.

Snelling, Clarence H., and Oliver R. Whitley
1974 "Problem-solving behavior in religious and parareligious groups: an initial report." In *Changing Perspectives in the Scientific Study of Religion,* edited by Allan W. Eister. New York: Wiley.

Stark, Rodney
1964 "Class, radicalism, and political involvement in Great Britain." *American Sociological Review* 29 (October):698–706.

Steinberg, Stephen
1965 "Reform Judaism: origin and evolution of a church movement." *Journal for the Scientific Study of Religion* 5 (Fall):117–129.

Takayama, K. Peter
1975 "Formal polity and change of structure: denominational assemblies." *Sociological Analysis* 36 (Spring):17–28.

Talmon, Yonina
1965 "Pursuit of the millennium: the relation between religious and social change." In *Reader in Comparative Religion,* 2d ed., edited by William A. Lessa and E. Z. Vogt. New York: Harper & Row.

Thompson, Kenneth A.
1970 *Bureaucracy and Church Reform: The Organizational Response of the Church of England to Social Change, 1800–1965.* London: Oxford University Press.

Troeltsch, Ernst
1931 *The Social Teachings of the Christian Churches.* Translated by Olive Wyon. New York: Macmillan.

Warburton, T. Rennie
1967 "Organization and change in a British holiness movement." In *Patterns of Sectarianism: Organization and Ideology in Social and Religious Movements,* edited by Bryan R. Wilson. London: Heinemann.

Whitley, Oliver R.
1955 "The sect to denomination process in an American religious movement: The Disciples of Christ." *Southwestern Social Science Quarterly* 36 (December):275–282.
1959 *Trumpet Call to Reformation.* St. Louis: Bethany Press.

Wilson, Bryan R.
1959a "An analysis of sect development." *American Sociological Review* 24 (February):3–14.
1959b "The Pentecostal minister: role conflicts and status contradictions." *American Journal of Sociology* 44 (March):494–504.

1967a Introduction to *Patterns of Sectarianism: Organization and Ideology in Social and Religious Movements*. London: Heinemann.

1967b "The Exclusive Brethren: a case study in the evolution of a sectarian ideology." In *Patterns of Sectarianism: Organization and Ideology in Social and Religious Movements*. London: Heinemann.

1970 *Religious Sects*. New York: McGraw-Hill.

Wuthnow, Robert, and Charles Y. Glock

1973 "Religious loyalty, defection and experimentation among college youth." *Journal for the Scientific Study of Religion* 12 (June):157–180.

Young, Frank W.

1960 "Adaptation and pattern integration of a California sect." *Review of Religious Research* 1 (Spring):137–150.

Yinger, J. Milton

1970 *The Scientific Study of Religion*. New York: Macmillan.

Zygmunt, J. F.

1970 "Prophetic failure and chiliastic identity: the case of the Jehovah Witness." *American Journal of Sociology* 75 (March):926–947.

6

Political Activism Among the Clergy:
Sources of unchurchlike behavior

During the decade of the sixties and into the early seventies, significant numbers of clergy became involved with efforts to bring about meaningful social change for the first time since the involvement of clergy with the ill-fated pre-World War I temperance movement and the pre-World War II pacifist movement. In the eyes of some observers (e.g., Cox, 1967), those who participated in recent movements seeking social change constituted a "new breed" of American clergy.[1] Whether new or not, however, they were a breed of clergy who sought to make religion relevant to crucial secular issues, despite the often presumed irrelevance of religion to such issues (see p. 84).[2] Moreover, the new breed of clergy stressed the prophetic aspects of ministry more than the roles of priest, preacher, or parish administrator.[3] They sought to implement their deeply held religious convictions through involvement in efforts to reform the secular status quo. Interestingly, they did so even though they themselves typically served congregations which were identified with and even representative of the very status quo which the new breed sought to reform.

In the terms of the sect-church legacy and the choice-point approach (see Chaps. 4, 5), the new breed of politically active reformist clergy were engaging in unchurchlike behavior. They refused to accept the secular status quo as it was.[4] Nevertheless, they typically served congregations with churchlike memberships drawn from the middle or upper socioeconomic status, memberships identified with and accepting of the secular status quo.[5] In short, paradoxical though it may appear, congregations whose external relations were churchlike in terms of their views on the secular status quo and their audience were often led or at least represented by clergy who, being politically active reformists, were not churchlike in their relations to the secular status quo. The aim of this chapter is to understand how such an apparently paradoxical situation could occur, that is, how clergy whose behavior was not churchlike with respect to the status quo might still have served congregations which were churchlike in that respect.

The key to understanding the apparent paradox lies in recognizing that the behavior of such politically active reformist clergy is not merely contrary to the expectations of sociological theory, but contrary to the expectations of the churchlike congregations such clergy serve. Put more strongly, the key is to recognize that the new breed of politically active reformist clergy can properly or at least plausibly be regarded as engaging in deviant behavior—behavior that violates norms defining the role of clergy and that is negatively sanctioned by such important others as local congregations and denominational superiors. This chapter defends the view that politically active reformist clergy serving churchlike congregations are engaged in what can be called deviant behavior. Sources and supports for the deviance of the politically active reformist clergy are identified in an attempt to understand how they can serve churchlike congregations while engaging in unchurchlike behavior. The sources and supports in question will be found in the role and training of clergy and in the various structural arrangements which shield politically active clergy from negative sanctions.

Clergy Activism as Deviant Behavior

As just stated, it can be argued (albeit not definitively) that politically active reformist clergy be regarded as engaging in deviant behavior. Unfortunately, there is only scant evidence available relevant to resolving the issue of whether or not activism by clergy *is* deviant. Hence, even though the evidence cited below is suggestive and supportive of the position taken here, the case for regarding activist clergy as deviant is not fully convincing from a scientific point of view.[6]

The basis for regarding political activity among the clergy as deviant is threefold: (1) Such activity is violative of the expectations of significant others, namely, the church laity. (2) It is defined as deviant

176

by such others. (3) It meets with negative sanctions from significant others.[7] Empirical studies suggest that on all three counts political activism among the new breed of clergy—an activism which takes priority over their roles as priest, preacher, and parish administrator and which is reformist both in goals and tactics—is deviant.

Glock and Stark (1965:150) conclude that the results of their study of the views of Lutheran parishioners as to how clergy spend their time

> suggest that the pastoral (including evangelistic) and preaching functions of the ministerial role are paramount to the parishioner, that he wants his minister to focus his energies on these tasks, and that he is prone to be critical where these expectations are not met.

The politically active new breed of clergy, who, as described above, stresses the prophetic aspects of ministry more than the roles of pastor and preacher, is violating the expectations of parishioners and not focussing their energy where it is expected to be.

Data from Hadden's national sample indicate that laity neither expect nor wish their clergy to be politically active, and, in addition, they actively disapprove of or reject such behavior. Hadden (1970:154) concludes that his data show that "there is a striking consistency in the rejection of clergy involvement in the struggle for social justice." Furthermore, he notes (1970:251),

> The . . . bold stance of clergy on civil rights and other social issues . . . left a large proportion of the laity bewildered and resentful. Many feel the church has no business speaking out on social and political issues. Others question the competency of the clergy to make pronouncements on such issues. For them, the church is a source of comfort in a troubled world. . . . For them the church is not an agent of change, but a buffer against it. They do not understand what clergy are saying and doing. . . . The result is that the clergy and laity are on a collision course. In a very real sense, the laity have one church and the clergy have another.

Political activism on the part of the clergy is not merely behavior which the laity neither expect nor desire, but behavior which they regard as alien to their conceptions of proper behavior for the clergy. Such behavior involves the church in matters they regard as an illegitimate concern and none of its business. Indeed, active involvement in political issues appears so alien to the laity that they may well regard those who engage in it as not of their faith, that is, as deviant from their conceptions of proper religious behavior.

Political activism by clergy is not only *defined as* deviant by the laity, but is *responded to* as deviant in that it elicits a variety of negative sanctions designed to punish it and prevent its repetition. Such sanctions may take passive forms, such as declining attendance and decreasing financial contributions, or more active forms, such as seeking the removal of an activist minister. Firing activist clergy as a sanction for activism is illustrated in the studies of Campbell and Pettigrew (1959) and of Hadden (1970).[8] Hadden (1970:214–215) summarizes the relevant points from both studies:

> . . . [Among the] Little Rock clergy during the 1957 school desegregation crisis, those who did attempt to speak out paid a price. . . . By early 1959 at least nine ministers had left their pulpits as a reasonably direct result of the integration conflict.
>
> In January 1965, . . . a group of twenty-eight young, native-born, Mississippi Methodist clergymen jointly signed and read from their pulpits . . . a carefully worded affirmation that they stood united in their belief that the Christian tradition does not permit discrimination because of race, color or creed. *By mid-1965 only nine of these clergymen remained in the state of Mississippi, and only two occupied the same pulpit as they had before they signed the statement* [italics in original].

Political activism even as mild as that of the Little Rock ministers studied by Campbell and Pettigrew or the Mississippi clergy in the Hadden study may, then, be negatively sanctioned by parishioners. In addition, such activism is not what parishioners expect and desire of their clergy and is generally defined as deviant by them. In sum, political activism on the part of the new breed of clergy can reasonably be regarded as deviant behavior in that it is violative of the expectations of significant others, is defined as deviant by them, and elicits negative sanctions from them. Such reform-oriented activism also departs from what sociological theory regards as churchlike behavior. Nevertheless, clergy who lead or represent churchlike congregations have engaged in such behavior. The next section considers some sources and supports for it.

Sources and Support of Political Activism Among the Clergy

Two sets of factors may provide support for the unchurchlike involvement of clergy in activist movements which seek significant reform in the secular status quo: (1) the role and training of the clergy, and (2) the availability of protections from sanction by the laity.

Clergy role and training. Three aspects of the role and training of the clergy are of particular importance as possible sources of participation in political activism: (1) the obligations of the clergy as professionals, (2) the expectation that the clergy, more than all other people, will serve ultimate values, and (3) the training of the clergy with respect to secular issues. The first two factors provide room for the development of what Sykes and Matza (1957:667) have called "techniques of neutralization." These are justifications of deviant behavior which imply a commitment "to the dominant normative system and yet so qualify its imperatives that violations are 'acceptable,' if not 'right'." The third factor is more determinative of the form and duration of clergy activism.

As professionals, the clergy are trained and obligated to think of the basic rights and duties of those in their chosen profession before acting on a specific issue, secular or otherwise. A student activist may not consider how his obligations as a student clash with his activism, but his professor and his clergyman are obligated and expected *not* to enter into activism so blithely. They are expected to consider their professional roles, as well as the merits of the specific issues. A professional must not only determine whose views are *in* the right on a given issue, but whether he himself *has* the right to act on his own views. If a clergyman does become active, he can be expected to articulate a conception of his role which legitimates his activism, lest he be considered unprofessional. Clergy who join with activists must not only be able to argue that the activists are in the right on the issue at hand, but that they, *as clergy*, have a right to be active on *any* secular issue, let alone the one in question. In other words, activist clergy must develop techniques of neutralization vis-à-vis the expectation that clergy will shun activism; that is, they must develop justifications which imply a commitment to the dominant normative system of their Church but yet so qualify its imperatives that violations, such as activism, are acceptable, if not right.

Research indicates that clergy who are involved in social action, or at least view it favorably, are more likely than other clergy to accept a conception of their ministry which facilitates the development of techniques of neutralization with respect to opposition to political activism. They are more likely than others to accept the legitimacy of a prophetic social witness as part of a Christian ministry and to believe that Christian love is best expressed through participation in attempts to eliminate political and economic injustice. Furthermore, clergy who participate in social action, or at least favor it, may be expected to hold theological beliefs which support the high value they place on the prophetic social witness as a component of ministry.[9] As research indicates, political activists among the clergy tend to reject the more orthodox theology, which stresses one's role as worshiper of God and one's finiteness and sinfulness in the eyes of God, in favor of a theology which stresses one's role as a partner with God in the creation of the human community (Blume, 1970; Hadden, 1970; Jeffries and Tygart, 1974; Johnson, 1967; Quinley, 1969, 1974*b*; Shupe and

Wood, 1973; Tygart, 1973; Winter, 1970a, 1971).[10] The more orthodox theology encourages a focus on liturgy and prayer, distrusts social reform movements, and regards them as doomed to futility or corruption. The more liberal view encourages one to help reshape society so that it conforms more closely to Divine guidelines. Thus, as professionals who must defend their actions as consistent with the rights and obligations of their positions, activist clergy can be expected to have a theology and a conception of mission which make their efforts to obtain change in the secular status quo appear acceptable, if not right within the context of normative Christian doctrine. That is, activist clergy may be expected to have a theology and conception of mission which support the development of appropriate techniques of neutralization.

Of course, the availability of appropriate techniques of neutralization does not ensure clergy participation in activist movements. The issue of the acceptability of the means used in the political struggles which activism entails must also be faced. The nature of the means used is of specific import to the clergy because they, more than all others, are expected to serve ultimate values. They are expected to deny that the ends justify the means and to choose means not in terms of their worldly or political efficacy but in terms of their ethical qualities. Clergy are expected not to use a political means merely because it will advance acceptance of their views, but to pass judgments on the practices of politics.

In Weber's (1958) terms the clergy are expected to follow the "ethic of ultimate ends", which calls for the use of morally pure means even if their use precludes worldly success, and to recoil from the politician's ethic, which calls for him to be successful even if through morally impure means. Yet, as Weber recognizes (1958:122), "in numerous instances the attainment of 'good' ends is bound to the fact that one must be willing to pay the price of using morally dubious means or at least dangerous ones." Thus, since the ethic of ultimate ends "logically . . . has only the possibility of rejecting all action that employs morally dangerous means," (1958:122), the clergy may find themselves immobilized. They may find that since they cannot be both moral and successful in the political realm, and since being moral is more important to them, they must withdraw from the activist involvement in political struggles to remain on the sidelines as persons with a concern, but no movement. Weber is suggesting that involvement such as entailed by activism in practical political affairs is corrosive to a commitment to avoid the use of morally impure means. He suggests (1958:122) that the crucial element in the corrosive process is that the "proponent of an ethic of ultimate ends cannot stand up under the ethical irrationality of the world." That is, he finds it difficult to live with the fact that undesirable even evil consequences may result from adament insistence on the use of morally pure means. For example, racism and poverty will persist if one refuses to make effective albeit morally impure use of political power.

However, a politically active clergyman, with the use of appropriate techniques of neutralization, may deny the existence of the dilemma which Weber poses and thus defend his activism and deny that his moral purity is soon to be corroded. Such denial may be sustained in two ways. First, the clergy may simply maintain a faith that from good comes only good and from evil only evil follows. They may, for example, participate only in nonviolent movements contending that the use of violence is not only immoral but counterproductive as well, and that nonviolence, the moral way, is the only truly effective way. That is, clergy may have faith that in the long run they can be both moral and successful. Faith in the eventual political success of the movement may suffice to preclude one's falling victim, as Weber predicts, to the temptation to use morally impure means to ensure success. Secondly, clergy may come to define as morally pure the means they find they must use to be effective. For example, they may adopt a situational ethic which justifies rejection of the clergy's traditional role as reconciler and mediator in time of conflict in favor of a role as active protagonist in given circumstances. They may come to deny that conflict is incompatible with Christian love, as did the activists studied by Winter (1970a, 1970b) and by Winter, Mills, and Hendricks (1971:29–56). They may assert that "Christian love may require one to use or create conflict," and come to view the use of conflict (which seems to many to be at best a morally dubious means) as justifiable and moral in the situation facing them. Similarly, they may even contend that while honesty may be the *best* policy, it is not the only *good* one. They may be willing, as are the more active clergy in the population studied by Winter (1970b), to support a group which uses bluffs and other techniques to misrepresent their true intentions. Finally, the active clergy may come to defend some forms of criminality or civil disobedience, noting with Shepherd, (1971:796) that

> . . . the biblical tradition . . . sounds at times very much like a criminal record: Moses, a "wanted" man who had to flee from Egypt; . . . Isiah and Jeremiah, accused of conspiracy and treason, spending time in jail and in the stocks; Jesus arrested, tried and executed as a criminal.

In short, armed with a belief, however unorthodox, in the moral acceptability of the means they use, clergy have available techniques with which to neutralize the claim that they are faced with the necessity of choosing between political success and morality, as Weber claims they must be. Clergy who participate in activist movements may be expected, both normatively and empirically, to have developed, firstly, a theology and conception of mission which facilitate the development of techniques of neutralization that support and legitimate such participation; secondly, a faith that the movement they have joined can be both moral and successful. Such faith may well be based on unorthodox definitions which neutralize common sense views of the moral quality of the means employed by the movement.

To say that clergy have developed appropriate techniques of neutralization, based on a supportive theology, legitimating conception of mission and justifications for means they employ as activists is essentially to say that clergy may be *willing* to join a social reform movement. However, it also implies something about the *role* clergy may play in reform movements, what they may be *able* to do in and for the movement. It implies that role is to offer the movement an appropriate ideology to support its claims and justify its existence and tactics; that is, to help the movement develop its own appropriate techniques of neutralization and thereby attain legitimacy and respectability for itself. This is not, of course, to imply that clergy are equally able to aid all activist movements in their struggle for legitimacy. Quite the contrary is the case. The reforms demanded by a given movement may call for an ideology which the clergy is not readily able to provide. For example, efforts by the ecology movement to combat exploitation of the environment may call for an ideology which clergy may find difficult to provide.[11] As a group of Protestant theologians recently noted (Fiske, 1970:12),

> ... the traditional Christian attitude toward nature had given sanction to exploitation of the environment by science and technology and contributed to air and water pollution, overpopulation, and other ecological threats.

Similarly, as members of organizations which have few women (if any) among their leaders and which may trace Original Sin to the original woman, clergy may find it difficult (albeit possible) to find a plausible basis for supporting attacks on male chauvinism.[12] In the early twentieth century, it was much easier for Protestant clergy to support the temperance movement than to support the labor movement. The concerns of the former were consistent with the prominent strain in Protestant thought at that time, which viewed social ills as rooted in the loss of self-discipline, which drinking could cause. The latter challenged the equally central notion that individual material advancement must be the result of individual effort, not collective effort. More recently, however, what Gilkey (1967:73) identifies as a "shift in Christian ethical concern from personal holiness to love of neighbor as the central obligation" has provided fertile grounds for supporting attacks on racism, poverty, and other forms of social injustice.

In sum, clergy can often, although not always, play a significant role in helping movements gain legitimacy. Moreover, given the content of the traditional training of clergy, with its lack of social science, there may be little else the clergy can do in and for a movement for social change. For example, armed with courses on Biblical bases for opposing racism or poverty or male chauvinism or what-have-you, but with none on the social, political or economic causes or cures for these situations, the typical clergyman has little to offer with respect to specific practical problems. Thus, clergy may be very crucial in the *early* stages of a movement, when the main task is to convince others that the situation they seek to correct is bad and the tactics they use are good. In the later stages, when the problems involve choosing targets for change and offering programs for action, the clergy may have little to offer, if anything. Thus, as the movement becomes established and legitimacy, with its goals and tactics no longer under attack, clergy may find themselves with no significant role to play and withdraw into inaction; or they may become involved in another movement in its earlier stages. For example, one may expect to find clergy more deeply involved in the early stages of an antipoverty movement, when the problem is to legitimate the claims of the poor, than in the latter stages, when the issue is specific reform of welfare programs. The process of early relevance and later inadequacy is also illustrated by Underwood's account of the experience of a Pastor Richardson in the 1930s and 1940s. The pastor had been involved in the early struggles of labor unions to gain acceptance in his town, but after that acceptance was gained he found his contributions irrelevant and withdrew from the unions. As Underwood puts it (1957:271–273):

> In the early years of labor organization in the community Richardson had believed that he saw the relevance of the Christian gospel with clarity and concreteness. . . . When members of the first unions were refused the right to work, the young pastor proclaimed . . . that this action was un-Christian and an affront to God. The pastor was welcomed at labor meetings and was invited to speak whenever he appeared. The pastor saw his role then chiefly as that of giving morale to the movement, to help men see their part in developing a just and free society. After many years of organizing, the unions gained a more accepted position. . . . Leaders of labor and management settled down to making the day-to-day decisions involved in contract negotiations and administration of them. As the years passed, the decisions became increasingly specialized and complex. For a while the pastor tried to keep up with the technical discussions. . . . But the pastor could no longer feel that he saw as he had in the old days the specific relevance of the Gospel to what went on among the labor unions. . . . He confided to friends, with genuine

183

sadness, that the union people "no longer need me, or want me to advise them." . . . Over the years, Richardson . . . withdr[e]w from positions of influence in . . . labor organization.

Pastor Richardson's experience is not unique. As Underwood notes (1957:273), it represents a development in many churches; "a withdrawal from the concrete, specialized activities of society as too 'temporal' or 'technical' to be interpreted by moral and religious thought."

Many activist clergy have come to realize that if they are to be as important in the later days of a movement as they are earlier and if they are not to be forced to withdraw in the face of concrete and specialized activities and questions, they had best become familiar with the social, political, and economic factors which cause and help cure the problem at hand. Thus, in the 1960s, a number of Action Training Centers were created across America to help meet the needs of clergy for greater knowledge of the more technical and specialized aspects of social change. Typically, an Action Training Center seeks to provide understanding of social scientific knowledge about the causes and cures of social problems as well as familiarity with the specific resources available in the clergy's home environment for dealing with a given problem.[13] These centers and (increasingly) seminaries offer programs to help clergy and seminarians understand what to do and how to do it; all, of course, provide guides for using whatever secular training the clergy has, within the framework of the theology, conception of mission, and ethical code they are expected, as professional religionist, to employ.

Vulnerability to sanction. So far, this discussion of clergy involvement in activist social reform movements has focussed largely on factors which might be included in what Campbell and Pettigrew (1959:513) call the clergy's self-reference system, which "may be thought of as what the actor [clergy] would do in the absence of sanctions from external sources." However, clergy, as professionals in a voluntary association (the congregation), do not operate in the "absence of sanctions from external sources." Typically, the clergy continually face sanctions from two important bodies: (1) the congregation or constituency which they serve, and (2) the authority structure or hierarchy of which they are a part.

As Hadden (1970) argues, the increasing involvement of American clergy in social reform movements threatened a "gathering storm" of lay protest and resistance. The storm is particularly evident in local congregations with churchlike external relations. That is, the problems facing the prophetic or activist clergy is strongest where their congregants tend to represent or support the very status quo which the clergy's prophetic judgments challenge. For example, clergy who criticize American society for its racist tendencies and who decry white America's resistance to racial integration are not only attacking racism, but most likely implicitly criticizing the stance of their own congregants. In such an event, the congregants can be expected to protect their own interests and to oppose the attempts of their clergy to challenge established ways, in which they have made material or symbolic investments. The resistance of congregations to clergy involvement in social reform movements also stems from differences between their conception and that of the activist clergy concerning the minister's obligations. As Hadden puts it (1970:234),

> [activist] clergy have come to see the church as an institution for challenging men to new hopes and new vision of a better world. Laity, on the other hand, are in large part committed to the view that the church should be a source of comfort for them in a troubled world.

As noted earlier, the Glock and Stark (1965:150) study finds that

> the pastoral (including exangelistic) and preaching functions of the ministerial role are paramount to the parishioner, that he wants his minister to focus his energies on these tasks, and that he is prone to be critical where these expectations are not met.

Since the activist clergy are apt to focus their energies on efforts to attain social reform, they are open to criticism and sanctions from congregants who expect and wish them to concentrate on their needs not on the ills of the larger society.

As noted above, resistance by the congregation may take passive forms (e.g., declining attendance and decreasing financial contributions) or more active forms (e.g., seeking the removal of an activist pastor). Whatever the form, as research indicates, such resistance or the threat of it has deterred local parish clergymen from involvement in social reform movements (Pope, 1942; Campbell and Pettigrew, 1959; Hadden, 1970). Thus, as Hadden (1970:185) observes,

> . . . a large proportion of the activist clergy have been located in positions within the denominational structure which are insulated from direct reprisals from laity. In short, the most active group of clergy has not been parish pastors.

They have, instead, been campus clergy, urban affairs specialists from the regional or national office, or others with no direct ties to local residential parishes (see Hammond and Mitchell, 1965).

It should also be noted that insulation from lay protest and resistance varies not only within denominations according to one's position in a given structure, but between denominations. Clergy in the more congregationally oriented denominations such as the Baptists are less insulated from lay resistance than those in the more hierarchically organized churches such as the Episcopal Church and the Roman

Catholic Church. Thus, denominational leaders are, as Wood (1970: 1064) finds, "more likely to press for policy in controversial areas when they have formal authority insulating them from member resistance."

Obviously not all parishes oppose the prophetic or reformist activities of their clergy; such activism may not challenge any of their vested interests. For example, a stance against the military establishment need not be objectionable to a congregation if none of its members are employed in defense industries. Moreover, the congregation may be willing to tolerate clergy activism if it has found that such involvements do not detract from performance of congregation-oriented duties as pastor, preacher, and administrator.[14] Quinley found in his study (1969) of hawks and doves among California clergy that some congregants may actively support rather than oppose prophetic tendencies. The importance of such support is illustrated in Quinley's discussion (1969:17–18) of the experience of clergy active in the anti-war movement:

> While those ministers active in anti-war activities experienced severe negative sanctions as a result of their involvement in the issue, they also received assistance from a substantial number of their parishioners. For such dovish clergymen this parishioner support appears to have been a major factor in their extensive involvement in the issue. . . . Thus, the "active parishioner" may well be a crucial factor in encouraging the "activist clergyman." The activist's ministry may suffer as a result of his behavior but he can take some comfort in the fact that he will often be able to rally parishioner support behind his position and may attract some new members and financial contributions to his church.

The activist parish clergy may also take comfort in denominational officials, who, relatively insulated from the protest of parishioners, support their critique of the status quo. However, the support or opposition of denominational officials can be expected to be more crucial to parish clergy in a hierarchically organized denomination, where the views of the local congregation can be overridden, than in a congregationally oriented one, where the views of the local congregation tend to prevail. Thus, Quinley (1974b:276–277) finds that "clergymen in denominations organized along episcopal or presbyterian lines expect to receive much greater assistance from their church leaders . . . than clergymen in denominations organized along congregational principles," if their participation in social action results in conflict with their local congregation.[15]

However, as Quinley (1974b:273) reports, regardless of the formal structure of the denomination, whether hierarchical or congregational, local congregations exert a great deal of control in the formulation of the policies of the local congregation. The import of the support of denominational officials may be muted by their lack of resources or power to reward parish clergy for their activism or protect them from the wrath of angry congregations. As Quinley (1974b:280) observes, "despite the sympathy of many denominational leaders for clergy activism . . . it remains unclear how much assistance church leaders are able to offer." It is also unclear how much support denominational officials may be *willing* to offer. Their support may depend on their willingness to tolerate the loss in membership or financial support which clergy activism may entail. Where denominational officials measure the success of local clergy in terms of the size of their congregation and the amount of its financial contributions, local activist clergy may find little comfort in the verbal support of denominational officials. The muting of the support for clergy activism by denominational officials is noted by Campbell and Pettigrew (1959:514):

> The church hierarchy . . . does not like to see divided congregations, alienated ministers, reduced membership or decreased contributions. . . . However exalted the moral virtue the minister expounds, the hierarchy does not wish him to damn his listeners to hell—unless somehow he gets them back in time to attend services next Sunday. Promotions for him are determined far less by the number of times he defends unpopular causes, however virtuous their merit, than by the state of the physical plant and the state of the coffer. . . . If . . . moral imperative and church cohesion are mutually incompatible, there is little doubt that the church superiors favor the latter. . . . Under these circumstances pressure from the national church to take an advanced position . . . loses much of its force. The minister is rewarded *only* if his efforts do not endanger the membership of the church [italics in original].

In sum, as professionals in an organized voluntary association, the clergy will respond not only to their own desires and values, but to approval and disapproval (positive and negative sanctions) applied by the congregation or constituency they serve and to the authority structure or hierarchy of which they are a part. The relative import of the two sanctioning bodies, membership and hierarchy, will vary from denomination to denomination. The former is more important in congregationally oriented denominations where local autonomy and democratic forms are stressed; the latter is more important in hierarchically oriented denominations where authority is said to flow from the highest officers down to the membership.

Summary

This chapter sought to understand how the apparently paradoxical situation might occur in which clergy whose behavior is not churchlike with respect to the secular status quo might be serving congregations which are churchlike in that respect. Specifically, it sought to understand how politically active, reform-oriented clergy might serve congregations who support the status quo and draw their membership from the middle and upper classes. The key to understanding the apparent paradox was said to lie in regarding the new breed of politically active, reform-oriented clergy as engaging in deviant behavior.

A reasonable argument to that effect was presented based on the contention (supported by empirical evidence) that such behavior violates the expectations of significant others, namely, church laity, is defined as deviant by these others and negatively sanctioned by them. Nevertheless, clergy do engage in such behavior. Sources or supports for their deviance were found in aspects of the role and training of the clergy and in various structural arrangements which shield political activists among the clergy from negative sanctions.

FOOTNOTES

1. Cox (1967:147) recognizes that the new breed of clergy have been preceded by other activist clergy. A history of clergy activism in America may be reconstructed from the work of Bodo (1964), Carter (1954), Hopkins (1961), May (1963), Meyer (1960), Odegard (1928), and Yinger (1946:129–218). For more specific discussions focussing on the activism of the 1960s and early 1970s, see Callahan (1967) and Garrett (1973). Quinley (1974a; 1974b:1–22) discusses the decline of clergy activism in the mid-1970s.

2. Quinley (1974b:297) suggests that the involvement of clergy in political activism may even have been a reaction against the presumed irrelevance of religion. He writes: "The widespread involvement of modernist church leaders in the political upheavals of the 1960s . . . appears as a means for [them] to renew their influence and prestige in a highly secular society in which . . . religion itself had come under attack for moral irrelevance."

3. Discussions of the various components of the role of the clergy generally follow suggestions found in Blizzard (1956, 1958). For developments of Blizzard's original suggestions, see Fukuyama (1972:60–81), Lauer (1973), Nelsen, Yokley, and Madron (1973), and Whitley (1964:135–167). For an alternative approach, see Fukuyama (1972:117–130), Gustafson (1965), and Gannon (1971), who discuss the role of the clergy within the context of a consideration of the status of the occupation of the clergy as a profession.

4. The new breed of activist clergy are not quite sectlike in their attitudes and behavior. Unlike those who take a sectlike response, the activist clergy remain neither indifferent to nor merely angry with the secular status quo. They seek to reform it. Thus, the response of activist clergy is something of a third type, not quite churchlike, but yet not quite sectlike either.

5. The congregations served by the new breed were typically churchlike in their internal characteristics as well. That is, they typically emphasized birthright memberships with minimal tests for membership, segmented involvement, which was largely formal and impersonal, and an educated, full-time non-lay leadership. These characteristics are not directly relevant to the concerns of this chapter, however.

6. Until the various disputes over just what constitutes deviance are resolved, no discussion of whether or not politicaly active reform-oriented clergy are

deviant can be definitive. For discussions of sociological disputes over the definition of deviance, see Akers (1968) and Gibbs (1966).

7. Politically active clergy may be deviant in the statistical sense as well, that is, they may constitute a decided minority of all clergy. Little data, if any, are available to enable one to estimate definitely the percentage of clergy who are politically active. Stark et al. (1971:118) estimate that no more than 12 percent of their sample of California clergy "can conceivably be called New Breed . . . and that a nationwide estimate would probably be substantially smaller." Their estimate is based on the sample used in Quinley's (1974b) study of activist clergy.

8. The various negative sanctions available to congregants who wish to object to some behavior on the part of their clergy and the vulnerability of clergy to these sanctions are discussed by Brannon (1971), Campbell (1971), Lauer (1973: 194–198), Quinley (1974b:209–258), and Wood and Zald (1966). Fray (1969) and Hadden and Longino (1974) provide case studies of local congregations which sought to organize themselves so that sanctions would not be used to inhibit reform-oriented political activity by the clergy and others in the congregation.

9. Davidson's study (1972) indicates that the presence or absence of similar beliefs may also effect the activism of the laity. However, the salience of these beliefs must be relatively high before they influence the behavior of the laity, as Bahr, Bartel, and Chadwick (1971) and Gibbs, Mueller, and Wood (1973) find.

10. Rojek (1973) offers some evidence which he implies is contrary to the view that orthodox theology inhibits a prophetic witness. His study population includes clergy as well as laity, but the salience of the beliefs of the latter are not measured. As noted above, Bahr et al. (1971) and Gibbs et al. (1973) have found that studies of the relationship of lay religious beliefs to behavior can be quite misleading if their salience is not controlled for. Furthermore, Rojek is concerned, as was Johnson earlier (1962, 1964, 1966) with political party preferences. The other studies cited here define reform-oriented political activism more broadly and do not equate it with any particular party preference. The relationship between theology and definition of mission by both clergy and laity is further discussed in Hoge and Faue (1973). Hammond (1974) and Vinz (1972) present analyses which indicate that orthodox theological beliefs do not always inhibit, and may even support, reform-oriented political activism.

11. For a further exposition of the view that traditional Christian creeds are one source of the ecological crisis, see White (1967). For responses to White, see Barr (1972) and Richardson (1972). For other views on the relationship between concern for the ecology and Christian theology, see Fackre (1971) and Jung (1972).

12. For discussions of possible bases for attacking sexist tendencies within Judeo-Christian creeds and congregations, see Daly (1973) and Harkness (1972). For discussion of the image of woman in traditional creeds, see Ruether (1974), Tavard (1973) and Wagner (1973).

13. For descriptions and evaluation of Action Training Centers for clergy, see Bonthius (1970) and Winter, Mills, and Hendricks (1971).

14. Quinley (1974b:242–243) finds that activist clergy do not in fact "appear to be ignoring their other clerical roles or to be dealing with their parishioners on a less personal basis than [non-activist] clergymen." Winter (1970a:61) finds a somewhat different relationship between clergy activism and their performance of other duties, as do Winter, Mills, and Hendricks (1971:21), who report that while clergy "do not generally find it necessary to choose between the pastoral and prophetic aspects of ministry[,] . . . time spent on social problems seems to be at the expense of administrative work." In any case, none of the above studies directly relate the performance of activist clergy in the nonprophetic aspects of ministry to the willingness of their congregations to tolerate their activism.

15. For further discussion of the role of denominational officials and structures in-

fluencing the extent of clergy activism, see Shupe and Wood (1973). Taylor (1975) discusses the impact of denominational structure on the success or failure of different modes of prophetic efforts to seek social change.

REFERENCES

Akers, Ronald L.
1968 "Problems in the sociology of deviance: social definitions and behavior." *Social Forces* 46 (June):455–465.

Bahr, Howard M., Lois Franz Bartel, and Bruce W. Chadwick
1971 "Orthodoxy, activism and the salience of religion." *Journal for the Scientific Study of Religion* 10 (Summer):69–75.

Barr, James
1972 "Man and nature—the ecological controversy and the Old Testament." *Bulletin of the John Ryland's University of Manchester* 55 (Autumn): 9–32.

Blizzard, Samuel W.
1956 "The minister's dilemma." *Christian Century* 71 (April 25):508–509.
1958 "The Protestant parish minister's integrating roles." *Religious Education* 53 (July–August):13–15.

Blume, Norman
1970 "Clergyman and social action." *Sociology and Social Research* 54 (January):237–248.

Bodo, John R.
1954 *The Protestant Clergy and Public Issues: 1817–1848*. Princeton University Press.

Bonthius, Robert
1970 Editor, "Theme: Action Training Centers' challenge to theological education." *Theological Education* 6 (Winter):82–186.

Brannon, Robert C. L.
1971 "Organizational vulnerability in modern religious organizations." *Journal for the Scientific Study of Religion* 10 (Spring):27–32.

Callahan, Daniel
1967 "The quest for social relevance." *Daedalus* 96 (Winter):151–179.

Campbell, Ernest Q., and Thomas F. Pettigrew
1959 "Racial and moral crisis: the role of the Little Rock ministers." *American Journal of Sociology* 64 (March):509–516.

Campbell, Thomas C.
1971 "The meaning of local 'vulnerability' in modern religious organizations: a response to Robert Brannon." *Journal for the Scientific Study of Religion* 10 (Spring):33–35.

Carter, Paul A.
1954 *The Decline and Revival of the Social Gospel: Social and Political Liberalism in American Protestantism, 1920–1940*. Ithaca, N.Y.: Cornell University Press.

Cox, Harvey
1967 "The 'new breed' in American churches: sources of social activism in American religion." *Daedalus* 96 (Winter):133–150.

Daly, Mary
1973 *Beyond God the Father*. Boston: Beacon Press.

Davidson, James D.
1972 "Religious belief as an independent variable." *Journal for the Scientific Study of Religion* 11 (March):65–75.

Fackre, Gabriel
1971 "Ecology and theology." *Religion in Life* 60 (Summer):210–224.

Fiske, Edward B.
1970 "Christianity linked to pollution." *New York Times*, May 1, p. 12.

Fray, Harold R.
1969 *Conflict and Change in the Church*. Boston: Pilgrim Press.

Fukuyama, Yoshio
1972 *The Ministry in Transition: A Case Study of Theological Education*. Pennsylvania State University Press.

Gannon, Thomas M., S.J.
1971 "Priest/minister: profession or non-profession?" *Review of Religious Research* 12 (Winter):66–79.

Garrett, William R.
1973 "Politicized clergy: a sociological interpretation of the 'new breed.'" *Journal for the Scientific Study of Religion* 12 (December):384–399.

Gibbs, David R., Samuel A. Mueller, and James R. Wood
1973 "Doctrinal orthodoxy, salience and the consequential dimension." *Journal for the Scientific Study of Religion* 12 (March):33–52.

Gibbs, Jack P.
1966 "Conceptions of deviant behavior: the old and the new." *Pacific Sociological Review* 9 (Spring):9–14.

Gilkey, Langdon
1967 "Social and intellectual sources of contemporary Protestant theology." *Daedalus* 96 (Winter):69–98.

Glock, Charles Y., and Rodney Stark
1965 Editors, *Religion and Society in Tension*. Skokie, Ill.: Rand McNally.

Gustafson, James M.
1965 "The clergy in the United States," In *The Professions in America*, edited by Kenneth Lynd. Boston: Houghton-Mifflin.

Hadden, Jeffrey K.
1970 *The Gathering Storm in the Churches*. Garden City, N.Y.: Doubleday (Anchor Books).

Hadden, Jeffrey K., and Charles F. Longino, Jr.
1974 *Gideon's Gang: A Case Study of the Church in Social Action*. Philadelphia: Pilgrim Press.

Hammond, John L.
1974 "Revival religion and anti-slavery politics." *American Sociological Review* 39 (April):175–186.

Hammond, Phillip E., and Robert N. Mitchell
1965 "Segmentation of radicalism—the case of the Protestant campus ministry." *American Journal of Sociology* 71 (September):133–143.

Harkness, Georgia
1972 *Women in Church and Society: A Historical and Theological Inquiry*. Nashville: Abingdon Press.

Hoge, Dean R., and Jeffrey L. Faue
1973 "Sources of conflict over priorities of the Protestant Church." *Social Forces* 52 (December):178–194.

Hopkins, Charles H.
1961 *The Rise of the Social Gospel in American Protestantism, 1865–1915.* New Haven: Yale University Press.

Jeffries, Vincent, and Clarence E. Tygart
1974 "The influence of theology, denomination, and values upon the position of clergy on social issues." *Journal for the Scientific Study of Religion* 13 (September):309–324.

Johnson, Benton
1962 "Ascetic Protestantism and political preference." *Public Opinion Quarterly* 26 (Spring):35–46.
1964 "Ascetic Protestantism and political preference in the Deep South." *American Journal of Sociology* 69 (January):359–366.
1966 "Theology and party preference among Protestant clergymen." *American Sociological Review* 31 (April):200–208.
1967 "Theology and the position of pastors on public issues." *American Sociological Review* 32 (June):433–442.

Jung, Hwa Yol
1972 "Ecology, Zen and western religious thought." *Christian Century* 89 (November 15):1153–1156.

Lauer, Robert H.
1973 "Organizational punishment: punitive relations in a voluntary association—a minister in a Protestant church." *Human Relations* 26 (April):189–202.

May, Henry F.
1963 *Protestant Churches and Industrial America.* New York: Octagon Books.

Meyer, Donald B.
1960 *The Protestant Search for Political Realism: 1914–1941.* University of California Press.

Nelsen, Hart M., Raytha Yokley, and Thomas Madron
1973 "Ministerial roles and social actionist stance: Protestant clergy and protest in the sixties." *American Sociological Review* 38 (June):375–386.

Odegard, Peter H.
1928 *Pressure Politics: The Story of the Anti-Saloon League.* New York: Columbia University Press.

Pope, Liston
1942 *Millhands and Preachers.* New Haven: Yale University Press.

Quinley, Harold E.
1969 "Hawks and doves among the clergy." *Ministry Studies* 3 (October):5–23.
1974a "The dilemma of an activist church: Protestant religion in the sixties and seventies." *Journal for the Scientific Study of Religion* 13 (March):1–22.
1974b *The Prophetic Clergy: Social Activism Among Protestant Ministers.* New York: Wiley.

Richardson, Cyril C.
1972 "A Christian approach to ecology." *Religion in Life* 41 (Winter):462–479.

Rojek, Dean G.
1973   "The Protestant Ethic and political preference." *Social Forces* 52 (December):168–177.

Ruether, Rosemary Radford
1974   Editor, *Religion and Sexism: Images of Woman in the Jewish and Christian Traditions*. New York: Simon & Schuster.

Shepherd, J. Barrie
1971   "Christianity and criminality." *The Christian Century* 86 (June 30): 796–798.

Shupe, Anson D., Jr., and James R. Wood
1973   "Sources of leadership ideology in dissident clergy." *Sociological Analysis* 34 (Autumn):185–201.

Stark, Rodney, Bruce D. Foster, Charles Y. Glock, and Harold E. Quinley
1971   *Wayward Shepherds: Prejudice and the Protestant Clergy*. New York: Harper & Row.

Sykes, Gresham, and David Matza
1957   "Techniques of neutralization: a theory of delinquency." *American Sociological Review* 22 (December):664–670.

Tavard, George H.
1973   *Woman in Christian Tradition*. Indiana: University of Notre Dame Press.

Taylor, Mary G.
1975   "Two models of social reformation in a normative organization." *Sociological Analysis* 36 (Summer):161–167.

Tygart, Clarence E.
1973   "Social movement participation: clergy and the anti-Vietnam war movement." *Sociological Analysis* 34 (Autumn):202–211.

Underwood, Kenneth
1957   *Protestant and Catholic: Religious and Social Interaction in an Industrial Community*. Boston: Beacon Press.

Vinz, Warren L.
1972   "The politics of Protestant Fundamentalism in the 1950s and 1960s." *Journal of Church and State* 14 (Spring):235–260.

Wagner, Walter
1973   "The demonization of women." *Religion in Life* 42 (Spring):56–74.

Weber, Max
1958   "Politics as a vocation." In *From Max Weber: Essays in Sociology*, edited and translated by Hans H. Gerth and C. Wright Mills. New York: Oxford University Press.

White, Lynn, Jr.
1967   "The historical roots of the ecological crisis." *Science* 155 (March 10): 1203–1207.

Whitley, Oliver R.
1964   *Religious Behavior: Where Sociology and Religion Meet*. Englewood Cliffs, N.J.: Prentice-Hall.

Winter, J. Alan
1970a   "The attitudes of societally-oriented and parish-oriented clergy: an empirical comparison." *Journal for the Scientific Study of Religion* 9 (Winter):58–66.

1970*b* "On the mixing of morality and politics: a test of a Weberian hypothesis." *Social Forces* 49 (September):38–41.
1971 "Pastor or prophet? clergy reaction to hypothetical parish unrest over a clergyman's social activism." *Social Compass* 18 (2):292–302.

Winter, J. Alan, Edgar W. Mills, Jr., and Polly Hendricks
1971 *Clergy in Action Training: A Research Report.* New York: IDOC—North American.

Wood, James R.
1970 "Authority and controversial policy: the churches and civil rights." *American Sociological Review* 35 (December):1057–1069.

Wood, James R., and Mayer N. Zald
1966 "Aspects of racial integration in the Methodist Church: sources of resistance to organizational policy." *Social Forces* 45 (December):255–265.

Yinger, J. Milton
1946 *Religion in the Struggle for Power.* Durham, N.C.: Duke University Press.

III

the
sociology
of
religious
communities

America's Three
Religious Communities:
Herberg revisited

This chapter examines evidence bearing on the relationships among
what Herberg (1960) has called "America's three religious communities":
Protestants, Catholics, and Jews.[1] Individuals and groups not generally
regarded as Protestants, Catholics, or Jews, such as atheists, agnostics,
Muslims, and devotees of one or another Oriental tradition, are common
in America,[2] but they are seen as peripheral to the American system
of interfaith relations. That system, as Herberg (1960:259) describes it,
is thought of as one of "the stable co-existence of three equi-legitimate
religious communities."[3]

The first part of this chapter identifies and defines the central
components of a *community* as the term is applied to Protestant,
Catholic, and Jewish groupings. This discussion is based primarily on
Herberg's study of the history and dynamics of the three religious
communities in America: *Protestant—Catholic—Jew* (1960). Evidence
is then examined bearing on the validity of the three-generation
hypothesis and the three-community hypothesis developed by Herberg.

Central Components of a Community

Herberg's (1960) analysis of religious communities in the United States fails to distinguish between two important sets of activities which occur within a community. One of these includes "activities of the general civic life which involve earning a living, carrying out political responsibilities, and engaging in the instrumental affairs of the larger community"; the other includes the "activities which create personal friendship patterns, frequent home intervisiting . . . and communal recreation" (Gordon, 1961:279). Sociologists refer to the latter set of activities as constituting *primary relationships* and to the former as constituting *secondary relationships.* Primary relationships are thought of as intimate, informal, and personal, involving the core of one's personality. Secondary relationships are thought of as cold and impersonal, involving only the more superficial segments of one's personality. Families and friendship circles are the more common settings for primary relationships; politics and business are common arenas for secondary relationships.

Some relationships involve elements of both primary and secondary relationships. For example, one's relationhip to a doctor, dentist, or other medical professional may well be cold and impersonal as befits relationships involving cash payments and the objectivity required for medical diagnosis. Nevertheless, such relationships are intimate in that they may involve the most personal and often secret aspects of one's life, especially if the medical professional is a psychiatrist or an old-fashioned family physician of the Marcus Welby type. Similarly, a family's relationship to the local school may be a mixture of primary and secondary relationships. The relationship may be primary insofar as it involves frequent visits and friendships among schoolmates and their families. On the other hand, relationships with school personnel may be formal and impersonal, that is, secondary. The school itself may be regarded either as a neighborhood institution and thus within the ambit of primary relationships or as a setting for secondary relationships inasmuch as it prepares one for roles in the larger economic and political systems. Consequently, it is possible to speak, as does Yinger (1970:238–244), of a "scale of communality" which ranges from the essentially primary relations of family and friends through the mixed relations of neighborhood associations and schools to the essentially secondary relationships of politics and business.

Although the term *community* as applied to groupings of Protestants, Catholics, and Jews may refer to either primary or secondary relationships, the research evidence generally offered to document the existence or dynamics of the three religious communities in the United

States focusses almost exclusively on primary relationships.[4] The reason for the focus on primary relationships is not difficult to comprehend if one recognizes that Herberg's study (1960) provides the theoretical or conceptual framework for these studies. To understand why the term *community* as applied to Protestant, Catholic, and Jewish groups in America has come, in practice, to mean a network of or setting for a system of primary relationships rather than of secondary relationships, it is necessary to review Herberg's analysis of the Protestant, Catholic, and Jewish communities.

Herberg's Analysis of Religious Communities

The ultimate significance for the sociology of religion of Herberg's analysis of religious communities is his conclusion concerning the meaning or function of such communities for the individual in American society. This conclusion provides the rationale for the tendency among sociologists of religion to define America's religious communities in terms of primary relationships rather than secondary relationships. Herberg concludes that membership in a religious community helps the individual to resolve the "problem of self-identification and self-location, the problem expressed in the question, 'What am I?' " (1960: 12). Furthermore, he holds that the resolution of the problems of self-identification and self-location in American society is primarily a matter of differential sociability, that is, of differences as to whom one is willing or able to socialize with or befriend—a matter of primary, rather than secondary, relationships. As Greeley (1972:108), paraphrasing Herberg, expresses it, America's religious communities help their members "define who they are and where they stand in a large and complex society." The mechanism through which religious communities provide such self-definition is that of providing a "pool . . . from which man could choose his friends, his spouse . . . his doctor, his lawyer and contractor, his dentist, . . . his real estate man and his psychiatrist" (Greeley, 1972:113). That is, religious communities provide a pool from which one selects those with whom to socialize and to experience the primary relationships of family and friendships. The pool also includes those one deals with on matters involved in selecting and maintaining a home (the setting of many primary relationships). Finally, the pool includes those one engages with in the nearly primary relationships between doctor and patient and lawyer and client.

In sum, Herberg's analysis has been said to hold that "the religiousness characteristic of America today is . . . a way of sociability or 'belonging' " (1960:260) and that as such it provides one means of defining who or what one is. However, Herberg (1960:40) ultimately goes beyond asserting that membership in a religious community is *one* way of answering the question "What am I?" and concludes that it is *the* way an American answers that question:

> Unless one is either a Protestant, or a Catholic, or a Jew, one is a "nothing"; to be "something," to have a name, one must identify oneself to oneself, and be identified by others, as belonging to one or another of the three great religious communities in which the American people are divided.

To understand why Herberg regards religious identification as *the* way in which Americans identify and locate themselves within the larger society, and to understand why secondary relationships are not used to define one's identity, it is necessary to recall that Herberg's analysis is based on an historical study of the experience of immigrant populations and of their children and grandchildren. Herberg's study is largely focussed on the great influx of immigration which began in the late nineteenth century and which ended with the initiation of the National Origin Quota System in the 1920s.[5] Thus, while Herberg's analysis often appears to be couched in terms which apply to all Americans, it is most directly applicable to the largely Eastern and Southern European immigrants who arrived in America during the period from 1880 to 1924 and to their descendants. His analysis begins with a study of the characteristic modes of self-identification and self-location among the immigrants themselves and then moves on to consider how these modes were altered by the experiences of the immigrants and those of their children and grandchildren.

The first generation: the immigrants. Herberg begins his analysis of the immigrant experience by noting that most of the immigrants in question "were men of their village or region (province), . . . intent upon transplanting . . . their village church [or synagogue] with all its ways," (1960:11) and that "men of their village or province [were] known by that name." That is, they were, in their own minds, not to be identified or located by national names, but by reference to their village or province: "They were not Italians, but Apulians or Sicilians. They were not Poles, but Poznansikers or Mazhovoers; not Germans, but Bavarians or Saxons or Prussians; not Greeks, but Thracians or men from Epirus" (1960:18). However, in America, where people from different villages and regions found themselves living and working side by side in the same ghetto neighborhood, even in the same tenement, and in the same factory, mill, or mine, such parochial identification could not survive. American life would not, Herberg contends (1960:12), "permit the indefinite perpetuation of these local identities." Still the immigrant needed an identity, he needed to know where he fit into the American scheme; and at least for the first generation he needed an identity which, while permitting an adjustment to conditions in America, did not break all ties to his European past. Greeley (1971:39) notes:

> If you weren't able to find someone from your own village, then you searched for someone from your area of the country; even though you may never have met him before, you could depend on him to have some of the same values you had, and you shared some sort of common origin. . . . Village or regional groupings . . . in their turn sought protection and some power against the strange world in which they found themselves by banding together. . . .

Initially, the new groupings and the new identity based on them focussed on a commonality of language as much as (or more than) on a common national origin. Hence, the immigrants became Italians, Poles, Germans, Russians, Slovaks, Greeks, Swedes, Hungarians, not just Apulians, Poznansikers, and Bavarians,—not just persons from this or that village or province—but persons who spoke this or that language. Herberg notes (1960:13) in citing Handlin (1951, 1954) that

> . . . immigrants found themselves drawn together by a larger affiliation the basis of which was the language that permitted them to communicate with each other. . . . So generally immigrant groups named themselves by their language rather than their place [town or province] of origin.

The new form of social identification and social location which the immigrants developed is, as Herberg notes (1960:14), what we now call the *ethnic group*, a group with a common linguistic heritage together with a common cultural background and national origin.[6] The ethnic group, in Herberg's view (1960:14), thus became "for so many millions of Americans the primary content of identification and social location." Moreover, since one of the primary concerns of the immigrants was to preserve their churches or synagogues (Herberg, 1960:14),

> as the ethnic group began to emerge, so did the ethnic church, the church that transcended "old country" particularism and grouped together believers according to the newly relevant ethnic (linguistic, cultural, "national") lines.

The ethnic group and the ethnic church were, then, adaptive innovations forged by the immigrants in response to their experiences in America. Moreover, they were innovations which provided the immigrant generation with "something of the old life, something that gave an appearance of continuity and security in their existence" (Herberg, 1960:16). For the next generation, Americans born of immigrant parents, the "ethnic existence was full of perplexities and conflict," (Herberg, 1960:16), which they and the third generation, the grandchildren of the immigrants, had to work out.

The second and third generation: the immigrants' children and grand-children. The children of the immigrants generally "spoke English as their first language and thought and felt about things in American ways" (Herberg, 1960:16), rather than in the ways of the European heritage of their parents. Moreover, while they still shared part of the ethnic life of their parents, "they could not help but realize that their ethnic status was a deprivation, a limitation, which shut many doors of American advancement in their faces" (Herberg, 1960:16). Consequently, most, although by no means all, of the second generation were anxious to rid themselves of the ethnic background which was dear to their parents, and to enter the mainstream of American life in hopes of taking advantage of the many opportunities for socioeconomic mobility they saw in America. Nowhere were the problems of self-identification and self-location "more troublesome than in religious life." Here the clash with their parents and their background was the strongest, since, as Herberg notes (1960:18),

> the church and religion were for the parents the one element of real continuity between the old life and the new. It was for most of them a matter of deepest concern that their children remain true to the faith.

Whether or not to identify with the religion or church of one's parents became for many children of immigrant parents the focal issue in their struggle to find self-identification and a place in what they took to be the melting pot of American society. That is (Herberg, 1960:19), "those who rejected their ethnic identification or felt uncomfortable in it transferred their rejection to the church and religion of their immigrant parents." Ironically, however, the rejection of their parents' religion caused not only the dismay of their parents, but engendered the "distaste of better acculturated Americans" (Herberg, 1960:19). The source of the dismay lay in the process of the assimilation or acculturation of immigrants throughout American history as it was understood by the older or (more) original Americans.

Acculturation calls for the newcomer "to change many things about him as he becomes American—nationality, language, culture" (1960:23) —as both the older Americans and the children of the immigrants knew. However, the former already knew, and the newer Americans were to learn, that there is "one thing . . . he is *not* expected to change— and that is his religion" (1960:23, italics in original). A change in religion was not expected, and indeed, was not even desired. The logic of the American system, with its absence of an established church and with the separation of church and state, favored and fostered religious pluralism. That is, since there has never been an established national church in America to which all are expected to belong, as there has been a Church of England or a Church of Sweden, the existence of a multiplicity of religious groups has been commonplace. Moreover, the separation of church and state implies that the practice of religion is not a public but a private affair and thus not a matter on which Americans have to agree. Indeed, to act as if Americans *had* to agree on religious matters or *had* to join a given church would be tacitly to reject basic American tradition and practice. Thus, older or (more) original Americans might well find it distasteful should a descendant of an immigrant act as if they required newcomers to change their religion, that is, as if they were compelling them to convert. Such distaste would be based primarily on the insulting implication that the older Americans were party to compulsion, something they "would never do," of course.

Thus, as Herberg contends, the logic of the American system places a limit on the processes of acculturation and assimilation. One need not change one's religion. The system works to encourage or at least permit the use of religion as an element to differentiate one American from another. Religion is one legitimate arena for differences and distinctions among Americans,[7] and thus, potentially, it is a context for or basis of self-identification and self-location. After much travail and anxiety, the bulk of the second generation, the children of the immigrants, and more readily the third generation, the grandchildren of the immigrants, came to understand the limits of assimilation and acculturation. Soon (Herberg, 1960:31) "religious association . . . became the primary context for self-identification and social location for the third generation as well as for the bulk of the second generation, of American immigrants." However, as Herberg (1960:31) is quick to add,

> in thus becoming the primary context of social location, religious association itself underwent significant change. . . . Men were Catholics, Protestants or Jews, categories based less on theological than on social distinction. A new and unique social structure was emerging in America, the "religious community."

Moreover, the new structure changes the relationship between religious and ethnic concerns (1960:34).

> Formerly, religion has been an aspect of the ethnic group's culture and activities; it was merely a part; . . . now the religious community was growing increasingly primary, and . . . fast becoming . . . the over-all medium in terms of which remaining ethnic concerns are preserved, redefined and given appropriate expression.

The part became the whole. Ethnic concerns, concerns with national, cultural, and linguistic heritage, were rapidly being replaced by a concern with perpetuating the religious community, with perpetuating a network of ties with family and friends, a network of primary relations.

According to Herberg (1960:37) "self-identification in ethnic terms, while it was a product of the American environment was also a sign of incomplete integration into American life." That is, self-identification in ethnic terms was an innovation which was adaptive for the first generation of immigrants only. Complete integration (desired by later generations) came with the acceptance of the American language, culture, and nationality as truly one's own regardless of one's ethnic origins. Nevertheless, complete integration permitted and even encouraged the maintenance of the religious identification of one's heritage, be it as a Protestant, Catholic, or Jew. Indeed, as Herberg notes (1960:39),

> . . . being a Protestant, Catholic or Jew is understood . . . increasingly [as] perhaps the only way of being an American and locating oneself in American society. It is something that does not in itself necessarily imply actual affiliation with a particular church, participation in religious activities, or even the affirmation of any definite creed or belief, it implies merely identification and social location.

In other words, being a Protestant, Catholic or Jew has come, in Herberg's view, to mean that one associates primarily with other Protestants, Catholics, or Jews. It does not necessarily mean that one is involved with a religious congregation or committed to a particular religious creed. The creeds and congregations of the various religious communities are *not* what differentiates members of one community from those of another. Differences in creeds, in beliefs and practices, are especially disregarded. In American eyes, there is only one basic American culture, one American way of life. The existence of significant creedal differences is denied. Where differences in religious beliefs and practices are acknowledged at all, they are regarded as no more proof of the existence of different cultures or importantly different creeds than the differences among Southern, Midwestern, and New York accents are regarded as evidence for the existence of more than one basic American language. The cultural or creedal components of religion are not seen as the distinctive aspects of the various religious communities; to the contrary, differences among Protestant, Catholic, and Jewish creeds are regarded as insignificant. The three creeds are taken (Herberg, 1960:87) to be "three diverse, but . . . equally American expressions of an over-all American religion, standing for essentially the same 'moral ideals' and 'spiritual values'." However, while creedal differences are essentially denied, structural differences are acknowledged more openly. Unfortunately, Herberg does not explicitly explain why the relevant structural differentiation involves primary relationships, the realms of family and friends, rather than secondary relationships, the realms of business and politics. However, a possible explanation, to which we now turn, is implicit in Herberg's work.

As noted above, the processes of self-identification and self-location of interest to Herberg occur within the context of the tensions attendant upon the assimilation and acculturation of immigrants and their descendants into American society. These tensions come to focus first on ethnic and then on religious differences. Consequently, if secondary relationships were to be the basis of self-identification and self-location, they would be secondary relationships heavily influenced by religious and/or ethnic background. Specifically, they would include religiously influenced business and politics. However, American standards generally regard business and politics as arenas into which religion and national origin should not intrude. Any overt attempt to perpetuate the influence of ethnic or religious background in politics or business, therefore, would be a sign of a failure to assimilate properly, a sign of a defect in the process of acculturation. In short, the secondary relationships in the group's social structure would have to become Americanized. Thus, even though different religious communities may persist, they can no more retain exclusive secondary relationships than they can retain a unique language or creed. Secondary relationships and culture are, in America's self-image, matters in which religion and national origin should make no significant difference. Thus, if a religious community is to retain any distinctive element, it is left to focus only on its primary relationships. Its members must, consequently, focus on primary relationships in their attempts to define and locate themselves within the larger American society.

Herberg sums up his thesis as to the nature of religious communities in the United States by referring to what he calls Hansen's Law: "what the son forgets, the grandson remembers" (see Hansen, 1938,1952). That is, the religion which the son forgets, the grandson remembers. However, Herberg adds what the grandson remembers is not quite what the grandfather knew. For the grandfather religion was merely a part of a larger ethnically based reality or community. It was this ethnically based religion which the son sought to forget. The religion the grandson remembers is one essentially stripped of its ethnic ties; it is now an Americanized religion, one not especially mindful of its European roots. Nevertheless, self-identification and self-location, for the grandson, occur within a religious community, albeit one of which ethnicity is a minor, fading part. In other words, Herberg's thesis may be summarized as saying that over time, from the generation of the immigrant grandparents to that of the native-born grandchildren, the culture and the secondary relationships of a given ethnic group are Americanized. In the realms of creed and secondary relationships, all Americans are thought to be essentially alike and within these realms, all are expected to be treated equally, without regard to religion or national origin. Nevertheless, in primary relationships, America appears to be a land where its various religious communities, while legally equal, prefer to be separate and distinct.[8] As noted above, "the American system is one of stable co-existence of three equilegitimate religious communities" (Herberg, 1960:259). We turn now to examine evidence bearing on the validity of Herberg's views as to the nature and development of America's religious communities.

Some Relevant Studies

Sociologists of religion who have sought to test the validity of Herberg's analysis of the development and present character of the so-called religious communities in the United States have tended to concentrate on two of his central hypotheses: the three-generation hypothesis and the three-community hypothesis. The *three-generation hypothesis* holds that within all ethnic groups, religious identification is high among the first generation (the immigrants), declines greatly in the second, and rises again in the third generation. The *three-community hypothesis* holds that the primary relationships of Protestants, Catholics, and Jews tend to involve coreligionists rather than individuals of different religious backgrounds; for example, Catholics tend to befriend other Catholics more often than they do Protestants. The three-community hypothesis, as interpreted within Herberg's framework, also implies that within each of the three broad religious communities, national origin or ethnic differences are residual and have largely disappeared. That is, for example, the three-community hypothesis implies that a Polish-American Catholic is as apt to marry an Irish-American Catholic as she is another Polish-American Catholic, or that a Jew of German heritage is as apt to befriend a Jew of Russian background as he is another German-American Jew.

Tests of the three-generation hypothesis. Lenski's (1963:43–47) report of data from a 1958 survey of the Detroit area presents the first quantitative evidence purporting to test Herberg's three generation hypothesis. Herberg himself does not provide quantitative data to support his hypothesis; instead, as noted above, he relies on qualitative historical accounts such as those provided by Hansen (1938, 1952).[9] Lenski's data lead him to suggest (1963:44) that "important modifications are necessary to make it [the three-generation hypothesis] conform to . . . [the] facts" of his study. Specifically, his data show that among Protestants and Catholics religious activity as measured by the frequency of church attendance is, contrary to Herberg's prediction, no less among second-generation Americans than it is among first-generation Americans.[10] Indeed, among Catholic Americans, the second generation shows "a marked increase in attendance over the first" (1963:45) and among Protestants, the two generations are alike in terms of church attendance. Lenski also finds that among Protestants and Catholics, the third (and subsequent) generation is more religiously active than the second. He concludes (1963:45): "Instead of the pattern of decline and return which Herberg speaks of, our data suggest a pattern of increasing religious activity linked with increasing Americanization."

In a study of church attendance based on data collected from over two thousand residents of New York City in 1963 and 1964, Nelsen (1973) finds a pattern somewhat like that found by Lenski. Specifically, he finds, that church attendance is no less among second-generation Protestant and Catholic Americans than it is among the first generation. Moreover, Nelsen finds an increase of church attendance among second-generation Catholics, as did Lenski. Among second-generation Protestants, while there is a slight decline in attendance, it is not statistically significant. Thus, as was the case in Lenski's study of Detroit Protestants, the church attendance of first- and second-generation New York City Protestants can be regarded as similar. Nelsen also finds that there is an increase in church attendance between the second and third generation for both Protestants and Catholics. However, Nelsen did not find the differences between the second- and third-generation Protestants to be statistically significant. Finally, Nelsen examined the synagogue attendance patterns of Jewish Americans in his sample. Here he finds a pattern of decreased attendance from the first to the second generation and from the second to the third. In sum, then, Nelsen (1973) finds no support for the decline-and-return pattern predicted by Herberg (1960). Among Jews, he finds a pattern of steady decline, among Protestants a pattern of no change, and among Catholics a pattern of steady increase. This last finding is like that by Lenski.

Lenski's finding also receives some support from the overall data of a study by Lazerwitz and Rowitz (1964) of the responses to two national surveys. The two surveys were conducted in 1957 and 1958, that is, they are roughly contemporaneous with Lenski's Detroit area survey and with the writing of Herberg's book (1960). In the Lazerwitz and Rowitz study the overall picture is one of small increases in church attendance with each succeeding generation in America among both Protestants and Catholics. However, the differences from generation to generation are quite small and not statistically significant; that is, they could well be random variations. Moreover, believing that the overall picture could well hide important variations, Lazerwitz and Rowitz explored generational differences after additional controls were applied for urbanization, education, occupation, and income. Interestingly, they then find that within their control classifications, Protestants follow the Lenski pattern of increases with each generation, while Catholics follow the Herberg pattern of a decline in the second generation, and then an increase in the third.

In addition, Lazerwitz and Rowitz find that the generational patterns of men differ from those of women for both Protestants and Catholics. They find (1964:534) that for Protestants the pattern among men "is more akin to Herberg's decline-and-return pattern" and the "women's pattern conforms more to Lenski's Detroit pattern" of increases from generation to generation. Catholic men like Protestant men "display the Herberg pattern. . . . On the other hand, Catholic women have no meaningfully consistent intergenerational differences." In short, the Lazerwitz and Rowitz study suggests that the relationship between religious activity (as measured by attendance at religious services) and Americanization (as measured by generation-in-America) is a complex one in which differences between Protestants and Catholics and between men and women both play a role.[11]

The results of two surveys of attendance at religious services by Jews, one conducted in Providence in 1963 (Goldstein and Goldscheider, 1968:188–190) and the other in the Chicago area in 1966 and 1967 (Lazerwitz, 1970), lend support to the Lazerwitz and Rowitz finding that both religious and sex differences affect the relationship between attendance at religious services and generation-in-America. Both studies find that the overall pattern of synagogue attendance is one of continuing decline from one generation of Jewish Americans to another and both find that the frequency of synagogue attendance among men and women is approaching a level of equality. The overall pattern shows attendance among Jewish men declining to equal the low level which characterized first-generation Jewish American women. The rate of decline among men has been greater than among women. Indeed, Lazerwitz finds relatively little change among women. Compared to the other groups, the pattern of continuing decline among Jewish men differs from the decline-and-return pattern found by Lazerwitz and Rowitz among Protestant and Catholic men (1964). Moreover, the pattern among Jewish women differs from the pattern of steady increase found among Protestant women. In short, the relationship between religious activity (as measured by attendance at religious services) and Americanization (as measured by generation-in-America) would appear to differ for Prostestants, Catholics and Jews, according to studies by Lenski (1963), Lazerwitz and Rowitz (1964), Goldstein and Goldscheider (1968), Lazerwitz (1970), and Nelsen (1973), and contrary to the implications of Herberg's analysis (1960). Furthermore, the relationship appears to be affected by differences between men and women within each of the three religious groups.

In addition to the differences among the religious groupings and between the sexes, Abramson (1973:110–116) and Nelsen and Allen

(1974) find in their studies of Catholics that differences in church attendance from generation to generation vary with ethnic (national origin) background.[12] The Abramson study is based on a national survey of white Catholic Americans conducted in 1964. The Nelsen and Allen study uses data collected in New York City during 1962.

Abramson finds that Catholics of German, Polish, and Eastern European background show a pattern of increase in church attendance from the first to the second generation and from the second generation to the third and later generations. The pattern among Catholics of Italian origin is, according to Abramson's study, one of persisting low church attendance. Among those of Irish descent, there are only slight changes, but these do follow the pattern predicted by Herberg of a decline followed by an increase in church attendance. Among Catholics of French-Canadian background the generational differences are relatively large and also conform to the decline-and-return pattern predicted by Herberg. As Abramson notes, it is only among Catholics of German, Polish, and Eastern European background that the Lenski pattern of continual increases is found. Thus, it is noteworthy, as Abramson points out (1973:113), that "the Catholic population of Detroit . . . is biased toward these three ethnic backgrounds . . . and may well have comprised the majority of Detroit's Catholic sample in the Lenski study." The findings of the Abramson and Lenski studies would appear, then, to be mutually consistent.

Nelsen and Allen (1974), in a study focussing on first- and second-generation Catholics, find that church attendance among those of Southern European background decreases from the first generation to the second, but among those of Eastern European background it increases, as it does among those of Western and Northern European backgrounds. Moreover, as with the earlier studies by Lazerwitz and Rowitz (1964) and Lazerwitz (1970), the direction and extent of generational differences found among men and women of similar background are not necessarily the same. For example, while Eastern European men evidence a decrease in attendance from the first to the second generation, Eastern European women evidence an increase. Among Southern Europeans, both men and women evidence a decline, but the decline is greater among men; while among Western and Northern Europeans, men and women evidence a similar degree of increase in church attendance from the first to the second generation.

These studies of attendance at religious services among first-, second- and third-or-more generation white Americans of European extraction lend support to Nelsen and Allen's fence-straddling assessment of the viability of the original three-generation hypothesis and Lenski's suggested modification (Lenski, 1963; Goldstein and Goldscheider, 1968; Lazerwitz and Rowitz, 1970; Abramson, 1973; Nelsen,

1973; Nelsen and Allen, 1974). Nelsen and Allen (1974:919) suggest that

> we can at least tentatively accept both the [Lenski] theory of attendance increasing over generations and the [Herberg] hypothesis of second-generation decline in religious interest as long as the conditions under which one or the other holds true are specified.

The conditions affecting which hypothesis holds true would appear to include differences among Protestants, Catholics, and Jews, differences between the sexes, and differences in ethnic (national origin) background. Given the importance of these differences, it is tempting to accept Lazerwitz's claim (1970:58) that "careful analysis of Jewish . . . Protestant and Catholic data . . . demolish(es) [Herberg's] simplistic notion of a pious immigrant generation, a rebellious second generation, and a returning third generation."

However, the value of the evidence cited by Lazerwitz, and even of the later evidence cited above, as a test of the validity of Herberg's analysis may be challenged on at least two grounds. In the first place, the use of attendance at religious services as a measure of the religiosity discussed by Herberg is of questionable value. As noted above, according to Herberg, the religion to which the third generation returns is not quite the religion the first generation practiced or the second abandoned. The religion of the third generation "does not in itself necessarily imply actual . . . participation in religious activities" (Herberg, 1960:39). The frequency of synagogue or church attendance is clearly an imperfect measure of a religiosity which "does not in itself necessarily imply" such attendance. Granted such attendance *may* reflect an interest in or identification with the religious community in question; however, it *need not* do so. Clearly, more appropriate measures of the religiosity of which Herberg speaks are needed.[13] Such measures would have to take cognizance of the two primary characteristics of that religiosity: (1) that it is a "way of sociability or 'belonging' " (Herberg, 1960:260), and (2) that it is a way of self-identification and self-location. Such measures might include, for example, attempts to measure participation in a network of primary relationships within a given religious community in order to assess religion as a way of sociability.[14] Future studies might also reflect the clearer understanding and measurement of religious self-identification called for by Dashevesky (1972) and undertaken by Goldstein and Goldscheider (1968), Lazerwitz (1973), and Dashefsky and Shapiro (1974). (See Glaser, 1958, for a related discussion of ethnic identification.) Future studies might also inquire, as have Wilensky and Ladinsky (1967) into the relevant strengths of religion and other bases for self-identification such as one's occupation or profession. They might inquire, as well, into Greeley's suggestion (1971:120–134) that membership in the intellectual elite constitutes a basis for self-identification and self-location in American society.[15] In any case, since Herberg claims that religion now answers the question "What am I?" (1960:12), future studies of the three-generation hypothesis could make use of a variant of Kuhn and Mc-Partland's Twenty Statement Test (1954) which calls for the respondent to write twenty answers to that question. Future studies might also adapt the questions used by Goering (1970:381). In his study of ethnicity among Irish and Italian Americans, Goering simply asked his respondents, "Do you think of yourself as Irish/Italians?" and "Do you feel that being Irish/Italian is important to you?"[16] Substitution of the words "Protestant," "Catholic," or "Jew" for "Irish/Italian" in a sample of first-, second-, and third-generation Americans could well provide the most direct test yet made of Herberg's three-generation hypothesis.

The second reason for a reluctance to abandon Herberg's three-generation hypothesis stems from the fact that Herberg's is an historical analysis. The first generation of whom he speaks immigrated to the United States in the late nineteenth and early twentieth century. The second generation, whose tensions over religious identification Herberg discusses, thus, is a generation largely reaching adulthood before the 1950s. Studies, such as those cited above, using data collected in the late 1950s or the 1960s refer to a time when the conditions of the country and the experiences of its people, both immigrant and non-immigrant, may have been quite different. The relevance of the possible differences is captured by Abramson (1973:116) when he writes:

> The rejection of some portions of immigrant culture by the second generation might have been truer of the nineteenth century . . . [and] the first third of the twentieth century than the more recent . . . period in which the children of immigrants may be experiencing less marginality or cultural dissonance.

Consequently, the attendance at religious services of first- or second-generation Americans in 1958 or 1966 may not mirror the behavior they would have evidenced in the earlier period of interest to Herberg. For example, second-generation Americans who ignored religious services because they were discomforted by a Jewish or Catholic background in the immigrant-conscious America of the 1920s or 1930s might not be so discomforted in an America of the 1950s or 1960s which did not concern itself as much with the presence of immigrants. Thus, in the later period, they might not ignore religious services. In other words, the experiences and hence the attendance at religious services of two sets of second-generation Americans, or of the same set at different times, may well be different, reflecting differences in the times in which they live. In short, the evidence provided by the studies cited above, all using data collected in post-World War II America, does not demolish the three-generation hypothesis. Nevertheless, it does suggest that Herberg's analysis is timebound, that it very likely does not apply to America today. However, it is not surprising that an historical analysis applies only to the period studied and not to a later one.

Tests of the three-community hypothesis. As noted above, the three-community hypothesis holds that for Protestants, Catholics, and Jews, primary relationships tend to involve coreligionists rather than individuals of different religious backgrounds. Furthermore, within the context of Herberg's analysis (1960), the three-community hypothesis also implies that within each of the three religious communities differences in national origin are residual and disappearing. In short, as Mueller (1971:18) notes, "Herberg argues, religious boundary lines have replaced national origin lines as the significant form of . . . differentiation among whites in American society."

In studies relevant to the testing of the three-community hypothesis, the primary relationships of interest have been those of marriage and friendship. Herberg (1960:30–34) cites studies of interreligious and interethnic marriages by Kennedy (1944) and Hollingshead (1950) to support his hypothesis. He also believes (1960:34) that Thomas' (1951) findings (see note 19) "do not materially alter the basic thesis" despite Thomas' own reservations. The following discussion of evidence bearing on the validity of the three-community hypothesis turns first to the fairly numerous studies of marriage and then to the relatively few studies of friendships within and across religious and ethnic lines.

Studies of marriage rates. Studies of the rates of marriage within and across religious and ethnic groupings face four methodological problems which bear on the relevance of their findings to the three-community hypothesis (see Besanceney, 1965; Cavan, 1970; Rodman, 1965; Yinger, 1968). First, such studies must choose between reporting rates for marriages or couples, on the one hand, and rates for individuals, on the other. For example, if a study examines marriages among a group of 50 Protestant men and 50 Protestant women, and finds that 25 of the men and 25 of the women married non-Protestants for a total of 50 intergroup marriages, while each of the remaining 25 men married one of the 25 remaining women for a total of 25 intragroup marriages, it may report its finding in one of two ways: (1) the intermarriage rate was two-thirds—50 intergroup marriages out of a total of 75 couples; or (2) the intermarriage rate was only one-half—50 intermarried individuals out of a total of 100 Protestants. For purposes of testing the three-community hypothesis within the framework of Herberg's analysis, the rate for individuals is clearly the more ap-

212

propriate one inasmuch as Herberg is basically concerned with the role of religion and ethnicity in the processes of an individual's self-identification or self-location. Unfortunately, many early studies of intergroup marriages, including the Kennedy study (1944) cited by Herberg and her follow-up of it (1952), do not clearly indicate whether a rate for couples or a rate for individuals is being used. Other relevant studies clearly have, for their own purposes, used a rate for couples. However, in these instances, it is possible, using a formula derived by Rodman (1965) to convert the rate for couples into the rate for individuals. Thus, wherever possible, the rates discussed below will be rates for individuals.

A second problem facing studies relevant to the testing of the three-community hypothesis is how to classify marriages involving individuals who have converted to a religion other than that of their birth.[17] For example, should a marriage in which the husband has converted from the Protestantism of his birth to the Catholicism of his wife be defined as an interreligious marriage? It is an intermarriage in terms of the partners' religions at birth, but not in terms of their present religions. Herberg's analysis does not resolve the question of how to define a marriage in which one or both partners have converted. On the one hand, much of the focus of Herberg's analysis is on a person's origins. Thus, the religion at birth should be the determinative one.[18] On the other hand, the three-community hypothesis is presented within a context of concern with self-identification and self-location. It is not claimed that Americans always locate and identify themselves as members of the religious community into which they were born. Indeed, Herberg's discussions of the tensions of second-generation Americans clearly implies that some Americans, at least, reject their origins and define themselves in new terms. Thus, one's present religion would be the more appropriate measure of the community to which one belongs and with which one identifies and locates oneself. In short, a case can be made for rates based on either religion at birth or one's present religion. Where possible, both rates will be reported.

The third methodological question to be faced by studies of interreligious and interethnic marriages is whether to report raw or unadjusted rates or to adjust the rates according to the size of the groups involved. Most studies report the former. However, doing so fails to adjust for the mathematical limits which the varying sizes of relevant groups set on their respective intermarriage rates. For example, in a study population of 10 Jews, 50 Catholics, and 100 Protestants, the intermarriage rates of the Jews and Catholics may reach 100 percent, since the study population makes it possible for all of them to marry a non-Jew or non-Catholic. However, the rate for Protestant individuals cannot exceed 60 percent, since that is the rate attained when they have intermarried with all available non-Protestants in the study population. As Besanceny (1965:719) puts it,

> . . . the smaller the group relative to the total population, the faster its rate goes up with each intermarriage; it can quickly reach a *real* upper limit of 100 percent. . . . A majority group, on the other hand, will find not only that its intermarriage rate goes up more slowly, but that it can never reach a *real* limit of 100 percent simply because there are not enough mates available outside the group. [italics in original]

Ideally, the reported rate of intermarriage should be adjusted for the differing sizes of the groups concerned. The most common form of doing so is to compare the actual rate of intermarriage with that expected at random. Without the necessary adjustments, differences between intermarriage rates can be misleading.

Finally, in order to ensure its relevance to the three-community hypothesis, a study should have data on both religion and ethnicity. Failure to have such data could render findings ambiguous. For example, a study with data only on religion may appear to indicate a low rate of religious intermarriage reflecting a tendency to confine one's primary relationships to coreligionists. However, it may really reflect a tendency for people to associate with those of a similar ethnic background, the great majority of whom happen to have the same religion. Thus, the low interreligious marriage rate would be an artifact of the low interethnic rate. It should be noted that a finding of a high rate of marriage across religious lines would tend to disprove the three-community hypothesis even without data on ethnicity. Since the hypothesis predicts a low rate of religious intermarriage, a finding of a high rate, whatever the underlying reason, would contradict that prediction.

In addition to variations in the resolution of the four methodological problems just discussed, studies relevant to the testing of the three-community hypothesis vary according to the scope of the study population. Studies may examine a population in a local or metropolitan area, a statewide area, or a national area. The following discussion of tests of the three-community hypothesis begins with an examination of the studies of local or metropolitan areas. Among these, are the New Haven studies by Kennedy (1944) and Hollingshead (1950), cited by Herberg (1960:30–34) in support of his hypothesis, and a follow-up study by Kennedy (1952).

Kennedy's first study examines the rates of intermarriage in New Haven for the years 1870, 1900, 1930 and 1940; the second, for the year 1950. Her general conclusion, on the basis of both studies, is that the rate of interreligious marriage was relatively low and the rates of interethnic marriage were declining among the ethnic groups she studied, namely, British, Irish, Italian, German, Polish, and Scandinavian Americans. She states her belief (1944:322) that "future cleavages will be along religious lines rather than along nationality lines as in the past." This belief was heartily accepted by Herberg and reformulated as his three-community hypothesis. Kennedy's data reveal that the rates of both interreligious and interethnic marriage have generally declined during the period she studied. The decline is somewhat greater in the rate of interethnic marrages, so that interreligious marriage rates appear greater than interethnic marriage rates. Kennedy's conclusion is suspect, however, on two methodological grounds. First, as Besanceney (1965:718–719) notes, she fails to adjust the intermarriage rates reported for the relative sizes of the religious and ethnic groups in the New Haven population. Such a failure is important because, as he notes (1965:719):

> since a religious group is larger than any of the ethnic groups that constitute it, we must expect that . . . ethnic intermarriage rates will be larger than the corresponding religious intermarriage rates—from mathematical necessity.

In short, a finding that interethnic marriage rates tend to be lower than interreligious marriage rates may be an artifact of the relative sizes of religious and ethnic groups. Kennedy's conclusion is also suspect because she has no direct and independent measure of religion. She merely assumes that all German, Scandinavian, and British Americans are Protestant, and all Irish, Italian, or Polish Americans are Catholic. Thus, her so-called inter*religious* marriage rates are really inter*ethnic* rates and may be inflated by the number of marriages within her so-called religious groupings which actually cross religious lines. For example, if a German American Catholic married a Scandinavian American Protestant, Kennedy would list such a marriage as *intra*religious, rather than *inter*religious, since she assumed all German Americans are Protestants. However, Hollingshead (1950:623) observes that in New Haven, "a minority of the Germans were Catholics." Of course, such errors may or may not have been compensated for by the erroneous classification of other marriages. For example, Kennedy would classify a marriage between a British American Catholic and Irish American Catholic as a Protestant-Catholic marriage.[19] However, such is not always the case. (See Abramson, 1973:57–65, for a discussion of Irish-English marriages among Catholics.)

The doubt concerning Kennedy's findings is not cleared up by Hollingshead's study (1950) of a 1948 survey conducted in New Haven. While Hollingshead did not confound religion and ethnicity, having correctly determined each independently, he did not tabulate interethnic marriage rates. He found (1950:624) "religion and ethnicity so closely related" that he could not "discuss how ethnicity is related to the selection of a marriage mate apart from religion." However, Hollingshead is willing to conclude on the basis of his data (1950:624) that "ethnicity within a religious group has been a very potent factor in influencing the mate selection process." It appears that the support which Herberg (1960:30–34) felt he could find for his three-community hypothesis in the local studies done in New Haven may not be there at all.[20]

Turning to statewide studies produces a similar lack of clear support for the three-community hypothesis. The statewide studies, however, involve interreligious marriages only and not interethnic marriages. Moreover, the statewide studies use data from either Indiana or Iowa, since these are the only two states which have required a report of religious affiliation on their marriage record forms.[21] (Indiana began the practice in 1959; Iowa began it in 1952, and stopped it in 1972. See Monahan, 1973:195–196.) None of the studies of Iowa records adjusts the reported rate of interreligious marriage for the differing sizes of the groups concerned, and only one by Rosenthal (1963) discusses trends over time, and that only for rate of interreligious marriage among Jews.[22] Thus, the studies of the Iowa records are not especially helpful in determining the validity of the three-community hypothesis.

The studies of the Indiana records are useful, however. The interreligious marriage rates among Protestants, Catholics and Jews married in Indiana has now been studied for 1960 by Christensen and Barber (1967), for 1960 and 1961 by Barber (1967, as reported by Monahan, 1973:196), and for 1962 through 1967 by Monahan (1973). In addition, Rosenthal (1967, 1968) has studied the rate of interreligious marriage among Jews for the period from 1960 to 1963. Only the data presented by Monahan have been adjusted for the different numbers of Protestants, Catholics, and Jews married in Indiana.[23] Specifically, he finds (Monahan, 1973:197) that the rate with which Protestants marry Protestants is only 1.10 times that expected by chance during the period from 1962 to 1967, while Catholics marry Catholics at 4.11 times the randomly expected rate, and Jews marry Jews at the rate of 171.11 times the randomly expected level for the same period. Moreover, when Barber's figures for 1960 and 1961 are compared with those reported by Monahan for 1962 to 1964 and 1965 to 1967, there is a steady increase in the rate of interreligious marriage for Protestants, Catholics, and Jews alike. In sum, the Indiana data indicate that as of 1967 the three-community hypothesis held only slightly, if at all, for Protestants, held somewhat better for Catholics, but held rather well among Jews. However, the "hold" seems to be slipping among all three so-called religious communities, at least among those married in Indiana.

Similar results are found from the examination of the findings of nationwide studies. Unfortunately, none of the nationwide studies of intergroup marriages have simultaneously studied both interreligious and interethnic marriages. Thus, their relevance to the testing of the three-community hypothesis may be somewhat limited depending, as noted above, on the direction of their findings. Caution is called for when examining these studies. Nationwide studies of interreligious marriages are examined first and then those on interethnic marriages. The few nationwide studies of intermarriage generally present their findings in one of two forms: either they present data on marriages at a given point in time, namely, the time of data collection, or they attempt to analyze trends over time. Interestingly, only the study by Mueller and Lane (1972) has sought to do both. However, it has a drawback, discussed below, which limits its relevance to the three-community hypothesis. The study by Monahan (1971) is examined for information it yields on the rate of interreligious marriages at a given point in time, March, 1957. Studies by Bumpass (1970) and by Mueller and Lane (1972) are examined for information on trends over time for all three so-called religious communities. Studies by Reiss (1965) and Wagner (1970, reported in Mueller, 1971) provide data on trends among Catholics. Cohen (1974) provides data for trends among Jews.

Monahan (1971) has analysed the data on interreligious marriages collected by the U.S. Bureau of the Census in its March, 1957 study.[24] Moreover, Monahan analyzes the data, unlike others who have used it (see Glick, 1960; Mueller and Lane, 1972; Winch, 1963:327–336; and Yinger, 1968), in a manner which renders his results especially pertinent to the three-community hypothesis. Specifically, Monahan examines data on white Americans only. Since the three-community hypothesis pertains only to white Americans, other analyses of the 1957 data which examine rates based on the total population, both white and nonwhite, are not as pertinent to the hypothesis. Monahan reports the rates for couples based on their current religion, rather than on their religion at birth, since only information on the former was collected by the Bureau of the Census. Converting the couple rate, using Rodman's formula (1965), the rate of interreligious marriages among individuals is 6.5 percent among Protestants, 13.5 percent among Catholics and 4.3 percent among Jews. Among males, the intermarriage rates are 5.6, 11.9 and 5.2 percent for Protestants, Catholics and Jews, respectively; while among women, the corresponding rates are 7.5, 14.5 and 2.7 percent. Moreover, while Monahan does not report the ratio of actual to randomly expected intermarriages, he does correct for the effects of the different sizes of the Protestant, Catholic, and Jewish populations by reporting the ratio of actual to expected *intra*marriages. He finds, as of March, 1957, that Protestants were married to Protestants at 1.38 times the rate expected at random; that Catholics were married to Catholics at 3.21 times the rate expected at random; and that Jews married Jews at 25.16 times the rate expected at random. Of course, these figures based on current religion show a higher rate of *intra*religious marriage than would be found using religion at birth, due to the unknown number of conversions.[25] In any case, the Census Bureau data indicate that as of March, 1957, at about the time Herberg was formulating the three-community hypothesis, it did not hold very well among Protestants, held somewhat better among Catholics, but held rather well among Jews.[26]

Bumpass (1970) seeks to determine the trend in the rate of interreligious marriage rates over time, rather than at one point in time, as did Monahan. Bumpass' rates are based on a study of a 1965 national sample of once-married white women. He presents rates based on both differences between the woman's current religion and that of her husband and differences between her parents' religion and that of her in-laws. The latter difference, of course, reflects differences in religion at birth insofar as her parents' religion reflects her own religion at birth and that of her in-laws reflects her husband's. Bumpass groups his sample in terms of the year of their marriage and finds that the rate of interreligious marriage, whether based on current religion or religion at birth, has increased slowly but steadily among both Protestants and Catholics. For example, the rate of interreligious marriage among Protestant women, based on current religion, rose from 5 percent among those married between 1935 and 1939, to 8 percent among those married between 1950 and 1954, to 11 percent among those married between 1960 and 1965. Among Catholics, the corresponding figures are 12, 14 and 20 percent, respectively for those years. Based on religion at birth, the corresponding figures for Protestant women are 7, 11 and 12 percent; and for Catholics, 23, 26 and 30 percent. However, among Jews in Bumpass' sample there is no apparent trend in the rate of interreligious marriage.

Mueller and Lane (1972) find similar results when they analyze the March, 1957 Census Bureau data in terms of respondents' ages. They find (1972:79) that when the interreligious marriage rates for individuals 14 to 29 years of age, 30 to 44 years of age, and 44 and over are compared, "for both Protestants and Catholics there is a clear and steady trend toward a greater amount of intermarriage. For Jews, in contrast, no such trend is evident." Of course, since they include both whites and nonwhites in their analysis, the relevance of their findings to the three-community hypothesis may be questioned.[27] In any case, an increase in the rate of interreligious marriage is, of course, contrary to the three-community hypothesis, which implies that a common religious affiliation is increasing, not decreasing, as a desideratum in marriage. As with the Monahan study of the 1957 Census Bureau data, the hypothesis appears to hold better for Jews than it does for either Protestants or Catholics.

However, Cohen's nationwide study (1974), which included members of over nine thousand marriages in which at least one partner was Jewish, indicates that the "hold" of the three-community hypothesis is decreasing among Jews in America.[28] Specifically, his figures indicate that while the rate of interreligious marriages among Jewish individuals was 1.4 percent for marriages which took place between 1930 and 1939, the rate rose to 4.8 percent for marriages which took place between 1950 and 1959. The rate is 17.7 percent for marriages which took place between 1960 and 1971; 11.2 percent for those between 1960 and 1965; 25.9 percent for those between 1966 and 1971. Even at 25.9 percent, the rate of interreligious marriages is less than the 97 or 98 percent rate which would occur among the 2 or 3 percent of the population who are Jewish.

Some evidence that the interreligious marriage rates may *not* be increasing is offered by Reiss (1965) and Greeley (1970), although neither is necessarily telling. Reiss, using the *Official Catholic Directory*, tabulated the rate of valid (performed by a priest) interreligious marriages among Catholics from 1943 to 1962.[29] He finds that the post-World War II rates are less than the rates during the war years of 1943 to 1945. Moreover, he finds that the postwar rates have held fairly steady at a level of about 15.6 percent, if his reported rate for couples is converted to the rate for individuals. However, Wagner (1970, as reported in Mueller, 1971:20–21) has examined the *Directory* and finds that the rate of valid interreligious marriages among Catholics has risen to 19.5 percent for 1967 and 20.5 percent for 1969, again converting the reported couple rate to a rate for individuals.

In a 1968 follow-up study of a national sample of June, 1961, college graduates, Greeley (1970) finds that the rate of interreligious marriage among his sample population is not much different from that found eleven years earlier in the 1957 Bureau of the Census data.[30] He contends that the rate of interreligious marriage has not changed. However, Greeley's data and that of the Bureau of the Census may not be strictly comparable since the latter includes people who are not college graduates and who cover a wider age distribution. Furthermore, Greeley does not exclude nonwhites from his analysis as called for in the three-community hypothesis. Nevertheless, his study does remain the one nationwide study to offer support for the three-community hypothesis.

Abramson's study (1973:49–100) of interethnic marriages, using a 1964 national sample of white Catholic Americans, like the studies of interreligious marriages by Bumpass (1970), Monahan (1971), and

Mueller and Lane (1972), fails to support the three-community hypothesis. Abramson's study (1973:66) indicates that the influence of ethnic (national origin) background is not residual and has not yet disappeared, at least not among Catholics: "expectations of widespread intermarriage among American ethnic groups, even with the limitation of marriage within a shared religion [Catholicism] simply have not yet materialized."[31] He finds that the rate at which individual respondents marry someone of the same ethnic background, as measured by the reported national origin on the father's side of the respondent's family and that of his or her in-laws, ranges from about one-quarter to one-half in all but the English in the seven groups of European origin he studied (see Table 2). Moreover, Abramson's 1964 figures are reasonably similar to those based on a November, 1969 study conducted by the U.S. Bureau of the Census (1971), except for the case of those of English descent, where the Census figures show a much higher rate of interethnic marriage. The differences between the rates reported by the two studies for the other ethnic groups show the Census rates to be approximately 10 percent lower for each group of non-English, European origin. These differences may, of course, reflect a genuine drop in the intraethnic rate between 1964 and 1969. On the other hand, the differences may merely reflect three differences between the methodologies of the studies: (1) the inclusion of non-Catholics in the Census Bureau study and their exclusion from the Abramson study, a factor of importance in considering the predominately non-Catholic English ethnic group; (2) a rate based on males or females in the Abramson study, but on males only in the Census Bureau study; and (3) the use of the total

Table 2 PERCENTAGE OF INTRAETHNIC MARRIAGES
BY INDIVIDUALS[a]

Ethnic Origin	As of 1964[b]	As of 1969[c]
Italian	50%	36%
Lithuanian	33	NA[d]
Russian	NA[d]	31
Polish	33	20
Irish	27	19
Eastern European	24	NA[d]
English	6	31

a. All rates are converted from rates reported for couples by use of Rodman's formula (1965).
b. Abramson (1973:63).
c. United States Bureau of the Census (1971:7).
d. Not ascertained; this category of ethnic origin not used in study.

population for determining rates of intermarriage by the Census Bureau while Abramson's base includes only the various ethnic groups studied. Neither set of data seems to indicate that ethnicity is a residual factor in the choice of a marriage partner. Correcting for the varying sizes of the groups in question, as Abramson does, further supports a claim that ethnicity plays a role in mate selection, at least among many Catholic Americans. Abramson (1973:64) finds the following ratios of the number of actual Catholic intraethnic marriages to the number expected at random among Americans of European origins: Lithuanian:16.7, Eastern European:5.6, Polish:4.5, Italian:3.1, German:2.8, Irish:2.7, English:1.7. The ratios indicate that the rate of intraethnic marriage (by couples) exceeds that expected at random. Ethnicity, then, would appear to remain a factor in determining with whom to establish the primary relationship of marriage, at least among Catholics.

The studies of interreligious and interethnic marriages fail to yield much support, if any, for Herberg's three-community hypothesis. Insofar as the primary relationship of marriage is concerned, white America does not appear to be a society simply divided into communities of Protestants, Catholics, asd Jews. If white America is divided at all, and it appears to be, the communities are most likely identifiable as Jewish and Christian (both Protestant and Catholic) and communities of ethnic Catholics who are primarily Italian-American but also Irish-American and Polish-American, with perhaps others as well.

Studies of friendship patterns. The formation of interreligious and interethnic friendships has not been investigated as often or as thoroughly as has marriage across religious and ethnic lines. For example, only local or metropolitan studies of interreligious and interethnic friendship patterns have been done. Of the local studies, two were conducted in Detroit (Lenski, 1963 and Laumann, 1969), one in three unnamed cities in Utah and two neighboring states (Anderson, 1968), and one in northern California (Stark and Glock, 1968).[32] The limited number and scope of the studies of friendship patterns is unfortunate, since, as Mueller (1971:22) observes, "friendship, being a much less permanent and [more] free-floating structure than marriage, may actually be a more sensitive indicator" of the validity of the three-community hypothesis. The discussion of interreligious and interethnic friendship patterns begins with the studies that deal exclusively with friendships within and across religious lines and then moves to the one which deals with both interreligious and interethnic friendships.

Of the three studies which focus on interreligious friendships, only Anderson's compares the rate of reported friendships to that expected by chance. Specifically, he finds (1968:504) that the percentage of

Protestants reporting that all three of their closest friends are Protestant is 58 in a predominately Protestant city, 41 in a predominately Catholic city, and 23 in a predominately Mormon city.[33] The rate of three such friendships expected by chance is 34 percent, 5 percent and near zero, respectively, in the three cities studied.[34] The rate of intra-Catholic friendships was not studied in the predominately Mormon city; and the rate of intra-Jewish friendship was not studied at all. In the predominately Catholic city, 45 percent of the Catholics reported that all three of their closest friends were also Catholic, compared to a rate of 25 percent expected by chance. In the predominately Protestant city, 17 percent of the Catholics reported that all three of their closest friends are Catholics compared to a rate of only 2 percent expected at random. Anderson's study yields support for the three-community hypothesis, at least among Protestants and Catholics in the cities studied.[35]

Further support for the hypothesis is found in Lenski's study (1963: 36–39) of friendship patterns in the Detroit area. He reports that 38 percent of white Protestants state that all or nearly all their closest friends are Protestants, 44 percent of the Catholics state that all or nearly all their closest friends are Catholic, and 77 percent of the Jews state that all or nearly all their closest friends are Jewish. As noted above, Lenski does not compare the reported rates of intra-religious friendships to the rates expected at random. However, it is possible to do so using Anderson's method of estimation (see note 29), and assuming that the phrase "all or nearly all of my closest friends" refers to a group of at least three people.[36] The percentages expected if the selection of closest friends is a random process are 13, 8.5, and virtually zero, for Protestants, Catholics, and Jews rather than the reported 38, 44, and 77 percent, respectively.

Stark and Glock (1968:165–167) studied friendship patterns among church members, both Protestant and Catholic, in northern California. They find that among white Protestants, 29 percent reported that three or more of their closest friends are not only Protestant, but belong to the same congregation. Among Catholics, 36 percent reported that three or more of their closest friends are not only Catholic, but belong to the same parish church. Since the percentage of the relevant total population in the respondents' congregation or parish is very small, the randomly expected percentage reporting that three closest friends belong to one congregation would be virtually nil. Once again the three-community hypothesis receives support from a study of friendship patterns. However, as was noted when discussing tests of the hypothesis using intermarriage rates, a high intrareligious rate may reflect the influence of ethnicity as well as that of religion. Thus, it is extremely valuable to examine Laumann's study, the only one to investigate the influence of both religion and ethnicity on the selection of friends.

Laumann (1969:189–196; 1972:42–72) examined the friendship patterns among over twenty different *ethnoreligious groups*, that is, groups defined by religion *and* ethnicity. These groups include, for example, German Lutherans and Irish Catholics. His religious categories include several Protestant denominational groupings, as well as a single category for Catholics and one for Jews. His ethnic categories include Anglo-American, French, German, Irish, Italian, Polish, Scandinavian and Slavic.[37] Laumann obtained his data on friendship patterns by asking each of his respondents to report the religious preference and the national origin of each of their three closest friends. However, rather than compute the number or percentage of individual respondents with a given number of friends of one category or another (as do Anderson, Lenski, and Stark and Glock), Laumann uses a very sophisticated computerized statistical technique (the smallest space analysis of indexes of dissimilarity) to compare simultaneously the entire distribution of friendship choices of each ethnoreligious group with that of the others. On the basis of his statistical analyses, Laumann is able to determine that three factors influence the friendship patterns of the men in his sample.[38] The most important of these factors, as Herberg's three-community hypothesis would predict, is religious preference. That is, the friendship patterns of the men studied clearly divide them into the three broad groupings, Protestant, Catholic, and Jew. Only one Protestant group, the Scandinavian Lutherans, seem "closer" to the various Catholic groups than to the other Protestants. All of the various Catholic groups are relatively "close" to each other; while the Jews are "quite isolated from all other groups" (Laumann, 1969:191). The second most important factor is socioeconomic status, while the third is ethnicity.[39] Within *both* the larger Protestant and Catholic communities, the Anglo-Americans (mainly those of English, Scottish and Welsh background) are somewhat separated from their coreligionists. That is, contrary to the three-community hypothesis, ethnicity is an important, rather than residual, factor in the determination of friendship patterns.[40] Thus, despite the importance of the tripartite grouping of Protestant, Catholic, and Jew in the formation of friendships, Laumann (1969:195) concludes,

> In sum, the results of the smallest space analyses . . . clearly indicated that a single dimension by itself (presumably ordering the groups into Herberg's tripartite division) is totally inadequate for representing the structure of intimate associations among religious groups. . . . [Another] model which stresses the continuing significance of underlying social compositional differences among the various groups appears to represent more adequately the social structure of religious groups. . . .

These compositional differences include ethnic (and socioeconomic) differences, among Protestants and Catholics at least. If American society is divided into communities at all, as it appears to be, there are not merely three, Protestant, Catholic and Jew, but a multiplicity of ethnic Protestants, ethnic Catholics and Jews. As Greeley (1971:82) notes, although "Herberg's insight that the three major religious groups played an [identification] function was extremely important, . . . it would seem now that his prediction of the vanishing of nationality groups was premature." A more accurate description of the situation would hold (Greeley, 1971:85), that probably "some Americans choose religion as their principal, primordial self-definition, while others choose nationality, and still others some sort of subtle combination of both."

Summary

Herberg (1960) has analyzed the role of religion and ethnicity in the experiences of the European immigrants who came to America during the period from the 1880s to the 1920s and those of their children and grandchildren. His analyses have led to the formulation of two hypotheses.

The three-generation hypothesis predicts what has been called a decline-and-return pattern in the religious activities of the immigrants and their descendants, that religious activity will decline among the second generation, the children of the immigrants, below that found among the first generation, but rise in the third generation. The evidence from the available relevant studies indicates that the decline-and-return pattern is not found at all among Jews, but is found among some groups of Catholics and Protestants. Moreover, ethnic and sex differences are found to influence the relationship between generation-in-America and the level of religious activities. It is also suggested that the three-generation hypothesis may apply better to the period discussed by Herberg than to more recent times in America.

The three-community hypothesis holds that the primary relationships of Protestants, Catholics, and Jews, tend to involve coreligionists rather than individuals of different religious backgrounds and thus that they constitute three distinct communities. Furthermore, within the context of Herberg's analysis, the three-community hypothesis implies that within each of the three so-called religious communities, ethnic (national origin) differences are residual and disappearing. However, the evidence from available studies of the primary relationships of marriage and friendship within and across both religious and ethnic lines indicates that if America is divided into communities at all, as it very likely is, there are not merely three, but a multiplicity of ethnic

224

Catholics, Protestants, and Jews; that is, that religious and ethnic identification are subtly mixed, each contributing, sometimes separately, sometimes together, to one's self-identification and social location within American society.

FOOTNOTES

1. It must be acknowledged, as Glazer and Moynihan (1963:324) contend, that not only religion, but "religion and race seem to define the major groups [in] American society." However, discussion of interracial relations is generally beyond the scope of this work in the sociology of religion. Some aspects of race relations are, however, discussed in Chapter 9, where the concept of religious community is applied in an examination of Black religion. Nevertheless, it must be borne in mind that this chapter refers to white Protestants, Catholics and Jews and not to their black or brown coreligionists.

2. A poll conducted in 1973 and 1974 indicates (Gallup Opinion Index, 1975:24) that among white Americans, some 5 percent have no religious preference and 4 percent have a preference other than Protestant, Catholic or Jew; 59 percent indicate they are Protestant, 29 percent indicate Catholic, and 3 percent indicate Jewish. In addition, the poll reveals (1975:17) that 9 percent of Americans are agnostic, that is, they are "not sure there is a God or vital force"; 11 percent are atheists, that is, they are "sure there is no God or vital force." On the other hand, 40 percent believe "there is a personal God," and an additional 37 percent believe "there is some kind of Spirit or vital force in the world." (Three percent gave no response.)

3. In addition to noting the racially parochial limit of the discussion in this chapter, it is also well to note that sociologically informed materials on interfaith relations in other nations are insufficent to permit extensive discussion. Thus, this chapter is nationally as well as racially parochial. However, mention should be made of religious pluralism in other nations, such as that studied by Gulick (1965) in Lebanon, and by Moberg (1961) and Lijphart (1968) in the Netherlands.

4. For exceptions to this rule, that is, for studies which focus on secondary relationships involving members of religious communities, see Glazer and Moynihan (1963) and Greeley (1974b). It should be noted that these studies deal with ethnoreligious communities rather than with religious communities per se.

5. Herberg's focus on the period from 1880–1924 helps explain why he does not discuss racial aspects of self-identification or problems facing Spanish-speaking or Chicano groups. Questons involving these latter groups on a national scale are largely a phenomenon of post-World War II America.

6. For other and more extensive discussions of the nature of ethnic groups and their place in American life, see Francis (1947), Glazer and Moynihan (1963, 1975), Gordon (1964), and Newman (1973).

7. Of course, the system referred to here is the normative or official view which stresses religious tolerance and does not countenance the existence of religious prejudice. Nevertheless, such prejudices existed even if they were not acknowledged in Herberg's analysis. The contradictions between the norms of religious tolerance and the existence of religious prejudice may well have added to the anxiety and travail which matters pertaining to religion caused the descendants of immigrants.

8. This summary follows closely Gordon's analysis (1964) of assimilation in America.

9. For discussion which predates and differs from Herberg, see Mead (1942, chap. 3) and Koenig (1952). For dissenting views see Thomas (1951) on the experience of Catholic Americans and Gans (1965a, b) on the experience of Jewish Americans. See also Bender and Kagiwada's commentary (1968) on Hansen's original formulations and Herberg's application of them.

10. Lenski (1963:43) does present some data on the applicability of the three-generation hypothesis to Jews. Here he finds, as predicted by Herberg, that synagogue attendance among second-generation Jews is less than that among the first generation. However, the number of respondents involved is quite small. Moreover, there is no data on third-generation Jewish Americans. Hence, it is not possible to tell from Lenski's data if there is a return to religion among third-generation Jewish Americans.

11. Lazerwitz and Rowitz (1964:537) also note that Herberg's discussions do not clarify the "issue of what to do about respondents one of whose parents is native-born and the other foreign-born." They classified these respondents as second-generation Americans, but note that doing so does change the patterns of results. Specifically, the grouping of those with mixed parentage, one native and one foreign born, with fully second-generation respondents results in a "different pattern for Protestant men and somewhat obscures the patterns for Protestant women and Catholic men" (1964:537).

12. Greeley and Rossi (1968:36–41) also find that generation-in-America and ethnicity both have an effect on another measure of Catholic religiosity, namely, enrollment in Catholic schools.

13. The confusion which can result from focussing on inappropriate measures of religious identification is illustrated by Sharot's conclusion based on a review of published and unpublished studies of synagogue attendance and other religious observances among Jewish Americans. Sharot concludes (1973: 162) that "in respect of American Jews the evidence does not support Herberg's three generation thesis." Yet, he notes, there is "unambiguous evidence of a possible 'return' in the rise in synagogue membership" (1973:162). Of course, as he adds (1973:162), a "high rate of synagogue membership is not strongly predictive of a high level of religious observance." However, he notes (1973:162) that "the synagogue has become a central institution for social activities and for transmitting Jewish identity." Moreover, he observes (1973:162) that "the synagogue has increased in importance as an *institutional* focus of Jewish identity because . . . no other . . . organization (nationalist, secularist, etc.) can provide . . . for such an identity" (italics in original). The synagogue, then, as Sharot himself notes, has served as a vehicle for religious identification—the phenomenon of interest to Herberg. Whether synagogue membership is related to increased religious observance is not central to the Herberg hypothesis, but what is central is whether or not it serves as a basis for religious identification. Thus, Sharot, contrary to his own conclusion, which mistakenly focusses on religious observances, has found some evidence supporting Herberg's three-generation hypothesis if synagogue membership is, as it appears to be, a more appropriate measure of religious identification than is synagogue attendance.

14. It should be noted that two of the studies cited above purporting to test the three-generation hypothesis do measure involvement in a network of primary relationships with others of the same religion. However, the studies by Goldstein and Goldscheider (1968) and Lazerwitz (1970) pertain only to the applicability of the hypothesis to Jewish Americans. Both studies fail to find the Herberg pattern of decline-and-return, even with the more appropriate measures of involvement in primary relationships.

15. Interestingly, Wilensky and Ladinsky in their study of lawyers, engineers, and college professors in Detroit, found that a common religious preference is a stronger factor in friendship selection than either occupation or work place. Specifically, they find (1967:47) that "43 percent of their professionals find *all* of their three best friends among men with the same religious pref-

erence" (italics in the original). Unfortunately, they do not study the friendship choices of Protestants, Catholics, and Jews separately. Nevertheless, their results do indicate that membership in a religious community is a factor influencing the choice of primary relationships and, thus, self-identification. Greeley (1971) offers no quantitative evidence to support his argument concerning the intellectual elite.

16. Similar adaptations may be made by substituting references to religious communities in the items used by Plax (1972:100) and by Pavlak (1973:227–228). Plax's items include: "Thinking of your [national] background, what would you call yourself?" and "Do you ever think of yourself as being a [name of national group]?" Pavlak's items include: "Do you feel at home among the [national group] people?" and "Do you agree or disagree that a [person of a national group] should never hide the fact . . . but should gladly represent himself as [such]?"

17. Studies of interethnic marriages do not, of course, face the problem of conversion inasmuch as one cannot change his national *origin*, even if he changes his present nationality.

18. The use of religion at birth has the added advantage of making the conceptual properties of religion and ethnicty more alike. That is, it renders religion an ascribed status just as ethnicity is an ascribed status (see note 14 above).

19. Thomas (1951:469) expresses further doubt about the New Haven studies. Specifically, he questions the low rate of interreligious marriage reported for Catholics. Ilis own study of valid interreligious marriages (those performed by a priest) among Catholics in Connecticut reveals a higher rate than that reported for both valid and nonvalid marriages in the New Haven studies. Thus, Thomas believes that New Haven is not typical of its own state of Connecticut, let alone the nation.

20. Further studies in local and metropolitan areas have also not clarified the doubts. First of all, none of them study interethnic marriage rates, only interreligious marriage rates. Moreover, only the study by Besanceney (1965) in the Detroit area in 1955, 1958, and 1959 corrects for the relative size of the groups involved. However, he only reports data on Protestant-Catholic marriages and not for Jewish-Gentile marriages. (He finds the Protestant intermarriage rate is 53 percent of that expected by chance for individuals and the Catholic rate 56 percent of that expected by chance for individuals.) Heiss (1960) reports rates for Protestants, Catholics, and Jews in a 1957 study in New York City's borough of Manhattan, but does not correct for size. Rosenthal (1963:16) reports the rate of interreligious marriage among Jews in Washington, D.C., in 1956. Goldstein and Goldscheider (1968) found a rate of intermarriage of only 2.5 percent among Jewish individuals in Providence in 1963. Schwartz (1970) summarizes the results of a number of similar studies in various communities during the 1960s. None of the studies of the rate of interreligious marriages finds a rate exceeding 10 percent for individual Jews and most find the rate under 5 percent. For further relevant studies, see Besanceney's comprehensive review of the literature (1970:48–74).

21. The Indiana and Iowa records report current religion and thus not necessarily religion at birth. Both sets of state records list all marriages performed in the state whether or not the persons involved reside in the state.

22. Rosenthal (1963:37) finds that the rate of interreligious marriage among Jews married in Iowa has fluctuated up and down from 1953 to 1959, the general trend being upward. The average intermarriage rate among Jews for the period was 42 percent for couples, or 27 percent for individuals. For studies of the interreligious marriage rates for Protestants and Catholics in Iowa, see Burchinal and Chancellor (1962) and Chancellor and Monahan (1955).

23. Monahan's (1973) data include both whites and Blacks, and not just whites as called for by the three-community hypothesis. However, he reports (1973:196) that Blacks comprise only 6 percent of the relevant population.

24. These 1957 data were collected in the only study by the Bureau of the

Census in the post-World War II era to inquire about religious affiliation. For something of the history of the availability of the 1957 data, which were not widely available for about ten years, and for relevant original tables, see Mueller and Lane (1972).

25. Attempts have been made by Yinger (1968) and Mueller and Lane (1972) to estimate the number of conversions. However, both attempts are based on very limited data gathered in the Detroit area by Lenski (1963) and Besanceney (1965) and may be inappropriate for use with nationwide data.

26. Greeley (1970) also reports data on interreligious marriage for a given point in time. However, his study is not discussed here primarily because it does not make necessary corrections for the different sizes of the relevant groups and includes both whites and nonwhites in the study population. In addition, Greeley does not report rates for Protestants as a whole, as called for by the three-community hypothesis, but for each of four major denominations. He does, however, report figures for Catholics and Jews as a whole. The latter figures have been subjected to careful scrutiny as reported in Schwartz (1970:108–110).

27. However, Mueller and Lane (1972:80) note that at least in the 1957 Census Bureau data "the ratios for whites are virtually identical for those for whites and Blacks combined."

28. For a report of figures on rates of Jewish-Gentile marriages in Canada, see Frideres and Goldstein (1974) and Bumpass (1970:254).

29. The exact ratio of valid to nonvalid interreligious marriages among Catholics is not known. However, one study (Burchinal et al., 1962) indicates that in Iowa, at least, from 1953 to 1957, the rates of valid and nonvalid marriages are highly correlated.

30. Again it should be noted that Greeley reports rates for Catholics and Jews as a whole but not for Protestants as a whole. Instead, he reports rates separately for Baptists, Lutherans, Methodists, and Presbyterians. For further criticism of Greeley's study (1971:86–89) of interreligious marriage, see Mueller (1974); see also Greeley's (1974a) response.

31. For discussions of the very scattered studies of ethnic intermarriage among Protestants, see Anderson (1970) on Americans whose origins are British (pp. 24–26), Dutch (p. 91), Finnish (p. 37), German (pp. 84–86), Norwegian (pp. 67–68), Scottish (p. 39), and Swedish (pp. 53–55).

32. Although he does not study friendships per se, mention should also be made of Greeley's study of patterns of social interaction between Catholics and non-Catholics in an upper middle class Irish Catholic parish in suburban Chicago. He finds (1962:61) support for the three-community hypothesis on the basis of "fieldwork observations, distribution of home ownership, intermarriage, norms of social acceptability [among female high school seniors] and choice of recreational [golf club] companionship."

33. Anderson (1968) does not include Mormons in his Protestant group.

34. Anderson (1968:504) calculates the expected rate of interreligious friendships by raising the percent of the given religion in the total city population by a power of three, the number of friends. For example, in the predominately Protestant city, Protestants constitute 70 percent of the population. If friendship selection was a purely random process, only 34 percent (0.70 × 0.70 × 0.70) of the Protestants would report that all three of their closest friends are Protestant.

35. Anderson (1969) analyzes these data still further and finds that the tendency for Protestants to have Protestants as their three closest friends is greater among Protestants in conservative denominations (Lutheran, Baptist and sects) than in liberal denominations (Congregational, Methodist, Episcopalian, Presbyterian, and Christian).

36. The calculation of the percentages of white Protestants, Catholics, and Jews in the total population needed to make the estimate is based on Lenski's

report of the relevant proportions of his total sample (1963:21). The relevant figures are 51 percent white Protestant, 44 percent Catholic and 5 percent Jewish.

37. The various ethnic categories were applied only to Protestants and Catholics, not to Jews. That is, in Laumann's study (1969) all Jews fall into one ethnoreligious group, while Protestants and Catholics are each divided into many.

38. While not presenting the data, Laumann (1972:72) notes that analyses of intermarriage data from his sample indicate that the underlying structures of the choice of friends and wives are quite similar.

39. Laumann (1969:194) observes: "there is some ambiguity with regard to interpreting this 'third factor,' to wit: is it a factor of ethnicity or religious involvement?" He implies that the confounding of *ethnicity* and the *religious* activities and beliefs used to measure religious involvement is so great that one is perfectly justified in calling it either. In either case, Herberg's analysis is challenged. If the factor is interpreted as ethnicity, then Herberg's claim that ethnicity is a residual factor is challenged. If the factor is interpreted as one of religious involvement, then Herberg's view that contemporary religiosity is not one for which differences in religious activities and beliefs are important is challenged. Thus, interpreting the third factor as ethnicity challenges the three-community hypothesis; while interpreting it as religious involvement challenges the assumption underlying the three-generation hypothesis.

40. It should be noted that ethnicity, while important in its own right, is, as Herberg predicts, subordinated to religion. That is, for example, a German Catholic is more apt to befriend a non-German Catholic than a non-Catholic German.

REFERENCES

Abramson, Harold J.
1973   *Ethnic Diversity in Catholic America.* New York: Wiley.

Anderson, Charles H.
1968   "Religious communality among white Protestants, Catholics and Mormons." *Social Forces* 46 (June):501–508.
1969   "Denominational differences in white Protestant communality." *Review of Religious Research* 11 (Fall):66–72.
1970   *White Protestant Americans.* Englewood Cliffs, N.J.: Prentice-Hall.

Barber, Kenneth E.
1967   *An Analysis of Intrafaith and Interfaith Marriage in Indiana.* Ph.D. dissertation, Purdue University.

Bender, Eugene I., and George Kagiwada
1968   "Hansen's Law of Third Generation Return and the study of American religio-ethnic groups." *Phylon* 29 (Winter): 360–370.

Besanceney, Paul H.
1965   "On reporting rates of intermarriage." *American Journal of Sociology* 70 (May):717–721.
1970   *Interfaith Marriage: Who and Why.* New Haven: College and University Press.

Bumpass, Larry
1970   "The trend of interfaith marriage in the United States." *Social Biology* 17 (December):253–259.

Burchinal, Lee G., and Loren E. Chancellor
1962 "Ages at marriage, occupation of grooms and interreligious marriage rates." *Social Forces* 40 (May):348–354.

Burchinal, Lee G., William F. Kenkel, and Loren E. Chancellor
1962 "Comparison of state- and diocese-reported marriage data for Iowa: 1953–57." *American Catholic Sociological Review* 13 (March):21–29.

Cavan, Ruth Shonle
1970 "Concepts and terminology in interreligious marriage." *Journal for the Scientific Study of Religion* 9 (Winter):311–320.

Chancellor, Loren E., and Thomas P. Monahan
1955 "Religious preference and interreligious mixtures in marriage and divorce in Iowa." *American Journal of Sociology* 61 (November): 233–239.

Christensen, Harold T., and Kenneth E. Barber
1967 "Interfaith versus intrafaith marriage in Indiana." *Journal of Marriage and the Family* 29 (August):461–469.

Cohen, Leland B.
1974 "Jewish intermarriage: analysis of the national Jewish population study." Paper delivered to the American Sociological Association, Montreal.

Dashefsky, Arnold
1972 "And the search goes on: the meaning of religioethnic identity and identification." *Sociological Analysis* 33 (Winter):239–245.

Dashefsky, Arnold, and Howard Shapiro
1974 *Ethnic Identification Among American Jews: Socialization and Social Structure.* Lexington, Mass.: Heath.

Francis, E. K.
1947 "The nature of the ethnic group." *American Journal of Sociology* 52 (March):393–400.

Frideres, Jane L., and Jay Ellis Goldstein
1974 "Jewish-Gentile intermarriage: definitions and consequences." *Social Compass* 21 (1): 69–84.

Gallup Opinion Index
1975 *Religion in America: 1975.* Report no. 114. Princeton, N.J.

Gans, Herbert
1956a "American Jewry: present and future. Part I: present." *Commentary* 21 (May):422–430.
1956b "The future of American Jewry: II." *Commentary* 21 (June):555–563.

Glaser, Daniel
1958 "Dynamics of ethnic identification." *American Sociological Review* 23 (February):31–40.

Glazer, Nathan, and Daniel Patrick Moynihan
1963 *Beyond the Melting Pot.* Cambridge: M.I.T. Press and Harvard University Press.
1975 Editors, *Ethnicity: Theory and Experience.* Cambridge: Harvard University Press.

Glick, Paul C.
1960 "Intermarriage and fertility patterns among persons in major religious groups." *Eugenics Quarterly* 7 (March):31–38.

Goering, John M.
1970 "The emergence of ethnic interests: a case of serendipity." *Social Forces* 49 (March):379–384.

Goldstein, Sidney, and Calvin Goldscheider
1968 *Jewish Americans.* Englewood Cliffs, N.J.: Prentice-Hall.

Gordon, Milton M.
1961 "Assimilation in America: theory and reality." *Daedalus* 90 (Spring): 263–285.
1964 *Assimilation in American Life.* New York: Oxford University Press.

Greeley, Andrew M.
1962 "Some aspects of interaction between religious groups in an upper middle-class Roman Catholic parish." *Social Compass* 9 (1):39–61.
1970 "Religious intermarriage in a denominational society." *American Journal of Sociology* 75 (July):949–952.
1971 *Why Can't They Be Like Us?* New York: Dutton.
1972 *The Denominational Society.* Glenview, Ill.: Scott, Foresman.
1974a "Andrew Greeley replies to his critics." *Journal for the Scientific Study of Religion* 13 (June): 228–232.
1974b "Political participation among ethnic groups in the United States: a preliminary reconnaissance." *American Journal of Sociology* 80 (July):170–204.

Greeley, Andrew M., and Peter H. Rossi
1968 *The Education of Catholic Americans.* Garden City, N.Y.: Doubleday (Anchor Books).

Gulick, John
1965 "The religious structure of Lebanese culture." *International Yearbook for the Sociology of Religion* 1:151–187.

Handlin, Oscar
1951 *The Uprooted.* Boston: Little, Brown.
1954 *The American People in the Twentieth Century.* Cambridge: Harvard University Press.

Hansen, Marcus Lee
1938 *The Problem of the Third Generation Immigrant.* Rock Island, Ill.: Augustana Historical Society.
1952 "The third generation is America." *Commentary* 14 (November): 492–500.

Heiss, Jerold S.
1960 "Premarital characteristics of the religiously intermarried in an urban area." *American Sociological Review* 25 (February):47–55.

Herberg, Will
1960 *Protestant—Catholic—Jew.* Garden City, N.Y.: Doubleday (Anchor Books).

Hollingshead, August B.
1950 "Cultural factors in the selection of marriage mates." *American Sociological Review* 15 (October):619–627.

Kennedy, Ruby Jo Reeves
1944 "Single or triple melting pot? intermarriage trends in New Haven: 1870–1940." *American Journal of Sociology* 49 (January):331–339.

1952 "Single or triple melting pot? intermarriage trends in New Haven: 1870–1950." *American Journal of Sociology* 58 (July):56–59.

Koenig, Samuel
1952 "Second and third generation Americans." In *One America*, edited by Francis J. Brown and Joseph S. Roucek. Englewood Cliffs, N.J.: Prentice-Hall.

Kuhn, Manford, and Thomas S. McPartland
1954 "An empirical investigation of self-attitude." *American Sociological Review* 19 (February):68–76.

Laumann, Edward O.
1969 "The social structure of religious and ethno-religious groups in a metropolitan community." *American Sociological Review* 34 (April): 182–197.
1972 *Bonds of Pluralism.* New York: Wiley.

Lazerwitz, Bernard
1970 "Contrasting the effects of generation, class, sex and age on group identification in the Jewish and Protestant communities." *Social Forces* 49 (September):50–59.
1973 "Religious identification and its ethnic correlates: a multivariate model." *Social Forces* 52 (December):204–220.

Lazerwitz, Bernard, and Louis Rowitz
1964 "The three generation hypothesis." *American Journal of Sociology* 69 (March):529–538.

Lenski, Gerhard
1963 *The Religious Factor.* Garden City, N.Y.: Doubleday (Anchor Books).

Lijphart, Arend
1968 *The Politics of Accommodation: Pluralism and Democracy in the Netherlands.* University of California Press.

Mead, Margaret
1942 *And Keep Your Powder Dry.* New York: Morrow.

Moberg, David O.
1961 "Social differentiation in the Netherlands." *Social Forces* 39 (May): 333–337.

Monahan, Thomas P.
1971 "The extent of interdenomination marriage in the United States." *Journal for the Scientific Study of Religion* 10 (Summer):85–92.
1973 "Some dimensions of interreligious marriages in Indiana: 1962–67." *Social Forces* 52 (December): 195–203.

Mueller, Samuel A.
1971 "The new triple melting pot: Herberg revisited." *Review of Religious Research* 13 (Fall):18–33.
1974 "The empirical point of view: review essay on the sociology of Andrew Greeley." *Journal for the Scientific Study of Religion* 13 (March):90–97.

Mueller, Samuel A., and Angela V. Lane
1972 "Tabulations from the 1957 current population survey on religion." *Journal for the Scientific Study of Religion* 11 (March):76–98.

Nelsen, Hart M.
1973 "Intellectualism and religious attendance of metropolitan residents." *Journal for the Scientific Study of Religion* 12 (September): 285–296.

Nelsen, Hart M., and H. David Allen
1974   "Ethnicity, Americanization, and religious attendance." *American Journal of Sociology* 79 (January):906–922.
Newman, William M.
1973   *American Pluralism.* New York: Harper & Row.
Pavlak, Thomas J.
1973   "Social class, ethnicity and racial prejudice." *Public Opinion Quarterly* 37 (Summer):225–231.
Plax, Martin
1972   "On studying ethnicity." *Public Opinion Quarterly* 36 (Spring):99–104.
Reiss, Paul
1965   "The trend in interfaith marriage." *Journal for the Scientific Study of Religion* 5 (Fall):64–67.
Rodman, Hyman
1965   "Technical note on two rates of mixed marriage." *American Sociological Review* 30 (October):770–778.
Rosenthal, Erich
1963   "Studies of Jewish intermarriages in the United States." *American Jewish Yearbook* 64:3–53.
1967   "Jewish intermarriage in Indiana." *American Jewish Yearbook* 68: 243–264.
1968   "Jewish intermarriage in Indiana." *Eugenics Quarterly* 15 (December): 277–287.
Schwartz, A.
1970   "Intermarriage in the United States." *American Jewish Yearbook* 71: 101–121.
Sharot, Stephen
1973   "The three-generation thesis and the American Jews." *British Journal of Sociology* 24 (June):151–164.
Stark, Rodney, and Charles Glock
1968   *American Piety: The Nature of Religious Commitment.* University of California Press.
Thomas, John L.
1951   "The factor of religion in the selection of marriage mates." *American Sociological Review* 16 (August): 487–492.
U.S. Bureau of the Census
1971   "Characteristics of the population by ethnic origin: November, 1964." *Current Population Reports,* ser. P-20, no. 221.
Wagner, Carol
1970   "Religious intermarriage in the United States and Canada." Paper, Department of Sociology, Indiana University as cited in Mueller (1971).
Wilensky, Harold, and Jack Ladinsky
1967   "From religious community to occupational group: structural assimilation among professors, lawyers and engineers." *American Sociological Review* 32 (August):541–561.
Winch, Robert F.
1963   *The Modern Family,* rev. ed. New York: Holt, Rinehart and Winston.
Yinger, J. Milton
1968   "A research note on interfaith marriage statistics." *Journal for the Scientific Study of Religion* 7 (Spring):97–103.
1970   *The Scientific Study of Religion.* New York: Macmillan.

Tensions in Church-State Relations in the United States:
The three-community system and the constitution

The empirical evidence presented in the previous chapter, while not confirming all of the details of the three-community hypothesis, generally supports Herberg's view of American society as containing a system involving the "stable co-existence of three equi-legitimate religious communities" (1960:259). The evidence presented indicates that at least the Protestant and Catholic communities are further subdivided into ethnic communities, and, thus, the more complete picture is one of *ethno*religious communities rather than merely one of *religious* communities. Still, whether associated with ethnicity (national origin) or not, religion is shown to be an important and even basic determinant of the boundaries of primary relationships in American society. Thus, the evidence is compatible with Herberg's depiction (1960:259) of religion "as a basic form of American 'belonging' " and supports the view that religion is a crucial factor in the self-identification and self-location of Americans.

The crucial role of religion in self-identification and self-location in the United States is a source of potential tension in church-state relations and may even pose a challenge to the maintenance of the separation between church and state, which Americans traditionally cherish. Specifically, the role of religion in self-identification sets into motion processes which may call for the establishment of religion or for prohibitions on the free exercise of religion in contravention of the First Amendment. Such implications or processes may flow first from the tendency inherent in the three-community system for religion to be viewed as good and acceptable and for irreligion to be viewed as neither good nor acceptable. They may also flow from the question of the status of religious and irreligious individuals and groups who remain outside any of the three equilegitimate communities. If those outside the three religious communities are not as legitimate and acceptable as those within them, America will have moved toward the establishment of a religion, albeit a tripartite religion, and toward the restriction of the religious liberties of those who are not Protestants, Catholics, or Jews.

This chapter identifies and discusses sources of potential tension between the norms of the three-community system and the tradition of church-state separation. First the chapter focusses on tensions rooted in the preference for religion over irreligion and inherent in the three-community system. Then it focusses on the question of the legitimacy of those who remain outside the three religious communities. The discussions focus on relevant Supreme Court cases and decisions, following a long and honored tradition within sociology of examining legal codes for clues to the underlying normative structure of a given society. This tradition dates, at least, from the original publication in 1893 of Durkheim's study of the division of labor (1961). The application of that tradition to the study of American society has been supported by Hammond (1974:129), who observes that "an expanding judiciary in American history . . . has adopted the task of articulating the collective moral architecture," that is, of articulating America's normative structure.

Of course, in focussing on Supreme Court cases, there is no implication or claim that the law, even as interpreted by the Supreme Court, is automatically or always followed. Indeed, there is evidence that such is not the case with decisions of the Court on matters pertaining to religion.[1] Nevertheless, a review of relevant Court decisions could yield insight into potential tensions between the norms underlying the three-community system and the traditional American values favoring the separation of church and state.[2] Such insights cannot take the place of needed empirical studies; however, they can prove useful in guiding the conduct of such studies. It is in hopes of finding suggestions and insights, rather than definitive facts, that attention is turned to Supreme Court decisions in the discussions which follow.

236

Religion, Irreligion, and the Schools

As indicated above, one source of potential tension between the three-community system and the separation of church and state called for by cherished American traditions is the preference for religion over irreligion inherent in a central tenet of the three-community system. This tenet holds (Herberg, 1960:40) that

> unless one is either a Protestant, or a Catholic, or a Jew, one is a "nothing"; to be a "something," to have a name, one must identify oneself to oneself, and be identified by others, as belonging to one or another of the three great religious communities in which the American people are divided.

According to Herberg (1960:84), since religion is the basis for being something rather than nothing, "religion is a 'good thing,' a supremely 'good thing' for the individual." Inasmuch as Protestantism, Catholicism, and Judaism serve equally well, " 'religion' here means not so much any particular religion" but "religion as such, religion-in-general." The three-community system merely prefers religion to irreligion; that is, it supports a faith in religion, a belief that religion is good and acceptable, and irreligion is not. Thus as Herberg notes (1960:257), the "picture that emerges is one in which religion is accepted as a normal part of the American Way of Life."[3] Moreover, "the American faith in religion implies . . . that every right-minded citizen is religious" (Herberg, 1960:266). That is, no right-minded citizen is irreligious, and no irreligious citizen is right-minded. Furthermore, given the American faith in religion engendered by the three-community system, being irreligious may connote as Herberg (1960:258) says, "being obscurely 'un-American,' as is the case with those who declare themselves atheists, agnostics, or even 'humanist.' " Moreover, what is held to be good for the individual is generalized as being good for the nation. That is, the American "faith in religion involves the conviction . . . that every decent and virtuous nation is religious; that religion is the true basis of national existence" (Herberg, 1960:265–266). Both the good individual and the good nation are held to be religious, and, more generally, religion itself is held to be a good thing. Religion is seen as the source of other good things, and is the basis of being something or somebody rather than nothing or nobody. All in all, the three-community system as described by Herberg implies that religion is good and acceptable and irreligion, bad and unacceptable.[4] Interestingly, however, attempts to implement the preference for religion over irreligion could involve an illegitimate breach of the wall of separation which Americans seek to maintain between church and state.

According to the Supreme Court, as it ruled in the landmark *Everson* case [(330 U.S. 1 (1947)] as reprinted in Tussman (1962:210), the "wall between church and state . . . must be high and impregnable." Furthermore, under the Constitution, the Court held (see Tussman, 1962:210), that

> neither a state nor the Federal Government can . . . pass laws which aid one religion, aid all religion, or prefer one religion over another. Neither can force . . . a person . . . to prefer a belief or disbelief in any religion. No person can be punished for entertaining or professing religious beliefs or disbeliefs.

If there is a preference for religion over irreligion inherent in the three-community system, it would appear to be one which could not be legally enforced. Rather than preferring religion to irreligion, the Court held, in the *Everson* case (quoted in Tussman, 1962:211), that government must "be a neutral in its relations with groups of religious believers and non-believers." Insofar as the Supreme Court interprets basic American values, religion is not necessarily preferred to irreligion, or at least not officially. Ironically, then, if Americans sought to enforce the notion inherent in the three-community system that irreligion is somehow un-American, they might themselves be acting in an un-American fashion, threatening the cherished separation between church and state by inappropriately seeking to establish religion over irreligion in America. Such a threat is greatly reduced if religion is confined to the role assigned it by the three-community system, the role of serving as the basis for determining the boundaries of primary relationships such as in family and friendship circles (see Chap. 7). Since such relationships do not generally involve federal or state government, the separation of church and state is not much affected. Families may thrive and friendships come and go with very little, if any, involvement of government officials or regulations. Although the maintenance of the three-community system may continue without any significant involvement of the state, the potential for challenges or threats to the separation of church and state do exist.

The primary area of challenges or threats is the role or place of religion in America's schools. It is unclear as to whether the schools should be considered (1) simply an arena for secondary relationships and, thus, outside the ambit of the three community system, or (2) at least partly a setting for primary relationships and, thus, within the ambit of the system (see pp. 204ff.). In addition to being the setting for the beginning of many a friendship, schools are often thought of as *neighborhood* institutions. As part of the neighborhood they are part of a most important arena for face-to-face intimate primary relationships.[5] If schools are considered to be related to networks of primary relationships, then it is reasonable to expect, at least in matters dealing with the schools, that the three-community system could threaten the separation of church and state. It could be expected that there would be pressure to establish a role for religion in American schools. At a minimum, such pressure might call for the use of the public school system to aid religious instruction, at least to the point of supporting the preference for religion over irreligion if not to further the child's identification with his respective religious community. At a maximum, such pressure might call for support of a parochial or religiously differentiated school system in the interest of furthering self-identification and self-location within the boundaries of the three-community system.[6] Such pressures are indeed evident. Moreover, they have been dealt with directly and indirectly in Supreme Court cases in the post-World War II era during which the three-community system has been developing. The sets of cases dealing (1) with pressure for the use of the public school system to aid religious instruction[7] and (2) with aid to parochial schools are examined below.

Religion, irreligion, and the public schools. The Supreme Court has issued four landmark decisions covering five cases dealing with pressures to use the public schools to aid religious instruction: *McCollum* v. *Board of Education* [(330 U.S. 203, (1948)], reprinted in Tussman (1962: 241–264); *Zorach* v. *Clauson* [(343 U.S. 306, (1952)], reprinted in Tussman (1962: 264–274); *Engel* v. *Vitale* [(370 U.S. 421, (1962), in United States Supreme Court, 1963: 601–619]; *Abington School District* v. *Schempp* [(374 U.S. 203, (1963) in United States Supreme Court, 1964: 844–914].[8] The ruling in the last case also decided the case of *Murray* v. *Curlett*.

The issue in the first two cases is the constitutionality of released-time programs, which permit students to be released from regular secular classes to spend time in religious instruction. In the *McCollum* case, the released-time religious instruction program took place on public school property and involved an expenditure of public funds. In the *Zorach* case, the program did neither. The absence of use of public property and funds is important to the Court. The issue in the second pair of decisions is the constitutionality of religious exercises as part of a regular school program. In the *Engel* case, the exercise was the recitation of a prayer composed by the Board of Regents which governed the schools; in the *Murray* case (included in the *Schempp* decision), it was recitation of the Lord's Prayer; and in the *Schempp* case, the recitation of Bible passages. In each case, the practice in question was thought of as nondenominational in that it recognized the claims of Protestants, Catholics, and Jews alike. The program at issue in the *McCollum* case resulted from what the Court called the efforts of "interested members of the Jewish, Roman Catholic and a few of the Protestant faiths [who] formed a voluntary association called the Champaign [Illinois] Council on Religious Education" (quoted in Tussman, 1962:243). The programs in question, in other words, are examples of a system of the stable coexistence of three equally legitimate religious communities. Nevertheless, the Court ruled that only the program at issue in the *Zorach* case (in which public property and funds were not used) was constitutional. Although the programs in the other cases were declared unconstitutional, the decisions do not directly contravene the norms of the three-community system. To the contrary, they are, to some extent, supportive of them. From the standpoint of the norms of the American three-community system, the matter of religious instruction and of religious exercises in the public schools bears on two fundamental norms. First, they are relevant to the norm which confines religion largely to its role in determining the boundaries of primary relationships. This norm does not require, and indeed generally forbids, the involvement of religion in the secondary relationships of government and business. Second, the decisions in question are relevant to the norm which calls for a preference for religion over irreligion. The import of the Court's decisions for each of these norms is discussed below.

As noted earlier, it is not clear whether the schools are part of a network of primary relationships or secondary relationships. In fact, the schools involve elements of both. On the one hand, the legal or formal status of the schools is fundamentally that of an agency of government. As such, the schools are an aspect of the secondary relationships within American social structure. On the other hand, the informal or extralegal status of the school is often a part of the network of primary relationships involving family, friends, and neighborhood. In deciding the cases at issue here, the Court viewed the schools entirely in their role as agencies of government. It considered only their legal status, which involves secondary relationships, ignoring their role in primary relationships. In ruling that religion had no place in the schools, the Court was saying that religion had no place in a network of secondary relationships. Such a decision is compatible with the norms of the three-community system, which, as noted above, confines the role of religion within the network of primary relationships but excludes it from secondary relationships. Thus, the norms of the three-community system were not contravened when the Court ruled in the *Engel* case that "in this country it is no part of the business of government to compose official prayers for any group of the American people to recite as a part of religious program carried on by government" (United States Supreme Court, 1963:604). Moreover, the norms of the three-community system are not contravened when, by extension, it is held that it is no part of the business of government to select prayers or Bible passages for recitation or to finance religious instruction.

The norms of the three-community system are compatible with the decision in the *Zorach* case which held that since the religious instruction did not take place on school property and did not involve public funds, it was not a government program and therefore was not unconstitutional. Both the Court and the norms of the three-community system recognize that religion may play a role so long as government is not involved. More importantly, the *Zorach* decision gives some support to the second norm of the three-community system, the view that religion is good and acceptable. In the *Zorach* decision, the Court pronounced that "we are a religious people whose institutions presuppose a Supreme Being" (quoted in Tussman, 1962:267). A similar pronouncement is found in the *Schempp* ruling where it is held that "today, as in the beginning, our national life reflects a religious people" (United States Supreme Court, 1964:853). Moreover, in the *Zorach* case, the Court added (quoted in Tussman, 1962:268):

> When the state encourages religious instruction or cooperates with religious authorities by adjusting the schedule of public events to sectarian needs, it follows the best of our traditions. For it then respects the *religious nature of our people*. . . . To hold that it may not would be to find in the Constitution a requirement that government show a callous indifference to religious groups. That would be preferring those who believe in no religion over those who do believe. . . . We find no constitutional requirement which makes it necessary for government to be hostile to religion and to throw its weight against efforts to widen the effective scope of religious influence [italics added].

In speaking of Americans as a religious people and in referring to the religious nature of our people the *Zorach* decision lends support to the tendency of the three-community system to picture religion as a normal part of the American way of life. However, the Court stops short of preferring religion to irreligion. The *Zorach* decision does not contradict the earlier *Everson* ruling calling for government to be neutral as between religion and irreligion. The earlier ruling was *not* a call for a neutrality of equal hostility; indeed, *Zorach* specifically enjoins government against any hostility toward religion, an injunction also found in the *McCollum* ruling, which noted (quoted in Tussman, 1962: 244) that manifestation of "a governmental hostility to religion or religious teachings . . . would be at war with our national tradition." A similarly protective attitude toward religion is found in the *Engel* ruling, where it was held (United States Supreme Court, 1963:610) that "the First Amendment, which tried to put an end to governmental control of religion and of prayer, was not written to destroy either." In sum, the Court's decisions on cases involving the use of the school system to aid religion do not contravene the norms of the three-community system. Indeed, they lend it some support, as is perhaps most evident in the closing paragraphs of the *Schempp* decision (United States Supreme Court, 1964:880–881) which held:

> The place of religion in our society is an exalted one, achieved through a long tradition of reliance on the home, the church and the inviolable citadel of the individual heart and mind.

In so speaking the Court lends support to the tendencies of the three-community system to exalt and praise religion and its place in American society while confining its role to the dynamics of networks of primary relationships such as those found in the home, the church and the intimate relations involving the individual heart and mind.

State aid to parochial schools. Since World War II, during the period when the three-community system has been developing, the Supreme Court has evaluated legislation resulting from pressures for state support of parochial or religiously differentiated school systems in eight different opinions.[9] The first of these opinions came in the *Everson* case. The Court, while expressing deep concern about keeping the "wall between church and state . . . high and impregnable" (Tussman, 1962: 212), nevertheless affirmed the constitutionality of a New Jersey statute authorizing the expenditure of public funds to reimburse parents for the cost of bus transportation in sending their children to parochial schools.[10] Twenty-one years later, the Court similarly affirmed the constitutionality of a New York statute which required public schools to lend secular textbooks free of charge to all students in grades seven to twelve, including those attending parochial schools (see *Board of Education* v. *Allen*, 392 U.S. 236 (1968), in United States Supreme Court, 1969a:1060–1081). Three years after that, however, the Court struck down as unconstitutional laws in Rhode Island and Pennsylvania which provided state aid to elementary and secondary parochial schools and to their teachers for instruction in secular matters (see *Lemon* v. *Kurtzman*, 403 U.S. 602, (1971), in United States Supreme Court, 1972b: 745–789).

Other programs for providing financial support for elementary and secondary parochial schools or their students were struck down as unconstitutional in three related but separate opinions at the close of the 1972–1973 Court term, although a fourth decision upheld the constitutionality of a program of aid to a church-related college. The three programs which were declared unconstitutional were as follows: In *Committee for Public Education and Religious Liberty* v. *Nyquist*, the

Court struck down a New York statute which provided for direct money grants for the maintenance and repair of parochial school facilities and equipment (413 U.S. 756 (1973), in United States Supreme Court, 1974:948–992). The *Nyquist* decision, and that of *Sloan* v. *Lemon* (413 U.S. 825 (1973), in United States Supreme Court, 1974:939–947) also struck down programs which provided for reimbursement from state funds to parents for tuition expenses incurred by sending their children to elementary or secondary parochial schools. In addition, the Court declared unconstitutional the New York state law providing state reimbursement of parochial schools for costs incurred in giving tests and keeping records required by the state (*Levitt* v. *Committee for Public Education and Religious Liberty*, 413 U.S. 472, (1973), in United States Supreme Court, 1974:736–744).

In the fourth case, *Hunt* v. *McNair* (413 U.S. 724 (1973), in United States Supreme Court, 1974:923–930), the Court upheld as constitutional a South Carolina law which involves the state's issuing revenue bonds for the benefit of the Baptist College in Charleston. The bond issuance did not include any buildings or facilities to be used for religious purposes. Finally, the Court has recently reaffirmed the constitutionality of a program, like the one involved in the *Allen* ruling, which provided for loans of secular textbooks to students in nonpublic schools, including those attending parochial schools (see *Meek et al.* v. *Pittinger et al.*, United States Supreme Court, 1975). However, in the same decision the Court struck down as unconstitutional programs which would have provided for the loan of other instructional materials and equipment, such as audiovisual aids and laboratory paraphernalia. In addition, the Court also declared unconstitutional programs providing so-called auxiliary services (e.g., guidance counseling, testing, remedial and accelerated instruction, speech and hearing services) to students of parochial schools on their school's premises.

The primary concern of the Court in all eight opinions has been to define just what constitutes a "law respecting the establishment of religion," a law which the Constitution, through the First and Fourteenth Amendments, forbids either the federal government or a state to make. By the time of the *Nyquist* decision in 1973, after over a quarter of a century of struggling with the problem, the Court (1974: 962) announced,

> . . . it is now firmly established that a law may be one "respecting the establishment of religion" even though the consequence is not to promote a "state religion," . . . and even though it does not aid one religion more than another but merely benefits all religions alike.

In so doing, the Court affirmed the doctrine of the separation of church and state, although earlier, in *Lemon* v. *Kurtzman*, it (1972b:756) had noted that "prior holdings do not call for total separation between church and state" and that "the line of separation, far from being a 'wall,' is a blurred, indistinct and variable barrier depending on all the circumstances of a particular relationship" (1972b:757). Thus, it is possible that "not every law that confers an 'indirect,' 'remote,' or 'incidental' benefit upon religious institutions is, for that reason alone, constitutionally invalid" as the Court (1974:962) said in the *Nyquist* decision. In its assessment of "all the circumstances of a particular relationship" for a determination of whether or not the barrier between church and state has been overstepped and whether the benefits it provides are constitutionally valid or invalid the Court has devised three tests or guidelines. However, it cautions (United States Supreme Court, 1975:8) that "the tests must not be viewed as setting the precise limits to the necessary constitutional inquiry, but serve only as guidelines." The tests (1975:8) are:

> First, the statute must have a secular legislative purpose. . . . Second, it must have a "primary effect" that neither advances nor inhibits religion. . . . Third, the statute and its administration must avoid excessive government entanglement with religion. . . .

In devising and defining these three tests of what constitutes a "law respecting the establishment of religion" the Court has not, of course, contravened any norm of the three-community system. To the contrary, the Court has merely refined the conception of the barriers surrounding a class of relationships, namely, the secondary relationships involving government, which the three-community system also forbids religion to intrude upon. Consequently, if there is popular disapproval with the Court decisions, it may simply reflect disagreement as to where the barrier lies, rather than disagreement over the legitimacy of erecting such a barrier somewhere.

The Court itself has occasionally supported the erection of such a barrier on the grounds that doing so minimizes the potential for civil or political strife along religious lines, which may accompany attempts by one or another religious group to gain or maintain government support of its institutions. For example, in the *Everson* case, the Court briefly reviewed the history of "turmoil, civil strife, and persecution, generated in large part by established sects determined to maintain their absolute political and religious supremacy" (Tussman, 1962:207–208). In *Lemon* v. *Kurtzman*, the Court observed (1972b:761) that

> . . . political division along religious lines was one of the principal evils against which the First Amendment was intended to protect. . . . The potential divisiveness of such conflict is a threat to the normal political process.

244

A concern over "the potential for political divisiveness related to religious belief and practice" was echoed in *Nyquist* (1974:976) and *Meek* (1975:22).[11] The expression of such concerns marks something of a departure from the exaltation and praise of religion inherent in the three-community system. The Court is at least noting that whatever the benefits of religion in general, religious differences are not necessarily beneficial when intruded into the political arena and may indeed bring quite harmful results.

However, despite its fears over potentially divisive political struggles over government support for parochial schools, the Court has not criticized or disapproved of the existence of parochial schools per se. To the contrary, the Court has said, "nothing we have said can be construed to disparage the role of church-related elementary and secondary schools in our national life. Their contribution has been and is enormous" (United States Supreme Court, 1972b:762–763).

The right of students to attend parochial schools, first affirmed in 1925 (see *Pierce* v. *Society of Sisters*, in Tussman, 1962:45–49), does not appear to be in jeopardy, certainly, not from a Court which believes (United States Supreme Court, 1974:975) that "certainly private parochial schools have contributed importantly" to raising levels of "knowledge, competency and experience." Nevertheless, while not challenging the legitimacy of parochial schools per se, but only that of some forms of state aid to them, the Court may have created what dissenting Justices in *Lemon* v. *Kurtzman* called "an insoluble paradox for the State and the parochial schools" (1972b:787). The paradox is created, they argue (United States Supreme Court, 1972b: 787), because

> the State cannot finance secular instruction if it permits religion to be taught in the same classroom; but if it exacts a promise that religion not be so taught—a promise the school and its teachers are quite willing and on this record able to give—and enforces it, it is then entangled in the "no entanglement" aspect of the Court's Establishment Clause jurisprudence.

No similar paradox, however, faces those seeking to find a place for religion itself within the confines of American society. Here the admonitions of the Constitution are held to be clear. Even though the Court has held that "religious values pervade the fabric of our national life" (1972b:762), it adds (United States Supreme Court, 1972b:763):

> Under our system the choice has been made that government is to be entirely excluded from the area of religious instruction and churches excluded from the affairs of government. *The Constitution decrees that religion must be a private matter for the individual, the*

family and the institutions of private choice, and that while some involvement and entanglement are inevitable, lines must be drawn [italics added].

The norm of the three-community system providing a role for religion in primary relationships (the arenas of the family and private or personal choice) but not in secondary relationships (politics or government) has been given the sanction of the Constitution by the Supreme Court itself. Thus, the potential for tension between the norm of the three-community system and the cherished tradition of the separation of church and state has been dealt with by the Court without serious threat to either.

The potential for tension between the norm of the three-community system which prefers religion to irreligion and the tradition of church-state separation has been dealt with somewhat differently from that pertaining to secondary relationships. The Court, while noting the exalted place of religion in American society in general, has nevertheless issued pronouncements which require government to be neutral as between religion and irreligion. In effect, the Court has agreed with the three-community system that religion is good and acceptable, but disagrees with the notion that irreligion must be seen as bad and unacceptable. Thus, the tendency of the three-community system to prefer religion over irreligion has not been given Constitutional sanction. The next section examines Court opinions which pertain to the preference for religion over irreligion, as well as the question of whether full legitimacy is to be extended only to those who are members of one of the branches of the three-community system and not to those outside the system.

The Court and Those Outside the Three-Community System

The norms of the three-community system clearly regard those who do not identify with any of the three religious communities as unorthodox. However, the consequences of being unorthodox are not entirely clear. They may simply be that an unorthodox person remains generally unmentioned, ignored, and shunned as a nothing by those who identify themselves as Protestants, Catholics, or Jews. Such a person may be regarded "as being foreign, as in the case when one professes oneself a Buddhist, a Muslim, or anything but a Protestant, Catholic or Jew, even where one's Americanness is otherwise beyond question," as Herberg notes (1960:257–258) or as "obscurely un-American," as in the case of atheists, agnostics, or humanists (see Herberg, 1960:258).

246

If the plight of those who remain outside the three-community system involves no more than being the objects of name-calling or being ignored and shunned by private citizens in their private capacities, no constitutional issue, no question of the separation of church and state is involved. However, the unorthodox in America do, at least occasionally, find themselves involved in disputes with government officials or government regulations.[12] These disputes have implications for defining the proper relationship between church and state in America. More importantly, from the perspective of this chapter, these disputes have provided occasions to determine if full legitimacy in America is extended only to Protestant, Catholic, and Jewish members of the three-community system or if it extends beyond to the religiously unorthodox outside the system. That is, these disputes have provided occasions for insight into whether the United States is merely a system of three equally legitimate religious communities, or one of greater variety, where legitimacy is also granted to other religious and nonreligious communities and individuals.

One of the clearest instances of a dispute involving the rights or legitimacy of the claims of somebody outside the three-community system came in the case of *Torcaso* v. *Watkins* (367 U.S. 488 (1961), in United States Supreme Court, 1962: 982–988). The appellant in the case, Roy R. Torcaso, had been appointed to the office of notary public by the governor of Maryland. However, he was refused a commission because he would not declare his belief in God as required by a provision of the Maryland state constitution. The Court ordered Torcaso to be given his commission as a notary public and installed in office. The reason for the judgment was (United States Supreme Court, 1962:987) in part, that

> . . . neither a State nor the Federal Government . . . can constitutionally pass laws or impose requirements which aid all religions as against nonbelievers and neither can aid those religions based on a belief in the existence of God as against those religions founded on different beliefs.

The ruling was also based on the logic of the Court's opinion in the *Everson* case (Tussman, 1962:204–212) and others discussed above, which call for government to treat not only all religions, but religion and irreligion equally. In the *Everson* opinion, it was held (see Tussman, 1962:211) that the Constitution forbids the exclusion of "Catholics, Lutherans, Mohammedans, Baptists, Jews, Methodists, Non-believers, Presbyterians, or the members of any other faith, because of their faith, or lack of it, from receiving benefits of public welfare legislation." The Court has held, in effect, that those who are unorthodox from the standpoint of the three-community system are nonetheless entitled

247

to equal treatment before the law. That is, the American system under the Constitution is not merely a system of three equally legitimate religious communities, namely, Protestants, Catholics, and Jews. Those outside the three-community system are guaranteed equal treatment before the law. Their legitimacy is equal to that of those within the system.

Nevertheless, disputes still arise between the religiously unorthodox and the state. However, these disputes generally do not involve claims to public office, nor do they generally involve claims to benefits from public welfare legislation. In short, they do not generally fall within the specific categories dealt with in the *Torcaso* and *Everson* cases. To the contrary, contemporary disputes between the religiously unorthodox and the state generally involve claims that the unorthodox should, by virtue of their religious or nonreligious beliefs, be exempted from some obligation created by a given government regulation or law, such as the obligation of an adult to perform military service or of a child to attend school.[13] That is, the religiously unorthodox have claimed that where their beliefs forbid their meeting obligations created by law, requiring them to do so would be tantamout to denying them equality with the religiously orthodox. However, it should be clear that the unorthodox are not necessarily claiming that there is any direct or intentional effort at religiously based oppression or discrimination between the orthodox and the unorthodox. The conflict between the unorthodox and the State may result from unintended and indirect consequences of a law or regulation enacted for purely secular reasons. Nevertheless, laws or regulations may come into conflict with some unorthodox belief or practice. As shall be shown in the cases to which we now turn, the attempts of the Supreme Court to resolve such indirect conflict between government-established secular obligations and unorthodox religious beliefs or practices throw some light on the extent to which the rights of the unorthodox are protected.

Perhaps the classic illustration of such indirect conflict between secular governmental regulation and an unorthodox religion is the controversy over the Mormon practice of polygamy in the late nineteenth century. In the late 1870s, Congress enacted legislation against polygamy which applied to the Territory of Utah, where the great majority of Mormons then lived.[14] Mormon doctrine, however, permitted polygamy. George Reynolds, a Mormon, was convicted of violating the antipolygamy law and his case eventually reached the Supreme Court. The Court upheld his conviction (see *Reynolds* v. *United States*, 98 U.S. 145, 1879, reprinted in Tussman, 1962:20–27). Moreover, in doing so, the Court claimed that there had been no unconstitutional restriction of Reynolds' free exercise of his religion. The basis for the Court's claim lay in the distinction it made between religious belief and religiously inspired action. The former it acknowledged was beyond the legitimate scope of governmental concern. However, the latter could be the subject of legislative prohibition if such prohibition is in pursuit of an otherwise legitimate secular end. The Court held that (Tussman, 1962:23–24), "congress was deprived of all legislative power over mere opinion, but was left free to reach actions which were in violation of social duties or subversive of good order."[15] That is, as the Court explained (Tussman, 1962:25),

> laws are made for the government of action, and while they cannot interfere with mere religious beliefs and opinions, they may with practices. Suppose one believed that human sacrifices were a necessary part of religious worship, would it be seriously contended that the civil government under which he lived could not interfere to prevent a sacrifice? . . . Can a man excuse his practices to the contrary [of law] because of his religious belief? To permit this would be to make the professed doctrines of religious belief superior to the law of the land, and in effect to permit every citizen to become a law unto himself. Government could exist only in name under such circumstances.

In short, religious practices, but not belief, could be restricted on the basis of an otherwise valid secular regulation of government. To do otherwise would be to prefer religious doctrines to the secular law of the land.

Nearly a century later, however, in another case of conflict between secular regulations and a religiously based practice (*Yoder* v. *Wisconsin*, 466 U.S. 205 (1972), in United States Supreme Court, 1973:15–44), the Court found that there were occasions when, under the Constitution, it was required to prefer religious doctrine over secular law. One such occasion arose when three Amish men, Jonas Yoder, Wallace Miller, and Adin Yutzy, refused for religious reasons to have their children continue their formal education after completion of the eight grades of their Amish-run schools. The state of Wisconsin required such attendance under its compulsory school attendance law. In the *Yoder* case, the Court noted (1973:28) that "in this context belief and action cannot be neatly confined to logic-tight compartments." The Court found that it could not and should not apply the findings of the *Reynolds* case, nearly a century old, to the instance of conflict between secular regulations and action stemming from the tenets of the Amish religion.

The Amish, or Pennsylvania Dutch as they are often called, can trace their origins to the sixteenth century Swiss Anabaptists who, the Court acknowledged (1973:22), "sought to return to the early, simple, Christian life de-emphasizing material success, rejecting the competitive spirit, and seeking to insulate themselves from the modern world." The Court further acknowledged (1973:22) that the "concept of life aloof from the world and its values is central to their faith." Moreover, the Amish refusal to send their children to school beyond the eighth grade was based on that concept. That is, the Amish, as the Court recognized, (1973:22), "view secondary school education as an impermissable exposure of their children to a 'worldly' influence in conflict with their beliefs." In addition, expert testimony before the Court held that "compulsory high school attendance . . . would . . . result in the destruction of the . . . Amish church community as it exists in the United States today" (United States Supreme Court, 1973:23).

The Amish live for the most part on self-contained and self-sufficient farms in rural America.[16] The conduct of their life, as the Court said (1973:22), "is regulated in great detail by the Ordnung, or rules, of the church community." Since the community is economically and socially self-contained and self-sufficient, the Amish, even though doctrinally Protestant, cannot be considered part of the three-community system. Their network of primary relationships, their family and friends, so largely exclude the non-Amish that they must be regarded as another distinct religious community. The *Yoder* case not only decided the right of the Amish to refuse to send their children to school beyond the eighth grade as required by Wisconsin law, but also throws some light on the legitimacy of those religious communities outside the three-community system. Unfortunately, the Court placed so much emphasis upon the particular qualities of the Amish that the light is not a particularly bright or searching one.

Specifically, the qualities to which the Court referred (1973:36) include

> . . . a history of three centuries as an identifiable religious sect and a long history as a successful and self-sufficient segment of American society . . . the sincerity of their religious beliefs, the interrelationship of belief with their mode of life, the vital role that belief and daily conduct play in the continued survival of . . . Amish communities and their religious organization . . . the adequacy of their alternative mode of continuing . . . education. . . .

In addition, the Court referred (1973:26) to the "hazards presented by the State's enforcement of a statute generally valid as to others." In the Court's view (1973:27) if the law were enforced against the Amish, they would face a situation which contained

> . . . a very real threat of undermining the Amish community and religious practice as they exist today; [in which] they must either abandon belief and be assimilated into society at large, or be forced to migrate to some other and more tolerant region.

Given what the Court called (1973:37) "this convincing showing, one that probably few other religious groups or sects could make" it ruled that the Amish did not have to comply with the secular governmental regulation in question. The legitimacy of the Amish claims for exemption, and by extension, the legitimacy of a religious community outside the three-community system was affirmed. However, since the Court believed "few other religious groups" could make as convincing a showing, it is not clear what other groups of the religiously unorthodox would receive similar constitutional protection under the Religion Clauses of the First Amendment, which forbid passage of any "law respecting an establishment of religion or prohibiting the free exercise therof." It is unclear whether more recently discovered religious beliefs would be similarly protected. It is also unclear what protection would be provided for sincerely held but nonreligious beliefs. The basis for such doubts may be found in the words of the *Yoder* opinion itself (United States Supreme Court, 1973:36):

> . . . Courts must move with great circumspection in performing the sensitive and delicate task of weighing a State's legitimate social concern when faced with religious claims for exemption from generally applicable . . . requirements. It cannot be overemphasized that *we are not dealing with a way of life* and mode of education *claiming to have recently discovered some "progressive" or more enlightened process* for rearing children for modern life [italics added].

Should a religious group base its claim for exemption from some generally applicable secular regulation (such as the restriction on the use of hallucinogenic drugs) on some recently discovered religious tenets or some new religious way of life, it is not clear that such a claim would be recognized as legitimate, even though an exception was granted in the *Yoder* case.[17]

Similarly, the Court's own words in the *Yoder* decision raise doubts about the Court's willingness to recognize the legitimacy of claims based not on religious grounds but on a nonreligious or secular ethic. The Court has said (1973:25),

> A way of life, however virtuous and admirable, may not be interposed as a barrier to reasonable state regulation . . . if it is based on purely secular considerations; to have the protection of the Religion Clauses, the claims must be rooted in religious belief. . . . Thus, if the Amish asserted their claims because of their subjective evaluation and rejection of the contemporary secular values accepted by the majority, much as Thoreau rejected the social values of his time and isolated himself at Walden Pond, their claims would not rest on a religious basis. Thoreau's choice was philosophical and personal rather than religious, and such belief does not rise to the demands of the Religion Clauses.

251

Although the *Yoder* decision affirmed the legitimacy of the claims of members of a long-established religious community, albeit one outside the three-community system, the decision itself indicates that similar claims from nonreligious persons or communities might not be honored. The *Yoder* opinion does not necessarily support the claims of the atheists, agnostics, humanists, or other nonreligious persons outside the three-community system for relief of the obligation to follow secular state regulations that they find morally or ethically repugnant and oppressive. The rights of such people to hold public office and to have the benefits of public welfare programs are affirmed in the *Torcaso* and *Everson* cases, respectively. Moreover, other Court opinions indicate a possible basis upon which the legitimacy of exemptions to otherwise applicable secular regulations may be granted to an atheist, agnostic, humanist, or indeed anyone not generally regarded as religious who nonetheless finds that a particular secular regulation requires action contrary to the dictates of conscience. However, such a basis is found in two cases, which deal not with the interpretation of the Constitution, but with that of one section of a specific federal law, namely, the Universal Military Training and Service Act, the Act which authorized the establishment of the Selective Service System after World War II.[18] Thus, the Court's opinion in these two cases does not necessarily establish precedents for cases not involving the specific law in question see *U.S.* v. *Seeger*, (380 U.S. 163 (1965), in United States Supreme Court, 1965:733–752); and *Welsh* v. *U.S.*, (398 U.S. 333 (1970), in United States Supreme Court, 1971:308–338). When constitutional issues involving the law were forced in *Gillette* v. *U.S.* (401 U.S. 437, (1971), in United States Supreme Court, 1971:168–195), the Court recognized limitations on the extent of conscientious exemptions from the obligations created by law.

The section of the Universal Military Training and Service Act, at issue in the *Seeger, Welsh,* and *Gillette* cases (6(j)) provides, in part, for exemptions from Selective Service to those "who, by reason of their religious training and belief are conscientiously opposed to participation in war in any form." The Act (see United States Supreme Court, 1971:317) defines religious training and belief as

> an individual's belief in a relation to a Supreme Being involving duties superior to those arising from any human relation, but does not include essentially political, sociological, or philosophical views or a merely personal moral code.

Daniel Andrew Seeger applied for exemption from Selective Service as a conscientious objector since he objected to participation in war in any form by reason of his religious beliefs. However, Seeger was an agnostic, that is (United States Supreme Court, 1965:737) "he

252

preferred to leave the question as to his belief in a Supreme Being open." He did, however, profess, as the Court noted (1965:737), "a belief in and devotion to goodness and virtue for their own sakes, and a religious faith in a purely ethical creed." The Selective Service System denied his claimed exemption on grounds that it did not involve a "belief in a relation to a Supreme Being" as required by Section 6(j). The sincerity, honesty, and good faith of his beliefs were accepted both by the Selective Service System and the Court. The Court granted Seeger his exemption as a conscientious objector, noting (1965:737) that under its interpretation of Section 6(j),

> . . . the test of belief "in a relation to a Supreme Being" is whether a given belief that is sincere and meaningful occupies a place in the life of its possessor parallel to that filled by the orthodox belief in God of one who clearly qualifies for the exemption.

Thus, the claims of theist and agnostic had equal standing under the law in the Court's view (1965:737), if they occupied "parallel positions in the lives of their respective holders." Had this view been expressed as an interpretation of the Constitution and not merely of the wording of Section 6(j), it would have had a broad sweep and could have provided a basis for the claims of agnostics, and perhaps of atheists and humanists as well, to exemptions from secular regulations they found morally or ethically repugnant.

The *Welsh* case extended the Court's interpretation of Section 6(j) still further. Elliot Ashton Welsh, II, an agnostic, applied for conscientious objector status. He did not define as religious the beliefs which led him to oppose participation in war. Welsh's objection to participation in war was, as the Court acknowledged (1971:320), based on his belief that the taking of anyone's life was morally wrong. The Court (1971:319) granted Welsh his conscientious objector status even though he himself did not regard his reasons as religious:

> If an individual deeply and sincerely holds beliefs that are purely ethical or moral in source and content but that nevertheless impose upon him a duty of conscience to refrain from participating in any war at any time, those beliefs certainly occupy in the life of that individual "a place parallel to that filled by . . . God" in traditionally religious persons. Because his beliefs function as a religion in his life, such an individual is as much entitled to a "religious" conscientious objector exemption . . . as is someone who derives his opposition . . . from traditional religious conviction.

Once more the agnostic and the atheist were granted equal status under Section 6(j). In so doing, the Court ruled that the function, rather than the source or content of one's beliefs, was the determining factor. While the Court did grant the religious and nonreligious equal treatment, it did so by denying the existence of any relevant differences between them. The Court in other words, defined the term "religious," as it appeared in Section 6(j), to include many who would generally be regarded as nonreligious or even irreligious. The Court acknowledged it was using a definition of religious not generally accepted by others when it admitted (1971:319) "very few . . . are fully aware of the broad scope of the word 'religious' as used in [Section] 6(j)." Had the Court been interpreting the Constitution and not merely a section of one federal law, a basis would have been clearly laid for establishing the legitimacy of the claims of atheists, agnostics, humanists, and others not generally regarded as religious for exemptions from government regulations they find morally repugnant. However, when the Court finally faced constitutional issues involving Section 6(j), as it had been urged to do in the *Welsh* case by Justice Harlan (United States Supreme Court, 1971:321–334), it stressed restrictions on the claims for exemption from governmental regulations based on religious beliefs, however defined.

The relevant ruling came in the case of *Gillette* v. *United States*, to which was joined *Negre* v. *Larsen* (401 U.S. 437 (1971), in United States Supreme Court, 1972a:168–195). Guy Porter Gillette and Louis A. Negre had each applied for conscientious objector status, although each objected only to participation in a particular war, the war in Vietnam, rather than to war in any form as Section 6(j) called for.[19] Gillette based his objection on a humanist approach to religion; Negre objected as a devout Catholic under Catholic doctrines which distinguish between just and unjust wars. The Court rejected both claims. However, it did so without explicitly facing the question of whether or not Gillette's humanistically based objections were religious. It simply ruled, in effect, that even if they were, they would not be valid in the case in question.

Thus, the Court did not, as do the norms of the three-community system, make any invidious comparison between the religiously orthodox and the unorthodox. It rejected alike both the claims of a Catholic and those of a humanist. It rejected claims which under its ruling in *Seeger* and *Welsh* could be regarded as religiously based, even though it was aware (1972a:180) that "petitioners ask how their claim to relief from military service can be permitted to fall, while other 'religious' claims are upheld" and while admitting that "it is a fact that [Section] 6(j), properly construed, has this effect." However, the Court indicated that such an effect was permissible; that it was permissible for a government regulation to provide relief to some religious claims but not others if in doing so it did not violate the "proposition that when Government activities touch on the religious sphere, they must be secular in purpose, evenhanded in operation, and neutral in primary impact" (1972a:181). In this case, the Government's purpose was secular and involved meeting the constitutionally sanctioned goal of raising and supporting an army. Moreover, the Court held (1972a:183) that "valid neutral reasons exist for limiting the exemptions to objectors to all war." These reasons involved the potential for excessive entanglement of government in the complex and subjective matters upon which objection to some but not all wars may be based. The Court feared that fair and consistent results could not be attained if a program of excusing objectors to particular wars was undertaken. It found (1972a:187) that there were "governmental interests of a kind and weight sufficient to justify . . . the impact of the . . . laws on those who object to particular wars," even though such an impact favored some religious beliefs over others. It recognized (1972a:188) that while "even as to neutral prohibitory or regulatory laws having secular aims . . . certain applications clashing with imperatives of religion and conscience" may be condemned by the Constitution, in other instances, religion and conscience do not relieve one from a "colliding duty fixed by a democratic government" (1972a:187).

In sum, the *Gillette* opinion recognizes that conflicts may arise between the claims of certain religious beliefs, on the one hand, and obligations created by the secular laws and regulations of government on the other. The Court, in that opinion, asserts that where the government's interests are of an appropriate kind and of sufficient weight, religious claims to exemption from obligations created by government may be overridden. However, the Court made no distinction between orthodox and unorthodox religious claims, and tacitly maintained its policy of neutrality between believers in specific religious doctrines and nonbelievers. Indeed, the Court noted (1972:182) that the Constitution "forbids subtle departures from neutrality, 'religious gerrymandering,' as well as obvious abuses." Thus, the *Gillette* ruling does not challenge the legitimacy of the religiously unorthodox established in the *Everson* and *Torcaso* opinions. It does not even seek to make the distinctions found in the *Yoder* opinion. Nevertheless, the opinion does permit de facto religious discrimination under certain circumstances. These circumstances exist where the de facto discrimination results despite government activities which are "secular in purpose, evenhanded in operation, and neutral in their primary impact," and where the government's interests are of an appropriate kind and of sufficient weight to override the need to eliminate the unintended secondary impact which creates the de facto discrimination. Thus, the Court has not denied the legitimacy of those outside the three-community system. Those outside the Protestant, Catholic, and Jewish communities retain their de jure or legal equality with those inside. Nevertheless, while the Court has not given constitutional sanction to the invidious distinction between religion and irreligion nor to the distinction between the three Judeo-Christian religions and other religions, it still has left room for de facto discrimination. Given the workings of the democratic political process, it can be expected that the majority, who are within the three-community system, may take greater care to avoid de facto discrimination against their own beliefs than against the beliefs of minorities, of the religiously unorthodox. The original wording and effect of Section 6(j) of the Universal Military Training and Service Act is clearly a case in point. It can be expected that if there are collisions between the duties fixed by a democratic government and one's religion and conscience, it will not be with the religion and conscience of the majority within the three-community system; it will be with that of the religiously unorthodox, such as agnostics, atheists, humanists, and the Amish. Democratic processes do, in the long run, reflect the wishes and values of the majority. Thus, while the legitimacy of the religiously unorthodox may be protected in principle, it may not always be protected in fact. Democratically enacted prohibitory or regulatory laws may clash with the imperatives of the religion and conscience of minorities.

The norms and tendencies of the three-community system to regard certain religious positions as foreign or obscurely un-American may prevail, even without explicit and unhesitating sanction from the Supreme Court and the Constitution. Clearly, they may prevail in the realm of primary relationships. Under the *Gillette* opinion, and perhaps the *Yoder* opinion as well, they may even prevail on occasion in the realm where secondary relationships are subject to government regulation.

Summary

This chapter identified two areas of tension between the norms of the three-community system and the tradition of the separation of church and state in the United States. The first area of tension is rooted in the preference for religion over irreligion inherent in the three-community system. The second area involves the question of the rights of the religiously unorthodox, who remain outside the three religious communities. Decisions of the United States Supreme Court were reviewed for evidence of the tensions and for indications of how they have been dealt with. Two issues illustrate the tensions between the preference for religion over irreligion inherent in the three-community system and the tradition of church-state separation: (1) the use of the public school system to aid religious instruction or as a place for religious exercises such as prayers, and (2) aid to parochial schools.

Supreme Court decisions do not contravene the norms of the three-community system on either issue. The Court has held (1972b:763), as does the three-community system, "that religion must be a private matter for the individual, the family and the institutions of private choice."

Contrary to the norms of the three-community system, however, the Court has rather consistently protected the rights of the religiously unorthodox. Although, there are indications, especially in the *Yoder* and *Gillette* decisions, that there may be limits to that protection. In the *Gillette* decision, the Court noted that certain government regulations that clash with certain imperatives of religion and conscience might be permissible. Presumably, even in a democracy, it is likely that more care will be taken to frame government regulations and laws so as to avoid clashes with the imperatives of orthodox religions than with those of unorthodox religions. Thus, even though the Supreme Court protects the de jure or legal rights of the religiously unorthodox, a degree of de facto discrimination may be tolerated.

FOOTNOTES

1. Studies of the compliance or lack of it with Supreme Court decisions on matters pertaining to religion have generally ignored the role of factors relating to the three-community system. Such studies have generally focussed instead on the dynamics of attitude change or on the influence of political elites in the process of attaining compliance. See Beaney and Beiser (1964), Birkby (1966), Dolbeare and Hammond (1971), Johnson (1967), Katz (1965), Muir (1967), Patric (1957), Reich (1968), Sorauf (1959) and Way (1968). See also Wasby's review (1970) of relevant studies.

2. For an historical overview of church-state relations in the United States, see Littell (1962), Marnell (1966), Morgan (1972) and Stokes and Pfeffer (1964). Legal and sociological theories of American church-state relations are discussed by Jones (1970). For a broad overview of church-state relations in other countries, see Pfeffer (1967:31–70). Menendez briefly discusses church-state relations in Ireland (1974a), Austria (1974b), Switzerland (1974c), Denmark (1974d), and the Netherlands (1974e). Latin American church-state relations are discussed by Mecham (1966) and Pike (1964); those in Russia by Murvar (1968) and Simon (1974); those in Eastern Europe by Bociurkiv and Strong (1975). Westhues (1975) examines church-state relations in Paraguay. Tammey (1974) surveys the views of students in five Southeast Asian universities on church-state relations. Krejci (1975) discusses religion and official antireligion in Czechoslovakia.

3. It is possible that this picture has changed in the years since Herberg wrote his analysis. According to the Gallup Opinion Index (1975:11–12), in 1974, 56 percent of adult Americans believed that religion as a whole was losing its influence on American life. This figure is lower than the 75 percent who thought, in 1970, that religion was losing its influence, but higher than the 14 percent who thought so in 1957 and the 31 percent who thought so in 1962 (about the time Herberg was writing his analysis). Even if religion

is losing its influence, it may still remain accepted as a normal and desirable part of American life. That is, it might be hoped that its influence would be increasing.

4. For discussion of the study of irreligion per se, that is outside the context of consideration of the three-community system, see Campbell (1971) and Pruyser (1974:186–200).

5. For a discussion of the institution of neighborhood or community schools in the experiences of Irish, Italian, and Jewish immigrants and the relevance of such schools to current Black experiences, see Mills (1974).

6. For a discussion of the public and parochial school systems in Canada, England, and the Netherlands, and of the lessons they may have for the United States, see Reller (1963). See also Himmelfarb (1966) for a defense of public aid to parochial schools.

7. Public reaction to these rulings is discussed in Murphy and Tannenhaus (1968) and Nagel and Erickson (1966). The Gallup Opinion Index (1971:25) indicates that as late as 1971 two-thirds of the public disapproved of the Court's ruling which forbids the reading of the Lord's Prayer or of Bible passages in the public schools.

8. In a related case, *Epperson* v. *Arkansas* (393 U.S. 97 (1968), in United States Supreme Court, 1969b:228–241), the Court held it was unconstitutional to forbid the use of a textbook simply because it conflicted with a particular religious doctrine. In the case in question, the conflict was between the use of a textbook teaching the biological theory of evolution and the Fundamentalist doctrine of the literal accuracy of the Biblical account.

9. *Tilton* v. *Richardson* (403 U.S. 672, in United States Supreme Court, 1972b: 790–809) also bears on the question of state aid to parochial schools. The Court upheld the constitutionality of the payment of grants to church-related colleges and institutions for the construction of academic facilities under a Connecticut law. In this case, the Court itself issued no opinion; there were only the separate opinions of individual Justices.

10. In dissenting from the Court's decision, Justice Jackson noted (Tussman, 1962:212) that,
    . . . the undertone of the opinion, advocating complete and uncompromising separation . . . seem[s] utterly discordant with its conclusion. . . . The case which irresistibly comes to mind as the most fitting precedent is that of Julia who according to Byron's reports, "whispering 'I will ne'er consent'—consented."

11. In his dissent from the *Meek* decision, Justice Brennan remarks that concern for the divisive potential of a given program may have become a fourth factor to test in determining the compatibility of the program with the Constitution (United States Supreme Court, 1975). For discussion of the potential for religiously based political conflicts in America, see Coleman (1956), Lee and Marty (1964), Parenti (1967), Raab (1964), Stedman (1964), Williams (1956), and Yinger (1967).

12. Burkholder (1974:27–50) and Pfeffer (1974:9–20) discuss the legal and constitutional issues raised by disputes involving unorthodox or marginal religions in the United States. They comment on the cases reviewed here and on cases that came before lower courts.

13. Of course, not all clashes between obligations created by secular law and religion involve the religiously unorthodox. Occasionally, even members of the three religious communities find that they have religious grounds for claiming an exemption from some government regulation. Some earlier cases involving the Jehovah Witnesses are discussed in Manwaring (1968). Other cases have involved challenges to so-called Sunday Blue Laws by Seventh Day Adventists and Jews who celebrate the Sabbath on Saturday. The constitutionality of laws recognizing Sunday as the common day of rest has been upheld (see *McGowan* v. *Maryland*, 366 U.S. 420 (1961); *Gallagher* v.

Crown Kosher, 366 U.S. 617 (1961); *Two Guys* v. *McGinley,* 366 U.S. 582 (1961); and *Braunfeld* v. *Brown,* 366 U.S. 599 (1961), all in United States Supreme Court, 1962:393–594). However, grounds for exemptions from such laws are recognized in *Sherbert* v. *Verner* (374 U.S. 398 (1962), United States Supreme Court, 1965:965–982).

14. For a discussion of early Supreme Court cases involving the Mormons, see Morgan (1972:40–44). For a sociological account of the Mormons and of Mormon history, see O'Dea (1957).

15. Problems involved in applying the belief versus action distinction to religion in contemporary America are discussed by Smith (1972:356–365).

16. For sociological accounts of life in the Amish community, see Hostetler (1968) Hostetler and Huntington (1971). For discussions of other disputes involving Amish resistance to state compulsory school attendance laws, see Casad (1969), Erickson (1968), and Rodgers (1969).

17. The convictions, under Tennessee law, of members of a farm commune for use of marijuana despite their claims that marijuana use is central to their religion (see Fiske, 1973) might be such a case. So might the California case, *People* v. *Woody,* in which the state sought to prohibit the use of peyote by the Native American Church, an American Indian religious organization. Peyote use is central to their ritual, and peyote itself is an object of worship (see Casad, 1969:67–69; Morgan, 1972:154–155). See also Burkholder (1974: 35–44) who discusses the Tennessee and California cases as well as others.

18. The rulings in *Seeger* and *Welsh* were applied in the case of *Clay* v. *U.S.* (403 U.S. 698 (1971), in United States Supreme Court, 1972b:810–819), involving the former heavyweight champion, Mohammed Ali. However, the decision itself was based on narrower technical grounds.

19. For discussion of other Court cases involving religiously based opposition to the Viet Nam war but not involving Section 6(j), see Bannan and Bannan (1974).

REFERENCES

Bannan, John F., and Rosemary S. Bannan
1974 *Law, Morality and Viet Nam: The Peace Militants and the Courts.* Indiana University Press.

Beaney, William, and Edward N. Beiser
1964 "Prayer and politics: the impact of *Engel* and *Schempp* on the political process." *Journal of Public Law* 13 (2):475–503.

Birkby, Robert
1966 "The Supreme Court and the Bible Belt: Tennessee reaction to the *Schempp* decision." *Midwest Journal of Political Science* 10 (August): 304–319.

Bociurkiv, Bohdan R., and John W. Strong
1975, eds. *Religion and Atheism in the U.S.S.R. and Eastern Europe.* University of Toronto Press.

Burkholder, John Richard
1974 " 'The law knows no heresy': marginal religious movements and the courts." In *Religious Movements in Contemporary America,* edited by Irving I. Zaretsky and Mark P. Leone. Princeton University Press.

Campbell, Colin
1971 *Toward a Sociology of Irreligion.* London: Macmillan.

Casad, Robert C.
1969   "Compulsory education and individual rights." In *Religion and Public Order: Number Five*, edited by Donald A. Giannella. Ithaca, N.Y.: Cornell University Press.

Coleman, James S.
1956   "Social cleavage and religious conflict." *Journal of Social Issues* 12 (3):44–56.

Dolbeare, Kenneth, and Phillip E. Hammond
1971   *The School Prayer Decisions.* University of Chicago Press.

Durkheim, Emile
1964   *The Division of Labor in Society.* Translated by George Simpson. New York: Free Press.

Erickson, Donald A.
1968   "The 'Plain People' and American democracy." *Commentary* 45 (June): 36–44.

Fiske, Edward B.
1973   "At Tennessee farm commune, marijuana is a part of religion." *New York Times*, February 17, pp. 33, 39.

Gallup Opinion Index
1971   *Prayer in the Public Schools.* Report no. 77. Princeton, N.J.
1975   *Religion in America: 1975.* Report no. 114. Princeton, N.J.

Hammond, Phillip E.
1974   "Religious pluralism and Durkheim's integration thesis." In *Changing Perspectives in the Scientific Study of Religion*, edited by Alan W. Eister. New York: Wiley.

Herberg, Will
1960   *Protestant—Catholic—Jew.* Garden City, N.Y.: Doubleday (Anchor Books).

Himmelfarb, Milton
1966   "Church and state: how high a wall." *Commentary* 42 (July):23–29.

Hostetler, John A.
1968   *Amish Society*, rev. ed. Baltimore: Johns Hopkins Press.

Hostetler, John A., and Gertrude Enders Huntington
1971   *Children in Amish Society.* New York: Holt, Rinehart & Winston.

Johnson, Richard M.
1967   *The Dynamics of Compliance: Supreme Court Decision-Making from a New Perspective.* Evanston, Ill.: Northwestern University Press.

Jones, J. P.
1970   " 'Religion' in religion and politics." *Journal of Public Law* 19 (2): 283–326.

Katz, Ellis
1965   "Patterns of compliance with the *Schempp* decision." *Journal of Public Law* 14 (2): 386–408.

Krejci, Jaroslav
1975   "Religion and anti-religion: experience of a transition." *Sociological Analysis* 36 (Summer): 108–124.

Lee, Robert, and Martin E. Marty
1964   Editors, *Religion and Social Conflict.* New York: Oxford University Press.

Littell, Franklin Hamlin
1962   *From State Church to Pluralism.* Garden City, N.Y.: Doubleday (Anchor Books).

Manwaring, David Roger
1968   *Render Unto Caesar. The Flag-Salute Controversy.* University of Chicago Press.

Marnell, William H.
1966   *The First Amendment: The History of Religious Freedom in America.* Garden City, N.Y.: Doubleday (Anchor Books).

Mecham, J. Lloyd
1966   *Church and State in Latin America,* rev. ed. University of North Carolina Press.

Menendez, Albert
1974a   "Church and state in Ireland." *Church and State* 27 (January):8–11.
1974b   "Church and state in Austria." *Church and State* 27 (February):6–8.
1974c   "Church and state in Switzerland." *Church and State* 27 (March):6–9.
1974d   "Church and state in Denmark." *Church and State* 27 (May):6–7.
1974e   "Church and state in the Netherlands." *Church and State* 27 (November):3, 6–8.

Mills, Nicholas
1974   "Community schools: Irish, Italians and Jews." *Transaction: Social Science and Modern Society* 11 (March–April):76–84.

Morgan, Richard E.
1972   *The Supreme Court and Religion.* New York: Free Press.

Muir, William K.
1967   *Prayer in the Public Schools: Law and Attitude Change.* University of Chicago Press.

Murphy, Walter F., and Joseph Tannenhaus
1968   "Public opinion and the Supreme Court: the Goldwater campaign." *Public Opinion Quarterly* 32 (Spring): 31–50.

Murvar, Vatro
1968   "Russian religious structures: a study in persistent church subservience." *Journal for the Scientific Study of Religion* 7 (Spring):1–22.

Nagel, Stuart, and Robert Erickson
1966   "Editorial reaction to Supreme Court decisions on church and state." *Public Opinion Quarterly* 30 (Winter): 647–655.

O'Dea, Thomas
1957   *The Mormons.* University of Chicago Press.

Parenti, Michael
1967   "Political values and religious cultures: Jews, Catholics and Protestants." *Journal for the Scientific Study of Religion* 6 (Fall):259–269.

Patric, Gordon
1957   "The impact of court decisions: aftermath of the *McCollum* case." *Journal of Public Law* 6 (February):455–464.

Pfeffer, Leo
1967   *Church, State and Freedom,* rev. ed. Boston: Beacon Press.
1974   "The legitimation of marginal religions in the United States." In *Religious Movements in Contemporary America,* edited by Irving I. Zaretsky and Mark P. Leone. Princeton University Press.

Pike, Frederick B.
1964   Editor, *The Conflict Between Church and State in Latin America.*
        New York: Knopf.

Pruyser, Paul W.
1974   "Problems of definition and conception in the study of unbelief,"
        Changing Perspectives in the Scientific Study of Religion, edited by
        Allan W. Eister. New York: Wiley.

Raab, Earl
1964   Editor, *Religious Conflict in America.* Garden City, N.Y.: Doubleday
        (Anchor Books).

Reich, Donald
1968   "The impact of judicial decision-making: the school prayer cases."
        In *The Supreme Court as Policy-Maker,* edited by David Everson.
        Carbondale, Ill.: Public Affairs Research Bureau, Southern Illinois
        University Press.

Reller, Theodore
1963   "Public funds for religious education: Canada, England, and the
        Netherlands." In *Religion and the Public Order,* edited by Donald
        A. Gianella. University of Chicago Press.

Rodgers, Harrell P.
1969   *Community Conflict, Public Opinion and the Law: The Amish Dispute
        in Iowa.* Columbus, Ohio: Merrill.

Simon, Gerhard
1974   *Church, State and Opposition in the U.S.S.R.* University of California
        Press.

Smith, Elwyn A.
1972   *Religious Liberty in the United States.* Philadelphia: Fortress Press.

Sorauf, Frank J.
1959   "*Zorach v. Clauson:* the impact of a Supreme Court decision."
        American Political Science Review 53 (September):777–791.

Stedman, Murray S., Jr.
1964   *Religion and Politics in America.* New York: Harcourt Brace Jovanovich.

Stokes, Anson Phelps, and Leo Pfeffer
1964   *Church and State in the United States,* rev. ed. New York: Harper &
        Row.

Tammey, Joseph B.
1974   "Church-state relations in Christianity and Islam." *Review of Religious
        Research* 16 (Fall):10–18.

Tussman, Joseph
1962   *The Supreme Court on Church and State.* New York: Oxford Uni-
        versity Press.

United States Supreme Court
1962   *United States Supreme Court Reports: Lawyers' Edition.* Rochester,
        N.Y.: Lawyers' Co-operative Publishing Co. Ser. 2, vol. 6.
1963   *United States Supreme Court Reports: Lawyers' Edition.* Rochester,
        N.Y.: Lawyers' Co-operative Publishing Co. Ser. 2, vol. 8.
1964   *United States Supreme Court Reports: Lawyers' Edition.* Rochester,
        N.Y.: Lawyers' Co-operative Publishing Co. Ser. 2, vol. 10.
1965   *United States Supreme Court Reports: Lawyers' Edition.* Rochester,
        N.Y.: Lawyers' Co-operative Publishing Co. Ser. 2, vol. 13.

1969a *United States Supreme Court Reports: Lawyers' Edition.* Rochester, N.Y.: Lawyers' Co-operative Publishing Co. Ser. 2, vol. 20.

1969b *United States Supreme Court Reports: Lawyers' Edition.* Rochester, N.Y.: Lawyers' Co-operative Publishing Co. Ser. 2, vol. 21.

1971 *United States Supreme Court Reports: Lawyers' Edition.* Rochester, N.Y.: Lawyer's Co-operative Publishing Co. Ser. 2, vol. 26.

1972a *United States Supreme Court Reports: Lawyers' Edition.* Rochester, N.Y.: Lawyers' Co-operative Publishing Co. Ser. 2, vol. 28.

1972b *United States Supreme Court Reports: Lawyers' Edition.* Rochester, N.Y.: Lawyers' Co-operative Publishing Co. Ser. 2, vol. 29.

1973 *United States Supreme Court Reports: Lawyers' Edition.* Rochester, N.Y.: Lawyers' Co-operative Publishing Co. Ser. 2, vol. 32.

1974 *United States Supreme Court Reports: Lawyers' Edition.* Rochester, N.Y.: Lawyers' Co-operative Publishing Co. Ser. 2, vol. 37.

1975 "Meek et al. v. Pittenger, Secretary of Education, et al." No. 73–1765 (Slip Opinion). Washington, D.C.: Government Printing Office.

Wasby, Stephen L.
1970 *The Impact of Supreme Court Decisions.* Homewood, Ill.: Dorsey Press.

Way, H. Frank, Jr.
1968 "Survey research on judicial decisions: the prayer and Bible reading cases." *Western Political Quarterly* 21 (June):189–205.

Westhues, Kenneth
1975 "Curses versus blows: tactics in church-state conflict." *Sociological Analysis* 36 (Spring): 1–16.

Williams, Robin
1956 "Religion, value orientations and intergroup conflict." *Journal of Social Issues* 12 (3): 12–20.

Yinger, J. Milton
1967 "Pluralism, religion and secularism." *Journal for the Scientific Study of Religion* 6 (Spring): 17–28.

Religion Among Black Americans:
A fourth religious community?

"It is impossible, of course, to speak of 'the' Negro church for there is," as Yinger (1970:326) notes, "a wide variety of . . . religious forms to be found among the various groups of Negroes." Indeed, the variety of religious preferences among the Negro or black minority in the United States clearly rivals that found among the white majority.[1] Black Americans are members of a myriad of sectlike and churchlike organizations across the broad range of Christianity, including the Roman Catholic Church and all forms of Protestantism. In addition, there are some blacks who regard themselves as Muslims, some who identify themselves as Jews, and others who, like the followers of Father Divine, pay no special attention to either the Bible or the Koran (see Fauset, 1944; Washington, 1972).[2] Nevertheless, the variety of religious preferences expressed by black Americans can be overstated since the vast majority are Protestants, mostly either Baptists or Methodists.[3] While it may be impossible or at least misleading to speak of one *Negro Church*, it is still possible that blacks constitute a single *religious community*. The existence of a religious community does not require uniformity of religious beliefs nor membership in a single religious organization. Jewish Americans are generally considered to be a single religious community despite the wide differences among Orthodox, Conservative, Reform, Reconstructionist, secular, and unaffiliated Jews.[4] Since the existence of a religious community "does not in itself necessarily imply actual affiliation with a particular church, participation in religious activities, or even the affirmation of any definite creed" (Herberg, 1960:39), a religious community may be evidenced simply by widespread self-identification and self-location rooted in a common religious heritage, even where such roots now feed a great variety of branches or expressions of the common heritage (see p. 204). A religious community could be said to exist among blacks in the United States to the extent that they define themselves and their place in the larger society in terms of a common religious heritage and to the extent that they are willing to say, "We blacks are really of one religion because of our common past, regardless of our present differences." If, as Williams (1971:267) claims, "blacks view themselves as a . . . community, and their religion as the source, together with color, . . . [of a] sense of 'oneness' [which] mitigates the differences that stem from varying denominations," then black Americans could be said to constitute a religious community in much the same sense as white Protestants, Catholics, and Jews do.

The character of a religious heritage which could form the basis of a religious community among blacks in the United States is outlined by Washington (1964:30–31) when he speaks of the folk religion of black Americans:

> The folk religion is not an institutional one. It is a spirit which binds Negroes in a way they are not bound to other Americans because of their different histories. Here and there this folk religion may be identifiable with a given congregation, yet, . . . it transcends all religious and socio-economic barriers which separate Negroes from Negroes. . . . This historical folk religion . . . unites all Negroes in a brotherhood which takes precedence over their individual patterns for the worship of God, or lack thereof.

The aim of this chapter is to assess the possibility that black Americans may constitute a religious community rooted in a common religious heritage. Of course, like the religious communities among whites (see p. 224), a black religious community may be infused with elements of ethnicity. Black religiosity and black nationalism may be subtly mixed, as are the religiosity and ethnicity of white Americans. Since this is a work in the sociology of religion, attention will be focussed on the religious components of the religious community. Nevertheless, in the attempt to assess the possibility of the existence of a black religious community, caution is needed concerning the potential influence of black ethnicity or nationalism. Two further considerations also require

266

caution. First, caution must be exercised because the attempt involves the always hazardous effort to predict the future as much as (or indeed more than) it involves the assessment of a present or past reality. This chapter considers both possibilities: that black Americans will constitute a religious community in the future and that they constitute such a community now. Second, caution must be exercised in the face of the paucity of sociological studies and analyses of black religion. The lack of such studies may be "curious," as Nelsen, Yokley, and Nelsen (1971:3) believe, especially given the prevailing assumption that religion has been at the center of the black community. Nevertheless, it is understandable, as Wilmore (1973:xi) says, that

> although religion has always been one of the most important aspects of the life of the Black people in the United States, it has been woefully neglected as an area of serious study by Black and white scholars alike. This partly because Black professional theologians, church historians and sociologists of religion have been few and far between . . . [and] white scholars, for their part, have rarely expressed great interest in Black religion in the United States.

The lack of interest on the part of white scholars stems, to a degree, as Wilmore (1973:xi) notes, from an assumption that the Protestantism of the majority of black Americans is "little more than a somewhat more noisy and colorful facsimile of the white rural Baptist and Methodist churches."[5] From the standpoint of such an assumption, studies of black Protestants are thought of as offering little likelihood of benefits to a white scholar which would warrant the possible pitfalls and extra effort of crossing the barriers between whites and blacks in America. Consequently, such studies of black religiosity as do exist tend to focus on the minority of blacks who are Catholics or non-Christians, that is, on the non-Protestant blacks. The resulting picture of black religiosity is apt, thus, to be incomplete and even distorted.

The cautious efforts of this chapter to assess the possibility that black Americans may constitute a religious community in the United States begin with a reexamination of the concept of religious community (see Chap. 7) and then focus on the applicability of the concept to black communities of the past and, possibly, of the future.

Reexaming the Concept of Religious Community

The application of the concept of religious community to the experience and conditions of black Americans constitutes an extension of the three-community hypothesis formulated by Herberg (1960). That hypothesis (see p. 212), in the generic form expressed by Mueller (1971:18), holds that "religious boundary lines [are] . . . the significant form of . . . differentiation among whites in American society." Operationally, that is, as actually tested in research, the hypothesis has been interpreted to predict that the primary relationships (family and friendship) of white Protestants, Catholics, and Jews tend to involve coreligionists rather than individuals of different religious backgrounds. However, reliance on rates of interreligious marriage and friendship (the same empirical measures employed to determine if white Americans comprise three religious communities) will not suffice to determine if black Americans constitute a religious community. Any tendency for blacks to befriend or marry other blacks may well reflect the existence of a nonreligious rather than a religiously based community.[6] For example, blacks may marry or befriend other blacks because they share a common ethnic (national origin) background as Afro-Americans. Even in studies of white Americans, the use of marriage and friendship rates leads to possible confounding of results by the influence of ethnic factors (see p. 214). In order to employ more definitive measures than those which deal only with the primary relationships of marriage and friendship, and to determine what other measures might be appropriate, it is necessary to reexamine the concept of religious community. The result of the requisite reexamination is a greater emphasis on the cultural or creedal heritage of a religious community than is found in the research on the three-community hypothesis (see pp. 212ff.). The reexamination also highlights the dynamic quality of the bases for religious community.

As may be recalled from Chapter 7, there are two basic components of a religious community, primary relationships and secondary relationships. Primary relationships are intimate, informal, and personal relationships, such as those typically found among families and friends. Secondary relationships are the cold, formal, and impersonal relationships which characterize business and political affairs. Measures of the degree of unity evidenced by a given religious community may refer either to the primary or to the secondary relationships in its social structure. Unfortunately, reliance on measures of secondary relationships, to assess the contention that black Americans constitute a single religious community, suffers from the same disability as does such reliance on measures of primary relationships. That is, any tendency for blacks to confine such relationships to other blacks may equally well reflect the existence of a nonreligiously based community as it would that of a religiously based community. For example, simply finding that blacks largely prefer to buy from or vote for other blacks, regardless of whether they are black Protestants, Catholics, Jews, Muslims, or what-have-you, would not decisively demonstrate the existence of a single black *religious* community which transcends denominational differences. Such a finding may merely reflect the existence of a common racial community or of a common ethnic community of Afro-Americans. Consequently, conclusive support of any contention that blacks constitute a single religious community must include the demonstration that the basis for the definition of the community as a distinctive unit is, to a significant degree, *religious* and not solely racial, ethnic, or otherwise purely secular in character. One way to determine whether the basis of a community is religious is to determine if either creedal or organizational elements help define membership. This is not to say that *belief* in a given creed is necessary or that membership in a congregation is required, but only that some relationship to creed or congregation is maintained. For example, the claim that blacks constitute a religious community can be substantiated if it can be shown that a significant part of what it means to be a black person in the United States involves recognition of a link to a religious heritage or to a culture common to black Americans. If such a link is demonstrated, then black Americans can be said to constitute a black *religious* community.

The use of measures of an individual black's relationship to the cultural heritage of black Americans is open to at least two objections. First is the objection that such use is not found in research on the three-community hypothesis among whites and, thus, that the meaning of the term religious community is being significantly changed in its application to the study of blacks. Second is the objection that whether or not the meaning of religious community is changed, there is no black cultural heritage in America, religious or otherwise, and hence no distinctive cultural components upon which to base a black religious community. Neither objection is convincing, although each is worthy of discussion. Their refutation requires further development of the concept of religious community. It is true, up to a point, that measures of one's relationship to the cultural heritage of a religious community are not found in research on the validity of the three-community hypothesis. Such studies have tended to rely (see pp. 212ff.) on measures of one aspect of social structure, the structure of a network of primary relationships. Nevertheless, the use of measures of one's relationship to a cultural heritage is not foreign to studies of religious communities among whites and involves no change in the definition of the term.

Studies of religious communities, whether white or black, refer to the existence of self-identification and self-location rooted in a religious heritage. While measures of self-identification and self-location may refer primarily to aspects of social structure, the claim that they are rooted in a *religious* heritage cannot. The heritage is, at least in part, a cultural heritage. Unfortunately, studies testing the three-community hypothesis among whites have generally employed an extremely primitive measure of one's relationship to a given religious heritage. Specifically, such studies have tended to accept the assertion of a religious preference as evidence that one stands in some meaningful relationship to the heritages of Protestantism, Catholicism, or Judaism. Such studies have generally failed to probe the nature or content of the stated preference or of the relationship to the past it presumably signifies. Nevertheless, the studies contend, implicitly or explicitly, that the discovery of a relationship between religious preference and some structural property, such as the pattern of mate selection, supports a claim that the property in question is that of a *religious* community. The identification of the community as religious, rather than otherwise, is generally based solely on the assessment of religious preference, a primitive measure of a link to some particular religious or cultural heritage. Thus, the use of a measure which explicitly refers to the cultural or creedal heritage of a religious community does not constitute a change in the meaning of the term religious community. To the contrary, use of measures referring to a religious heritage is based on an informed application of the term. Moreover, use of such measures would provide a more adequate basis for claiming that the community under study is, in fact, a religious community and not one based on ethnic, political, economic or other nonreligious factors. Such measures involve no change in the definition of the term *religious community*, but only a more sophisticated application of the accepted definition. To belong to a religious community means not only to confine one's primary or secondary relationships to coreligionists, but to do so because of a shared *religious* heritage rather than on the basis, for example, of a common ethnic or racial ancestry.

Of course, if no shared religious heritage exists, the claim that a given group constitutes a religious community could not be substantiated. Interestingly, the claim that black Americans have no distinctive heritage, religious or otherwise, has been quite common among sociologists and may even, as Blauner suggests (1970:418), have had some standing as accepted dogma. One of the clearer statements of the claim is made by Glazer and Moynihan (1963:53) when they assert that "it is not possible for Negroes to view themselves as other . . . groups view themselves because . . . the Negro is only an American, and nothing else." That is, they add (1963:53), "he has no [distinctive] values and culture to guard and protect." The roots of such a claim may be found in *The American Dilemma*, a study of black American life prior to World War II by Myrdal. In it, Myrdal observed (1944:928) that "American Negro culture is not something independent of general American culture"; and while he acknowledged (1944:930) "the fact that American Negro culture is somewhat different from the general

American culture," he believed that the differences "are *generally created* by American conditions even if some of the specific forms are African in origin" (italics in original). The more specific claim that black Americans lack a distinctive religious heritage is likewise found in Frazier's *The Negro Church in America* (1974) which first appeared in 1963. "In studying any phase of the character and development of the social and cultural life of the Negro in the United States," Frazier (1974:9) asserts, "one must recognize . . . they were practically stripped of their social heritage." He then (1974:13) applies his argument to the specific instance of black religious heritage: "It is impossible to establish any continuity between African religious practices and the Negro church in the United States." Furthermore, he continues (1974:14), "Negroes were plunged into an alien civilization in which whatever remained of their religious myths and cults had no meaning whatever."

The statements by Myrdal and Frazier suggest that the heritage of any black religious community in the United States may be viewed as one which began as a tabula rasa which drew upon white religion for its eventual content. However, as Brotz (1964:130) correctly observes, the tabula rasa argument that "the Negro lost his African heritage, and, hence, has nothing which is not derivative from or dependent upon white culture is ultimately misleading."

The argument misleads the student of religious communities for two reasons. First, it misdirects attention from the present to a search for ultimate origins. That is, as Brotz notes (1964:130), the argument elevates "the importance of the genesis of something to such a degree that it loses sight of the importance of the results." The issue in the study of religious community, black or white, is not what the *ultimate* origins of its heritage are, but whether or not in the process of its development a distinctive product has been created which is important in defining the *contemporary* relationships among members of that community and the relationships between them and nonmembers. Less attention should be paid to the ultimate source of the heritage, and more to its past and present role in defining self-identification and self-location in the larger society. The issue is less where the heritage ultimately comes from and more whether it has some past or history. The need is to discover longstanding continuity not ultimate origins.[7]

The tabula rasa argument is also misleading because it elevates the derivative or dependent character of the black heritage to a point where the claim that its content is "generally created by American conditions" (Myrdal, 1944:930) comes to be taken as tantamount to asserting that "it is not possible for blacks to view themselves as other . . . groups view themselves" (Glazer and Moynihan, 1963:53), that is, as a group with a distinctive heritage. However, as Herberg's three-generation hypothesis implies, religious community, even among whites in the United States, is a "new and unique social structure" (1960:31) which emerged under the impact of general American conditions. The immigrant generation did not regard themselves as members of a *religious* community. To the contrary (see pp. 200–201), they initially regarded themselves as members of parochial or *village* communities and only later began to view themselves as members of *ethnic* (national origin) communities. According to Herberg, it is not the immigrant generation which saw themselves as members of a religious community, but their grandsons, who wished to remember the religious heritage that the sons (their fathers) had sought to forget. The recognition of a membership in a religious community on the part of the third generation (the grandsons) was a reaction to general conditions prevailing in America (see pp. 202ff.), a reaction to the separation of church and state and the resulting reluctance of older (more original) Americans to see themselves as requiring religious conversions. The affirmation of one's religious heritage as the basis for self-identification and self-location is a relatively new phenomenon in America, derivative from, dependent upon, and thus generally created by American conditions. The heritages of the white religious communities cannot be distinguished from those of any black religious community on the basis of some presumed independence from general American conditions. A religious heritage is not passed from generation to generation like a family jewel, unchanged and unchanging, whatever its environment. The cultural or creedal heritage carried on by the younger generation is never quite an exact duplicate of what the older generations knew. Cultural transmission, like biological transmission, does not result in perfect replication. Parent and child never have the close resemblance of identical twins. The transmission of a religious heritage, as Herberg's three-generation hypothesis implies, is a dynamic process influenced by its own internal processes *and* the conditions of the larger society. The heritage of any religious community, whether black or white, is always dependent and derivative to some extent, whatever its ultimate origins.

While an attempt to assess the possibility of the existence of a single black religious community rooted in a common black religious heritage may suffer from a paucity of appropriate empirical studies, such an attempt does not entail any change in the meaning of the term religious community. Such an attempt should not suffer from doubt as to the ultimate origins of the black heritage nor from concern over the black heritage's complete independence from the conditions of its white American environs.

This chapter next examines evidence that blacks have been a religious community, at least in terms, of black definitions of what being a black person in the United States mean. Then it considers the possibility that black Americans will constitute a religious community in the future, whatever they may or may not have been in the past.

Evidence of a Black Religious Community in the American Past

The possibility that blacks in the United States constitute a religious community ultimately hinges on whether or not a significant part of what it means to be a black person in America involves a relationship with a religious heritage common to black Americans. That is, it depends on the extent to which black Americans define themselves and their location in American society in terms of a relationship to black religious heritage. Of course, for most of their more than three-and-a-half centuries in America, blacks have not been defined as a religious community. As Singer (1962) suggests, early black Americans, the slaves, were not a community at all. While they may have maintained something of their African cultural heritage, the social structures of their African communities were essentially destroyed and not immediately replaced. Moreover, slaves were thought of as property, not persons. In 1857, the Supreme Court, in the Dred Scott decision, asserted that the phrase "we the people" was not intended to refer to slaves and their descendants. After Emancipation and Reconstruction, black Americans were generally thought of as persons, but persons of a different *race*. That is, to be black was defined in terms of a presumed biological inheritance, not in terms of the transmission of any religious or cultural heritage.

The definitions of the black person as property or as a member of a racial group were basically the definitions of white America. They did not necessarily reflect the reality of black life. Blacks obviously knew they were persons even when treated as property; they also knew many of their number could "pass" as white even in the heyday of racism. Moreover, from the vantage point of black reality and black self-definition, the possibility that black Americans constitute a religious community is not new at all. To the contrary, as Lincoln observes (1974:116),

> the time was when the personal dignity of the Black individual was communicated almost entirely through his church affiliation. To be able to say that "I belong to Mt. Nebo Baptist" or "We go to Mason's Chapel Methodist" was the accepted way of establishing identity and status when there were few other criteria by means of which a sense of self or a communication of place could be projected.

The time when part of what it meant to be a black person included a relationship to a religious heritage extends back, beyond the point when first there was a Mt. Nebo Baptist or a Mason's Chapel Methodist, to the era of slavery. In other words, there is "a long tradition that looks back," as Lincoln (1974:116) observes, "to the time when there was only the Black Church to bear witness to 'who' or 'what' a man was as he stood before the bar of his [black] community." Two of the more important components of that long tradition are the "invisible institution" of the Negro Church among the enslaved blacks (see Frazier, 1974:23–25), and the black congregations which were organized by free blacks before the Civil War (see Frazier, 1974:26–34).[8]

The significance of the invisible institution of black religion among enslaved blacks is twofold. First, the camp meetings and revivals provided rare opportunities where "some social solidarity, even if temporary, was achieved, and they [the enslaved blacks] were drawn into a union with their fellow men" (Frazier, 1974:16). In short, at religious meetings black slaves could experience what it meant to be persons and to participate in a black community: "The religion of the Negro . . . expressed . . . faith and fellowship with his fellow slaves" (Frazier, 1974:24).

Similar expressions of faith and fellowship among blacks were found in the churches organized by free blacks in both the North and the South before the Civil War. "Every city," writes Wade (1971:68), "witnessed the spread of formal Negro organizations where slaves and free mingled in religious exercises." The concerns of the black churches were not confined to worship services. The efforts of free blacks to create and maintain "mutual aid societies and cooperation for economic welfare . . . including efforts to acquire an education, were generally tied up with their [black] churches" (Frazier, 1974:28). Thus, even before the Civil War, it could be said that "already the church had become the cardinal point of colored [i.e., black] affairs" (Wade, 1971: 72). Black congregations, and thus black religion, had become the center of a network of primary and secondary relationships. Black religion among both the free blacks and the slaves had become the center of what autonomous community there was among blacks in the United States.

Following Emancipation, and during the era of Reconstruction, the invisible black religious institutions of former slaves and the congregations organized by free blacks before the Civil War were fused (see Frazier, 1974:34–37; Mays and Nicholson, 1933:29–32). The impetus for the formation of the resulting new congregations included, in part, "a growing racial consciousness . . . [and] the desire of the Negro to manage and direct his own religious activities"

(Mays and Nicholson, 1933:36–37). The great majority of the resulting congregations were Baptist, with many of the remainder Methodist. More importantly, the result provided a basis for a religion-related community among blacks in the United States and forged yet another link in the long tradition whereby "the social identity of the Black-american (sic) as well as his self-perception are . . . refracted through the prism of his religious identity" (Lincoln, 1974:116).

The tradition and life of black communities, in which social identity and self-perception are related (through the "prism" of religious identity) to a religious heritage, first became the objects of empirical studies by sociologists and social anthropologists in the early 1930s. Most of these early empirical studies were conducted in the rural South, where the majority of black Americans lived until the mid-twentieth century; most of the studies employed the nonquantitative techniques of participant observation characeristic of the social anthropologists (Davis, Gardner, and Gardner, 1941:413–417, 527–533; Dollard, 1937: 220–229; Johnson, 1934:150–179; 1941:135–169; Powdermaker, 1939: 223–298). One study, Mays and Nicholson (1933), used both quantitative and qualitative techniques and examined urban as well as rural congregations. Only in the Mays and Nicholson study is the focus on black religiosity. The focus of the others was generally on the caste and class relations then common in the rural South under the prevailing system of Jim Crow segregation. Where black religion is examined in these early studies, attention is usually paid to the details of worship services and other aspects of the formal organization of religion. Nevertheless, it is possible to glean some information and insight from these early studies concerning the relationship between black religion and the processes of self-identification and self-location of blacks in the rural South under Jim Crow segregation.[9]

The key to understanding the role of religion in these processes is found in an observation by Davis et al. (1941:414): "The rural colored [black] church gains its strength not chiefly from the supernatural sanctions claimed for it by its dogma, . . . but rather from the social bonds it establishes among its participants." According to Mays and Nicholson (1933:270), these social bonds provide the "Negro church something that gives it life and vitality, that makes it stand out significantly above its buildings, creeds, rituals and doctrines." That is, in the definitions by blacks of their identity and location within their own and the larger American society, the role which religion played did not stem from promises of rewards or threats of punishment in the sweet-by-and-by after death; it stemmed from the congregation's role, in Dollard's apt phrase (1937:248), as "a center of social solidarity." To Johnson (1934:150) the black congregation was "the one outstanding institution of the community over which the Negroes themselves had control." The black congregation served a variety of functions; it was the center of a network of primary relationships and the arena for many secondary relationships as well. To Powdermaker (1939:285), the black congregation served the "vital function of maintaining the self-respect of the Negro individual" because (1939:285) it is

> the one institution where the Negro enjoys full and undisturbed control. . . . He can freely exert his talents and powers. A man may become an elder. . . . A woman may . . . take part in community undertakings which yield a gratifying sense of accomplishment. . . . Thus, the church contributes to the sense of respect and esteem from others which is so essential to the self-respect of most individuals, and which is so consistently refused to Negroes by the white society which dominates most of their lives.

For black Americans the black congregation, the rural Black Church, and the tradition it represented was generally a major source, often the only source, of positive meaningful self-identity and a gratifying self-location within the primary and secondary relationships, the social structure, of a community. The role of the Black Church in the rural, segregated South as a source of intimate, informal and personal (i.e., primary) relationships is aptly summarized by Johnson (1934:150):

> . . . The church is the most important center for face-to-face relations. It provides . . . recreation and relaxation. . . . It is the agency looked to for aid when misfortunes overtake a person. It offers the medium for a community feeling . . . the formal expressions of fellowship. . . . It is the agency which holds together the subcommunities and families physically scattered over a wide area.

In addition, the rural Black Church was the center of more formal and impersonal (i.e., secondary) relationships. For example, it was an agent of social control (see Frazier, 1974:37–40). It could, as Johnson (1934:150) observes, set up "certain regulations for behavior, passing judgments which represent community opinion, censuring and penalizing improper conduct." It was in the Black Church that one bore "witness to 'who' or 'what' a man was as he stood before the bar of his community" (Lincoln, 1974:116).

The Black Church was also a center for political life (see Frazier, 1974: 47–50; Washington, 1964:58–95). It brought blacks together for a common cause and could "train them for concerted action [and] . . . provide an organized followership for Negro leaders" (Myrdal, 1944:858). Such political functions were muted, however, in the rural

South, where black congregations were generally indifferent to current social and political issues and accommodated themselves to the prevailing patterns of segregation (see Mays and Nicholson, 1933: 249; Davis et al., 1934:417; Dollard, 1937:258; Johnson, 1941:135–136).[10] Nevertheless, as Frazier says (1974:49), the rural Black Church "had a political significance for Negroes in a broader meaning of the term." In the rural South, the local congregation represented the "widest social orientation and the largest social groups in which they [blacks] found an identification" (Frazier, 1974:49). Moreover, Frazier (1974:49) observes:

> Since the Negro was an outsider in the American community, it was the church that enlisted his deepest loyalties. . . . For the Negro masses, in their . . . isolation in American society, the Negro church community has been a nation within a nation . . .

or, in our terms, a community within the larger American society. To be black meant to be identified with a religious organization and a religious heritage, to locate oneself vis-à-vis others in terms of membership in the Black Church and as an heir to that heritage. In the era from the end of the Civil War to the mid-twentieth century, there was indeed a black religious community, based where most blacks were, in the rural South. That whites did not generally so define blacks does not necessarily make it less of a reality. The differences in definitions may merely reflect the existence of two contemporaneous, albeit different, social realities: one a white definition of black reality, the other, a black definition of black reality.

More importantly, the existence of a black religious community may well have survived the migration of blacks from rural areas to the urban centers of the North and South. Drake and Cayton (1945: 418) report, in their study of Chicago during the Depression years of the 1930s, that the "church managed to remain an important element in the life" of blacks in Chicago; and, that (1945:423),

> one of the most striking aspects of [black Chicago's] church life is a mutually shared core of religious customs that cuts across denominational lines. People "feel at home" in any of the major Protestant denominations and interdenominational visiting and shifts in church membership are widespread.

Black congregations, even in an urban center such as Chicago, provided something of the religious basis for community. As Washington (1964: 31) observes, black religiosity could unite all blacks "in a brotherhood or sense of community which takes precedence over their individual patterns for the worship of God."

The urban black congregations of the 1930s, like their rural counterparts, were run by blacks and were largely free of white control (see Drake and Cayton, 1945:427; Mays and Nicholson, 1933:168–197, 279–280). The urban congregation was one arena which could provide a place where blacks could be somebody. People who received little or no recognition in their daily jobs, if they were fortunate enough to have jobs, could, in the congregation, compete for prestige, be elected to office, exercise power and control, win applause and acclaim, in short, be complete and effective human beings. Other arenas in which one could be somebody in urban centers, such as, the Negro press and Negro business, were largely middle-class operations. For the mass of black people, the local congregation was the most likely and most accessible arena for a positive self-identity and for a gratifying location within a community. Thus, while in the 1930s the urban black "church [was] not the *center* of community life as it was in . . . the small towns of the South," it was still an "important element" in black urban life and for the black community (Drake and Cayton, 1945:418, italics in original).

Even after the Depression and World War II, in the 1950s and 1960s, "the churches [were] the most pervasive social institutions in the Negro [urban] ghettoes" (Clark, 1965:179). One reason for their pervasive influence is that, as Suttles (1968:45) discovered in his study of a Chicago slum area in the early 1960s, "the church is different"; because "of all the institutions in the area, the church is virtually the only one that local residents can potentially make their own and whose services they can feel are simply what is due them." More generally, Suttles (1968:41) found religion to be "one of the most significant ways in which . . . area residents assure one another of their willingness to sacrifice personal designs in favor of joint concerns." This is not to say, as Suttles adds (1968:41) that area residents "are particularly religious or moral." Rather it is to say (1968:41) that "religious affiliation must be taken for what it is—a public guarantee of one's amenability to group concerns," that is, community concerns. As Hannerz (1969:147) found in his study of black ghetto culture and community in Washington, D.C., in the late 1960s "religion is still part of the ghetto perspective, . . . it is something ghetto dwellers can more or less count on having in common." At least as late as the 1960s and presumably in the 1970s, religion remains an important element in the life of the black ghetto; one basis of the sense that blacks have something in common, something upon which to build a religious community. That is, something which indicates that a significant part of what it means to be a black person in the United States is to identify with a black religious heritage and to locate oneself within that heritage.

The Possibility of a Black Religious Community in the American Future

As noted above, black Americans could be said to constitute a religious community in much the same sense as white Protestants, Catholics, and Jews constitute religious communities if, as Williams claims (1971:267), "blacks view themselves as a . . . community, and their religion as the source, together with color . . . [of a] sense of 'oneness'." As was also noted above, the application of the concept of religious community to the experience and conditions of black Americans constitutes an extension of the three-community hypothesis (see p. 206) formulated by Herberg (1960). Indeed, the prediction that black Americans will constitute a religious community in the United States is tantamount to transforming the *three*-community hypothesis into a *four*-community hypothesis, that is, to claim that American society will contain four so-called religious communities: blacks, white Protestants, Catholics and Jews.[11] Such a transformation involves, in turn, two further predictions. First, it implies that America will be a society characterized by the existence of separate and distinct networks of primary relationships bounded or defined by religious lines. Although the boundaries may be somewhat permeable, they will still be discernible. Second, the transformation implies that participation in secondary relationships, unlike that in primary relationships, will increasingly be equally available to all on the basis of their individual merit without regard to one's group affiliation. While America will be a society in which family, friends, and other intimate and personal primary relationships are largely confined to coreligionists, political offices and jobs and other impersonal and formal secondary relationships are open to all qualified individuals.[12] In short, the now infamous separate-but-equal doctrine of *Plessy* v. *Ferguson* will be reinterpreted and reevaluated. Americans will be separate in things private and personal, but equal in things public and impersonal. The American dilemma or puzzle will then be how do we rationalize and justify the existence of four equilegitimate communities within one society. The answer, I think, will be to conceive of the communities as so-called religious communities, that is, as sources of self-identification and arenas for self-location rooted in differing religious heritages. Actual affiliation with a particular congregation, participation in religious activities, and affirmation of a specific creed need not be required if and when there are four religious communities, any more than they are now when there may be only three. Although, the view that America has four religious communities holds certain attractions for both whites and blacks, the acceptance of the four-community view requires some difficult adjustments. It will not, even if accepted, necessarily solve all problems in the relationships between whites and blacks.

To whites, the primary attraction of defining black Americans as just another religious community with its own distinctive religious heritage is that it will permit the desired separation of networks of primary relationships without challenging the image of an America free of the problems of prejudice and discrimination. Whites need only contend, to themselves and to blacks, that the separation of blacks from whites is not the result of antiblack prejudice and discrimination, but is voluntary on both parts, resuling from a preference for *one's own kind*, defined, of course, on religious lines not color or racial lines. Thus, the separation of primary relationships need not imply any un-American notion that blacks are inferior to nonblacks. It need only be claimed or believed that they are different, that is, different by virtue of a different religious heritage. The separation of primary relationships involving blacks from those involving white Protestants, Catholics, and Jews need no more imply antiblack feelings than the separations within these latter groups necessarily implies the existence of anti-Protestant, anti-Catholic or anti-Jewish feelings or actions. Americans may come to believe they can be for their own group without being prejudiced against another.[13] The acceptance of the four-community view would place the relationships between blacks and whites on the same basis as the relationships among whites. That is, just as white Americans with differing religious heritages may maintain separate networks of primary relationships, so too would those with a black religious heritage maintain a separate network of primary relationships. Of course, the claim that blacks are distinguished from whites on the same basis as whites distinguish among themselves, that is, on the basis of differing religious heritages, may be open to grave suspicion; suspicions that it covers up hatred and bigotry. Whether suspect or not, the claim may be attractive, and that is all that is being predicted here. Although the claim may be merely a legal or social fiction, it may well be a more attractive legal or social fiction than the now prevailing notion that blacks and whites constitute differing races.[14] The attraction of the view that black-white differences are religious or cultural rather than biological is presumably enhanced as America becomes a society where there is growing disbelief in the idea that one's role in life is determined by one's biology, for example, by one's sex. As disbelief in biological determination increases, the plausibility of a separation of blacks and whites on the basis of presumed biological differences should decline. Consequently, the idea of culturally based differences, such as those in religious heritages, should become relatively more and more attractive.[15]

The notion of America as a society with four religious communities may also be attractive to blacks. The basis for the attraction is hinted at by Clark (1965:177):

> The church is likely to be the last of the social institutions to be effectively integrated. Paradoxically, bedrock resistance to desegregation may be found more among Negroes than among whites, for only in the church have many Negroes found a basis for personal worth. If one demands that the Negro give up the Negro church . . . the demand will be rejected for the Negro has managed to salvage some personal self-esteem from his church, and until he achieves such self-esteem elsewhere, he will not give up his last and only sanctuary.

The view of blacks as just another religious community would permit blacks to retain control of the one institution they have essentially controlled since the era of slavery, one which has long been the center of their community. The notion of America as a nation of four religious communities would permit the continuation of the long tradition in the black community in which " the social identity of the Blackamerican (sic) as well as his self-perception are . . . to an important degree refracted through the prism of his religious identity" (Lincoln, 1974:116). The acceptance of the four-community view by blacks would minimize the disruption of black life. There would be no "threat" of the elimination of the Black Church and its replacement by integrated congregations. Furthermore, acceptance of the four-community view need not diminish or prejudice the demand for equality. Quite to the contrary, as noted above, acceptance of this view would put distinctions between whites and blacks on the same basis as distinctions now made among whites. Unlike race, which distinguishes whites from blacks, but not among whites, religious differences would be a standard equally applied to all and equally respectful of the dignity of all. It is a standard useful only to justify separate primary relationships. It will not justify unequal political or economic opportunities. Acceptance of the four-community view would permit blacks to demand equal political and economic opportunities, the goals of the Black Power movement, without requiring the elimination of the Black Church, the institution which has served as a haven and inspiration during black America's long struggle for equality and dignity.[16]

Although the four-community view may be attractive to both blacks and whites, its acceptance will entail at least two significant adjustments in the understanding of what it means to be black and of the nature of black religion. First, it implies a shift in the status of "blackness" from that of an ascribed or involuntary characteristic to that of an achieved or voluntary one. Secondly, it will entail the abandonment of the idea (see p. 267) that black religion is merely a noisy and colorful replica of elements of white Protestantism. Instead, black religion will have to be recognized as a distinct and meaningful heritage in its own right. The shift in the status of "blackness" from that of an involuntary characteristic to that of a voluntary one is part and parcel of the acceptance of the notion that blacks constitute just another religious community. That is, religious affiliation in the United States is a voluntary, not involuntary, characteristic. People need not, although they usually do, choose the religion of their parents. Thus, if being black, that is, being a member of the black community, is the same as being a Protestant, Catholic, or Jew, it will have to be, in some sense, voluntary.

If the black community is to be defined as just another religious community, people with black skins will have to have the option of rejecting the black heritage and people of white skins the option of accepting it, just as whites now have the option of selecting among the Protestant, Catholic, and Jewish heritages. The conversion of a person to and from the black religion will have to be defined as a real possibility. It will have to be recognized that to view "blackness" as unchangeable, as Lyman and Douglass (1973:365) note, is "to ignore the important consideration that in living out their lives human actors . . . engage regularly in the construction, manipulation and modification of social reality." Americans will have to become adjusted to recognizing that not everybody who is born black will stay black, just as it now recognizes that not all those born Protestants, Catholics, and Jews stay in their respective communities.[17] However, if blackness is really not a matter of skin color or some other biologically given trait and is really a matter of religious or cultural heritage, the adjustment should be possible. On the other hand, if the adjustment is not forthcoming, if some amount of movement to and from the black community is not a reality, the acceptance of the four-community view will be severely threatened. Its basis in reality will be undermined and its plausibility more difficult to maintain. Even if blackness can be transformed into a voluntary religious preference, one problem of adjustment at least will remain. The view that black religion is merely a noisy and colorful replica of elements of white Protestantism will have to be abandoned. Black religion will have to be defined as having a distinct and meaningful heritage and content in its own right. The historical links between black religion and white Protestantism need not be denied; after all, the historical links between Protestantism and Catholicism do not preclude viewing Protestantism as a distinct religion. If black religion is seen as nothing more than a derivative of white religion, as having no unique or distinct qualities of its own, it will not be truly equal to the religions of the other three

282

communities. The system of four equilegitimate religions envisioned in the four-community view will be threatened.

Although there is not yet widespread agreement as to what constitutes the core of distinctive attributes of black religiosity, a lively debate is taking place among black theologians (e.g., Barrett, 1974; Cleague, 1968, 1972; Cone . . . 1969, 1970a, 1970b; Jones, 1971; Roberts, 1971, 1974, and Washington, 1969).[18] The nature of any consensus which might evolve from the debate is not yet clear. Neither is it clear whether the eventual definition of the nature of black religiosity will be sufficiently broad to include all the current varieties of religious expression among blacks. For example, it is not clear if the definition will include black Roman Catholics as members of the black community; research by Nelsen and Dickson (1972) and by Denhardt and Salomone (1972) indicates that they so regard themselves.[19] Obviously, if black religiosity is defined as basically Christian, the inclusion of black Catholics as part of the black community would be possible, although their inclusion in the larger Roman Catholic community must also be regarded as a possibility. The inclusion in the black community of such non-Christian groups as the Black Jews, the Black Muslims, and the followers of Daddy Grace could be difficult if black religiosity is defined as Christian. Of course, the eventual consensus may recognize variations in black religiosity just as it does among whites, so that there may be not one but many black religious communities. If so, all blacks would not be alike; one would have to inquire as to a black's religious preference in order to properly "locate" him in the social structure of America, just as one now does with white Americans.

Even if the problems of adjustment are overcome and the four-community view is accepted by blacks and whites, not all the problems in the relationships between whites and blacks will be resolved. There will be problems in the application of the "separate in things private and personal, but equal in things public and impersonal" doctrine. Such problems will stem in large part from the lack of agreement on what constitutes a personal and private (primary) relationship and what constitutes an impersonal or public (secondary) relationship. As noted above (see p. 198), the line between primary and secondary relationships is not a clear or firm one. Many relationships have strong elements of both types. For example, primary schools may be defined as part of a neighborhood institution and the setting of pupil-to-pupil friendships and thus fall within the ambit of primary relationships. However, since education prepares one for roles in political and economic systems, the schools may be defined as part of the network of secondary relationships. Similar conflicts may flare up whenever a neighborhood is changing from a white to a black neighborhood or vice versa. Since such changes result from business transactions, the buying and selling of real estate, or the construction of new homes, they involve secondary relationships. On the other hand, since the neighborhood is the setting of the activities of many family and friendship circles, the change involves networks of primary relationships as well. In short, the acceptance of the four-community view will not be a panacea. Problems will still remain. Nevertheless, the acceptance of blacks as a separate and equal religious community may represent progress beyond the present system of so-called race relations.

SUMMARY

This chapter has sought to assess the possibility that black Americans constitute a religious community rooted in a common religious heritage. That is, it has sought to determine whether there are four religious communities, black, white Protestant, Catholic, and Jewish, and not just three as Herberg (1960) asserted. The application of the concept of religious community to the study of black Americans requires development of the concept beyond that used in studies of white Americans. For example, it is first necessary to clarify the role of one's relationship to a religious heritage in defining the community as religious rather than as ethnic or political. Reliance on measures of primary and secondary relationships alone are insufficient. In addition, the dynamic, adaptive quality of religious community must be stressed. Religious community is an adaptation to the conditions of American society used by many groups. Examination of evidence referring to blacks both before and after slavery is compatible with the claim that blacks have long constituted a religious community, whether whites recognized them as such or not. Moreover, the black religious community persisted despite the migration of blacks from the rural South to urban areas outside the South. There is a possibility that in the future blacks will be viewed as constituting a religious community. Should such a possibility actualize, advantages and disadvantages will accrue to blacks and whites and to relations between whites and blacks in America.

FOOTNOTES

1. For sociological analyses of the development and sources of the variety of religious preferences among black Americans, see Frazier (1974), Glenn (1964), and Pope (1967). A discussion of developments among black Protestants is

found in Johnston (1956). Hamilton (1972) examines the relationship between the role of the black preacher and forces influencing black religion in general.

2. The rather awkward phrases "regard themselves" and "identify themselves" are used here when speaking of Black Muslims and Jews, respectively, in light of the tenuous ties of the former to the Islam of the Near East, and of the latter to the Judaism of Europeans and white Americans, to whom the terms Moslem and Jew are usually applied. (See Lincoln, 1973:233–250 and Brotz, 1964:46–59, for discussions of, respectively, the relationship between Black Muslims and Islam and the relationship between Black Jews and Judaism). The strengthening of such ties and the claims to be regarded as Moslems and Jews rather than as distinctively Black Muslims and Black Jews, is not of much present concern to either group. For further discussion of the Black Muslims, see Essien-Udom (1962), Howard (1966), Kaplan (1969), Laue (1964), Massen (1970) and Tyler (1966). The Black Jews are discussed in Fauset (1944) and Washington (1972), as is the Father Divine movement. The latter movement is also discussed by Cantril and Sherif (1938), Harris (1971), and Burnham (1974).

3. In the last nationwide census of religious preferences in 1957 (United States Bureau of the Census, 1958), over 88 percent of black Americans were Protestants, with 61 percent Baptists and 17 percent Methodists. Erskine (1969:154–155) reports on a nationwide survey by the National Opinion Research Center in 1964 which shows 57 percent of blacks reporting they are Baptist, 14 percent Methodist, and a total of 87 percent Protestant. The *Gallup Opinion Index* based on 1973 and 1974 surveys (1975:24), reports among nonwhites, most of whom are black, 72 percent report they are Protestant, 12 percent Catholic, less than 1 percent Jewish, 10 percent other religions, and 6 percent no preference. In an earlier survey (*Gallup Opinion Index*, 1971:71), it was found that among nonwhite Protestants, 69 percent were Baptists and 18 percent Methodists; the remaining 13 percent were scattered among all other Protestant denominations.

4. For discussions of the diversity within the Jewish community, see Glazer (1972), Neusner (1972), Sklare (1971), and especially Glazer and Moynihan (1963: 143–175).

5. It should be noted that this assumption received support from Myrdal (1944:866), who claimed that "the Negro [Protestant] church is quite like any lower class white Protestant church. Negro churches have made no innovations in theology or in the general character of the church service." Boling (1975), however, does find differences between the religiosity of white and black lower-class individuals in his study of Springfield, Ohio. The point is debated among black churchmen. On the one hand, Washington (1964:95–96) concurs that "there is nothing unique in the worship life of the Negro [Protestant]. What is taken for uniqueness is but the extreme of what may be found in comparable white congregations." On the other hand, Watts (1971:25) believes that "the notion, held by many, that there is only an imperceptible or in-distinguishable difference between the black church and the white church is incorrect." Recent attempts to define the unique aspects of black theology are presented and discussed in Gardiner and Roberts (1971) and Jones (1973).

6. Studies reporting the extremely high rate with which blacks befriend and marry other blacks is summarized in Mueller (1971). See also Erskine (1973).

7. Interestingly, Myrdal seems to have understood the basic irrelevance of the question of the ultimate origins of black culture. From the practical point of view of its significance "for Negroes and the relations between Negroes and whites," he noted (1944:929–930), "the problem of the historical origin of the divergence of American Negro culture becomes irrelevant."

8. For alternative perspectives on pre-Civil War black religion, see Hamilton (1972), Washington (1964) and Wilmore (1973).

9. For a more recent social anthropological study of black life in the South, but not the Deep South, see Lewis (1955).

10. The relationship between black religiosity and acceptance of the prevailing

patterns of segregation are subjected to an empirical study of urban blacks in the 1960s by Marx (1969), Altson, Peck and Wingrove (1972), and Nelsen and Nelsen (1975). Marx (1969:104) found that while "the net effect of religion is clearly to inhibit attitudes of protest . . . nevertheless . . . a religious orientation and a concern with racial protest are certainly not mutually exclusive." Alston et al. report that the inhibiting effect of religion on black militancy may be waning among younger adults, women, and non-Baptists. Nelsen and Nelsen conclude (1975:134), on the basis of published surveys and their own data that "it cannot be said that black religiosity in general dampens militancy" and (1975:136) that "black religion serves in part as a channel through which feelings about society can be voiced and protest expressed in a routinized way." For discussion of the contemporary role of the black preacher in protests against discrimination, see Johnstone (1969) and Hamilton (1972). For an historical perspective on the relationship between black religion and black militancy, see Harding (1968, 1969) and Wilmore (1973).

11. Precedent for the notion that blacks constitute a separate religious grouping in America is found in Lenski's treatment (1963) of black Protestants as a group distinct from white Protestants, Catholics, and Jews.
12. Grounds for doubting the common sociological assumption that full integration or assimilation is inevitable are discussed in Metzger (1971).
13. For studies which suggest that resistance to interaction with blacks need not be based on antiblack prejudice, see Kelley (1974) and Ransford (1972). For a somewhat differing view, see Pettigrew (1969).
14. For a discussion of the history of the pseudoscientific uses of the concept of race, see Newman (1973:250–285).
15. The cultural basis of differences between whites and blacks may be seen as linked to national rather than religious heritages, that is, as ethnic in nature. It is also possible that the notion of the so-called culture of poverty will replace the current racist basis for distinction. Such a possibility is discussed by Ryan (1971:112–135) and Lewis (1971:71–98).
16. For an historical overview of the Black Church as a haven and inspiration, see Wilmore (1973). See also note 10 above, and Nelsen and Nelsen (1975:9–14; 125–137), who discuss the view that black religion serves both as a basis for black community and identity, on the one hand, and as a voice for equality and civil rights, on the other.
17. Lyman and Douglass (1973) discuss strategies which may be used to reveal or hide one's religious or ethnic identity.
18. See Gardiner and Roberts (1971) for further contributions to black theology. For an insightful, critical analysis of black theology, see Jones (1973).
19. These studies tend to confirm Lenski's (1963:4) belief that black Catholics "share in the subculture of the dominant Negro Protestant majority." Further indication that black Catholics and Protestants are in one community is found in Mueller and Lane (1972:80), who report, on the basis of 1957 United States Bureau of the Census figures, that the rate of intermarriage between nonwhite Protestant and Catholic individuals is 28 percent of that expected at random and that such marriages are "relatively more common among non-whites than among whites." For further studies of black Catholics, see Feagin (1968), Collins (1971), Alston, Alston and Warrick (1971), and Hunt and Hunt (1975).

REFERENCES

Alston, Jon P., Lettita T. Alston, and Emory Warrick
1971 "Black Catholics: social and cultural characteristics." *Journal of Black Studies* 2 (December):245–255.

Alston, Jon P., Charles Peek, and Ray C. Wingrove
1972 "Religiosity and black militancy: a reappraisal." *Journal for the Scientific Study of Religion* 11 (September):252–261.

Barrett, Leonard E.
1974 *Soul-Force: African Heritage in Afro-American Religion.* Garden City, N.Y.: Doubleday (Anchor Books).

Blauner, Robert
1970 "Black culture: myth or reality?" In *Americans from Africa: Old Memories, New Moods,* edited by Peter I. Rose. Vol. 2. New York: Atherton.

Boling, T. Edwin
1975 "Black and white religion: a comparison in the lower class." *Sociological Analysis* 36 (Spring): 73–80.

Brotz, Howard
1964 *The Black Jews of Harlem.* New York: Free Press.

Burnham, Kenneth E.
1974 "Father Divine: a case study of charismatic leadership." Mimeographed. Philadelphia: Sociology Department, Temple University.

Cantril, Hadley, and Muzafer Sherif
1938 "The kingdom of Father Divine." *Journal of Abnormal and Social Psychology* 33 (April):147–167.

Clark, Kenneth B.
1965 *Dark Ghetto.* New York: Harper & Row.

Cleague, Albert B., Jr.
1968 *The Black Messiah.* New York: Sheed and Ward.
1972 *Black Christian Nationalism: New Directions for the Black Church.* New York: Morrow.

Collins, Daniel T.
1971 "Black conversion to Catholicism: its implications for the Negro church." *Journal for the Scientific Study of Religion* 10 (Fall):208–218.

Cone, James H.
1969 *Black Theology and Black Power.* New York: Seabury Press.
1970a *A Black Theology of Liberation.* Philadelphia: Lippincott.
1970b "Black consciousness and the black church: a historical-theological interpretation." *Annals of the American Academy of Political and Social Science* 387 (January):49–55.

Davis, Allison, Burleigh B. Gardner, and Mary R. Gardner
1941 *Deep South: A Social Anthropological Study of Caste and Class.* University of Chicago Press.

Denhardt, Robert B., and Jerome J. Salomone
1972 "Race, inauthenticity, and religious cynicism." *Phylon* 33 (Summer): 120–131.

Dollard, John
1937 *Caste and Class in a Southern Town.* New Haven: Yale University Press.

Drake, St. Clair, and Horace E. Cayton
1945 *Black Metropolis.* New York: Harcourt Brace Jovanovich.

Erskine, Hazel
1969 "The polls: Negro philosophies of life." *Public Opinion Quarterly* 33 (Spring):147–158.

1973   "The polls: interracial socializing." *Public Opinion Quarterly* 37 (Summer):253–274.

Essien-Udom, E. U.
1962   *Black Nationalism: A Search for Identity in America.* University of Chicago Press.

Fauset, Arthur
1944   *Black Gods of the Metropolis.* University of Pennsylvania Press.

Feagin, J. R.
1968   "Black Catholics in the United States: an exploratory study." *Sociological Analysis* 29 (Fall):186–192.

Frazier, E. Franklin
1974   *The Negro Church in America.* New York: Schocken Books.

Gallup Opinion Index
1971   *Religion in America: 1971.* Report no. 70. Princeton, N.J.
1975   *Religion in America: 1975.* Report no. 114. Princeton, N.J.

Gardiner, James J., and J. Deotis Roberts
1971   Editors, *Quest for a Black Theology.* Philadelphia: Pilgrim Press.

Glazer, Nathan
1972   *American Judaism*, rev. ed. University of Chicago Press.

Glazer, Nathan, and Daniel Patrick Moynihan
1963   *Beyond the Melting Pot.* Cambridge: M.I.T. Press.

Glenn, Norval
1964   "Negro religion and Negro status in the United States." In *Religion, Culture and Society*, edited by Louis Schneider. New York: Wiley.

Hamilton, Charles V.
1972   *The Black Preacher in America.* New York: Morrow.

Hannerz, Ulf
1969   *Soulside: Inquiries into Ghetto Culture and Community.* New York: Columbia University Press.

Harding, Vincent
1968   "The religion of Black Power." In *The Religious Situation: 1968*, edited by Donald R. Cutler. Boston: Beacon Press.
1969   "Religion and resistance among antebellum Negroes, 1800–1860." In *The Making of Black America*, edited by August Meier and Elliott Rudwick. New York: Atheneum.

Harris, Sarah
1971   *Father Divine: Holy Husband*, rev. ed. Garden City, N.Y.: Doubleday.

Herberg, Will
1960   *Protestant—Catholic—Jew.* Garden City, N.Y.: Doubleday (Anchor Books).

Howard, John R.
1966   "The making of a Black Muslim." *Trans-Action* 1 (December):15–21.

Hunt, Larry, and Janet G. Hunt
1975   "A religious factor in secular achievement among Blacks: the case of Catholicism." *Social Forces* 53 (June):595–605.

Johnson, Charles S.
1934   *Shadow of the Plantation.* University of Chicago Press.
1941   *Growing Up in the Black Belt.* Washington, D.C.: American Council on Education.

Johnston, Ruby Funchess
1956 *The Religion of Black Protestants.* New York: Philosophical Library.
Johnstone, Ronald L.
1969 "Negro preachers take sides." *Review of Religious Research* 11 (Fall):
      81–88.
Jones, Major
1971 *Black Awareness: A Theology of Hope.* Nashville: Abingdon.
Jones, William R.
1973 *Is God a White Racist? A Preamble to Black Theology.* Garden City,
      N.Y.: Doubleday (Anchor Books).
Kaplan, Howard
1969 "The Black Muslims and the Negro American's quest for communion."
      British Journal of Sociology 20 (June):164–176.
Kelley, Jonathan
1974 "The politics of school busing." *Public Opinion Quarterly* 38 (Spring):
      23–40.
Laue, James
1964 "A contemporary revitalization movement in American race relations:
      the 'Black Muslims.'" *Social Forces* 42 (March): 315–323.
Lenski, Gerhard
1963 *The Religious Factor.* Garden City, N.Y.: Doubleday (Anchor Books).
Lewis, Hylan
1955 *Blackways of Kent.* University of North Carolina Press.
1971 "The culture of poverty? What does it matter?" In *The Poor: A Culture
      of Poverty or a Poverty of Culture,* edited by J. Alan Winter. Grand
      Rapids, Mich. Eerdmans.
Lincoln, C. Eric
1973 *The Black Muslims in America,* rev. ed. Boston: Beacon Press.
1974 *The Black Church Since Fraizer.* New York: Schocken Books.
Lyman, Stanford M., and William A. Douglass
1973 "Ethnicity: strategies of collective and individual impression manage-
      ment." *Social Research* 40 (Summer):344–365.
Marx, Gary T.
1969 *Protest and Prejudice,* rev. ed. New York: Harper & Row.
Massen, William A.
1970 "Watchtower influences on Black Muslim eschatology: an exploratory
      study." *Journal for the Scientific Study of Religion* 9 (Winter):321–325.
Mays, Benjamin E., and Joseph Nicholson
1933 *The Negro's Church.* New York: Institute of Social and Religious
      Research. As reprinted by Arno Press and The New York Times, Inc.,
      New York: 1969.
Metzger, L. Paul
1971 "American sociology and black assimilation." *American Journal of
      Sociology* 76 (January):627–647.
Mueller, Samuel A.
1971 "The new triple melting pot: Herberg revisited." *Review of Religious
      Research* 13 (Fall):18–33.
Mueller, Samuel A., and Angela V. Lane
1972 "Tabulations from the 1957 census population survey on religion."
      Journal for the Scientific Study of Religion 11 (March):76–98.

Myrdal, Gunnar
1944   *The American Dilemma*. New York: Harper & Row.

Nelsen, Hart M., and Lynda Dickson
1972   "Attitudes of black Catholics and Protestants: evidence for religious identity." *Sociological Analysis* 33 (Fall):152–165.

Nelsen, Hart M., and Anne Kusener Nelsen
1975   *Black Church in the Sixties*. University Press of Kentucky.

Nelsen, Hart M., Raytha L. Yokley, and Anne K. Nelsen
1971   Editors, *The Black Church in America*. New York: Basic Books.

Neusner, Jacob
1972   *American Judaism: Adventure in Modernity*. Englewood Cliffs, N.J.: Prentice-Hall.

Newman, William M.
1973   *American Pluralism: A Study of Minority Groups and Social Theory*. New York: Harper & Row.

Pettigrew, Thomas F.
1969   "Racially separate or together?" *Journal of Social Issues* 25 (January): 43–70.

Pope, Liston
1967   "The Negro and religion in America." In *The Sociology of Religion: An Anthology*, edited by Richard D. Knudten. New York: Appleton-Century-Crofts.

Powdermaker, Hortense
1939   *After Freedom: A Cultural Study in the Deep South*. New York: Viking Press.

Ransford, H. Edward
1972   "Blue collar anger: reactions to student and black protest." *American Sociological Review* 37 (June):333–346.

Roberts, J. Deotis
1971   *Liberation and Reconciliation: A Black Theology*. Philadelphia: Westminster Press.
1974   *A Black Political Theology*. Philadelphia: Westminster Press.

Ryan, William
1971   *Blaming the Victim*. New York: Random House.

Singer, L.
1962   "Ethno-genesis and Negro Americans today." *Social Research* 29 (Winter):419–432.

Sklare, Marshall
1971   *America's Jews*. New York: Random House.

Suttles, Gerald D.
1968   *The Social Order of the Slum: Ethnicity and Territory in the Inner City*. University of Chicago Press.

Tyler, Lawrence
1966   "The Protestant Ethic among the Black Muslims." *Phylon* 27 (Spring): 5–14.

U.S. Bureau of the Census
1958   "Religion reported by the civilian population of the United States: March, 1957." *Current Population Reports*, ser. P-20, no. 79.

Wade, Richard C.
1971 "Beyond the master's eye." In *The Black Church in America*, edited by Hart M. Nelsen, Raytha L. Yokley, and Anne K. Nelsen. New York: Basic Books.

Washington, Joseph R., Jr.
1964 *Black Religion.* Boston: Beacon Press.
1969 *The Politics of God.* Boston: Beacon Press.
1972 *Black Sects and Cults.* New York: Doubleday.

Watts, Leon W.
1971 "The reality of the black church." In *Ministry in the Seventies*, edited by Jack I. Biersdorf. New York: IDOC North America.

Williams, Preston N.
1971 "Toward a sociological understanding of the black religious community." *Soundings* 54 (Fall): 260–270.

Wilmore, Gayraud S., Jr.
1973 *Black Religion and Black Radicalism.* Garden City, N.Y.: Doubleday (Anchor Books).

Yinger, J. Milton
1970 *The Scientific Study of Religion.* New York: Macmillan.

Author Index

Elder, Glen H., Jr., 53, 71
Eliade, Mircea, 15 n, 18
Ellwood, Robert S., Jr., 165 n, 169
Engels, Frederick, 33–36, 39, 39 n, 40
Erickson, Donald A., 259 n, 260
Erickson, Robert, 258 n, 261
Erskine, Hazel, 285 n, 287–288
Estus, Charles, 120, 126, 128–130, 133 n, 134
Essien-Udom, E. U., 285 n, 288

Fackre, Gabriel, 95 n, 98, 189 n, 191
Fallding, Harold, 159, 169
Faue, Jeffrey L., 166 n, 170, 189 n, 192
Faulkner, Joseph E., 11–12, 14, 16 n–17 n, 17–18
Fauset, Arthur, 265, 288
Feagin, J. R., 286 n, 288
Featherman, David L., 53–54, 56, 71
Feifel, Herman, 38 n, 39
Feld, Sheila, 56, 76
Feldman, Kenneth A., 96 n, 101
Fenn, Richard K., 84–85, 95 n, 98
Festinger, Leon, 142, 169
Feuerbach, Ludwig, 38 n, 39
Fichter, Joseph, 16 n, 18, 165 n, 169
Fischoff, Ephraim, 43, 67 n, 71
Fisher, Victor, 76
Fiske, Edward B., 182, 191, 259 n, 260
Flippen, Charles C., 96 n, 101
Flora, Cornelia Butler, 140, 169
Forcese, Dennis P., 43, 71
Fortune, 58, 71
Foster, Bruce D., 193
Fox, William S., 53–54, 71, 73
Francis, E. K., 153, 169, 225 n, 230
Fray, Harold R., 189 n, 191
Frazier, E. Franklin, 271, 274, 276–277, 284 n, 288
Freud, Sigmund, 38 n, 40, 89
Frideres, Jane L., 228 n, 230
Friedrichs, Robert W., 97 n, 99
Fukuyama, Yoshio, 16 n, 18, 188 n, 191

Galbraith, John Kenneth, 57, 61–62, 68 n, 71
Gallup Opinion Index, 225 n, 230, 257 n–258 n, 260, 285 n, 288
Gannon, Thomas M., S. J., 188 n, 191

Gans, Herbert, 226 n, 230
Gardiner, James J., 285 n–286 n, 288
Gardner, Burleigh B., 275, 287
Gardner, Mary R., 275, 287
Garrett, William R., 38 n, 40, 188 n, 191
Geertz, Clifford, 15 n, 18
Gerlach, Luther P., 153, 169
Gerth, H. H., 45, 72
Gibbs, David R., 189 n, 191
Gibbs, Jack P., 189 n, 191
Gibbs, James O., 12, 17 n, 18
Gilkey, Langdon, 69 n, 72, 182, 191
Gladden, James W., 12, 17
Glaser, Daniel, 210, 230
Glazer, Nathan, 225 n, 230, 270–271, 285 n, 288
Glenn, Norval D., 53, 72, 284 n, 288
Glick, Paul C., 217, 230
Glock, Charles Y., 4, 7–15, 16 n, 18, 20, 69 n, 76, 116, 134, 142–143, 165 n, 169, 172, 177, 185, 191, 193, 221–222, 233
Gockel, Galen L., 53, 72
Goering, John M., 211, 231
Goldscheider, Calvin, 208–210, 226 n–227 n, 231
Goldstein, Bernice, 55, 72
Goldstein, Jay Ellis, 228 n, 230
Goldstein, Sidney, 53, 72, 208–210, 226 n–227 n, 231
Goode, Erich, 108–109, 120, 126–130, 132 n–133 n, 134
Gordon, Milton M., 198, 225 n, 231
Gouldner, Alvin, 97 n, 99
Greeley, Andrew M., 39 n, 40, 53–54, 72, 76, 92, 97 n, 99, 199, 201, 210, 219, 224, 225 n–228 n, 231
Green, Robert W., 43, 67 n, 72
Greenwald, David E., 81, 99
Gulick, John, 225 n, 231
Gurin, Gerald, 56, 76
Gustafson, James M., 188 n, 191
Gustafson, Paul, 107, 135

Hadden, Jeffrey K., 177–179, 184–185, 189 n, 191
Halevy, Elie, 67 n, 72
Hamilton, Charles V., 285 n–286 n, 288
Hamilton, William, 63, 70

Subject Index

Sectlike congregations, 111, 131, 159, 161–164, 165 n–167 n
external relations of, 114–116, 140, 149, 152, 154–155, 157–158, 164
internal characteristics of, 112–114, 140, 149, 152, 154–155, 157, 164
rise of, 139–148, 164
types of, 132 n See also Adventists, Conversionists, Gnostics, Introversionists
Sectlike religiosity, 117, 124–125
Section 6(j), 256
as it defines "religious," 252
as its definition is interpreted by Supreme Court, 253–254
Sect-to-church hypothesis, 139, 148–164, 166 n–167 n
modification of, 159–164, 166 n
Niebuhr's explanation of, 154–156
Niebuhr's formulation of, 149–151, 165 n–167 n
Pope's explanation of, 154, 157–158
Pope's formulation of, 151–152
Secularization, 2, 67 n, 80, 95 n, 108. See also Differentiation, Disenchantment
Seegar case, 252–253, 259 n
Self-identification, 199–202, 205, 211–212, 225 n, 227 n, 235–236
as a black, 266, 273–278, 281–284
in ethnic terms, 201, 203–204
among immigrants, 200–201
measurement of, 211, 226 n, 264–270
as Protestant, Catholic, or Jew, 200, 204, 237, 246
and religious community, 199–200, 205, 239, 266
among second- and third-generation Americans, 202–206
Self-location. See Self-identification
Separation of church and state, 202–203, 236–238
and three-community system, 236–240, 246–247. See also Three-community system, and Supreme Court decisions
SES hypothesis, 111, 132 n
evidence on, 120–131
roots of, 117–120
Sloan v. Lemon, 243

Social involvement approach
to sociology of theism, 38 n
Societal integration, 79, 81, 85, 88–89, 94, 95 n. See also Functional integration; Normative integration
Sociology
defined, 2
Sociology of religion
continuity in. See Continuity in the sociology of religion
defined, 3
and religious discourse, 38 n
Socius. See Subjective presuppositions, ultimate reservoirs of
Sovereign groups, 29–30, 29 n
Spirit of capitalism, 54, 56, 67 n See also Entrepreneurial ideology, Ideology of management, Managerial ideology
as defined by Weber, 46
and entrepreneurial ideology, 44
as ideology of management, 57
Spirits, 4, 7, 30, 93, 225 n
Subjective presuppositions, 92–93
of knowledge, 90–91, 94
of science, 90–92, 97 n
ultimate reservoirs of, 92–94
Substantive continuity, 1, 108–110
defined, 3
Supernatural, 4, 7, 13, 29, 34, 89, 105
Symbolic reductionism, 38 n
Synagogue attendance, 207, 226 n
in tests of three-generation hypothesis, 207–208, 210

Techniques of neutralization, 179–182
defined, 179
Temperance movement, 175
Theism, 24–26, 38 n See also Functionalism, Metaphoric parallelism, Marxian viewpoint; Monotheism, Polytheism
defined, 38 n
functions of, 24–27, 35–37
sociology of, 23–39
as Supreme Court defines Section 6(j), 253–254
Theology, 11, 95 n, 97 n, 184, 189 n. See also God